Pharmaceutical Freedom

Pharmaceutical Analysis

Pharmaceutical Freedom

Why Patients Have a Right to Self-Medicate

JESSICA FLANIGAN

OXFORD
UNIVERSITY PRESS

OXFORD
UNIVERSITY PRESS

Oxford University Press is a department of the University of Oxford. It furthers
the University's objective of excellence in research, scholarship, and education
by publishing worldwide. Oxford is a registered trade mark of Oxford University
Press in the UK and certain other countries.

Published in the United States of America by Oxford University Press
198 Madison Avenue, New York, NY 10016, United States of America.

© Oxford University Press 2017

CIP data is on file at the Library of Congress
ISBN 978-0-19-068454-9

1 3 5 7 9 8 6 4 2

Printed by Sheridan Books Inc., United States of America

CONTENTS

ACKNOWLEDGMENTS

I am grateful to my mentors, friends, and colleagues for their support and guidance as I wrote this book. I began writing about pharmaceutical regulation at Princeton University, where Stephen Macedo, Peter Singer, and Annie Stilz supervised my dissertation on this topic and provided invaluable encouragement and guidance. I am also grateful to the Princeton University Center for Human Values, where students and faculty provided much appreciated comments and suggestions during that time. I especially want to recognize my friend Ryan Davis. Ryan's friendship and reassurance emboldened me to write this book. And our conversations over the past thirteen years have been exceptionally intellectually rewarding and indelibly informed my views about morality and meaning.

I completed my dissertation as a visiting scholar at the Brown University Political Theory Project (PTP). I wish to thank John Tomasi and the 2011 PTP post-docs for welcoming me into their vibrant intellectual community. I then enjoyed productive conversations about paternalism and political authority with my colleagues at the University of Richmond, where I wrote this book. I wish to thank colleagues and students in the Jepson School and the Political Philosophy Learning Community in particular. Students and faculty at James Madison University, Harvard Medical School, Harvard Law School, University of Pennsylvania, the Manhattan Institute, Duke University, University of North Carolina, University of Virginia, University of North Carolina Greensboro, and St. Edwards University also provided valuable comments and suggestions.

I would also like to thank audiences at the Inspire2Live 2015 annual meeting, especially Peter Kapitan and Stephen Friend for very helpful conversations about patient advocacy and the future of drug development. In addition, it has been a privilege to learn from the many patients, advocates, and health workers whose experiences pressed me to challenge and refine my thoughts about public health and medical ethics. I hope this book is a useful resource for patients and health workers and that the arguments I develop can in some way contribute to a better future for patients everywhere.

In 2015 I presented the book manuscript at the Georgetown Junior Faculty Manuscript Workshop. I am grateful to the participants of that workshop for reading the manuscript with such care, to Michael Kates for organizing the workshop, and to Sarah Conly, David Sobel, and Alex Tabbarok for presenting exceptionally helpful commentary and suggestions. I am also indebted to those who provided written comments on the manuscript, including Jonny Anomaly, Jason Brennan, Chris Freiman, Lance Stell, Thomas Stossell, and Kevin Vallier. Two reviewers for Oxford University Press, Allen Buchanan and Douglas Husak generously provided extensive comments and my arguments are much stronger for having responded to their objections and incorporated their suggestions. Peter Ohlin and Andrew Ward also provided excellent editorial guidance, and I am fortunate that Tammy Tripp and Elizabeth DeBusk Maslanka provided proofreading assistance.

Finally, I certainly owe the most to Javier Hidalgo, both with respect to this book and also the rest of my life. I was able to travel and present parts of this book over the years because of Javier's support for my career and commitment to our family. He also provided comments on several drafts and I learned so many things that influenced this book from our daily conversations. Just about everything I've made is better because of Javier, to whom I dedicate this book.

INTRODUCTION

People use drugs to save their lives, to end their lives, or to make their lives better. Sometimes people end up making their lives worse by using drugs. On the other hand, policies that limit access to drugs can also make people's lives worse. People suffer and die while waiting for regulators to approve new drugs. People must pay physicians and pharmacists to obtain life-sustaining prescription drugs. People face criminal penalties if they use illegal drugs.

In all developed countries, public officials adopt a prohibitive approach to therapeutic and recreational drugs, meaning that people are legally prevented from purchasing and using certain drugs without authorization, and other drugs are banned entirely. This approach is at odds with officials' non-prohibitive approach to most other products and services. A prohibitive approach conflicts with widespread ethical commitments in medicine that protect patients' rights to make medical decisions without being deceived and in the absence of coercive interference. And drug prohibition is also at odds with liberal values, such as the presumption of liberty and anti-paternalism.

A prohibitive approach to drugs cannot be justified without undermining principles such as informed consent or anti-paternalism. My central claim is that it is wrong for public officials to prohibit people from purchasing and using therapeutic or recreational drugs. These policies not only cause needless death and suffering, they also violate patients' rights of self-medication, bodily rights, rights to make intimate and personal decisions, and general rights against interference. And they violate the rights of producers who are forbidden from selling or advertising pharmaceuticals without authorization.

Proponents of the current prohibitive approach to drugs face a dilemma—either they must abandon widely held moral commitments to respect and freedom of choice or abandon their support of prohibitive pharmaceutical regulations and drug policies. The dilemma arises because whatever reasons one may cite in favor of a prohibitive approach to buying or selling drugs can also be deployed against a range of other dangerous activities where the same values are at stake.

For example, one may argue, "drugs are different" and should be prohibited or regulated differently from other products on the grounds that the decision to use therapeutic medicines is complex and that patients are poorly equipped to understand the relevant medical literature or to appreciate the risks associated with using pharmaceuticals. Yet, in the very same jurisdictions that regulate the use of pharmaceuticals by enforcing premarket approval and prescription drug requirements, physicians are legally required to respect patients' rights to make medical decisions in accordance with the doctrine of informed consent.

If the decision to use a drug is so complex that patients must be protected from themselves, then one should also hold that the decision to refuse a drug, a decision that is based on the very same complex information and assessments of risk, would also be a choice that patient's should not be permitted to make for themselves. But the same reasons for rejecting medical paternalism in clinical contexts are reasons to reject paternalistic drug policies as well. The doctrine of informed consent is the fundamental principle of medical ethics, so proponents of informed consent should rethink existing limits on patients' medical autonomy with respect to pharmaceutical choices.

Or, one may argue that patients should be prohibited from using unapproved drugs because they often make the choice out of desperation, when they are extremely emotional and are easily manipulated. But we do not generally think that public officials can prohibit people from making intimate choices out of desperation in times when they are emotional and easily manipulated. For example, some people choose to marry bad partners because they are desperate for companionship and they judge that their other prospects are worse. These lonely hearts are likely to be easily manipulated by their bad partners too. But despite the presence of desperation, heightened emotions, and the potential for manipulation, public officials nevertheless permit people to make terrible romantic decisions on the grounds that the freedom to form intimate associations is foundational to a liberal society.

Even if decisions about drugs are not generally intimate and personal choices, they can be for patients whose treatment choices are a matter of life and death and for chronically ill patients who must make difficult decisions about whether to take risks to improve their quality of life. At least in these cases, people should not be disqualified from choosing to use unapproved drugs on the grounds that they may be emotionally compromised when making those decisions. Moreover, even if the freedom to use particular drugs is not particularly important to people, public officials ought to respect people's more general freedom to make choices about their bodies, including private and personal decisions about health and medicine.

More generally, liberal societies tolerate a range of dangerous decision-making for the sake of goals that are as weighty as self-preservation and as seemingly trivial as recreation. People are allowed to mortgage their homes to pay for approved pharmaceuticals that are unlikely to work; yet public officials prohibit them from risking their health by using an unapproved medicine. The right to refuse lifesaving treatment is widely affirmed, yet people are not permitted to use deadly drugs.

Adults are permitted to play football and rugby, to go base jumping and to kayak through rapids, to swim alone at night, to ride motorcycles, to hang glide, scuba dive, or take up boxing. Most people are permitted to drink alcohol and smoke cigarettes too. And public officials tolerate citizens' choices when they eat junk food and watch television every day, even though people risk their health and well-being by doing so. Yet recreational activities that involve drugs are prohibited even when the health risks of a drug are much lower than the risks of these other recreational activities.

These examples highlight an inconsistency between drug policy and policies that protect people's right to make risky decisions, but they do not straightforwardly support a permissive approach to drugs. Rather, these considerations challenge justifications for existing drug policy. But there are two other ways to reconcile drug policy with officials' permissive approach to other risky products and activities. First, one could attempt to justify the current policy of treating drugs differently. Second, proponents of paternalism may reply that the parallels to football, bodily modification, boxing, cigarettes, and junk food do not suggest that officials should permit people to use drugs but rather that they ought to prohibit or require authorization for risky activities that are as or more dangerous than drugs.

One may think that drugs are different because their sole purpose is to change some aspect of a person's body, usually to improve one's health. But the aforementioned risky choices also change people's bodies and psychologies. And if anything, bodily choices merit greater protection, not less, since respecting a person's autonomy generally requires respect for her bodily rights (consistent with the bodily rights of others). When defenders of abortion rights invoke the slogan "my body, my choice" they highlight the widely shared conviction that public officials are not generally entitled to legislate what people can do with their bodies, unless someone else's rights are threatened. Similarly, transgender activists assert the legal right to access gender confirmation surgery on similar grounds. In these cases, policies that prevent people from accessing the necessary means to change their bodies violate their bodily rights. Even if laws against abortion do not directly prohibit women from having abortions but only prohibit physicians from providing them, such laws violate women's rights to terminate pregnancy. So too, even when public officials only prohibit the sale of pharmaceuticals or recreational drugs but do not penalize users, if people have rights of self-medication, then such policies would violate them.

The conviction that people have presumptive rights to make decisions about their own bodies also explains why people ought to be permitted to change their bodies in ways that are seemingly irresponsible. For example, it would be wrong to legally forbid adults from getting face and hand tattoos, purchasing buttock augmentation, practicing poor dental hygiene, earlobe stretching, or tanning, even though these choices are often imprudent. Perhaps some people think that these imprudent choices ought to be illegal, since people's interests in face tattoos or tanning is not especially important or urgent. But these interests could be. The decision to purchase a face tattoo is a form of self-expression, and there is no reason to assume that self-expression through bodily modification is less important than expressing oneself through art or writing. Even if most people do not generally think of specific opportunities for self-expression as being especially significant, people's freedom of expression, considered broadly, is a significant right which requires general protections that extend to even insignificant instantiations of the right. And if people are permitted to express themselves by modifying their bodies for aesthetic purposes, why are pharmacological forms of self-expression and bodily modification not similarly deserving of legal protections?

Similarly, some people care a lot about their dietary choices. People culturally identify with each other on the basis of the foods they purchase, prepare, and consume. Because nutrition so closely affects health, many people highly value their ability to access healthy food. Vegetarians and vegans purchase manufactured plant-based protein products and refrain from eating meat for ethical reasons. Religious people also make dietary choices in ways that reflect their conceptions of the good life. On the other hand, imprudent food and drink choices cause a great deal of suffering due to obesity and alcohol-related diseases. Is there a principled way to distinguish drugs from dietary choices though? Many unhealthy foods are made with non-natural ingredients and specifically designed to evoke a pleasurable physical and psychological response. Some recreational and therapeutic drugs are grown on organic farms. Both food and drugs can be used to promote health or for recreation. Both can play an important role in people's cultures or religion. Both can be very harmful, depending on how they are used. And yet people are permitted to make a very wide range of food choices without government authorization while most drugs are either banned or require premarket approval and a prescription. Insofar as the dangers of imprudent consumption justify premarket approval requirements for potential cures, prescription requirements for cholesterol medication, and a ban on medical marijuana, such dangers could justify premarket approval for snacks, a ban on Twinkies, and prescription requirements for soda and alcohol as well. Those who view such policies as impermissible should question support for existing drug policy in light of the reasons in favor of protecting dietary choices.

One may also resist analogies between drug use and other risky choices on the grounds that public officials are qualified to regulate drugs but not other products and activities. After all, judgments about whether a drug is likely to undermine a person's health and well-being depend on scientific expertise in a way that judgments about whether a person should become a vegetarian, take up boxing, or get a face tattoo do not. Even if this were so, when justifying prohibitive regulations the relevant question is not whether using a drug, boxing, or getting a tattoo is likely to undermine a person's health and well-being. Scientific experts can convey their opinion that some drugs are very likely to injure users without prohibiting people from using them. Rather, the relevant question is whether public officials are qualified to judge whether a drug is acceptably risky. Though officials may know the ways that boxing and face tattoos are likely to undermine people's health and well-being, they are not well placed to know whether the risks associated with these imprudent activities are worth it to people, given their other values and their overall circumstances. Whether it is worth it to make a risky decision is not a scientific judgment. It is a normative judgment that each person is generally in the best position to make for herself. So even if experts and officials are more qualified to judge the likely effects of a drug, as with other choices, patients are in the best position to judge whether the risks are acceptable.

Other attempts to find a principled distinction between drugs and other products and services also fail. The fact that pharmaceuticals are bought and sold within the healthcare industry doesn't render manufacturers liable to be censored and regulated more than other industries. The fact that people who use drugs may harm their families and loved ones by harming themselves does not justify prohibiting drugs either. Not everyone who uses drugs harms people in these ways, and officials are not typically permitted to forbid people from being bad family members or friends anyhow. The fact that people who use dangerous drugs may subsequently require medical care does not justify preemptive prohibitions of potentially risky self-medication either. In both cases, if a person has an inalienable right to receive medical care, then she is not liable to be forced to make prudent decisions on the grounds that taxpayers would then be required to give her the medical care she is entitled to. If she does not have a right to receive medical care, then she also is not liable to be interfered with on the grounds that her fellow citizens would feel compelled to beneficently provide her with medical care if she were injured.

It may seem revisionary to adopt a more permissive approach to drug policy, but if proponents of paternalistic pharmaceutical policies cannot justify treating drugs differently then they must instead rethink officials' permissive approach to football, bodily modification, boxing, cigarettes, and junk food. Paternalists may welcome this conclusion, but if drugs are not different from other risky choices then the same reasons to support status quo drug policies are reasons to support even more revisionary conclusions in clinical contexts as well. After all, the same reasons to reject medical paternalism in clinical contexts are reasons to reject paternalism with respect to pharmaceuticals. So paternalists who endorse the claim that prohibitions of very unhealthy or dangerous choices are generally justified because people's rights and interests in making unhealthy dangerous choices are outweighed when the costs and risks are substantial must not only rethink existing rights to make risky recreational or dietary choices but also the doctrine of informed consent and people's rights to make imprudent comments, risky investments, and costly personal decisions. To support restrictions on a range of decisions that include recreation, diet, medical choices, expression, property rights, and association, whenever restrictions on those decisions would protect people from risk is to substantially diminish liberalism's fundamental commitment to individual rights as a constraint on public officials' conduct. For those who judge that it would be better to abandon informed consent and these other fundamental liberal values than to permit self-medication, my argument still would have revisionary implications relative to the status quo.

In this book I argue that drugs are not morally different from other products and that the same considerations that justify other rights, such as informed consent, the right to make intimate and personal decisions, the right to die, bodily rights, economic freedoms, freedom of expression, and rights of self-preservation, also justify rights of self-medication. Additionally, I suggest that the existing system of pharmaceutical regulation has bad consequences. Instead, patients and physicians should assert their rights of self-medication and advocate for reform.

The main reform that I support is a non-prohibitive, certificatory approach to almost all pharmaceuticals (except antibiotics). If public officials treated drugs more like other products and treated patients as capable trustees of their own health, people could still consult medical experts and agency recommendations when making decisions about their health. But the decisions would be their own, in contrast to the current system that requires regulators, physicians, and pharmacists to act as the gatekeepers of most medical treatment. And within a certificatory system public officials would not be empowered to withhold access to potential cures or imprison recreational drug users for the sake of public health.

This conclusion calls for substantial changes to the current system. But the current system is untenable, not only for the moral reasons I develop in this book but also in light of new technology that facilitates patient-driven drug development, personalized medicine, and human enhancements, as well as recent political movements such as the right to try campaigns in the United States, and the increasingly vivid evidence that officials' current approach to pharmaceuticals and recreational drugs is ineffective and counterproductive. The need for reform is urgent. For every year that the current system of premarket approval persists patients needlessly die while waiting for treatment and more lives are lost because existing requirements discourage innovation. Every year that prescription requirements persist is a year that public officials violate patients' rights and force some patients to spend their time and money unnecessarily consulting with physicians and pharmacists. Every year that officials continue to prohibit people from purchasing and using recreational drugs is a year that subjects innocent people to criminal penalties. Comprehensive drug policy reform is necessary. This necessity presents an opportunity for adopting reforms that promote health and well-being while respecting patients' rights.

The rise of liberal values and the development of lifesaving pharmaceuticals are two of the greatest collective achievements of the twentieth century. Yet as pharmaceuticals became more powerful and pervasive and individuals' rights expanded throughout the twentieth century, officials increasingly violated citizens' medical rights by enforcing prohibitive drug regulations. These policies persist worldwide even though the same values that justify other important rights also justify rights of self-medication. Today, twenty-first century medicine necessitates a new approach. It's time to embrace the values of freedom and respect in our approach to pharmaceuticals. It's time for pharmaceutical freedom.

Pharmaceutical Freedom

A Defense of Self-Medication

Mary Schloendorff was admitted to New York Hospital in the winter of 1907, suffering from abdominal pain and indigestion.[1] Before she was discharged, a physician found a lump in her side during a physical examination. The physician, Dr. Frederick H. Bartlett, advised that Mary be examined under anesthesia to determine what the lump was. Mary replied that she did not want to undergo any operation, but Dr. Bartlett assured her that the exam was only investigational and that she could decide later if she wanted surgery. Still, Mary decided to go home and wrote to her landlady that she was returning.

The night before Mary was to leave the hospital, she was awakened several times in preparation for an examination, and each time she stated that she did not want an operation. Mary's ability to understand her circumstances and make decisions was not impaired during this time. Nevertheless, the next morning she was physically restrained and anesthetized. When she woke up, she learned that a surgeon discovered uterine fibroids and that she had been given a supravaginal hysterectomy. Screaming in pain, she was confined to the hospital. As she recovered, Mary was transferred to a series of hospitals and convalescence homes for months. She developed painful complications related to the surgery, including the amputation of some of her fingers as a result of gangrene.

The most significant development in twentieth-century medical ethics is the rejection of medical paternalism of the sort that Mary Schloendorff experienced. Though people may disagree about how exactly to define medical paternalism, or paternalism, a fairly uncontroversial characterization is that medical paternalism consists in interference with a person's medical choice, which is motivated or justified for her own sake, without her consent. So if interference against a person's will is motivated or justified to promote her well-being, to protect her from injury, to make her healthier or more autonomous, or to benefit her in some other way, then it is paternalistic interference. There may be other forms

---

[1] This account is informed by Paul Lombardo's reconstruction of Schloendorff's case. Paul A. Lombardo, "Phantom Tumors and Hysterical Women: Revising Our View of the Schloendorff Case," *The Journal of Law, Medicine & Ethics* 33, no. 4 (2005): 791–801.

of paternalism that do not take the form of interference, such as paternalistic gift-giving, but these are not central cases. The three main ways to paternalistically interfere with a person against her will is to force, coerce, or deceive her to make her better off.

Before the twentieth century, physicians routinely deceived patients, withheld diagnoses, and even performed unwanted medical interventions. In the United States, a series of court cases, including Schloendorff's lawsuit against New York Hospital, secured legal and professional recognition of the doctrine of informed consent. However, the rejection of medical paternalism happened gradually. A 1967 survey of internists and surgeons found that almost 90 percent of physicians had a general policy of withholding cancer diagnoses from patients. [2] Some even reported that they falsified diagnoses of patients in advanced-stages of their diseases.

Today, though some parts of the world still permit deception by physicians, most developed countries protect patients' rights to be informed about treatment options and require consent for medical procedures. Even when a patient's treatment choice is medically inadvisable, courts and physicians now recognize the principle of self-determination that Judge Benjamin Cardozo famously articulated in his opinion for *Schloendorff v. New York Hospital*:

> Every human being of adult years and sound mind has a right to determine what shall be done with his own body; and a surgeon who performs an operation without his patient's consent commits an assault.[3]

At the same time, the twentieth century also altered the scope of patients' rights outside the clinical context. Just as patients were gaining ever more rights as part of the newly developing doctrine of informed consent, administrative agencies began enforcing legal limits on the kinds of medicines patients could purchase and use. These limits included premarket testing requirements and the prescription drug system.

Today, pharmaceutical regulation is pervasive. In all developed countries government agencies control the drug industry at every level. As Daniel Carpenter writes, the US Food and Drug Administration (FDA) is the most powerful regulatory agency in the world, in part because "an American model for pharmaceutical regulation has been perhaps the primary institutional export of the United States."[4] I will therefore focus mainly on the United States because the FDA is the clear global leader in crafting legal standards for drug approval and access,

---

[2] A. Buchanan, "Medical Paternalism," *Philosophy & Public Affairs* 7, no. 4 (1978): 370–90.

[3] In re *Schloendorff v. Society of New York Hospital* (NYS 1914).

[4] Daniel Carpenter, *Reputation and Power: Organizational Image and Pharmaceutical Regulation at the FDA* (Princeton, NJ: Princeton University Press, 2014), 22.

though the philosophical arguments I develop apply more generally to all administrative agencies that prohibit patients from accessing pharmaceuticals without authorization.

My thesis is that the same considerations that justify rights of informed consent also justify rights of self-medication. Paternalism is just as wrong at the pharmacy as it is in the doctor's office. Medical autonomy is an important value in both contexts, so states should protect patients' rights against unwanted medical interventions from physicians and from unwanted limits on access by public officials. Both informed consent requirements and rights of self-medication will permit people to make decisions that their physicians would advise against. For example, rights of self-medication would require that patients can legally purchase and use dangerous medicines without a prescription and without authorization from a regulatory agency.

This is not to say that patients *should* use pharmaceuticals without seeking medical advice. Patients who are interested in protecting their health should generally consult physicians and other experts on medical choices. Patients also should comply with treatment recommendations, exercise routines, and diets. Yet, in all these cases, the fact that a recommended option is better for a person's health does not authorize physicians or public officials to force the patient to choose that option. Similarly, even when unapproved pharmaceutical use will undermine a patient's health, it is wrong to forbid use.

Like other rights, rights of self-medication are interpersonal. So when I argue that people have a moral right to use drugs, I mean that they have rights against others who would forcibly or coercively interfere with their drug use. The right of self-medication does not establish that people have rights to inexpensive drugs or that people have rights to pharmaceutical innovation. In this way too, rights of self-medication parallel rights of informed consent and bodily rights more generally. The right of self-medication only establishes rights against public officials' prohibition of drug sales, but a person could still lack effective access to pharmaceuticals if the drugs she needs have not yet been developed or if manufacturers are unwilling to provide her with drugs (assuming the manufacturer has a property right in the drug). Yet as I will argue, though rights of self-medication do not entail rights to access affordable drugs or rights to drug development, respecting patients' rights of self-medication would promote innovation and could make drugs more affordable too.

Like informed consent, the right of self-medication does not rely on a single, potentially controversial normative premise. Consequentialists and non-consequentialists, liberal egalitarians and libertarians, all have sufficient reasons to endorse both informed consent and the right of self-medication. From a consequentialist perspective, patients should be entrusted with making choices for themselves because they are generally most knowledgeable about which decision will further their interests. From a rights-based perspective, medical decisions are often intimate and personal choices that are especially significant to patients. And even if a medical choice is not intimate, personal, or especially significant, people are more generally entitled to choose how they live their lives without being subjected to benevolent interference by physicians or public officials. Furthermore, even if people do not have general rights to make medical choices, it is wrong to force, coerce, or deceive people, and effectively constraining a person's medical choices often requires force, coercion, or deception. These arguments in favor of patients' rights to make medical decisions are often deployed on behalf of informed consent requirements, but they also justify rights of self-medication.

1.1　Two Motivating Cases

The following two cases illustrate the current state of medical paternalism:

> *Risky Refusal*: Debbie has diabetes and her physician advises her to start insulin treatment. Debbie understands the risks of refusing insulin but is also unwilling to live by a schedule and monitor her medication. Against medical advice, Debbie decides to try to manage her diabetes with diet and exercise. Debbie's physician is morally and legally prohibited from injecting Debbie with insulin against her wishes.
>
> *Risky Access:* Danny has diabetes and his physician advises him to treat his condition with diet and exercise. Danny doesn't want to invest the time or energy in diet and exercise and would prefer to just begin using insulin right off. Against medical advice, Danny wishes to try to manage his diabetes with insulin. However, Danny cannot legally access diabetes medication without a prescription from his physician.

Why is Debbie's right to refuse treatment against medical advice legally protected and widely recognized while Danny's right to make a similarly risky treatment decision is not? Many of the same considerations that justify Debbie's refusal right also support Danny's right to access treatment. For example, one justification for informed consent is that patients like Debbie know better than anyone else whether the risks of a particular treatment decision are justified given the potential benefits. But patients like Danny are also especially well placed to evaluate whether a risky treatment decision is justified. In addition, patients like Debbie and Danny both have rights to make intimate and personal decisions about their own bodies. If it is wrong for public officials or physicians to treat Debbie paternalistically, then it is wrong to paternalistically interfere with Danny's treatment decisions as well because the two cases are relevantly similar with respect to the moral considerations in favor of respecting Debbie's choice.

One seeming dissimilarity between Debbie's rights and Danny's rights is that it would be morally worse for Debbie's physician to forcibly inject her with insulin than it is for Danny to simply be barred from buying medication without a prescription. Yet informed consent protects patients from more than just forced treatment. It would be wrong for Debbie's physician to deceive her or to trick her into consenting to treatment, or to pressure, threaten, or coerce her. Even if he doesn't violently force her to use insulin, insofar as he deprives her of the ability to choose insulin he has violated her medical rights.

In Danny's case, public officials prohibit him from accessing medication by using coercion. If Danny tries to use insulin, he could be forcibly prohibited from doing so or he could face criminal penalties, which are backed by force and threats of force. Even though few patients who seek access to pharmaceuticals directly encounter forceful interference by public officials, it is only because people preemptively comply with laws to avoid legal penalties, such as fines or prison sentences. If public officials legally prohibited patients like Debbie from refusing medical treatment, then patients' consent would be invalid even if the prohibition were never enforced because everyone would comply with the law. So too, the mere threat of a legal penalty constrains patients like Danny's ability to decide whether to use drugs, even if coercive penalties are rarely enforced because patients generally comply with the law.

For these reasons, a commitment to medical autonomy requires more than the protection of a person's bodily integrity, which would prohibit forced treatment or battery. Deception and threats of force can invalidate medical consent too. And laws that prohibit people from accessing drugs are backed by threats of force, which are ultimately threats to a person's bodily integrity. A physician can fail to obtain a patient's consent even if he does not forcibly administer treatment or treat her when she is unconscious. If her treatment decision was a result of coercion or deception, then, even if she appears to consent, her consent is invalid. Similarly, public officials violate patients' entitlements to make treatment decisions when they coercively enforce penalties for particular treatment choices.

1.2 Patients Know Best

In making the case for rights of self-medication for patients like Danny, I am assuming that rights of informed consent for Debbie are justified and that the rejection of paternalistic deception and coercion in the twentieth century is an example of moral progress in medicine. Of course, one may argue that neither

Debbie nor Danny should have the right to make inadvisable medical choices, but I regard this as too high a price to pay for rejecting self-medication since the reasons in favor of informed consent, which I will now review, are widely affirmed and independently compelling.

The first argument in favor of informed consent can be stated thus:

> (P1) Each patient is typically in the best position to determine which treatments are in his or her overall interest.
>
> (P2) Health workers should aim to promote patients' overall well-being.
>
> (P3) In general, the most reliable way to promote overall well-being is to defer to the expert.
>
> (C) Health workers should defer to patients' judgments about treatment options.

In other words, medicine should respect patients' choices because doing so is the most reliable way to promote patients' well-being on balance.

The first premise of this argument is meant to establish that each patient is generally in the best position to judge whether treatments are in his or her interest relative to other people who may decide. It is not meant to suggest that each patient is in an optimal position to make treatment decision or that people always will make the best decisions. Rather, people are generally sufficiently capable of judging what treatments are in their interest, and they have a presumptive advantage over other potential decision-makers. This premise originates with John Stuart Mill's claim that no one but a person himself can judge whether a risk is worth taking because each person understands and cares about his own interests more than anyone else.[5] Mill was not saying that patients are always the best judges of their own interests, but rather that they ought to be treated as if they were experts regarding their own interests because they have insight into their well-being and incentives to promote their well-being that everyone else necessarily lacks.

In the medical context, bioethicists, including Allen Buchanan and Robert Veatch, have affirmed the principle. Veatch writes, "There is no reason to believe that a physician or any other expert in only one component of well-being should be able to determine what constitutes the good for another being."[6] This principle

---

[5] Mill famously argued in *On Liberty*: "Neither one person, nor any number of persons, is warranted in saying to another human creature of ripe years, that he shall not do with his life for his own benefit what he chooses to do with it. He is the person most interested in his own well-being, the interest which any other person, except in cases of strong personal attachment, can have in it, is trifling, compared with that which he himself has." John Stuart Mill, *On Liberty and Other Essays*, ed. John Gray (Oxford; New York: Oxford University Press, 2008), 83–104.

[6] Buchanan, "Medical Paternalism"; Robert M. Veatch, "Abandoning Informed Consent," *Hastings Center Report* 25, no. 2 (1995): 5–12; Robert Young, "Informed Consent and Patient Autonomy,"

is compatible with various theories of well-being. Patients generally understand their own desires better than others; they know what causes pleasure or pain; and they know how they weigh their own values. In other words, doctors may be experts on health, but patients are the experts on themselves.

A person's overall well-being is whatever is non-instrumentally good for her.[7] Health is an important part of well-being according to most theories of well-being, but it is not the ultimate non-instrumental good for all people. For example, a hedonist may acknowledge that health is important for the experience of pleasure and that disease is bad because it often causes pain, but it needn't always be so. Imagine a life-threatening hypothalamic brain tumor that causes euphoria. According to a hedonist, the tumor might promote well-being, at least in the short-term, but not health. The same can be said for other theories of well-being. People often desire good health but not to the exclusion of other goods. Health may be one good on an objective list of things that constitute well-being, but other things are also on the list.

The second premise also assumes that health is only one part of a patient's overall well-being and states that health workers should aim to promote overall well-being. Better health does not guarantee a better life. We can imagine a person who pursues health to the exclusion of other values and has a worse life for it. And we can imagine someone who has a wonderful life despite the presence of a disease or disability.

A myopic focus on health mistakes the means to a good life for the good life itself, just like an obsession with money or admiration would. Health workers risk making a similar mistake if they focus too narrowly on patients' health. Instead, they should keep in mind that the purpose of health is to facilitate a good life for the patient, not to make a patient's body function as well as it can. This principle dates at least to Maimonides, who wrote that physicians should treat patients and not diseases.[8] It's easy for that message to get lost in an era of increasing specialization where physicians define themselves in terms of the kinds of diseases and conditions they treat. An orthopedic surgeon treats people who need new hips, not damaged femoral heads. Oncologists treat people with cancer, not tumors.

The third premise states that, in general, the best way to promote a person's well-being is to defer to the expert, who is generally the person whose well-being is being considered. This claim is not committed to the view that judgments about well-being are subjective. Rather, even if we accepted an objective

in *A Companion to Bioethics*, ed. Helga Kuhse and Peter Singer (Chichester: Wiley-Blackwell, 2009), 530–40.

[7] Roger Crisp, "Well-being," *Stanford Encyclopedia of Philosophy*, Summer 2008, http://seop.illc. uva.nl/archives/sum2008/entries/well-being/#4.1.

[8] F. Rosner, "Moses Maimonides' Treatise on Asthma," *Thorax* 36, no. 4 (April 1981): 245–51.

theory of well-being (such as the view that well-being consists in an objective list of goods), it would still be true that people could generally assess their own well-being in terms of any theory of well-being better than other people could because a competent adult generally knows more about his or her life than others do.

There are also other moral reasons to defer to peoples' judgments of their own well-being beyond the claim that people are generally the experts on what is good for them. When we defer to a person's testimony about her experiences when deciding how to treat her, we are more likely to avoid practical problems of testimonial injustice—where a marginalized or eccentric person's experiences are treated as less credible in virtue of unfamiliarity or systematic prejudices.[9] If observers have reason to doubt a person's testimony about her values and experiences, they may attempt to encourage reflection, to provide time or resources for disadvantaged groups to engage in meaningful deliberation, and to provide people with an opportunity to improve their critical thinking skills. But even in the absence of these measures, each person's testimony should be treated with deference, even if her judgments about her well-being or values differ from expert or peer observers' judgments.

Therefore, in light of patients' epistemic advantage in knowing which medical options will promote their well-being on balance, physicians should defer to patients about treatment choices. One limit of this epistemic argument is that some theories of well-being state that what is non-instrumentally good for a person consists in what she would reflectively endorse if she were fully informed, or more informed, or more rational. But people's reflective judgments about well-being (what they would judge as good for them with more information and better deliberative conditions) often depart from the judgments they act on or initially state about themselves.

And yet I am arguing that officials and physicians should defer to people's stated judgments rather than the judgments they would hold on reflection. Though I would encourage people to reflect on their projects and ends and to think seriously about which choice would be best, there are three compelling reasons to reject the claim that people should only defer to a person's *reflective* judgment about what is good for her. First, some people may reflectively judge that it is best if they do not overthink every choice. So while particular choices may not reflect their considered judgments, the choice to unreflectively make those choices does. In these cases, the epistemic argument for respecting a person's autonomy would require respecting some unreflective choices, even if we hold that reflective judgments are the only ones that merit deference. Second, even if there are comparatively stronger reasons for people to act on

---

[9] Miranda Fricker, *Epistemic Injustice: Power and the Ethics of Knowing* (Oxford; New York: Oxford University Press, 2009).

their reflective judgments (versus their stated judgments), there is no reason to think that those who paternalistically interfere generally interfere with stated judgments on the basis of what a person would reflectively endorse, or that their decision to interfere is not itself a rather unreflective choice. Third, those who are concerned that other people's stated judgments differ from what they would judge on reflection may provide resources for further deliberation and offer information and advice to encourage reflective decision-making while also deferring to people's stated judgments about well-being. So while we may grant that reflective judgments of well-being are more reliable or morally significant than stated judgments, this claim would not undermine the imperative to defer to people's claims about their well-being.

To illustrate this epistemic argument for medical autonomy, imagine a deeply religious Jehovah's Witness who believes that it is wrong to accept blood transfusions. While a physician might correctly judge that a blood transfusion is in the interest of her health, the physician might also agree that it is not in her interests all things considered, given her cultural identity and religious commitments. Or, we might imagine a cancer patient who refuses chemotherapy in an effort to preserve her fertility, even though alternative therapies are less likely to succeed than chemotherapy. Someone may forgo the best, most expensive daily medication in favor of a less effective but more affordable drug. A patient might refuse to schedule medically necessary treatment as soon as possible, so that she can participate in important life events such as her child's wedding or a vacation with her spouse.

In all these cases, the doctrine of informed consent holds that the patient's judgment about her *overall* interests ought to prevail. It would be wrong for a physician to force or trick a Jehovah's Witness into accepting a transfusion, to pressure a cancer patient into chemotherapy, to only provide an expensive treatment option when a less costly version is available, or to otherwise refuse to accommodate a patient's preferences on the grounds that those preferences would undermine the patient's health.

Beyond the doctrine of informed consent, other pervasive and widely accepted medical practices affirm this as well. For example, cosmetic surgery does not provide patients with any medical benefit, and it carries significant risks. But cosmetic surgeons act permissibly because their patients accept medical risks for the sake of non-medical benefits like larger breasts or a smaller nose. Similarly, physicians who treat athletes may facilitate treatment plans that are medically risky with the goal of helping their patients achieve athletic goals.

For example, cortisone injections reduce pain and inflammation so that athletes can play while injured. But the shots are not a substitute for physical therapy, for allowing time for an injury to heal, or for surgery. Cortisone shots can cause cartilage damage or ruptured tendons, and the long-term health effects are unknown. Despite the absence of a clear medical benefit and the presence of significant risks, team doctors regularly administer injections to athletes so they can play. In these cases, physicians recognize that their duty is not to promote players' health above all else because patients' overall goals may necessitate endangering their health.

1.3 Patient Expertise and Drug Choice

This epistemic argument supports the doctrine of informed consent. It also explains why cosmetic surgeons can act permissibly even though they do not promote health. It explains why sports medicine can be an ethical industry. Additionally, this argument calls for the right of self-medication. Though proponents of an epistemic justification for the doctrine of informed consent often invoke Mill's argument for a liberty principle, when Mill applied his argument to medicine, it was not in favor of a principle of informed consent but for rights of self-medication. Mill wrote that prescription requirements were wrong because they would interfere with patients' choices and make some legitimate uses of drugs impossible, or at least more expensive.[10]

To extend on Mill's argument, when it comes to a patient's expertise about her own well-being, it doesn't matter whether she is making a judgment about accessing or refusing treatment. When Debbie decides to refuse treatment, against medical advice, it is because she judges that treatment is not in her overall interest. When Danny seeks treatment against medical advice, it is because he judges that forgoing treatment is in his overall interest. In both cases, the reason to defer to Debbie or Danny is that Debbie and Danny are experts on their overall interests. In both cases their choice is against medical advice. If proponents of informed consent truly take a principle of deference seriously, then they should defer to patients, whatever their choice. This means allowing not only risky refusal but risky access as well, at least for similar levels of risk.

Again, this argument relies on the idea that health is only one of many values. Whether a particular treatment is safe depends on whether the overall risks of a drug are justified in light of the overall benefits. Drug safety is not a scientific judgment that requires medical training and expertise about the physiological effects of a chemical. Drug safety is a normative judgment that requires knowledge about how the risks and side effects of a drug fit into a patient's life as a whole. Therefore, if the goal of pharmaceutical regulations were to ensure the safe use of medications, the epistemic argument would recommend that physicians and public officials defer to patients when it comes to drug choices

---

[10] Mill, *On Liberty*, 117.

since patients are experts on themselves. The patient likely knows best how side effects will fit into her life as a whole, or whether she experiences her condition as severe and burdensome relative to the effects of a medication.

When a physician makes a decision about whether to allow a patient to access a prescription-only drug, the decision is based on an analysis of how risky the drug is, which depends on the severity of the condition it treats and the expected side effects for a particular patient-type. But a physician cannot know whether using a drug is "worth it," which is precisely the question physicians are required to ask when they are designated as gatekeepers between patients and prescription drugs.

Pharmaceutical regulators are in an even worse position to judge whether a patient should have access to a drug. At least physicians meet the patients whose medication choices they have the power to constrain. Regulators make decisions for thousands of patients, whom they have never met, imposing the same risk-benefit calculus on a vast heterogeneous patient population. One patient may be extremely bothered by restless leg syndrome but tolerate dizziness with ease, whereas another may find that a side effect like dizziness is worse than a condition like restless leg syndrome. These patients will come to different judgments about whether taking a drug that is associated with dizziness to treat restless leg syndrome is worth it for them, but approval policies cannot capture these tradeoffs. It is impossible for a regulator to know whether the risks of a drug are acceptable in light of the potential benefits for each patient who is affected by the decision to prohibit a drug or limit access to an unapproved drug.

The distinction between what is medically advisable and what is a good choice is crucial to this argument. Even if it is medically inadvisable for a patient to use a dangerous, unknown, unapproved, untested drug, it may be advisable on balance. She may judge that the potential benefits will justify any health risk no matter how extreme. She may not care about a lack of information about a new drug. Some patients might seek dangerous and untested drugs out of desperation because no other treatments have worked and they suffer from terminal and degenerative illnesses. Proponents of drug regulations say that these patients decide against their interests when they seek ineffective drugs that have sickening effects. Yet even if it were true that allowing patients to choose medications would have negative health effects, healthcare professionals cannot know if allowing patients to choose medications would undermine patients' overall well-being.

When pharmaceutical policy empowers physicians and regulators to decide whether the risks of a particular treatment are worth it given the benefits, people who have scientific knowledge are empowered to make decisions about other people's values. Safety is a normative judgment. There is no pharmacological property of a substance or physiological property of a patient that a physician or regulator can point to as the thing that makes it safe to use a drug. A drug is safe if the effects are not too severe in light of its benefits, but physicians and regulators are not trained to judge what makes a risk too severe. Nor should health workers be trained about what makes a drug acceptably risky or not, because the truth about acceptable risk will depend on each patient's attitude, plans, and projects.

As a counterexample to the foregoing argument, we might imagine patients who genuinely do choose against their interests. Whether because of cognitive biases, stupidity, imprudence, or indifference, people make terrible choices all the time and later regret those choices. Yet for the epistemic arguments in favor of informed consent and self-medication to fail, it is not sufficient to simply point to examples where patients were mistaken about their interests. One would need to show instead that patients are more reliably mistaken about their interests than physicians and regulators.

Such an argument may go something like this.[11] Physicians and regulators are unbiased because they are not experiencing the pain and fear associated with an illness, and they also have much more experience seeing the effect of treatment choices not only on people's health but also on their lives as a whole. In contrast, patients' judgments are clouded by their emotions and limited experiences. Patients may also be unduly shortsighted and weak willed in circumstances where promoting long-term interests requires planning and distance from one's immediate impulses. For example, a patient may acknowledge that losing weight is in her overall interest, but change her mind about those interests when she encounters a dessert tray.[12]

I will address this kind of skepticism about patients' expertise throughout the following chapters, but for now I consider four responses. First, the price of this skepticism is to reject not only self-medication but also informed consent. If patients cannot make choices in their long-term interests, then as long as a deceptive or coercive intervention is not too burdensome, it shouldn't matter if it limits access or refusal choices on behalf of the patient. Those who are skeptical of patients' abilities to decide in their interests must either explain why it justifies limits on self-medication but not informed consent, or they must abandon informed consent as we generally understand it.

Second, even if patients suffer from reliable cognitive biases that impair their ability to perceive and act in their overall interests, physicians and regulators have cognitive deficits when it comes to perceiving another person's interests. I claimed that patients are more motivated to promote their interests and more informed about their interests simply because those interests are their own.

---

[11] I am grateful to Nir Eyal for prompting me to consider this objection to the epistemic argument.
[12] Richard Holton, "Rational Resolve," *Philosophical Review* (2004): 507–35.

Unlike most judgments, when it comes to judgments about oneself, partiality is a credential, not a bias.

Third, the claim that the relevant characterization of a person's overall interests refers to her long-term well-being is itself a controversial claim. Some people may value their long-term well-being a lot, but others may embrace a carpe diem outlook that values the benefits of having dessert today more than any troubles a choice may cause in the future. Those who cite patients' biases as a reason for skepticism about their qualifications to make medical choices must not only establish that patients are more biased than physicians but also defend the claim that certain ways of making decisions are biases—for example, deciding with a preference for the status quo or for short-term gains.

Fourth, even if patients' judgments about their well-being are not reliable, it doesn't follow that the judgments of physicians and regulators should prevail. Insofar as physicians and public officials can educate and inform patients in ways that ameliorate patients' judgments, they ought to, since patients still have greater knowledge of their own values and experiences than others would even if they are biased or misinformed.

Another reason in favor of deferring to patients is that patients' judgments about the effects of treatment choices can potentially become a self-fulfilling prophecy. The mere belief that a treatment will make a patient worse off could make it true that the treatment will make her worse off if she has it. Similarly, the belief that being denied a treatment would make a patient worse off may mean that denying treatment is harmful. Not only are patients generally experts on their interests, but also patients' beliefs and choices determine what is in their interests. When it comes to a patient's well-being, thinking that an intervention or prohibition is an injury might be sufficient to make it so.

This epistemic argument in favor of self-medication does not deny that medical experts are indeed experts on health and medicine. In most cases, an expert's advice is relevant to a patient's judgment about her overall interest. Many of us have a strong interest in preserving our health, so medical advice is tremendously valuable to us. Millions of people seek the advice of financial planners, consumer reports, and family therapists, even though citizens can legally manage their money, buy appliances, and navigate personal challenges without consultation or approval from an expert. Similarly, the freedom to choose which drugs to use would not undermine the importance or value of medical expertise. Anyone who values his or her health and is capable of accessing the advice of physicians, pharmacists, and regulators before using a risky drug is likely to seek out the relevant information.

However, prohibitive policies are not necessary for the provision of medical advice. The current system of pharmaceutical regulation doesn't just encourage people to make medically advisable treatment choices; it requires them to do so. This policy is a mistake because not all patients will judge that acting in accordance with medical advice is their best choice, and it is more likely that patients, rather than physicians, know which choices are in their interests. For this reason, where patients judge that their overall well-being departs from an expert's judgment, public policy should permit patients' judgments to prevail. This requires a right of self-medication—patients should be permitted to access their chosen treatment because they are best informed about their own values and interests.

1.4 Intimate Choices

If patients are generally the experts on their overall interests, then patients have a kind of epistemic authority that physicians and regulators lack. This is significant because many people think that medicine and government should promote overall well-being. Those concerned with overall well-being would then do well to consult the patients in matters of health. But even if I am wrong about patients' expertise about their well-being, the strongest reasons in favor of informed consent and self-medication do not rely on epistemic considerations or empirical conjectures about which policies would promote well-being. The most important reason to respect a patient's autonomy is that each person has the right to decide what happens to his or her own body.

Today, physicians and public officials must abide by the doctrine of informed consent, even when it is clear that a patient's choice will not promote her overall well-being on any plausible account of well-being. Insofar as it is possible to knowingly make a choice that is worse for one's well-being on balance, patients are entitled to do so when they make medical decisions.

Consider an analogy to romantic choices. Most of us can think of people in our lives who manage their romantic lives in ways that are terrible for their short-term and long-term well-being. This kind of a hopeless romantic might acknowledge this fact but, nevertheless, persist with her choices. She may not care about being happy, or having her desires satisfied, or living her life in a way that realizes an objective list of values. Or, she may care about those things but value other things more, such as her family's approval or societal acceptance. Or perhaps she is very accepting of risk and judges that a slim chance of finding her soul mate is worth the distress caused by bad relationships. In any case, you might think that she is making a series of poor choices, and you might be right. But even if you were right, you *still* would not be entitled to trick or coerce her into dating your preferred matches, and you would not have a right to forbid her from dating people who were bad for her well-being. You could make recommendations, such as "maybe you should try dating women instead," or "maybe you should stop dating your brother's friends," but enforcing these suggestions would be wrong even if doing so promoted her overall well-being.

Medical decisions are similarly intimate and personal, if not more so. Medical choices are bodily, ailments and diseases are often impossible to ignore, and a person's health has a substantial impact on every other choice and plan she makes. Anne Phillips argues that people are intrinsically embodied and that we cannot understand ourselves without reference to our bodies.[13] Because of this link between persons and bodies, Phillips argues that bodily harms are more morally serious than other harms, such as property crimes. Even if embodiment is not intrinsically linked to one's personhood and self-understanding, the fact that people attach special normative significance to their bodies is a reason to treat bodies as if they were morally distinctive.[14] Another reason to grant special moral significance to bodily choices is that bodies are especially closely linked to a person's autonomy. Most people require functioning bodies to carry out their plans and to write the story of their lives.

For these reasons, bodily choices have a distinctive quality that justifies distinctive protection for bodily rights. Patients are therefore justified in feeling violated when their physicians lie to them about the risks of treatment, just as it is a serious violation when people make other intimate choices under false pretenses.[15] In Judge Cardozo's ruling on Mary Schloendorff's case, he emphasized that Mary's rights to determine what should be done with her one body were sacrosanct. Other judicial affirmations of the doctrine of informed consent echoed this position. For example, in *Cobbs v. Grant*, the Supreme Court of California found that physicians must disclose the risks and benefits of alternative treatments on the grounds that "a person of adult years and in sound mind has the right, in the exercise of control over his own body, to determine whether or not to submit to lawful medical treatment."[16]

Even if a physician never touches a patient's body, if he fails to disclose relevant information about the patient's treatment choices, he can violate the patient's bodily rights. Philosophical justifications for informed consent also single out the particular importance of bodily choices. For example, Nir Eyal considers that a patient's interest in personal integrity, especially bodily integrity, could ground informed consent requirements.[17] There, he invokes Ronald

[13] Anne Phillips, *Our Bodies, Whose Property?* (Princeton, NJ: Princeton University Press, 2013), 11.

[14] Jessica Flanigan, "Review: Anne Phillips: *Our Bodies, Whose Property?*," *APA Newsletter on Feminism and Philosophy* 14, no. 1 (Fall 2014).

[15] For example, if a rapist leads his victim to falsely believe that he is her husband, the victim still has been raped, even if the rapist did not use force or coercion.

[16] *Cobbs v. Grant*. For more on the ethics of this case see Alan J. Weisbard, "Informed Consent: The Law's Uneasy Compromise with Ethical Theory Medical Jurisprudence Symposium," *Nebraska Law Review* 65 (1986): 749–67.

[17] Nir Eyal, "Informed Consent," *The Stanford Encyclopedia of Philosophy*, ed. Edward N. Zalta, Fall 2012, http://plato.stanford.edu/archives/fall2012/entries/informed-consent/.

Dworkin's idea of adopting "a prophylactic line that comes close to making the body inviolate."[18]

Just as patients have rights to make decisions about medical interventions, such as surgery, and to be informed about the risks of each available treatment, patients also have rights to make decisions about medication in virtue of their bodily rights. For example, it would be a significant violation of Debbie's bodily rights to trick or force her to use insulin. Yet, as in cases of informed consent and other intimate choices, the right to make decisions about medications not only prohibits unwanted interventions, it also prohibits people from concealing or prohibiting alternative choices. In this way, an official can therefore violate a person's right, even if he never physically interferes with the person whose rights are violated.

To further illustrate this point, consider an analogy to reproductive choice. Proponents of abortion rights will sometimes make an argument that says, "my body, my choice." By this they do not mean that their bodily rights entitle them only to refuse or consent to abortions when a physician or public official approves of that choice. Rather, "my body, my choice" is meant to imply that women are entitled both to choose to continue a pregnancy without interference *and* to access emergency contraception or abortion services from willing providers. The analogy to abortion is especially apt because it is another policy that reflects the misplaced sense of entitlement that public officials display when they legally limit what members of disadvantaged groups may do with their bodies, often in the guise of public health and safety. If women have rights to abortion, then laws that prohibit the provision of abortions violate women's abortion rights, even if women never face legal penalties for abortion and criminal sanctions only apply to providers.

An analogy to the right to die is also helpful on this point. In 1997, John Rawls, T. M. Scanlon, Thomas Nagel, Ronald Dworkin, Robert Nozick, and Judith Thomson jointly penned "The Philosophers' Brief," an amicus curiae brief for two Supreme Court cases arguing for a constitutionally protected right to die. In it, they argued that the Constitution ought to protect patients' right to die because the interest in making end-of-life decisions "is so central a part of the more general right to make 'intimate and personal choices' for himself that a failure to protect that particular interest would undermine the general right altogether."[19] The right to *refuse* lifesaving treatment was already protected as part of informed consent, but the philosophers in "The

---

[18] Ronald Dworkin, "Comment on Narveson: In Defense of Equality," *Social Philosophy and Policy* 1, no. 1 (September 1983): 24–40, doi:10.1017/S0265052500003307.

[19] Ronald Dworkin et al., "Assisted Suicide: The Philosophers' Brief," *New York Review of Books*, March 27, 1997, 41–47.

Philosophers' Brief" pointed out that the right to access deadly treatment was justified for the same reasons.

Both abortion and assisted dying are exceptionally personal decisions. In these cases the right to refuse treatment is not enough to respect a person's singular entitlement to terminate a pregnancy or end his or her life. For patients to truly have meaningful options when it comes to abortion or assisted dying, the right to use medical services or drugs is necessary as well. More generally, the examples of assisted dying and abortion illustrate how the decision to use a particular drug could be the kind of intimate choice that merits protection, since pharmaceuticals can be used to cause an abortion or to end a person's life.

But abortifacients and deadly drugs are not the only pharmaceuticals that might be required for a patient to live and die in accordance with her most deeply felt commitments. Similarly, choices about using or not using pharmaceuticals can be important for the expression of a person's identity or integral to a person's ability to live in accordance with her values. For example, some religions discourage people from taking psychotherapeutic drugs, and their members define themselves in terms of this choice. But other people may find that they cannot achieve their goals or act in accordance with their values without the assistance of psychotherapeutic drugs. For both groups, decisions about pharmaceutical use are intensely personal choices. Contraceptives are another class of drugs that are closely linked to people's interest in bodily integrity. Some women choose not to use contraception while others value the ability to have sex without getting pregnant or benefit from contraceptives in other ways. In this case, access to pharmaceuticals is necessary for women to effectively control their own bodies.

Dietary choices also helpfully illustrate the connection between self-medication and the right to decide what happens to one's body. Diabetic patients like Debbie and Danny are entitled to make risky food choices, even if doing so threatens their overall well-being. The risks of choosing unhealthy food can be as substantial as the risks of choosing to use a drug against medical advice. Millions of people suffer from conditions related to obesity that threaten their long-term health. Yet people are nevertheless entitled to eat unhealthily, and patients like Debbie are entitled to opt for a healthy diet instead of using pharmaceuticals. Why are people entitled to ingest unhealthy food in dangerous quantities but not comparably permitted to take dangerous drugs? This asymmetry cannot be sustained. If the freedom to make dietary choices is justified because food is an especially significant expression of a person's identity, or an important part of daily life, or an exercise of one's bodily rights, then it shouldn't matter whether someone is swallowing a pill or a piece of pie.

1.5 Anti-paternalism and Freedom to Choose

One may resist this line of argument by claiming that the fact that people tend to value intimate and personal bodily choices more than other choices does not mean that those choices merit special protection. This argument could go two ways. On one hand, perhaps resistance to violations of bodily integrity is mere squeamishness and taboo, and people shouldn't think their bodily choices are different from choices that affect their property or their reputations. But this view would seem to license a range of interventions that are deeply at odds with liberal values and foundational ethical commitments such as the doctrine of informed consent.

On the other hand, if people were unjustified in singling out bodily choices, then perhaps other sorts of entitlements, such as property rights or reputations, would merit further protection as well. Such a view would preserve the conviction that patients' rights of informed consent or self-medication merit protection even if intimate and personal decisions were not morally uniquely important. Instead, the duty to respect patients' autonomy would be justified by an appeal to the more general principle that all choices that patients value merit protection, whether they involve bodies or not.

This strategy highlights another justification for rights of self-medication that doesn't rely on the aforementioned arguments about the importance of medical autonomy. Even if one rejects the claim that people have specific rights of self-medication, it would not follow that public officials are entitled to use coercion or force to prevent people from making treatment decisions, because people do have more general rights against coercion and violence. So even if a person's treatment choice does not concern matters that are particularly intimate or personal, public officials should refrain from using coercion to limit his choices as long as he does not choose to violate other people's rights.

This idea, which is most firmly grounded in Kantian principles, is affirmed by a range of philosophical perspectives. One reason to endorse a presumption of respect for people's choices is that we are rationally required to acknowledge the value of our own and others' choice-making capacities, as Kant and contemporary Kantians have argued. On this view, a person would be inconsistent if he acted as if his plans and projects had authority in determining how he lived his life but did not recognize the authority of other people's plans and intentions in determining how they lived their lives.

Other normative ethicists arrive at similar conclusions. Stephen Darwall persuasively argues that paternalistically interfering with a competent adult's choices reflects a failure to recognize the respect that she is owed as a member of the moral community who has equal status to others. In other words, paternalism is incompatible with an assumption of moral equality. Darwall writes:

> The objectionable character of paternalism . . . is not primarily that those who seek to benefit us against our wishes are likely to be wrong about what really benefits us. It is not simply misdirected care or even negligently misdirected care. It is, rather, primarily a failure of respect, a failure to recognize the authority that persons have to demand, within certain limits, that they be allowed to make their own choices for themselves.[20]

According to these views, *even if* interference would benefit a person, it is still wrong to paternalistically interfere with a choice because it is disrespectful to the authority she has to make her own choices.

Similarly, egalitarians may agree that paternalistic interference is generally impermissible on the grounds that it expresses an infantilizing or offensive judgment of a person. As Jonathan Quong argues, paternalistic interference is *pro tanto* wrong because it is motivated by a negative and offensive judgment about another person's ability to choose well.[21] Paternalism is therefore incompatible with an assumption that all members of society are morally equal and entitled to equal freedoms. Seana Shiffrin similarly argues that paternalism always calls for further justification. Shiffrin writes:

> [Paternalism] directly expresses insufficient respect for the underlying valuable capacities, powers, and entitlements of the autonomous agent. Those who value equality and autonomy have special reasons to resist paternalism toward competent adults.[22]

These arguments do not entail that paternalism can never be justified, but they do set a high standard for proponents of paternalism to justify interfering with people's choices for the sake of their own well-being. On these accounts, any justification of paternalism must not only establish that the paternalism is effective (thereby overcoming the epistemic challenges to paternalism described in the previous sections) but also explain why the moral reasons against violating a person's rights and expressing an offensive view of her capacities are outweighed by the moral importance of forcing her to make the "right choice."

[20] Stephen Darwall, "The Value of Autonomy and Autonomy of the Will," *Ethics* 116, no. 2 (January 1, 2006): 263–84, doi:10.1086/498461.

[21] Jonathan Quong, *Liberalism without Perfection* (Oxford; New York: Oxford University Press, 2011).

[22] Seana Valentine Shiffrin, "Paternalism, Unconscionability Doctrine, and Accommodation," *Philosophy & Public Affairs* 29, no. 3 (2000): 205–50, doi:10.1111/j.1088-4963.2000.00205.x.

A presumption in favor of free choice is also justified by an appeal to the interests that everyone has in virtue of being autonomous beings. For example, Ryan
Davis has argued that because autonomy is a future-oriented capacity, every
autonomous person has an interest in effectively making decisions and plans,
which requires that people refrain from interfering with other people's plans.[23]
Similarly, Christine Korsgaard offers an interpretation of Kant's Formula of
Humanity that shows how we can deduce substantive moral principles, such as
the duty to refrain from paternalistic interference, by reflecting on what it is to
act.[24] She argues that we should think of moral reasons as the objective reasons
we have, whatever our inclinations or desires (in contrast to the subjective reasons we have only in virtue of our desires).[25] She then makes the case that people
have objective reasons to respect other people's choices because the only thing
that each person has reason to value is the capacity to value, which is same capacity as the capacity to choose. Crucially, well-being is *not* unconditionally valuable
for people in this universal way because the choices that promote one person's
well-being will not promote another's.[26] In contrast, each person does have an
unconditional reason to respect other people's choices because, once you recognize the value of your own ability to choose, "you must view anyone who has the
power of rational choice as having, in virtue of that power, a value conferring status."[27] In practice then, Kant's argument requires that each person refrain from
interfering with other people's choices, but people are not required to attend to
conditionally valuable features of others, such as features of their well-being.
Therefore paternalistic interference is impermissible because it involves interference with a person's ability to choose for the sake of her well-being.

All these arguments against paternalism share in the conviction that respect
sets the limits on what is permissible. Contrast these views with what is sometimes called a consequentialism of rights.[28] A consequentialist might hold that we
should promote autonomous choosing rather than respect autonomous choices.
If so, then interference with autonomous choices would be justified in those cases
where it promoted autonomy on balance. For example, a consequentialist might
argue that it is permissible to interfere with a person's decision to drink if being
drunk would undermine her autonomy on balance. The foregoing arguments in
favor of freedom of choice are different from a consequentialism of rights because

---

[23] Ryan Davis, "The Moral Significance of Respect for Persons," Working paper, Brigham Young
University, 2015.

[24] Christine M. Korsgaard, *Creating the Kingdom of Ends* (Cambridge, UK: Cambridge University
Press, 1996).

[25] Korsgaard, *Creating the Kingdom of Ends*.

[26] Though as I argued in the previous section, this is true too.

[27] Korsgaard, *Creating the Kingdom of Ends*.

[28] Michael Smith, "Two Kinds of Consequentialism," *Philosophical Issues* 19, no. 1 (October 1,
2009): 257–72, doi:10.1111/j.1533-6077.2009.00169.x.

they maintain that, even if interference would promote autonomy, it is still impermissible because it would violate the authority each person has to make her own choices.

There are other egalitarian reasons to oppose paternalistic interference by public officials too. Paternalism has long been used to justify violating the rights of vulnerable and oppressed groups. During the nineteenth century, American slavery apologists disingenuously justified slavery by an appeal to paternalism.[29] Women were historically denied economic liberties and political rights on the grounds that men could better secure women's interests. Even today, workers are prohibited from taking jobs that public officials deem degrading or dangerous, such as jobs as sex workers or jobs that violate maximum hour requirements. These considerations highlight the disproportionate harms of paternalistic policies. Furthermore, rich, well-connected, and socially advantaged people are able to avoid or pay the penalties associated with prohibitive policies, including paternalistic ones. Paternalism further subjects marginalized people to governmental interference without their consent, ostensibly for their own sake.

These arguments against paternalism support rights against self-medication insofar as prohibitive pharmaceutical policies are justified by an appeal to the interests or well-being of people who would access pharmaceuticals in the absence of restrictions. In light of these considerations, anti-paternalism is particularly important in medical contexts because patients are especially vulnerable. Like people who endure racism, patriarchy, and poverty, those who suffer from a disability or an illness are often marginalized, discriminated against, and disadvantaged. But a person's marginalized status does not justify treating her like a child, which only compounds the harms of marginalization. Paternalism toward children is only justified insofar as they lack the capacity to decide. Unlike children, adults who face oppression or misfortune are not rendered incapable simply because they cannot effectively overcome social or natural adversity.

Ultimately, I think the most compelling reasons for rights of self-medication are these more general reasons against paternalism. Patients not only have epistemic authority about their interests and well-being, they also have the normative authority to make treatment choices. Policies that prohibit people from accessing pharmaceuticals are disrespectful. They express a judgment by physicians and policymakers that people are not able to competently make a pharmaceutical choice and, like other forms of paternalism, treat adult patients as if they were children. The doctrine of informed consent is supported by each of these arguments against paternalism. Physicians cannot interfere with a patient's choice in order to benefit her because to do so is to violate her right to

---

[29] Howard McGary Jr. and Bill E. Lawson, *Between Slavery and Freedom: Philosophy and American Slavery* (Bloomington, IN: Indiana University Press, 1993), 20–21.

decide for herself, and it expresses the judgment that the physician has more of a claim to choose what happens to her body than she does.

1.6 Patient Protection

Another reason to support the doctrine of informed consent is that it protects patients from abuse. In particular, even if one is unconvinced by arguments in favor of a general right to choose, one may agree that people have rights against coercion, battery, or fraud. Medicine involves interactions between physicians and patients that would be impermissible without consent, which transforms actions that would ordinarily be immoral (e.g., cutting into someone's body) into something permissible.

This justification for informed consent is based on Manson and O'Neill's argument that the doctrine is best understood as a way of preventing physicians from acting wrongly.[30] On their account, informed consent is a way of ensuring that all physicians take due care to ensure that their patients are sufficiently informed so as not to be deceived and to protect patients from feeling coerced or pressured to make a particular decision. They therefore think of informed consent as a way of knowing whether a patient has waived her rights—the right to not be deceived or rights against battery, for example.

To see why this argument for informed consent also justifies a right of self-medication, it is helpful to focus on the insight that informed consent transforms what would otherwise be an impermissible violation into permissible conduct by a physician. For example, performing unwanted medical interventions is a form of battery, but providing a surgery to a consenting patient is permissible and even praiseworthy in most cases. As Manson and O'Neill discuss at length, withholding information and deceiving a patient is wrong, but if physicians have a conversation with patients and allow opportunities to ask questions and learn about a treatment, the patient cannot claim to have been misled or wronged. Finally, it would be abusive for physicians to threaten patients with penalties if they did not comply with medical advice, and it is difficult to see how informed consent requirements could permit this kind of behavior, so informed consent prohibits coercion by medical professionals.

Now consider whether pharmaceutical regulations constitute behaviors that would be abusive in other contexts, and whether patients have an opportunity to transform what would otherwise be mistreatment into something permissible by way of their consent. Pharmaceutical regulations are backed by threats of legal force, such as fines and, in some cases, criminal penalties. In ordinary circumstances, if a public official or a physician threatens to physically restrain

---

[30] Neil C. Manson and Onora O'Neill, *Rethinking Informed Consent in Bioethics* (Cambridge; New York: Cambridge University Press, 2007).

a patient, take her money, or imprison her for making an unhealthy decision; such conduct would be a kind of mistreatment unless the patient consented. That is, if it is wrong to coerce a patient so that she makes an advisable medical choice, then it shouldn't matter whether the coercion is done by a physician or by a public official.

Patients do not consent to the pharmaceutical regulations that are enforced by physicians, pharmacists, and public officials.[31] Therefore, just as informed consent requirements stand as a check against coercive treatments, informed consent should also stand as a check against the coercive practices of public officials, such as pharmaceutical regulations that deprive patients of their rights of self-medication.

1.7 Ignorance and Fraud

The idea that consent can alter the moral landscape between a patient and her provider is also helpful for understanding why the doctrine of informed consent and rights of self-medication include rights against being deceived about the known and unknown risks of drugs. However, not all instances of ignorance amount to deception, so not all forms of patient ignorance invalidate a patients' ability to consent to pharmaceutical use or refusal.

One source of patient ignorance is the inherent risks associated with many pharmaceuticals, which pose unknown dangers to those who use them. But in general, if a person can consent to an outcome, then she can also consent to the risks of that outcome. So if a person was entitled to take a drug that was guaranteed to have a particular effect (e.g., a deadly drug or a drug that only caused stomach cramps), then she is also able to consent to use a drug that carries a risk of that effect. Another source of patient ignorance is the cost of learning about a drug. But a reasonable person may choose to remain somewhat ignorant about the risks of a

---

[31] One may reply that this move from informed consent to self-medication is too quick because any plausible account of coercion will ultimately rest on an antecedent theory of people's entitlements not to be coerced. That is, the argument is circular if I am suggesting that people have rights of self-medication because they have rights against coercive pharmaceutical regulations because those regulations violate rights of self-medication. I am sympathetic to this reply. It stands as a serious objection to Manson and O'Neill's influential account of informed consent, insofar as their account aims to avoid resting on a controversial theory of rights but defines mistreatment in terms of a theory of rights. If successful, this objection shows that informed consent cannot be justified simply as a way of preventing wrongful behavior, because what counts as wrongful will depend on a background theory of patients' entitlements. We must therefore look at the arguments, such as those mentioned here, about whether people are entitled to make self-regarding choices about their bodies or self-regarding choices more generally. If those arguments succeed, however, then they will justify the informed consent requirements that Manson and O'Neill argue for, as well as rights of self-medication.

drug if she judges that the risks of remaining ignorant are justified in light of what she does know and the costs of learning more. In these cases, the mere presence of risk and uncertainty do not invalidate a patient's ability to consent to treatment.

There are three reasons to accept the principle that if a person can consent to drugs with certain outcomes that she can also consent to drugs that carry known and unknown risks. First, drugs with certain outcomes may be understood as drugs that have a 100 percent likelihood of a particular effect. It is unclear why a person would be permitted to consent to a 100 percent likelihood of a single outcome but not a 50-50 lottery between two outcomes. Second, the decision to forgo pharmaceutical use is also risky, so if the mere presence of risk overturned a person's ability to consent to pharmaceutical use, it would also threaten rights of informed consent. Third, imagine a person created a drug that had completely unknown risks and effects, such that it could cause death or immortality, pain or euphoria, disfigurement or incredible beauty, personality change and memory loss or perfect rationality and memory.[32] Further imagine that the likelihood of all these outcomes is also completely unknown. If the manufacturer of such a drug accurately represented the thoroughly mysterious nature of the drug, people could consent to use it. This example may seem far-fetched, but it reflects the idea that the first humans to use a newly developed drug after animal testing are in similar circumstances, yet few question their ability to consent to participate in early trials because the uncertain nature of the drugs are disclosed to them. But if a person can consent to a drug about which nothing is known, then, more generally, patients can consent to use drugs about which little is known.

On the other hand, patients who consent to take a drug do not necessarily automatically consent to all the risks associated with taking a drug. Voluntary assumption of a known risk does not amount to consent to the effects of the risk when the risk in question is associated with another person's wrongdoing.[33] After all, if a woman walks through a dangerous neighborhood on her way to work, she voluntarily walks on the street, where she may accidently step on some glass or trip on the sidewalk, but she does not consent to be robbed.[34] Similarly, when people consent to use drugs, they can consent to the disclosed risks of the drug, such as potential side effects. But people cannot consent to be deceived by manufacturers about the nature of a product.[35]

---

[32] I am thankful to Jason Brennan for discussing this example and its relevance to questions of risk and consent.

[33] I am thankful to Heidi Hurd for encouraging me to consider this point.

[34] This is true by definition, since robbery consists in taking another person's property without her consent.

[35] Arguments in favor of greater disclosure of the financial side effects of medical treatment reflect this ideal as well, to the extent that patients are sometimes mislead about the cost of treatment in clinical contexts. Alicia Hall, "Financial Side Effects: Why Patients Should Be Informed of Costs," *Hastings Center Report* 44, no. 3 (2014): 41–47.

Consent is a way of waiving one's general entitlement against interference, thereby altering the moral landscape between people. Deception is a form of interference that people cannot waive their entitlements against. If a person knew she was waiving her rights to be deceived, then deception would not be effective. Deception undermines a person's ability to consent to treatment in the same way that force or coercion does; by denying her the power to authorize treatment. If a physician or provider deceives a patient about a treatment, the patient cannot consent because she is unaware of what she is actually consenting to.

Both the epistemic and rights-based justifications for informed consent and rights of self-medication require protections against deception. Consider the epistemic argument first. A person is only in the best position to judge whether one treatment is better than another if she capable of learning about both treatments and of understanding the limits of her knowledge. Deception about drugs interferes with a patient's ability to know the truth about her treatment options. So a deceived patient's treatment choices may not reliably reflect her judgments about whether a treatment will promote her well-being on balance. In contrast, if truthful information about a drug is available to a patient and she chooses not to read it, then she consents to remain ignorant about the nature of a drug, and so we may assume that she judges that she would be better off on balance if she made an uninformed choice, perhaps because she judges that consulting an expert or learning about a new treatment is more costly in expectation than uninformed self-medication.

The deontological case against deception is more familiar. Following Kant, philosophers who defend people's rights against interference also tend to defend rights against deception. For example, Christine Korsgaard argues that lying is wrong because it is wrong to control another person's will. Since people cannot consent to be deceived, all acts of deception are a kind of interference with a person's natural authority to govern her own life.[36] By its very nature, the purpose of deception is to prevent one from acting as she would if she knew the truth. Alternatively, Tamar Schapiro argues that moral norms like honesty presuppose a reciprocal moral relationship between equals.[37] Paternalistic deception, and deception in general, violates these norms because it deprives only those who are deceived from having genuine control over their lives. People continue to discuss which background conditions mark out some locutions as deceptive and others as merely manipulative or misleading, and whether strategic reticence can ever amount to wrongful deception. But these debates about the scope of

---

[36] Christine M. Korsgaard, "The Right to Lie: Kant on Dealing with Evil," *Philosophy & Public Affairs* 15, no. 4 (October 1, 1986): 325–49.

[37] Tamar Schapiro, "Kantian Rigorism and Mitigating Circumstances," *Ethics* 117, no. 1 (2006): 32–57, doi:10.1086/508036.

wrongful deception do not undermine the more foundational claim that deception is wrong because it violates people's general rights to autonomously set and pursue their ends and to be treated as moral equals.

For these reasons, just as the doctrine of informed consent forbids physicians from knowingly withholding a cancer diagnosis or exaggerating the risks of a procedure, rights of self-medication forbid manufacturers from knowingly withholding information about the risks of a drug or from misleading patients about the risk of a treatment. In both cases, manufacturers are not entitled to deceive patients about the nature of a treatment, and public officials may rightly prevent and punish deception and fraud. Public officials may permissibly penalize fraud preemptively or in the event of harm, because, at either point, deceptive manufacturers are liable to be interfered with on the grounds that they are wrongfully deceiving consumers.

One may object to the claim that it is wrong for manufacturers to knowingly withhold information about the risks of their products. For example, James Child argues that an appeal to bodily rights (which he calls self-ownership) cannot on its own justify fraud protections, since such a view would seem to imply that a person's bodily rights can be violated by silence alone and this claim is in tension with the idea that each person is entitled (in virtue of his bodily rights) to simply remain silent and to refuse to provide others with information.[38] This point requires further clarification. If a manufacturer admits they are not disclosing all information about a product, or if norms develop where people assume that manufacturers withhold information about their products, then it may not be wrong for manufacturers to intentionally withhold information because patients would be able to knowingly consent to the risks of using drugs that potentially carry unknown risks. But if a manufacturer leads patients to believe they are disclosing all relevant information about a product and there are norms in place where people expect that manufactures disclose the contents and known information about their products unless stated otherwise, then it could be deceptive for manufacturers to knowingly withhold information about the risks of their products.

1.8 Self-Medication and Unapproved Drugs

Rights of self-medication require changes to the approval process for investigational drugs and changes to the prescription drug system. In the rest of this chapter, I will preview the arguments in favor of these policy reforms, which I will further defend in the next three chapters. For now, I will highlight the ways

[38] James W. Child, "Can Libertarianism Sustain a Fraud Standard?," *Ethics* 104, no. 4 (1994): 722–38.

that the foregoing arguments in favor of self-medication apply to these two policies in particular.

Consider first the approval process. Currently, patients are legally prohibited
from accessing investigational drugs until they have been approved safe and
effective by regulators at government agencies such as the FDA or the European
Medicine Agency (EMA). Yet safety is a normative judgment. Officials may certify a drug as safe even if there are some risks associated with its use, on the
grounds that the benefits outweigh the risks. Given that officials tolerate some
level of risk regarding drugs, the question is then how much risk is acceptable
given the benefits of a drug. This is a question that can be answered only by an
appeal to normative considerations, such as considerations about the value of a
drug's benefits or the value of avoiding side effects and risks, and considerations
about how best to make trade-offs between quality of life and life expectancy.
Just as physicians are not well placed to judge whether a course of treatment
is justified given her patients' other normative commitments, public officials
are not well placed to judge whether using an investigational drug is acceptably
safe for a large and heterogeneous patient population whose values and circumstances differ.

Premarket testing requirements that prohibit patients from accessing investigational therapies also violate patients' rights to make intimate and personal
decisions. The decision to use a drug in order to die is the kind of intimate and
personal decision that shapes the narrative of a person's life in a significant way.
And the decision to use a drug in order to live, which patients with terminal
and degenerative illnesses make when they seek access to investigational drugs,
is similarly as intimate and personal. In both cases, a person is choosing how
he or she wants to live and die, and, in both cases, access to drugs that are currently prohibited is required. Insofar as a drug could save a patient from death
or degenerative illness, self-medication rights are also a species of more general
rights of self-preservation.

More generally, prohibitions of experimental drugs are paternalistic,
and they interfere with patients' ability to access potentially therapeutic
drugs. Physicians and manufacturers are not legally permitted to provide
patients with unapproved drugs unless they are given special permission to
do so through compassionate access programs. This means that if a patient
wishes to purchase and use an unapproved therapy, even if her physician
agrees that doing so will improve her health and promote her overall well-
being, she may be legally prohibited from doing so on the grounds that
accessing unapproved drugs is dangerous. Laws that prohibit patients from
accessing unapproved drugs and physicians from using them are also coercive. Patients who aim to exercise their rights of self-preservation or their
bodily rights by using unapproved drugs face threats of fines and other legal
sanctions.

One concern is that approval requirements are necessary to ensure informed consent because otherwise patients and physicians would not have enough information to know whether a drug was safe or effective. Yet the off-label drug market in the United States demonstrates that a market in unapproved drugs is not incompatible with informed consent. In the United States, drugs are tested as effective treatments for particular patient-types with specific conditions. Once approved, those drugs can be prescribed off-label for any condition. Off-label prescribing gives us a glimpse into a world without prohibitive testing requirements. Without FDA approval for efficacy, physicians and patients rely on the available scientific evidence and decide whether the risks of an off-label treatment are justified. Off-label prescribing is common for children and pregnant patients, and most chemotherapy treatments are an off-label combination of drugs. The pervasiveness and success of the off-label market suggests that premarket efficacy testing requirements are not necessary to protect patients.

Patients' rights advocates have long argued for a right to try certain drugs, at least for people with serious and treatment-resistant conditions. The patients' rights movement has won significant victories in speeding the pace of approval and expanding access programs for investigational drugs. For example, more than twenty US states recently passed "right to try" legislation, which allows physicians and manufacturers to provide patients with access to investigational drugs outside the context of a clinical trial. Nevertheless, most patients still lack access to most investigational drugs, and the approval system remains prohibitive in all developed countries. Self-medication requires a right to try for all patients and citizens.

1.9 Self-Medication and Prescription Drugs

In addition to reforming the approval process, physicians and public officials should also rethink the prescription drug system in light of patients' rights of self-medication. Like premarket approval requirements, the prescription drug system violates rights of self-medication because it empowers physicians and regulators to prohibit patients from making treatment decisions. Prescription systems vary by country. Some places allow more drugs over the counter than others, and many European countries offer a third option of "behind the counter" drugs that do not require a prescription but do require authorization from a pharmacist. But all developed countries enforce prescription requirements for some drugs, such as painkillers.

Epistemic arguments in favor of self-medication support reforms to current prescription drug systems because the current systems all privilege physicians' and pharmacists' judgments about treatments, instead of patients' judgments about whether using a drug is the right choice. The example of Debbie and

Danny illustrated that this asymmetry is unjustified. In general, patients are more likely to be right about whether a treatment choice will promote their overall well-being. Patients are experts on their values and tolerance for risk, and choosing against medical advice should not undermine our belief that a patient is better equipped to decide what is best for her life on balance than her physician. Moreover, whether a patient chooses to refuse or access a treatment against medical advice does not undermine her epistemic advantage in knowing whether her treatment choice is in her interests.

To further illustrate this point, consider people who access neuroenhancing drugs, such as Adderall, without prescriptions. A growing number of students and professionals use neuroenhancements even though they do not have a medical condition that warrants the prescription of the drugs. Under the current system, people without a diagnosis of attention deficit disorder (ADD), or a similar condition, cannot legally buy Adderall because they cannot obtain a physician's prescription for the drug. One justification for a prohibition of Adderall is that the drugs are not safe enough to be used as neuroenhancements because they have significant health risks, such as high blood pressure, cardiovascular problems, anxiety, mania, and insomnia. Despite these significant risks, physicians are not equipped to judge whether the risks of Adderall are justified for the sake of the cognitive benefits it brings. Rather, some people with ADD may judge that the risks of using Adderall are not worth it despite the benefits, even if a physician recommends prescription treatment to manage the symptoms of ADD. And some people who do not suffer from ADD may judge that the risks of using Adderall are acceptable given the cognitive benefits of using the drug.

The example of Adderall also illustrates how the prescription drug system limits patients' rights to make intimate and personal decisions, and how the system is paternalistic and coercive. If a person goes on a diet to fit in a wedding dress, or enrolls in an extreme running program to complete a marathon, she may incur significant health risks because of her dietary or fitness choices, but she is permitted to do so on the grounds that she can make risky bodily choices for the sake of other values. People can permissibly use alcohol to make going to a club more enjoyable even though alcohol can be dangerous. Students are not forbidden from pulling all-nighters to gain an advantage on an exam, even though sleep deprivation is unhealthy. Similarly, a person who uses a neuroenhancing drug may accept the risks of drug use to make studying more enjoyable or to gain a professional advantage. The rights to incur bodily risks for the sake of important projects is a species of the more general right to decide what happens with one's own body, which is justified on the grounds that bodies are subjectively and objectively very important to people and that bodies are crucial for people to live their lives in accordance with their own values.

Prescription requirements are also paternalistic and coercive. Paternalism is wrong because it interferes with each person's natural entitlement to make self-regarding choices, and, in most cases, prescription drug requirements interfere with this entitlement by limiting the range of drugs a person can use. Paternalistic interference also expresses a negative and offensive judgment that a person is not equally entitled to make a decision as whoever is interfering. Prescription requirements express the judgment that patients are not entitled to make drug choices about their own bodies; they send the message that physicians and regulators have some authority to make pharmaceutical choices for other people.

Prescription requirements also coercively violate patients' rights of self-medication by using threats of legal penalty and state-sanctioned force to prevent people from exercising their normative authority to use pharmaceuticals without authorization. Returning to the example of Adderall, the US Drug Enforcement Agency (DEA) classifies Adderall as a Schedule II drug, meaning that only licensed practitioners can provide them to people and that patients must be authorized by a licensed practitioner to use them. Unauthorized possession or distribution of a Schedule II drug is punishable by up to five years in prison. Even if some prescription requirements are justified on the grounds that some drugs are addictive, which is an argument that I will address in the third chapter, officials' interference with non-addictive pharmaceutical choices could not be justified on these grounds.

1.10 Conclusion

Though different, the epistemic and rights-based justifications for informed consent agree that a patient has a special normative relationship to her own life. The epistemic justification focuses on a patient's authority in knowing what will promote her overall well-being, whereas rights-based justifications focus on a patient's authority in deciding what to do. The rights-based argument provides a less conditional foundation for rights of self-medication, whereas the epistemic justification for self-medication is more empirically contingent, especially for theories of well-being that do not give special weight to choice or desire-satisfaction.

In most cases though, both arguments deny the claim that physicians and public officials have the authority to either substitute their judgment for a patient or to decide on a patient's behalf. So the doctrine of informed consent and rights of self-medication are both supported by moral considerations that relate to the value of autonomy and the moral significance of well-being.

The same considerations that support the doctrine of informed consent support rights of self-medication because a person does not forfeit her moral status and authority to consent when she steps outside the clinic and into the pharmacy. Patients have superior knowledge about themselves and their own well-being, whether they are deciding to use or to refuse treatment. So proponents of informed consent should reaffirm their commitment to patients' rights by also advocating for self-medication. This may strike some as a revisionary conclusion, but the recognition of informed consent requirements in the twentieth century also faced significant opposition from members of the medical profession before they were widely affirmed. The current system of barriers and regulations is an injustice just as other forms of medical paternalism were unjust in the past. If we are to continue the moral progress that began in Mary Schloendorff's era, we should take patients' rights seriously for all kinds of medical choices, including pharmaceutical use.

Paternalism and Public Health

In the fall of 1937, more than one hundred people died slow and painful deaths after taking Elixir Sulfanilamide. Many of the victims were children who were given the drug to treat streptococcal infections. The drug caused abdominal pain and vomiting, renal failure, agonizing convulsions, and death.[1] Before 1937, Sulfanilamide was safely and effectively used in tablet and powder form, but the manufacturer, S.E. Massengil Co., reformulated it to be taken in liquid form. The new elixir formulation dissolved Sulfanilamide in diethylene glycol, a sweet poisonous substance that is similar to antifreeze. Harold Watkins, the chemist who developed the solvent for S.E. Massengil Co. did not test the mixture on animals or humans, or even review the medical literature that demonstrated the toxicity of diethylene glycol. Without any testing or oversight, the company distributed 633 shipments of the poisonous elixir.

Physicians reported the deadly effects of Elixir Sulfanilamide within a month of distribution, and members of the American Medical Association (AMA), the FDA, and S.E. Massengil Co. acted quickly to complete a national recall of the drug. The news media also participated in publicizing the dangers of the drug. As the recall continued, newspapers reported poisonings and near-poisonings, the shockingly minimal legal ramifications of S.E. Massengil Co.'s negligence, the CEO's seeming indifference to patients' deaths, and Harold Watkins's suicide in the wake of the tragedy.

One particularly powerful description of the Elixir Sulfanilamide tragedy was a widely publicized letter to President Roosevelt from Maise Nidiffer, a mother whose six-year-old daughter Joan died from taking the drug. Nidiffer wrote:

> The first time I ever had occasion to call in a doctor for [Joan] and she was given Elixir of Sulfanilamide. All that is left to us is the caring for her little grave. Even the memory of her is mixed with sorrow for we can see

---

[1] Carol Ballentine, "Taste of Raspberries, Taste of Death: The 1937 Elixir Sulfanilamide Incident," *FDA Consumer Magazine* (June 1981): http://www.fda.gov/aboutfda/whatwedo/history/product-regulation/sulfanilamidedisaster/default.htm.

her little body tossing to and fro and hear that little voice screaming with pain and it seems as though it would drive me insane. . . . It is my plea that you will take steps to prevent such sales of drugs that will take little lives and leave such suffering behind and such a bleak outlook on the future as I have tonight.[2]

Nidiffer's letter was included in a widely publicized report by Secretary of Agriculture Henry A. Wallace and FDA Commissioner Walter Campbell. The report called for unprecedented reforms to drug regulation, including premarket testing requirements, administrative authority to prohibit and recall drugs, the authority to regulate labels, and the requirement that manufacturers disclose all known properties of a drug.[3] These and other accounts of the disaster fortified public support for greater pharmaceutical regulation. In 1938, Congress passed the Food, Drug, and Cosmetic Act, which set the standards of drug regulation worldwide since its passage.

Maise Nidiffer's letter is one of the most compelling reasons to support pharmaceutical regulation. Drugs can be dangerous. Manufacturers cannot always be trusted. Someone should keep the public protected by ensuring that drugs are safe and effective. Premarket testing requirements and the prescription drug system were designed in part to ensure that patients do not unknowingly harm themselves by using dangerous drugs. However, *prohibitive* drug regulations, which violate patients' rights of self-medication, are not necessary to this end. If patients were adequately informed that a drug was not tested, if manufacturers disclosed the dangers of a drug, then patients could safely avoid dangerous drugs, like Elixir Sulfanilamide, even if such drugs were available.

There are other compelling reasons in favor of prohibitive drug regulations too. As in the case of informed consent, patients who are not sufficiently informed or mentally competent cannot give meaningful consent to treatment. If it were impossible to sufficiently inform people about drugs, or if people were not mentally capable of making choices about pharmaceuticals, then that could be grounds for prohibition as well.

Or, paternalists may argue that even if patients are capable of making choices about pharmaceuticals, prohibitive regulations are nevertheless permissible for the sake of public health. There are two versions of this defense of paternalism. Some paternalists argue that even competent citizens can rightly be prohibited from making self-destructive and unhealthy choices. Others argue in favor of

---

[2] Ibid.

[3] Daniel Carpenter and Gisela Sin, "Policy Tragedy and the Emergence of Regulation: The Food, Drug, and Cosmetic Act of 1938," *Studies in American Political Development* 21, no. 2 (September 2007): 149–80, doi:10.1017/S0898588X0700020X.

paternalism on the grounds that unhealthy choices are burdensome to the political community, which bears the cost of providing medical care to all citizens.

Proponents of prohibitive regulations must show not only that it is permissible to limit people's pharmaceutical choices for the sake of their health, they must also show that prohibitive policies promote public health on balance and that they are necessary to do so. Yet paternalistic arguments for drug regulation fail at each step. I argued in the previous chapter that it is not permissible to limit a person's treatment options on the grounds that she might make a bad choice. In this chapter I will argue further that the public health context is not morally different from the clinical context with respect to paternalism.

Furthermore, even if paternalistic policies were permissible, it is not clear that prohibitive pharmaceutical regulations are necessary to promote public health. In fact, prohibitions may actually undermine health, at least in some cases. Prescription requirements might not prevent accidental overdoses, for example, if the requirements make patients more deferential to physicians and tolerant of medical risks. Premarket testing requirements cause people to suffer and die waiting for new drugs to get approved, and they discourage new drug development.

This is not to say that regulation serves no purpose. Pharmaceutical regulators provide a valuable pubic good by overseeing testing for new drugs and by certifying drugs that they deem generally safe and effective. But the benefits of regulation do not require that the regulations be prohibitive, and prohibitive regulations not only violate patients' rights, they may also cost lives.

2.1 Prohibition and Protection

When S.E. Massengil Co. sold Elixir Sulfanilamide, the company did not disclose that the solvent was wholly untested. Patients who used the drug were led to believe that it was as safe as the previously available tablet and powder Sulfanilamide. The subsequent deaths were used to justify giving regulatory agencies the power to prohibit and recall drugs, but the 1938 Congress was also explicit that the new requirements ought not extend to prohibitions of existing and approved medicines. Rather, the initial legislation aimed to require that manufacturers show the FDA that new drugs were safe for use and appropriately labeled. The Act states it is "not intended to restrict in any way the availability of drugs for self-medication. On the contrary, it is intended to make self-medication safer and more effective."[4]

---

[4] Ronald Hamowy, *Government and Public Health in America* (Northampton, MA: Edward Elgar, 2007), 175.

Yet the 1938 Act did permit the FDA to prohibit new drugs until they were approved. Then, in 1951, Durham-Humphrey amendments to the 1938 Act introduced further limits on self-medication by allowing the FDA to require prescriptions for certain approved drugs.[5] Prescription-grade drugs were defined as those that are potentially toxic or harmful if used without authorization and supervision from a medical professional.[6]

The FDA's prohibitive power expanded again in 1962 when Congress passed the Kefauver-Harris amendments to the 1938 Act, which required that all manufacturers submit to safety and efficacy testing overseen by the FDA. Like the 1938 Act, the Kefauver-Harris amendments were passed after a public health crisis, when thousands of children in Europe were born with deformed limbs as a result of mothers' consumption of the morning sickness treatment thalidomide. The United States was spared from the thalidomide crisis because an FDA official, Dr. Francis Kelsey, delayed the manufacturer's application for approval. Kelsey became a national hero for protecting American families from the dangerous drug. Her story buoyed support for stronger drug regulations, though Kelsey acknowledged that an expansion of the agency's power was not necessary to prevent the marketing of dangerous drugs like thalidomide.[7] Finally, the US Congress passed the Comprehensive Drug Abuse Prevention and Control Act in 1970, which enabled the DEA to enforce prohibitions of prescription drugs and to distinguish between legitimate medical uses and illegitimate recreational drug use.[8]

Tragic incidents like the Elixir Sulfanilamide deaths and the thalidomide crisis heightened public support for the expansion of prohibitive pharmaceutical regulations from 1938–1970. But were prohibitive policies *necessary* to avoid these disasters? In both cases, had patients known that the drugs they were using were untested and potentially toxic, they most likely would not have used them. When patients died because they used these toxic medicines, the problem was not that people had access to a dangerous substance. After all, even today people can purchase antifreeze, bleach, and many other chemicals that would be toxic if ingested.

---

[5] Carpenter, *Reputation and Power: Organizational Image and Pharmaceutical Regulation at the FDA*. Princeton Studies in American Politics: Historical, International, and Comparative Perspectives (Princeton, NJ: Princeton University Press, 2010), 152.

[6] H. M. Marks, "Revisiting 'the Origins of Compulsory Drug Prescriptions,'" *American Journal of Public Health* 85, no. 1 (January 1995): 109–115, esp. 112.

[7] Kelsey wrote, "The Food, Drug, and Cosmetic Act passed in 1938 was indeed adequate to prevent marketing of thalidomide in this country, but the episode did serve to call attention to the inadequacies of this Act and hastened if not ensured its amendment in October 1962." Frances O. Kelsey, "Thalidomide Update: Regulatory Aspects," *Teratology* 38, no. 3 (June 6, 2005): 221–26.

[8] David T. Courtwright, "The Controlled Substances Act: How a 'big Tent' Reform Became a Punitive Drug Law," *Drug and Alcohol Dependence* 76, no. 1 (October 5, 2004): 9–15.

To achieve the 1938 legislation's purpose of making self-medication more effective, pharmaceutical regulators could have implemented a drug certification program rather than prohibitive requirements. Such a system could prevent accidental poisonings from dangerous drugs, but it would do so by providing information about the effects of a drug rather than by barring access to the drugs. The US Consumer Product Safety Commission (CPSC) is an example of a certification program that does not primarily prohibit people from purchasing dangerous products. The Commission regulates most consumer products that are not food, drugs, tobacco, medical devices, or firearms. It oversees some premarket safety testing to some extent, but this testing is mostly aimed at informing consumers about whether children's toys contain toxic materials.[9] In 2011, the CPSC launched an online database that catalogues and monitors consumer safety complaints, dangerous defects, and risks for all products, so that consumers can access the information necessary to make an informed choice. The CPSC also oversees voluntary recalls of dangerous products but has rarely used the legal system to force a manufacturer to comply with a recall.[10]

Despite the CPSC's apparent toothlessness, it promotes consumer safety through limited testing, voluntary recalls, information campaigns that discourage consumers from buying unsafe products, and labeling and safety disclosure requirements.[11] The CPSC works in part because companies are also legally liable for known but undisclosed safety hazards posed by their products. Anticipating CPSC oversight and potential liability encourages manufacturers to test products for safety and voluntarily disclose risk and warnings. [12] The CPSC's example demonstrates that protective policies needn't be prohibitive. If the risks associated with a product are disclosed, consumers can avoid products that are untested and refrain from purchasing products that they deem too dangerous.

So while access to dangerous drugs is a necessary condition for major drug disasters to occur, that fact does not imply that patients' access to drugs

[9] U.S. Consumer Product Safety Commission, "Toy Hazard Recalls," www.cpsc.gov/cpscpub/prerel/category/toy.Html. Also see Monica Becker, Sally Edwards, and Rachel I. Massey, "Toxic Chemicals in Toys and Children's Products: Limitations of Current Responses and Recommendations for Government and Industry," *Environmental Science and Technology* 44, no. 21 (2010): 7986–91.

[10] A recent study of the CPSC, which included a survey of recall reports and interviews with CPSC staff, also was unable to find any examples of non-voluntary recalls by the CPSC. See Seth M. Freedman, Melissa Schettini Kearney, and Mara Lederman, "Product Recalls, Imperfect Information, and Spillover Effects: Lessons from the Consumer Response to the 2007 Toy Recalls," NBER Working Paper No. 15183, July 2009.

[11] Ibid.

[12] Kenneth Ross and J. David Prince, "Symposium: The Products Liability Restatement: Was It a Success?: Post-Sale Duties: The Most Expansive Theory in Products Liability," *Brooklyn Law Review* 74 (Spring 2009): 963.

should be limited to avoid drug disasters. Perhaps pharmaceutical policies that promote informed decision-making by certifying drugs and publicizing risks could also avoid drug disasters without violating patients' rights of self-medication.

2.2 Soft Paternalism and Drug Regulation

One may respond to my call for certification by arguing that patients are not capable of understanding the consequences of using dangerous drugs, even if the risks of using a drug are disclosed. Paternalism that coercively interferes with someone's choice on the grounds that she is incapable of choosing is called soft paternalism. For some patient populations, soft paternalism is a valid reason to limit choice. For example, young children and mentally incompetent adults cannot give informed consent to treatment in the clinical context, in part due to their inability to understand the consequences of treatment decisions. In these cases, surrogate decision-makers ought to paternalistically choose a treatment on their behalf. Young children and mentally incompetent adults may also be unable to understand the consequences of using dangerous medications as well. And similarly, physicians, pharmacists, and public officials can also permissibly constrain treatment options for people who cannot make an informed and competent choice.

Yet prohibitive regulations apply to all citizens, including adults who are capable of making informed medical choices. For example, prescription drug laws forbid informed adult patients from using dangerous drugs without authorization from a physician. However, some philosophers doubt that even informed adult patients are capable of making medical decisions. For example, Sarah Conly defends a soft-paternalistic rationale for prescription requirements on the grounds that medicine is particularly complicated and even educated consumers cannot really understand information about prescription drugs. Conly writes:

> While [prescription requirements are] occasionally frustrating, there hasn't been any groundswell movement to eliminate the necessity for a doctor's visit for certain medications.... The idea seems to be that this isn't a judgment we can reliably make ourselves: the costs of a bad decision are great, expert knowledge is necessary and available, and we are thus, on the whole, better off having the decision taken out of our hands.[13]

---

[13] Sarah Conly, *Against Autonomy: Justifying Coercive Paternalism* (Cambridge: Cambridge University Press, 2012), 4.

And though people are generally capable of researching medications and learning about their effects, Conly is skeptical that research can substitute for the knowledge of a medical expert.

Following John Stuart Mill's claim that it would be permissible to stop someone from unknowingly trying to cross a broken or dangerous bridge, she suggests that prescription requirements can be defended on similar grounds. Yet, even if we grant Mill's claim that paternalism in emergency situations may be warranted, it would not establish that paternalism is justified whenever a person is irrational in a particular situation. Interference is only permissible in the broken bridge case because the bridge-crosser is not making an autonomous choice due to her lack of information. So, just as it is permissible to interfere with fundamentally incompetent decision-makers, such as children, it is permissible to interfere with temporarily incompetent bridge crossers. However, if she was informed and decided to cross anyhow, then paternalistic interference would be impermissible. Turning to prescription requirements, it is possible to inform people of the risks of using drugs. So Mill's argument in favor of emergency paternalism would not support paternalism in this case. This explains why Mill agreed that it was permissible to interfere with an uninformed choice, yet he opposed prescription requirements.[14]

But perhaps this is too quick. Conly suggests that the line between a competent person and an incompetent person is blurry, and that even competent adults can be irrational in some situations such that paternalistic interference could be warranted.[15] Steven Wall develops an argument like this too. Wall is skeptical that those who ground rights against interference in the value of autonomy can reject hard paternalism, for example, a policy that prevents competent and informed adults from using drugs, without those same considerations against hard paternalism also counting against soft paternalism, for example, stopping the person from crossing a broken bridge.[16] And whatever considerations one might cite in favor of soft paternalism would also count in favor of hard paternalism.

Wall's argument against my view goes like this. People make lots of non-autonomous choices that are not self-harming or destructive, so if interference were warranted whenever a person's choice fell short of full autonomy then "respect for the choices of idealized agents can go hand in hand with insufficient respect for the actual choices of people."[17] In this way, arguments in favor of soft paternalism can also be cited in favor of hard paternalism. On

---

[14] Mill, *On Liberty and Other Essays*, 107.

[15] Conly, *Against Autonomy*, 20–23.

[16] Steven Wall, "Self-Ownership and Paternalism," *Journal of Political Philosophy* 17, no. 4 (2009): 399–417.

[17] Ibid., 411.

the other hand, if only minimal autonomy is necessary to ground a duty of noninterference, then it is difficult to justify interfering with the uninformed crosser, since, except for her ignorance, she is generally an autonomous person. Wall then considers the possibility that a person's rights against interference vary with her autonomous capacity and notes that this response would still permit a lot of paternalistic interference that would strike us as hard paternalism.

In response, I think an anti-paternalist should deny the claim that the uninformed bridge crosser is sufficiently autonomous and adopt the view that a person's autonomous choices command our respect when her decision-making abilities exceed a certain threshold. It is permissible to treat people whose autonomous capacities are below the requisite threshold level of autonomy in order to promote their autonomy and bring them into a moral relationship. That is, people who lack the capacity to participate in a reciprocal moral relationship of mutual respect may be interfered with because their decisions are not the kinds of autonomous choices that people have a duty to respect. In contrast, when people are capable enough to make informed and autonomous decisions, paternalism for the sake of promoting their autonomy is wrong because they have rights against paternalistic interference in virtue of the value of their existing autonomy.

Tamar Schapiro defends a similar view regarding the paternalistic deception of children, and the analogy may serve as a useful illustration of this point.[18] Schapiro claims that nonautonomous beings that are capable of autonomy, such as children, should be brought into the moral relationship.[19] In some cases, bringing a person into the moral relationship may require paternalism that violates the norms that would govern a moral relationship between two autonomous people. For example, if lying to children about Santa Claus facilitated greater self-control and improved their ability to reason about morality, then it would be permissible to lie about Santa even though lying is generally wrong. When we interact with children, the context that usually gives norms of honesty their authority is deficient because the child is not autonomous. In these cases, the most choice-worthy action may be paternalism. Yet, as Schapiro notes, even when paternalism is warranted, it still makes sense to regret this way of realizing the moral relationship because it stems from a deficiency in one person's circumstances.

I will elaborate on children's medical rights in the next section. For now, the lesson to take from Schapiro's justification of paternalistic deception is that paternalism is warranted when a person's circumstances make autonomous

---

[18] Schapiro, "Kantian Rigorism and Mitigating Circumstances."

[19] Tamar Schapiro, "What Is a Child?," *Ethics* 109, no. 4 (July 1, 1999): 715–38, doi:10.1086/233943.

choice impossible. And in those cases, paternalistic interference should aim foremost to enable autonomous choice going forward, not to promote a person's well-being. This framework enables critics of paternalism to meet Wall's challenge and draw a line regarding paternalistic drug policy and soft-paternalistic interference with the bridge crosser. So if the bridge crosser were sufficiently autonomous, then interference would not be warranted. If she were not sufficiently autonomous, then paternalism should aim to enable autonomous choice.

At this point, one may reply that more people live below the threshold of autonomous decision-making than I seem to recognize. For example, Conly is skeptical about whether people really are autonomous and experts on their own well-being, as I have suggested. Conly cites evidence of cognitive biases, the fact that people are overly optimistic about their ability to make a choice, and the evidence that many people seem to regret their free choices when they are allowed to make them. And Conly is also skeptical that education and information can solve these problems. She argues that it is generally ineffective to teach people about the dangers of smoking or overeating and that it is more difficult still to convince people they are misinformed or in the grip of a bias. For these reasons, Conly thinks it is permissible to prohibit adult citizens from making bad decisions because they are incapable of making the right decisions on their own. She then concludes that public officials therefore ought to prohibit people from making bad decisions as long as the benefits outweigh the costs of doing so.

Say we grant Conly's pessimistic picture of human decision-making. For an argument like Conly's to succeed against rights of self-medication, one must show not only that patients and consumers reliably fail to be fully informed and that attempts to inform them are unsuccessful but also that public officials have an advantage in knowing what is best and that the benefits do not outweigh the costs. It is not at all clear that the health benefits of prohibitive pharmaceutical regulations outweigh the costs. But even if one could show that prescription requirements and other pharmaceutical regulations benefited people's health on balance, it would be even more difficult to show that they benefited people's overall well-being. Regulators who make decisions for a heterogeneous population are unlikely to understand patients' interests better than patients, if only because they lack information about each patient's values. And regulators and public officials are people too, so they are also subject to cognitive biases and deficiencies in decision-making such as risk-aversion and political incentives that could put patients at risk.

This argument also revives the arguments from the previous chapter. If it were true that public officials and physicians knew which decisions about drugs each patient ought to make and had the authority to prevent patients from choosing otherwise, then these arguments in favor of coercive paternalism would also justify some breaches of informed consent. For example, imagine that physicians adopted a policy of secretly removing tonsils, adenoids, appendices, wisdom teeth, and other unnecessary but potentially problematic parts whenever a patient was under anesthesia and would be unlikely to find out. If the benefits of covert paternalism outweighed the costs, it seems that Conly's arguments would support such a policy, even though it consists in removing body parts without patients' consent.

Conly is correct, however, to point out that some people do make terrible decisions because they lack information. But paternalistic policies do not remedy patients' lack of information. Even if a paternalistic policy prevents the bad effects of ignorant decision-making, it may cause patients to become even less informed as they develop learned helplessness in the face of restrictive policies.

Alternatively, public officials could work to promote medical literacy and to make information about treatment options more accessible and available. Pharmacists and physicians could still recommend drugs and answer patients' questions. Public officials could still certify drugs and recommend drugs. Technological advances such as online databases of drug information and websites that give targeted health advice can inform patients as well. Until patients are given the chance to access information and exercise their rights of self-medication, it is premature, even for a defender of paternalism, to cite patient ignorance as grounds for prohibition.

An analogy to financial literacy illustrates this point. In the nineteenth-century United States, married women were forbidden to own property or make contracts. This legal doctrine was called coverture, and it was justified in part on the grounds that women lacked the necessary education, status, and intelligence to manage finances, and that they were better off if a male patriarch handled money on their behalf. Institutions that prevented women from making financial decisions reinforced the sexist assumptions about women that justified those institutions. Defenders of coverture may even have been correct that women were less capable of managing money, but only because they had never been given the chance.

Similarly, institutions that prevent patients from making medical decisions may render patients incapable of making medical decisions. But prohibitive policies are not the solution to patients' seeming inability to make informed choices any more than coverture was the solution to women's seeming financial illiteracy. More generally, we should be reluctant to infer that members of marginalized or powerless groups are incapable of making decisions simply because they have not proven themselves as capable when they were subject to oppressive policies.

2.3 Children and Incompetent Adults

The Elixir Sulfanilamide and thalidomide disasters predominately affected children. Yet the system of pharmaceutical regulation that developed in response to these disasters limited the rights of everyone. I have argued that these policies violate competent, adult patients' rights of self-medication. But the initial impulse to protect the well-being of children was justified. Young children do not have rights of self-medication, and pharmaceutical policies should prevent children from using dangerous drugs. Similarly, some adults with severe cognitive disabilities have autonomous capacities that are relevantly similar to children. Policies that aim to protect these vulnerable groups are also justifiable.

In clinical and policy contexts, guardians or expert surrogates should make medical decisions on behalf of nonautonomous children. Where do we draw the line between children and autonomous people who have rights of self-medication? I propose that a person has rights of self-medication at the point that she has rights to make her own medical decisions in accordance with the doctrine of informed consent. As a rough guide, pediatricians sometimes use a "rule of sevens" to allocate decisional authority for minors. For children under the age of seven, pediatricians seek only parental permission for treatment. For children seven to fourteen years old, pediatricians seek parental permission and their patient's assent to treatment. If patients in this age range refuse treatment, there is a strong ethical presumption against forcing treatment or diagnosis unless the child's life is at stake and treatment cannot be deferred without substantial risk. And the AAP maintains that adolescents older than fourteen may have the same decisional capacities as adults and would therefore be entitled to the same medical rights that are protected by the doctrine of informed consent.[20]

According to this standard, there is no presumption in favor of parental rights to make medical decisions for their children. Parents may have important insight into their child's interests, but they may not decide in their child's interests, and parents do not have the authority to consent on behalf of their children.[21] As Tim Dare argues, even though parents may feel they know their child better than anyone, they may systematically fail to know what is in their child's overall interests for several reasons.[22] First, parents often project their values and preferences as their child's, but those values may not be the child's. Children may misrepresent their values and adopt a different disposition around their parents than they do around other caregivers and physicians. These family dynamics may distort parents' understanding of their children's interests.

[20] Committee on Bioethics, "Informed Consent, Parental Permission, and Assent in Pediatric Practice," *Pediatrics* 95, no. 2 (February 1, 1995): 314–17.

[21] Ibid.

[22] Tim Dare, "Parental Rights and Medical Decisions," *Pediatric Anesthesia* 19, no. 10 (October 1, 2009): 947–52, doi:10.1111/j.1460-9592.2009.03094.x.

Parents' partiality toward their own children may also obscure their judgment about treatment, meaning that parents could refuse treatment that is in a child's interest out of concerns about side effects, or they might overestimate their child's tolerance for treatment that is not in the child's interest.

Instead, the American Academy of Pediatrics approaches responsibility for a child's well-being as a duty that is shared by medical professionals, public officials, the courts, parents, and the child. I would add that people deciding in the interest of a child should not only aim to promote a child's well-being but her capacity to decide as well. The duty to develop a child's capacity to make medical decisions may require treating the child as if she has the authority to decide, informing her about the risks and benefits of treatment, and teaching her how to communicate with health professionals about her symptoms, medical history, and values.

Turning to self-medication, this framework can be used to justify prescription requirements for young children. As above, pharmacists and physicians should not presume that parents have the sole authority to medicate their children. Though parents do provide and administer pharmaceuticals to their children, paying for medical treatment does not generally entitle people to put their children in harm's way by making risky pharmaceutical choices. The prescription drug system is a model of the shared responsibility approach to medical decision-making because it requires that pediatricians and parents support the decision to use pharmaceuticals.[23]

As with children, physicians and patient representatives should make medical decisions in the interest of adults who are not capable of exercising their rights of informed consent. The possibility that children or incompetent adults could access dangerous pharmaceuticals may warrant designating some drugs as behind the counter so that pharmacists can screen for capacity when they sell drugs. In these ways, the right of self-medication is limited to only a subset of the patient population. Yet, just as the presence of some people who are incapable of giving informed consent for medical treatment does not support violations of autonomous patients' medical rights in general, the presence of some people who are incapable of informed medical decision-making does not support paternalistic limits on self-medication for the general population.

---

[23] On the other hand, parents should be permitted to purchase and administer some relatively safe pharmaceuticals for their children. Parents with sick children should not be required to visit a pediatrician anytime an antihistamine or analgesic is necessary. Nevertheless, if anything, there is too little oversight of drugs for pediatric uses. Access to dangerous pediatric products, such as children's acetaminophen, should be more closely monitored to ensure that parents use them properly. T. Christian Miller and Jeff Gerth, "Dose of Confusion," *ProPublica*, September 20, 2013, http://www.propublica.org/article/tylenol-mcneil-fda-kids-dose-of-confusion.

2.4　Hard Paternalism and Drug Regulation

Granting that most adult patients are capable of choosing which medications to use, paternalists may nevertheless oppose rights of self-medication on the grounds that some pharmaceuticals are unacceptably dangerous. Paternalism that coercively interferes with an adult's capable, informed choice is called hard paternalism. Several political philosophers have argued that while autonomy is valuable, it is not an absolute constraint on what public officials can permissibly do and that hard paternalism can be justified in some cases.

If we accept that most adult citizens are capable of making self-regarding medical choices, then defenders of paternalistic policies must show why physicians and public officials are nevertheless entitled to paternalistically interfere with people's drug choices. What is it about their roles as doctors and regulators that permit them to coercively limit treatment options? Citizens do not consent to public officials' coercion. Patients do not contractually entrust physicians to prevent them from making regrettable choices. Some paternalists write that "we" are entitled to enforce paternalistic policies. This language conflates citizens in a democratic society with public officials; ordinary citizens are not entitled to paternalistically coerce each other. Agents of the state enforce hard paternalism, so defenders of paternalism must explain why public officials are uniquely entitled to coerce.

In this section I will consider three justifications for hard paternalism that appeal to the idea that public officials should not be held to the same moral standards as other people. First, some political philosophers argue that while individuals are not permitted to paternalistically coerce each other, public officials can coerce people if a democratic majority authorizes them or if they can justify their conduct to reasonable citizens. Another alleged asymmetry between private individuals and public officials is that public officials collectively decide to enforce laws based on many reasons, and paternalism may only be one among them.[24] Therefore, diverse bodies like legislatures or electorates cannot be paternalistic because they do not act on a unified set of reasons that expresses disrespect for people. This seeming asymmetry addresses the expressive harms of paternalism to an extent—policies that benefit people by limiting their freedom needn't express any disrespectful judgments of their abilities to make decisions, but those policies could still be unjustified because they violate rights or have other costs.

Democratic theorists may claim that paternalistic prescription drug requirements and approval policies are permissible as long as they are democratically

[24] James Wilson, "Why It's Time to Stop Worrying About Paternalism in Health Policy," *Public Health Ethics* 4, no. 3 (November 1, 2011): 269–79, doi:10.1093/phe/phr028.

passed. Such an argument may go like this. First, imagine that a majority of citizens preferred to prevent themselves and others from making self-harming choices and a minority preferred unregulated access to pharmaceuticals. In these cases, democratic majorities may legitimately impose paternalistic policies on citizens who oppose paternalism.[25] If majorities were not entitled to enforce coercive paternalistic policies, then a single anti-paternalist's preferences would effectively veto everyone else in society who favors a paternalistic law.[26] Such a libertarian regime of strict anti-paternalism would only be attractive to libertarians, who would then force everyone else in society from satisfying their desire to protect themselves from their own bad judgment.[27] In these cases, proponents of paternalism suggest that anti-paternalists must compromise for the sake of the enormous good that paternalism can bring to society as a whole.[28]

This argument is at risk of proving too much. Democratic majorities are and ought to be constrained by their duty to respect people's rights. And the scope of a person's rights does not depend on how many of her compatriots are willing to recognize those rights. For example, if people have rights against surveillance, then the government acts unjustly by spying on them, even if a majority of citizens do not believe in privacy rights. Though people may overwhelmingly prefer limits on the rights of pharmaceutical users, the distribution of preferences in a society is irrelevant to a patient's claim to self-medication if she indeed has a right to use pharmaceuticals. In this way, democratic justifications of hard paternalism assume the conclusion they seek to establish. It only seems plausible that voters and their representatives are permitted to enforce pharmaceutical regulations if we already assume that people do not have rights of self-medication.

Say we concede that proponents of self-medication are mistaken about the scope of patients' rights and that people are not entitled to risk their safety in this way. Some people defend paternalism on the grounds that public officials and voters have epistemic advantages, relative to individuals deciding for themselves, because they can better assess the aggregate costs and benefits of regulations without being blinded by an individual's self-interested perspective.[29] For

---

[25] Elizabeth S. Anderson, "What Is the Point of Equality?," *Ethics* 109, no. 2 (1999): 287–337; Alan Wertheimer, "Liberty, Coercion, and the Limits of the State," *The Blackwell Guide to Social and Political Philosophy* (Oxford, UK: Blackwell, 2002): 38; Cass R. Sunstein, "Legal Interference with Private Preferences," *University of Chicago Law Review* 53, no. 4 (1986): 1129–74.

[26] Wilson, "Why It's Time to Stop Worrying About Paternalism in Health Policy"; Kalle Grill, "Liberalism, Altruism and Group Consent," *Public Health Ethics* 2, no. 2 (2009): 146–57.

[27] Wall, "Self-Ownership and Paternalism."

[28] Danny Scoccia, "The Right to Autonomy and the Justification of Hard Paternalism," in *Paternalism: Theory and Practice*, ed. Christian Coons and Michael Weber (Cambridge, UK: Cambridge University Press, 2013), 86.

[29] Bill New, "Paternalism and Public Policy," *Economics and Philosophy* 15, no. 1 (April 1999): 63–83, doi:10.1017/S026626710000359X; Sunstein, "Legal Interference with Private Preferences."

example, Robert Goodin argues that impersonality is a virtue of public officials, who ought to decide on the basis of consequentialist considerations rather than person-affecting principles when they are crafting policy.[30]

But taking an impersonal perspective is not impartial. Just as public officials and voters deciding on public policy are also subject to cognitive biases, they also systematically favor the median voter's self-interest and decide against marginalized minority groups. Plausibly, pharmaceutical regulators are more likely to focus a lot on the people who are killed by using dangerous pharmaceuticals, especially when these vivid tragedies are reported in the media. And officials are likely to overlook the costs of regulation that are disproportionately borne by a minority of anti-paternalists, sick patients who are seeking unapproved treatments, and people who want to use prescription drugs without a medical need. And cynically, we might also consider that health professionals have financial incentives to maintain a system of legal requirements that ensures patients consult with physicians and pharmacists before using pharmaceuticals.

Alternatively, one may defend pharmaceutical regulation from a broadly contractualist framework.[31] For example, drawing on Thomas Scanlon's arguments for contractualism, Peter deMarneffe writes:

> To value each other properly as rational beings is to act towards each other only in ways that we can justify to each other. We can justify our actions to each other if they are permitted by principles none of us could reasonably reject.... Because [paternalistic] reasons sometimes outweigh any reasons we have to insist on a principle that prohibits all forms of paternalistic interference, no one could reasonably reject a principle that permits some forms of paternalism.[32]

Like the soft-paternalist arguments for pharmaceutical regulation, by claiming that it would be unreasonable to use drugs against medical advice, this justification for paternalism asserts that there is some objective ideal of reasonableness

[30] Robert E. Goodin, *Utilitarianism as a Public Philosophy* (Cambridge, UK: Cambridge University Press, 1995).

[31] One version of this strategy is a Rawlsian argument that seatbelt mandates protect people's higher order interest in being able to pursue a conception of the good and participate as an equal in a fair society. Samuel Freeman makes an argument like this about paternalistic drug policies. Donald VanDeVeer sketched an argument like this for seatbelt mandates. This view is similar to the "autonomy promoting" view I consider later in this chapter, where I reply that coercive seatbelt mandates are more likely to limit autonomy, even when they aim to promote it. Samuel Freeman, "Liberalism, Inalienability, and Rights of Drug Use," in *Drugs and the Limits of Liberalism: Moral and Legal Issues*, ed. Pablo De Greiff (Ithaca, NY: Cornell University Press, 1999), 110–30; Donald VanDeVeer, "Autonomy Respecting Paternalism," *Social Theory and Practice* 6, no. 2 (July 1, 1980): 187–207.

[32] Peter de Marneffe, "Self-Sovereignty and Paternalism," in *Paternalism* (Cambridge, UK: Cambridge University Press, 2013), http://dx.doi.org/10.1017/CBO9781139179003.004.

or an ideal of full information and rationality that a person must meet, and that when people fall short of that ideal interference can be warranted. But contractualists needn't show that consumers of pharmaceuticals are not sufficiently autonomous. Even if one were to accept my claim that most adults are sufficiently autonomous, to justify paternalism on contractualist grounds, one must only show that they are unreasonable.[33]

Two responses. First, consider a conception of reasonableness that deems people who desire to use unapproved or prescription medicines without authorization as unreasonable. Such a conception of reasonableness may hold that unauthorized pharmaceutical users fail to promote their own interests or well-being, according to some objective conception of well-being or interests. As such, this standard of reasonableness would be perfectionistic because it would appeal to a conception of value that at least some people would reject. Namely, anyone who subjectively values self-medication would fall short of this perfectionistic standard.

On its own, perfectionism is not fatal to a liberal justification for paternalism, though many liberals think that there are at least *pro tanto* reasons against perfectionistic public policy.[34] But even if we were to accept standards of reasonableness that are based on an objective conception of people's interests, people may still reasonably reject pharmaceutical paternalism. To see why, we must distinguish between two questions. Is it reasonable to use unauthorized pharmaceuticals? And, is it reasonable to reject a mandate that requires authorization for pharmaceutical use? As evidence of the claim that pharmaceutical users have reason to act in accordance with paternalistic regulations, one may point to the fact that most people *would* defer to the judgments of their physicians and pharmaceutical regulators if they were acting in accordance with their idealized, fully informed, and rational desires. Thus, most people have reasons to comply with pharmaceutical regulations, so it is permissible to coerce their non-ideal actual selves into complying with these regulations. Danny Scoccia, for example, develops an argument like this. Scoccia claims that interference does not violate a person's autonomy if, based on his values, he would consent to it were he informed and rational.[35] Conly also argues that everyone has a reason to support coercive paternalism because we have reason to support policies that effectively get us what we really want, even if we fail to recognize it.[36]

---

[33] Scoccia and Dworkin also seem to endorse a version of this view. Scoccia, "The Right to Autonomy and the Justification of Hard Paternalism"; Gerald Dworkin, "Paternalism," in *The Stanford Encyclopedia of Philosophy*, ed. Edward N. Zalta, Summer 2014, http://plato.stanford.edu/archives/sum2014/entries/paternalism/.

[34] See for example Jonathan Quong's discussion of the hazards of appealing to perfectionist doctrines when justifying coercions. Quong, *Liberalism without Perfection*.

[35] Scoccia, "The Right to Autonomy and the Justification of Hard Paternalism," 80.

[36] Conly, *Against Autonomy*.

So say we grant that thinking of our more reasonable selves in light of some objective theory of well-being can give us guidance about what is good for a person and shed light on what we think people have reason to do. It is plausible enough that we ought to do either what our idealized selves would do or what they would advise us to do. Nevertheless, whether a fully informed and rational person would consult with a physician or regulatory agency before making drug choices is quite a separate question from whether he would endorse being coerced to comply with experts' recommendations. A pharmaceutical user, were he fully informed and rational, would plausibly consult with experts and his physician and advise his non-ideal self to do the same. But even an ideally informed pharmaceutical user would neither necessarily prefer coercive regulations (because he already consults with experts and would rationally desire to keep his options open) nor necessarily advise his non-ideal self to support pharmaceutical regulations (because his non-ideal self might not always comply with regulations, so he would be susceptible to penalties under a mandate).

One may reply that in some cases, people do have reasons not only to comply with whatever a paternalistic law would require but also to prefer a mandate as well. Peter de Marneffe argues that this kind of argument may justify prostitution regulations, prohibitive drug laws, and laws that prohibit suicide.[37] For example, de Marneffe argues that motorcycle helmet laws are permissible even if some people would have reason to reject the paternalistic law because the reasons for people to want the government to adopt a helmet law have greater weight.[38] So de Marneffe may grant that the relevant question is not whether a person could reasonably refuse to wear a helmet but whether a person could reasonably reject helmet laws. But de Marneffe claims that a paternalistic law can meet this standard if the reasons cited by the intended beneficiaries of a paternalistic law have greater weight than the reasons of those who oppose it. Similarly, one could argue that sex workers do not have very strong reasons to want the legal freedom to sell sexual services compared with the reasons that people have to prefer a legal environment that subjects them to a lower risk of engaging in sex work.[39]

Turning to drug prohibitions, de Marneffe's argument in favor of prohibiting heroin can illustrate how his defense of paternalism could apply to other drugs. De Marneffe claims that heroin and the social environment that would result from legal heroin are extremely destructive to young people's overall well-being. Therefore, "the reasons of at least one person to prefer her situation in a

---

[37] Peter de Marneffe, *Liberalism and Prostitution*, reprint (New York; Oxford: Oxford University Press, 2012), 65–66.

[38] Ibid., 129.

[39] But de Marneffe is skeptical of this strategy. Ibid., 119.

prohibition environment outweigh everyone else's reasons to prefer his or her situation in a legalization environment."[40]

Can a similar case be made for prohibitive pharmaceutical policies? Some prescription drugs are similar to heroin and some are more powerful. But most drugs are not as destructive as heroin. Moreover, while de Marneffe may plausibly sustain his claim that everyone else's reasons to prefer legalization are not very weighty with respect to heroin, those who seek access to therapeutic drugs generally have much weightier reasons than those who want to use drugs recreationally. Moreover, as some commentators have pointed out, de Marneffe's view seemingly allows a single individual's objectively weighty interest in the enforcement of a paternalistic policy to prevail even if that individual and all other citizens would prefer a non-paternalistic policy regime.[41]

A final justification for paternalism along these lines is James Wilson's claim that all public policy consists in coercing people in ways that would be impermissible if done by ordinary citizens. Wilson argues that there is nothing uniquely objectionable about a policy that coerces people for the sake of their own good and a policy that coerces people in order to provide public goods.[42] Elsewhere, I argued in response to Wilson's argument that for the same reasons that public health paternalism is often morally objectionable, so too are other coercive public policies.[43] Perhaps rejecting hard paternalism would have revisionary implications for how people see other coercive laws. Perhaps people should accept these revisionary implications and reconsider whether some non-paternalistic coercive policies are wrong too.

2.5 The Health Effects of Approval Requirements

I have argued that existing philosophical defenses of coercive paternalism cannot justify prohibitive pharmaceutical regulations, even if such regulations effectively promoted people's health and well-being. But perhaps the more compelling reason to reject paternalistic pharmaceutical regulations is that they are ineffective. By this I do not mean that public officials cannot effectively prevent people from accessing unapproved and prescription drugs. Rather, there is reason to believe that when public officials do effectively prevent people from accessing medicine, they do not promote people's health and well-being on balance.

---

[40] Doug Husak and Peter de Marneffe, *The Legalization of Drugs* (Cambridge; New York: Cambridge University Press, 2005), 161.

[41] William Hawk, "Review of Douglas Husak, Peter de Marneffe, *The Legalization of Drugs: For & Against*," *Notre Dame Philosophical Reviews* 2006, no. 8 (2006).

[42] Wilson, "Why It's Time to Stop Worrying About Paternalism in Health Policy."

[43] Jessica Flanigan, "Public Bioethics," *Public Health Ethics* 6, no. 2 (July 1, 2013): 170–84, doi:10.1093/phe/pht022.

Though prohibitive pharmaceutical regulations are justified on the grounds that they make people safer, the empirical record does not clearly support this claim. Consider first the effects of prohibitive approval policies, such as premarket safety and efficacy requirements. These requirements raise the price of drug development and thereby discourage manufacturers from creating new drugs. This phenomenon is known as drug loss. It refers to the drugs that are never invented because it would be too expensive and risky to bring them to market. People also die while waiting for new drugs to be approved. This is called drug lag. Furthermore, it is especially unlikely that prohibitive efficacy-testing requirements are necessary for protecting the public's health since many drugs are sold off-label, meaning they are prescribed for conditions for which they have never been tested for efficacy. There is also reason to believe that even safety requirements may not be necessary to protect the public from dangerous drugs. Reflecting on large-scale tragedies associated with dangerous drugs, prohibitive regulations did not protect citizens from drug disasters.

Drug regulation discourages innovation because it is very expensive to attain approval. The process can take up to fifteen years and cost up to $2 billion.[44] To test whether prohibitive policies discouraged innovation, economist Sam Peltzman developed a model to predict how many new drugs would have been introduced to the market were it not for the introduction of efficacy-testing requirements, which were established in 1962.[45] He found that two and a half times more drugs would have been introduced on average each year after 1962 (forty-one), than the average number of drugs that were actually introduced (sixteen). This hypothesis was subsequently supported by additional studies.[46] For example, when economists compared research and development productivity in the United States and UK, they found that productivity declined sixfold

[44] Brian Palmer writes, "It costs around $1.75 billion to develop the average cancer medicine. Only drugs for respiratory disorders, at $2 billion, can top that total. (AIDS drugs and anti-parasitic are the real bargains, at between $500 million and $700 million.)" Brian Palmer, "The $8,000 Pill," *Slate*, August 16, 2010, http://www.slate.com/articles/news_and_politics/explainer/2010/08/the_8000_pill.html. See also Gary S. Becker, "Big Ideas," *Milken Institute Review*, June 2004, 93–94, UNZ. org, http://www.UNZ.org/Pub/MilkenInstituteRev-2004q2-00093; and also Sam Peltzman, "An Evaluation of Consumer Protection Legislation: The 1962 Drug Amendments," *Journal of Political Economy* 81, no. 5 (1973): 1049–91.

[45] Sam Peltzman, "An Evaluation of Consumer Protection Legislation: The 1962 Drug Amendments," *Journal of Political Economy* 81, no. 5 (1973): 1049–91.

[46] For example, Grabowski and Vernon, argue, "In sum, the hypothesis that the observed decline in new product introductions has largely been concentrated in marginal or ineffective drugs is not generally supported by empirical analyses" (34). Henry G. Grabowski and John Mitcham Vernon, *The Regulation of Pharmaceuticals: Balancing the Benefits and Risks* (Washington, DC: American Enterprise Institute for Public Policy Research, 1983). See also Steven N. Wiggins, "Product Quality Regulation and New Drug Introductions: Some New Evidence from the 1970s," *The Review of Economics and Statistics* 63, no. 4 (November 1, 1981): 615–19.

in the United States and only threefold in the UK after the introduction of the 1962 testing requirements in the United States.[47] Economist Elizabeth Jensen later found more generally that regulatory stringency is inversely related to the expected number of new drug discoveries.[48] This hypothesis is supported by evidence that less regulated drug classes are more innovative, so it is plausible that less regulation for all drugs would increase innovation.[49]

In response to worries about drug lag, the US Congress passed the Orphan Drug Act (ODA) in 1983, to encourage companies to develop and seek approval for drugs for rare conditions, affecting fewer than 200,000 Americans. The ODA established tax incentives to develop drugs for rare conditions and seven-year market exclusivity provisions for approved drugs. The ODA worked, but it also confirmed that prohibitive regulations discouraged drug development. Significantly more drugs were developed for patients with rare diseases, and patients with rare diseases were significantly more likely to access and benefit from newly available drugs.[50] The success of the ODA illustrates that costly approval processes adversely affect pharmaceutical innovation and that efforts to mitigate the costs of approval positively affect innovation. Yet the ODA only helped patients with moderately rare diseases. For extremely rare diseases, even the benefits established by the ODA do not offer manufacturers enough of an incentive to invest in development and approval.

In response to these concerns, policymakers could encourage innovation by compensating manufacturers for high-development and approval costs, but this policy would be costly for citizens who would be asked to subsidize the research costs of for-profit corporations. Or policymakers could encourage drug development through deregulation, which would also lower the cost of development and approval. Nobel-winning economist Gary Becker argued in favor of deregulation for this reason. Becker wrote:

> A return to a safety standard alone would lower costs and raise the number of therapeutic compounds available. In particular, this would include more drugs from small biotech firms that do not have the deep

[47] This research indicates that even if innovation slowed in part because of fewer research opportunities, prohibitive testing requirements still had an adverse effect on innovation in the United States. Henry G. Grabowski, John M. Vernon, and Lacy Glenn Thomas, "Estimating the Effects of Regulation on Innovation: An International Comparative Analysis of the Pharmaceutical Industry," *Journal of Law and Economics* 21, no. 1 (April 1, 1978): 133–63.

[48] Elizabeth J. Jensen, "Research Expenditures and the Discovery of New Drugs," *The Journal of Industrial Economics* 36, no. 1 (1987): 83–95.

[49] R. A. Merrill, "Regulation of Drugs and Devices: An Evolution," *Health Affairs* 13, no. 3 (May 1, 1994): 47–69.

[50] Frank R. Lichtenberg and Joel Waldfogel, "Does Misery Love Company—Evidence from Pharmaceutical Markets Before and After the Orphan Drug Act," *Michigan Telecommunications and Technology Law Review* 15 (2009): 335.

pockets to invest in extended efficacy trials. And the resulting increase in competition would mean lower prices—without the bureaucratic burden of price controls.[51]

Drug lag costs lives because people suffer and die from diseases that might be treatable, if only there were more investment in finding a cure. Today, patient advocates privately organize to raise funds to subsidize the costs of drug development for rare diseases. Requirements that raise the cost of development make it less likely that they will succeed. Premarket testing requirements also cost lives because patients with conditions that could be treated or cured by unapproved drugs suffer and die while they are waiting for approval. We can see evidence of drug lag by comparing approval times between countries and across time. Both methods of comparison indicate that longer approval times are extremely costly but do not save lives.

The average drug took seven months to gain approval in 1962. Five years later, it took thirty months because of efficacy-testing requirements. Drug lag was first raised as a concern in the 1970s when pharmacologists William Wardell and Louis Lasagna estimated that tens of thousands of American patients' deaths could have been prevented if the FDA had approved available lifesaving drugs sooner and faster.[52] By then drugs took up to ten years to gain approval. In the late 1970s, American patients began traveling to European countries to buy pharmaceuticals that were awaiting approval in the United States, and the National Cancer Institute (NCI) clashed publically with the FDA over the agency's oversight of clinical trials for cancer treatments, which they alleged undermined potentially lifesaving research and subjected oncologists to unnecessary bureaucratic requirements.[53] In 1988, the HIV/AIDS advocacy organization AIDS Coalition to Unleash Power (ACT UP) staged large protests to encourage the FDA to expedite approval for medications that could fight opportunistic infections like HIV.[54]

In response to these concerns from the medical community and the public, Congress passed the Prescription Drug User Fee Act (PDUFA) in 1992 that, among other things, implemented expedited approval process for drugs that could potentially treat life-threatening diseases and relaxed premarket prohibitions for terminally ill patients. The PDUFA shortened the approval process, and today, the United States has one of the fastest approval processes in the world.

---

[51] Becker, "Big Ideas."

[52] L. Lasagna and W. M. Wardell, "The FDA, Politics, and the Public," *JAMA: The Journal of the American Medical Association* 232, no. 2 (April 14, 1975): 141–42, doi:10.1001/jama.1975.03250020015015.

[53] Carpenter, *Reputation and Power*, 393.

[54] Ibid., chap. 7.

In 2012, the Congress created a new category of expedited approval for break-through therapies, which encouraged the FDA to allow greater access to drugs that treat serious diseases and are likely to be effective based on preliminary evidence.[55]

Still, every month that an unapproved drug remains inaccessible to patients, people suffer and die because they lack access to treatment.[56] In light of the cost of withholding access to drugs, due to drug loss and drug lag, defenders of prohibitive requirements give three kinds of justifications for mandatory premarket efficacy testing. First, prohibitive requirements are intended to prevent manufacturers from selling drugs that do not effectively treat patients' conditions. Second, efficacy requirements may be justified on the grounds that consumers and physicians would otherwise be unable to learn about new drugs. Third, efficacy requirements may be used to further establish whether a drug is safe.

The first justification for efficacy-testing requirements is that they are necessary to prevent "snake oil" salesmen from selling useless potions that do not effectively treat anything. Patients are harmed when they forgo effective treatment and use an ineffective treatment instead. However, the evidence does not support the claim that efficacy-testing requirements prevent manufacturers from selling ineffective drugs or patients from taking them. For example, when efficacy requirements were introduced in the 1960s, the market share of ineffective drugs did not change.[57] Additionally, the practice of off-label prescribing has now grown to account for more than 20 percent of all prescriptions written, which means that more than 20 percent of all drugs are prescribed for conditions that they were not approved to treat on the basis of efficacy-testing requirements. And though off-label uses of drugs are not subject to efficacy testing, off-label prescriptions are no more dangerous than on-label prescriptions.[58]

[55] Jonathan J. Darrow, Jerry Avorn, and Aaron S. Kesselheim, "New FDA Breakthrough-Drug Category—Implications for Patients," *New England Journal of Medicine* 370, no. 13 (March 27, 2014): 1252–58, doi:10.1056/NEJMhle1311493.

[56] Kenneth I. Kaitin and Jeffrey S. Brown, "A Drug Lag Update," *Drug Information Journal* 29, no. 2 (April 1, 1995): 361–73. doi:10.1177/009286159502900203; L. G. Schifrin and J. R. Tayan, "The Drug Lag: An Interpretive Review of the Literature," *International Journal of Health Services: Planning, Administration, Evaluation* 7, no. 3 (1977): 359–81; Arthur Daemmrich, "Invisible Monuments and the Costs of Pharmaceutical Regulation: Twenty-Five Years of Drug Lag Debate," *Pharmacy in History* 45, no. 1 (January 1, 2003): 3–17; W. M. Wardell, "The Drug Lag Revisited: Comparison by Therapeutic Area of Patterns of Drugs Marketed in the United States and Great Britain from 1972 through 1976," *Clinical Pharmacology and Therapeutics* 24, no. 5 (1978): 499; Grabowski and Vernon, *The Regulation of Pharmaceuticals*.

[57] Peltzman, "An Evaluation of Consumer Protection Legislation."

[58] A. T. Tabarrok, "Assessing the FDA via the Anomaly of Off-label Drug Prescribing," *Independent Review* 5, no. 1 (2000): 25–53.

The off-label market is foundational to current prescribing practices for the treatment of adults, though the practice is not uncontroversial.[59] In some cases, off-label prescribing practices are not supported by causal research and may be harmful.[60] But even critics of off-label prescribing acknowledge the substantial benefits of the practice and do not propose that each drug undergo efficacy-testing requirements for every patient-type and condition. The pervasive, broadly successful practice of off-label prescribing indicates that manufacturers are capable of providing effective drugs to patients even when those drugs have not been officially approved for their conditions. So, efficacy testing is not required to deliver effective drugs to patients.[61]

A second defense of efficacy-testing requirements is offered by Patricia M. Danzon and Eric L. Keuffel, who argue that premarket testing solves the pharmaceutical market's failure to provide consumers and physicians with enough information about new drugs.[62] The idea is that drug companies will not disclose information about drugs on their own, so they must be compelled to do so by testing their drugs in publically available clinical trials. Data sharing is a legitimate concern about the current clinical trial system. Even with efficacy-testing requirements, the FDA does not release the data they gain during the drug approval process. More generally, manufacturers are not required to publish negative or compromising results of registered clinical trials, and published results do not include participant-level data. These practices leave patients and physicians in the dark about the effects of drugs. In a recent report by the Institute of Medicine, a committee of public and private stakeholders argued that the current system of clinical trials, which are overseen by the government, could be used to encourage more data sharing. Yet prohibitive policies, such as efficacy-testing requirements, are not necessary to ensure that patients and physicians have access to information about new drugs.[63] In addition to data

---

[59] Jerry Avorn and Aaron Kesselheim, "A Hemorrhage of Off-Label Use," *Annals of Internal Medicine* 154, no. 8 (April 19, 2011): 566, doi:10.7326/0003-4819-154-8-201104190-00010.

[60] N. Ghinea et al., "No Evidence or No Alternative? Taking Responsibility for Off-label Prescribing," *Internal Medicine Journal* 42, no. 3 (March 1, 2012): 247–51, doi:10.1111/j.1445-5994.2012.02713.x.

[61] An opposing position—Randall Stafford argued in the *New England Journal of Medicine* that the FDA ought to increase oversight of off-label uses as well. See R. S. Stafford, "Regulating Off-label Drug Use—Rethinking the Role of the FDA," *New England Journal of Medicine* 358, no. 14 (2008): 1427–29. As Klein and Tabarrok found in a survey of over five hundred physicians, this is a minority position. Klein and Tabarrok, "Do Off-label Drug Practices Argue Against FDA Efficacy Requirements? A Critical Analysis of Physicians' Argumentation for Initial Efficacy Requirements," *American Journal of Economics and Sociology* 67, no. 5 (2008): 743–75. See also Klein, Daniel B. "Colleagues, Where Is the Market Failure? Economists on the FDA." *Econ Journal Watch* 5, no. 3 (2008): 316–48.

[62] Patricia M. Danzon and Eric Keuffel, "Regulation of the Pharmaceutical Industry," NBER Chapters (National Bureau of Economic Research, 2011), http://ideas.repec.org/h/nbr/nberch/12572.html.

[63] This point is also made by economist Fredric Scherer, who writes, "An information market failure may need correction. But why doesn't the regulator merely require appropriate testing and

sharing, pharmaceutical regulators could also certify and recommend drugs for particular uses, as they do when they expand the list of approved uses for previously approved drugs.

The third defense of prohibitive efficacy-testing requirements is that faster drug approval makes drugs less safe. This empirical claim is controversial. One study shows that, as drug approval times decreased since 1992, there have also been more black-box warnings associated with new drugs and more market withdrawals.[64] But another study shows that the 1992 legislation did not cause a corresponding increase in drug recalls or public health crises that resulted from dangerous drugs.[65] A comparison between different countries' approval processes before 1992 suggests that a shorter approval process was not less safe.[66] Even if a faster approval process does cause more drug recalls, longer approval requirements also cost lives. In order to defend lengthy efficacy requirements for the sake of safety, one would need to show that the harm of faster approval was greater than the harm of prohibition. The harm of prohibition is clear—patients die waiting for drugs to be approved. The same cannot be said about the harm of a faster approval process.

These arguments against prohibitive efficacy requirements should prompt us to reconsider prohibitive safety requirements as well. When people use drugs that they do not know to be unsafe, drug disasters occur. For example, patients who used Elixir Sulfanilamide died because they were not aware that the drug's solvent had not been tested. If the manufacturer had been required to disclose its untested status, or if there was a system of certification, the disaster could have been avoided without prohibition. The thalidomide disaster in the 1950s

disclosure of test data, letting physicians decide from the data whether the drug is safe and efficacious? If there is an argument for regulation of whether new drugs may be marketed, it must lie in a further information market failure—e.g., from the possibility that most physicians are too busy to make well-informed independent decisions." F. M Scherer, *The Pharmaceutical Industry*, Handbook of Health Economics (Amsterdam, NL: Elsevier, 2000), 1315.

[64] Cassie Frank et al., "Era Of Faster FDA Drug Approval Has Also Seen Increased Black-Box Warnings And Market Withdrawals," *Health Affairs* 33, no. 8 (August 1, 2014): 1453–59, doi:10.1377/hlthaff.2014.0122.

[65] For example, Philipson et al. write, "By the most plausible measure, the [1992 PDUFA] act did not, in fact, have any effect on drug safety: neither the proportion of drugs eventually withdrawn (2 to 3 percent), nor the speed with which they were withdrawn, changed in any statistically significant way since the law's passage." Tomas J. Philipson et al., "Assessing the Safety and Efficacy of the FDA: The Case of the Prescription Drug User Fee Acts," National Bureau of Economic Research Working Paper Series No. 11724, 2005, http://www.nber.org/papers/w11724. See also Henry Grabowski and Y. Richard Wang, "Do Faster Food and Drug Administration Drug Reviews Adversely Affect Patient Safety? An Analysis of the 1992 Prescription Drug User Fee Act," *Journal of Law and Economics* 51, no. 2 (May 1, 2008): 377–406.

[66] Olav M. Bakke et al., "Drug Safety Discontinuations in the United Kingdom, the United States, and Spain from 1974 Through 1993: A Regulatory Perspective," *Clinical Pharmacology & Therapeutics* 58, no. 1 (July 1, 1995): 108–17.

and 1960s is also cited as a justification for a longer approval process and greater safety regulation on the grounds that the FDA spared the United States from the crisis because the drug was awaiting approval.

Despite this narrative, however, it is unclear whether prohibitive regulations should be credited for avoiding the thalidomide crisis. First, recall that the thalidomide tragedy occurred before the 1962 amendments that required efficacy testing. Therefore, the tragedy cannot be cited as a triumph of the current standards of regulation because thalidomide was one of the motivations for extensive and prohibitive safety and efficacy-testing requirements; it was not a product of them.[67] Furthermore, clinical trials are not usually conducted on pregnant women, so government testing even today could not have detected the adverse effects of thalidomide. At the time, thalidomide approval was delayed because of concerns that had nothing to do with pregnancy or birth defects but rather because of potential neurological effects, even though birth defects were the primary problem with thalidomide. Today, thalidomide is still available as an approved treatment for cancer patients and people with leprosy, so it is technically still available off-label as a morning sickness drug. The drug's legal status is thereby effectively the same as when it was prescribed in the 1950s, since all morning sickness drugs are off-label. Of course, no pregnant women would take thalidomide knowing the risks, despite the fact that it bears the same approval status as other morning sickness drugs that are widely used, such as Zofran. Therefore, if patients and physicians have access to information about drugs, they can avoid unsafe drugs even if the drugs are not prohibited.

Premarket testing requirements also cannot protect patients from the risks associated with long-term risks associated with drugs. For example, in the 1960s more than 3,500 children in Europe and Australia died after long-term continued use of the asthma drug Isoproterenol. The drug was also approved and sold in the United States and Canada, but manufacturers marketed safer inhalers in these countries for reasons unrelated to the approval system.[68] Similarly, when more than 27,000 American patients suffered heart attacks and sudden cardiac death between 1999 and 2003 after taking the popular arthritis treatment Vioxx, premarket testing requirements could not have effectively prevented the drug-related deaths because they resulted from long-term use.[69]

My claim is not that safety testing never saves lives. It is plausible that strict approval requirements prevented Japan's clioquinol tragedy from occurring in

[67] Carpenter, *Reputation and Power*, 259.

[68] D. H Gieringer, "The Safety and Efficacy of New Drug Approval," *Cato Journal* 5, no. 1 (1985): 177–201.

[69] http://www.consumeraffairs.com/news04/vioxx_estimates.html; Richard A Epstein, "Regulatory Paternalism in the Market for Drugs: Lessons from Vioxx and Celebrex," *Yale Journal of Health Policy, Law, and Ethics* 5 (2005): 741.

the United States. From 1956 to1970, more than 11,000 patients in Japan were severely disabled after using clioquinol as an over-the-counter treatment for intestinal problems.[70] In other countries, such as the United States, over-the-counter sales of clioquinol were banned, and the drug's use was discouraged as early as 1961 because of concerns about toxicity. This example illustrates that regulations can prevent deaths. The questions at hand, though, are whether the costs of drug lag and drug loss are justified for the sake of avoiding drug disasters, and whether drug disasters can be prevented in less costly ways.

Paternalists who defend prohibitive premarket testing requirements must show that limiting the right of self-medication does in fact promote citizens' health or well-being on balance, not just that prohibitive requirements have saved lives in some cases. Defenders of premarket testing requirements must also show that prohibitions are necessary to protect people from dangerous drugs. If giving patients access to quality information about drugs could also prevent drug disasters, then approval policies cannot be justified by an appeal to paternalistic concerns for people's well-being.

2.6 The Health Effects of Prescription Policies

Proponents of pharmaceutical regulation also speculate that greater access to prescription drugs would have disastrous consequences for patients. The prescription drug system is sometimes cited, along with helmet laws and seatbelt requirements, as paternalistic policies that are so uncontroversial they demonstrate the more general plausibility of all coercive paternalism.[71] But unlike helmet laws and seatbelt requirements, the prescription drug system does not clearly save lives. Rather, in some cases, its prescription requirements may endanger patients.

We can assess the health effects of prescription requirements by comparing public health outcomes before and after prohibitive prescription requirements between countries that do and do not enforce prohibitive requirements and between drugs that change from prescription-only to over the counter. For example, if a prescription drug system did prevent unsafe drug choices, then we would expect to see fewer medicine-related mortality rates after the introduction of prescription requirements. Yet an analysis of time-series data from the United States found that the introduction of a prescription drug system did not reduce overall mortality from accidental or suicidal poisonings, which suggests that prescription requirements did not clearly protect people from the risks of

---

[70] Gieringer, "The Safety and Efficacy of New Drug Approval."
[71] Conly, *Against Autonomy*.18.

drug use.[72] Rather, prescription requirements were correlated with more fatal poisoning incidents, perhaps because consumers were more likely to use potent and risky drugs when a physician endorsed their choice or suggested that they use a drug.

Another explanation for this result is that prescription-only designation coincided with an explosion of new and dangerous drugs. Perhaps fatal poisonings would have increased were it not for a prescription-only system. Yet international comparisons, between middle-income countries that enforced prescription drug regulations and those that did not, have similar results. Poisoning-related mortality did not increase in countries without prescription requirements. Instead, states that enforced prescription-only drug regulations had higher rates of poisoning than non-prohibitive countries.[73]

Prescription requirements also make drugs more expensive and limit access to potentially beneficial treatment. For example, one study of prescription requirements found that switching the approval status of cough and cold medicines and topical hydrocortisones from prescription-only to over the counter significantly lowered the costs of medical care for patients, expanded access, and improved health outcomes for people with colds.[74] The fiscal cost of prescription requirements may be paid either by pharmaceutical users or their insurance providers. If consumers directly bear the cost of visiting a physician for a prescription and paying a pharmacist to administer it, then the worst-off are likely to be harmed the most by the added expense of prescription requirements. If members of insurance-risk pools or taxpayers pay the cost of a prescription system, then people without access to insurance or publically financed healthcare may find it difficult to access affordable medicine. In contrast, if

---

[72] Peltzman writes, "My analysis of American time series suggests that [prescription] regulation did not reduce—indeed may have increased—poisoning mortality from drug consumption." I take Peltzman's research to establish that prescription drug requirements do not clearly cause a reduction in poisonings related to pharmaceutical use. Peltzman conceived of the introduction of prescription requirements as an exogenous event, so if it had an effect on rates of accidental and suicidal poisonings from pharmaceutical use, then the effect would be reflected in the overall poisoning rate. Because this research design is not a controlled experiment, it provides limited evidence in favor of the hypothesis that prescription requirements did not cause a reduction in pharmaceutical poisonings, and it does establish that, to the extent that prescription requirements are justified as a way of reducing fatal poisonings, this justification would require further evidence. Sam Peltzman, "The Health Effects of Mandatory Prescriptions," *Journal of Law and Economics* 30, no. 2 (October 1, 1987): 207–38. P. 235.

[73] Peltzman writes, "Poisoning mortality is higher, all else remaining the same, in countries that enforce prescription regulation. This is consistent with other evidence that drug consumption in these countries is shifted toward more potent drugs." Sam Peltzman, "The Health Effects of Mandatory Prescriptions," *Journal of Law and Economics* 30, no. 2 (October 1, 1987): 207–38. P. 235.

[74] Peter Temin, "Realized Benefits from Switching Drugs," *Journal of Law and Economics* 35, no. 2 (1992): 351–69; P. Temin, "Costs and Benefits in Switching Drugs from Rx to OTC," *Journal of Health Economics* 2, no. 3 (1983): 187–205.

officials did not enforce prescription requirements, people could still pay to consult with physicians and pharmacist about their treatment options, they just would not be required to.

Proponents of coercive paternalism may reply that prescription requirements have good health effects because they prevent people from abusing controlled substances, such as prescription stimulants and painkillers. I will address this possibility in more detail in a later chapter, but for now, note that prescription requirements for high cholesterol, asthma, heartburn, allergies, diabetes, neutropenia, multiple sclerosis, arthritis, and hypertension treatments surely cannot be justified for the sake of preventing abuse.

And even prescription requirements for stimulants and painkillers could only be justified on these grounds if the health effects of prohibitive policies and criminal sanctions were on balance positive. But criminal prohibitions of prescription drugs not only have devastating effects on users and communities, they also prevent patients with a legitimate need for painkillers and stimulants from accessing them.[75] When prescription requirements do effectively prevent people from accessing prescription drugs for recreational use, some users respond by switching to even more dangerous opioids, such as heroin. To justify the prohibitive prescription requirements in these cases, it isn't enough to point to overdose and abuse statistics. One must also show that prohibiting recreational prescription drug use is the best way to do promote public health despite the costs. In light of the negative effects of prohibitive policies, this burden of proof remains unmet. So even though people recreationally use some pharmaceuticals in dangerous ways, prescription requirements cannot be justified on the grounds that they promote the public's health.

2.7 The Regulatory Reversal Test

Public officials have made some progress in acknowledging that patients with urgent claims to investigational drugs should have access. For example, compassionate access programs and accelerated approval policies aim to give more patients earlier access to potentially lifesaving drugs. The FDA's current compassionate access program approves most requests for early access from patients who meet the criteria. Each year, about one thousand patients are permitted to access unapproved drugs, and the FDA grants more than 99 percent of

---

[75] G. Alexander, S. P. Kruszewski, and D. W. Webster, "Rethinking Opioid Prescribing to Protect Patient Safety and Public Health," *JAMA* 308, no. 18 (November 14, 2012): 1865–66, doi:10.1001/jama.2012.14282; A. L. Taylor, L. O. Gostin, and K. A. Pagonis, "Ensuring Effective Pain Treatment: A National and Global Perspective," *JAMA* 299, no. 1 (January 2, 2008): 89–91, doi:10.1001/jama.2007.25; "The Shame of Filling a Prescription," *Well*, accessed December 30, 2014, http://well.blogs.nytimes.com/2012/01/05/the-shame-of-filling-a-prescription/.

compassionate use requests.[76] In 2015, the agency streamlined the process for patients to get access to experimental drugs and promised faster approval for compassionate use requests. Additionally, the FDA is approving all drugs faster than ever and offers accelerated approval for drugs that could potentially treat cancer, HIV, and rare conditions. Health Canada and EMA have similar programs. Regulatory agencies have also redesignated some drugs to over-the-counter or behind-the-counter status and, in doing so, have given patients more affordable access to safe and beneficial drugs.

Regulatory agencies also allow over-the-counter access for drugs that once required a prescription. Today more than seven hundred products contain active ingredients that once required a prescription in the United States.[77] Agencies like the FDA move drugs over the counter on the grounds that expanded access to relatively safe or well-understood drugs benefits the public's health on balance. The decision to move drugs over the counter is increasingly common, as European agencies aim to lower the costs associated with providing medications and the FDA aims to expand patients' access to preventive medicines and drugs that treat chronic conditions.[78]

These policies recognize that the previous approval policies and prescription requirements caused unjustified harm to patients who were waiting for better access to drugs. Yet public officials are reluctant to deregulate further in order to prevent other patients from suffering the same harm on the grounds that the consequences of deregulation would be worse on balance. The evidence I presented in the previous sections suggest otherwise, though this evidence is not decisive. However, we should be suspicious of the hypothesis that deregulation would be harmful because this approach to regulation is plausibly informed by status quo bias.

When people overstate the risks of a change in the future while acknowledging that similar changes in the past have been for the good, their assessments of the risks may reflect a bias to endorse the status quo. Nick Bostrom and Toby Ord developed a useful heuristic called the Reversal Test, which can be used to diagnose whether resistance to new technologies or policies is a result of status quo bias or whether a preference for the status quo is justified.[79] The Reversal

---

[76] Alexander Gaffney, RAC, "From 100 Hours to 1: FDA Dramatically Simplifies Its Compassionate Use Process" (Regulatory Affairs Professionals Society, February 4, 2015), http://www.raps.org/Regulatory-Focus/News/2015/02/04/21243/From-100-Hours-to-1-FDA-Dramatically-Simplifies-its-Compassionate-Use-Process/.

[77] "FAQs About Rx-to-OTC Switch," *CHPA.org*, n.d., http://www.chpa.org/SwitchFAQs.aspx#whatisswitch.

[78] Joshua P Cohen, Cherie Paquette, and Catherine P Cairns, "Switching Prescription Drugs to Over the Counter," *BMJ: British Medical Journal* 330, no. 7481 (January 1, 2005): 39–41.

[79] Nick Bostrom and Toby Ord, "The Reversal Test: Eliminating Status Quo Bias in Applied Ethics," *Ethics* 116, no. 4 (2006): 656–79.

Test asks defenders of the status quo to explain why changing a parameter (e.g., approval times or patient access) was good in the past but is unlikely to be good in the future. This test shifts the argument from justifying a change to justifying the status quo. In order to justify resistance to faster approval times or patient access, proponents of the current system must show that while expanding access has been beneficial so far, even more access would be harmful.

Proponents of the current approval system agree that existing compassionate access and accelerated approval programs are morally better than a more restrictive system. Reclassifying some pharmaceuticals as over the counter has also meaningfully expanded access without causing great harm. Therefore, one must either agree that the system should become even less restrictive going forward or show that the current system is optimal. If the current system should become less restrictive then the scope of compassionate access should expand to include even more patients. Approval times should become shorter for all drugs, not just breakthrough therapies. And regulatory agencies should consider making more drugs available without a prescription.

Or, if the current system is optimal, then it was wrong to prevent patients from compassionate access programs in the past, but allowing more patients to have compassionate access today would also be wrong—and the current balance of prescription to over-the-counter drugs is just right. There is little reason to believe that the current system is optimal, even on consequentialist grounds. Patients continue to die waiting for drug approval. People cannot access beneficial drugs because of paternalistic prescription policies, even if those drugs are relatively safe and going without them is not. Though the empirical evidence is not decisive, it does indicate that the costs of existing regulations outweigh the benefits. The existing system is also coercive, and if coercion requires justification to those who are coerced then this is a further normative reason that the burden of proof should lie with defenders of the status quo to justify the current system of regulation. Policymakers should be less concerned about unsubstantiated empirical predictions about the potentially disastrous consequences of less regulation and more concerned about the costs of the current system.

2.8 Certification Versus Approval

Imagine a world without gatekeepers for pharmaceuticals. Imagine a world where most drugs are available over or behind the counter. In such a world, people would be able to access pharmaceuticals without authorization from a physician. People could purchase experimental medicines with unknown risks. But imagine that other parts of pharmaceutical policy stayed the same. In such a world, regulatory agencies could still test and certify drugs as safe and effective for particular conditions. Physicians could still recommend treatment plans and advise patients about their options. Manufacturers would still be required to disclose the known and unknown risks associated with every product. Patients could still know the anticipated effects of drugs, whether regulators deem a drug safe and effective, and if their physicians recommend it.

Unlike other consumer choices, the decision to use a pharmaceutical is generally motivated by concern for one's health. People use pharmaceuticals to make themselves healthier. Given that patients are motivated by their health, they should ask medical experts, such as physicians and regulators, about health effects of pharmaceuticals, even if they can access pharmaceuticals without authorization from experts. This is especially true if drugs carry warnings that they are potentially very dangerous, or if patients know they have medical conditions that make using pharmaceuticals risky.

In such a world, where drugs are properly labeled and certified and patients have access to expert advice from physicians and regulators, should we expect that patients would knowingly choose to take drugs that are diluted with untested solvents or drugs that have never been tested on humans? Would patients self-medicate with toxic and risky drugs without ever talking to a pharmacist or a physician? Would people ignore the certification of regulatory bodies in favor of their own judgment about drugs? Would patients use incredibly dangerous painkillers recreationally? Would you? People who are concerned with their health would realize that it is prudent to only use certified drugs in most cases, to consult with a physician, and to avoid the risks associated with recreational painkiller use.

For the majority of patients who value their health, not much would change if they could purchase and use pharmaceuticals without a prescription. People probably would not visit physicians as often if physicians were not required to prescribe medicine, but many drug-related choices are so complicated or dangerous that it would still be justified to consult with an expert before choosing to use a drug. And for the minority of patients who have other values, removing gatekeepers between pharmaceuticals and users would enable them to access experimental treatments when all other options have failed. Patients would be empowered to learn more about their drug choices and tailor their medications to fit their values. Patients would not be required to spend money paying an expert to tell them what they already knew. Allowing access to medications would not harm the patients who currently value the expertise of physicians and regulators because they would still have access to all that expertise. But allowing access would provide patients with an additional set of options for those circumstances when their own values and priorities depart from experts' judgments.

If prohibitive forms of paternalism are ever permissible, it is because prohibitions are necessary to protect people from making dangerous choices. But this thought experiment illustrates that prohibitions are not necessary to protect people. A certification system would be sufficient to warn patients about the dangers of using pharmaceuticals. The drug disasters that motivated public officials to increasingly limit citizens' rights of self-medication throughout the twentieth century could have been avoided had the risks of dangerous drugs been discovered and disclosed. More generally, simply disclosing the dangers of a drug can prevent people from using a deadly medicine.

Paternalists who are concerned that patients would harm themselves if given access to risky drugs should ask whether the harm is due to access or uninformed access. When dangerous drugs harm or kill patients, it is often because someone misunderstood the risks of the drug. Giving patients the option to use drugs against medical advice would not make patients worse off as long as patients still have access to medical advice. If the risks of a drug were disclosed, people who are interested in mitigating risks to their health would avoid using a drug that was more likely to be harmful than helpful. For this reason, certification of drugs is a worthwhile goal for public officials. But approval policies are not necessary to protect health for patients who value their health and they limit the options of patients whose judgment or values departs from those of experts. Therefore, even if paternalism were a permissible justification for some prohibitive policies, when it comes to pharmaceuticals, certification is sufficient.

2.9 Conclusion

When public officials pass prohibitive laws to protect citizens' health by preventing people from making unhealthy choices, those laws are paternalistic. I am skeptical that prohibitive forms of paternalism are ever permissible. But even if the strongest arguments in favor of paternalism could justify some prohibitive polices, they could not justify prohibiting most pharmaceuticals because pharmaceutical regulations do not clearly protect the public health and they are not necessary to promote informed self-medication.

3

Rethinking Prescription Requirements

The earliest accounts of governmental regulations of pharmaceuticals date to Roman law. In 331 BC, officials found hundreds of women guilty of administering deadly poisons and punished the offenders by literally giving them a taste of their own medicine.[1] Except insofar as drugs were used for crimes, abortions, or euthanasia, governments largely overlooked medicine throughout ancient history.[2] By the ninth century, private professional cooperatives began prohibiting fraudulent drug sales among their members.[3] As medicine developed as a prestigious, intellectual profession in the tenth century, governments took an interest in drug regulation.[4] And from then on, pharmaceuticals in Europe were regulated by legally certified professional guilds that were charged with upholding the standards of their profession.[5] These regulations coincided with more

[1] The Twelve Tables, one of the earliest legal codes, forbids poisoning in Table VI Law XIV. This code dates to 450 BC. Disturbingly, early accounts of Roman law did not address the conduct of physicians except insofar as their actions compromised the health of slaves, in which case malpractice was considered a form of property damage. Vivian Nutton, *Ancient Medicine* (London; New York: Routledge, 2012). The account of punishment from poisonings is from D. B. Kaufman, "Poisons and Poisoning Among the Romans," *Classical Philology* 27, no. 2 (1932): 156–67. See also Veatch, *Cross-Cultural Perspectives in Medical Ethics*, and L. Cilliers and F. P. Retief, "Poisons, Poisoning, and the Drug Trade in Ancient Rome," *Akroterion* 45 (2000): 88–100.

[2] Walter Pagel, "Prognosis and Diagnosis: A Comparison of Ancient and Modern Medicine," *Journal of the Warburg Institute* 2, no. 4 (April 1, 1939): 382–98.

[3] Beginning in the ninth century, private professional cooperatives called frankpledges recorded acts of deceitful trade and paid fines in cases where their members sold deficient goods, but, in general, governments did not directly regulate the availability of most consumer goods, including drugs. Walton H. Hamilton, "The Ancient Maxim Caveat Emptor," *Yale Law Journal* 40 (1931): 1133.

[4] By the tenth century, the Visigothic and Ostrogothic kingdoms and Welsh law empowered legislators and judges to regulate physicians and pharmacists, and governments subsidized licensed medical providers. John M. Riddle, "Theory and Practice in Medieval Medicine," *Viator* 5 (1974): 157–84.

[5] For example, in the thirteenth century, Parisian apothecaries were subject to inspections and licensing requirements. These regulations quickly spread throughout Europe. By the fourteenth century, German apothecaries were not permitted to sell drugs without authorization from a university-trained physician, and Italy adopted similar regulations in the fifteenth century. Vern L. Bullough, "Status and Medieval Medicine," *Journal of Health and Human Behavior* 2, no. 3 (October 1, 1961): 204–10.

general increases in state power because high-status medical professionals could then use public power to limit access to medicines, codify professional training, and legally enforce codes of ethics.[6]

Set against this historical narrative, the relatively laissez faire era of the nineteenth century marks a brief respite from the steady rise of regulatory states.[7] Unprecedented economic growth, democratization, and the rise of Enlightenment ideals in Europe and North America produced fairly laissez-faire policies, particularly in the United States and Australia where governments were relatively weak.[8] In the nineteenth century, American policymakers widely affirmed rights of self-medication.[9] Daniel Carpenter writes:

> Votaries of self-medication frequently voiced their support for stronger labeling disclosure requirements for drug manufacturers, in part out of the belief that the intelligent layman needed maximal information to render an informed pharmaceutical purchasing decision. Yet the supporters of auto-therapy usually disdained state and federal regulatory measures. One of the most relevant political implications of their ethic was a time-honored "right of self-medication." In operation, this

---

[6] For example, medical regulation persisted in France throughout the nineteenth century, though unlicensed pharmacology was still practiced but subject to prosecution. England regulated the practice of pharmacy but did not regulate specific pharmaceuticals (except for a few narcotics) until the end of the nineteenth century, and apothecaries were permitted in some jurisdictions. See Matthew Ramsey, "Medical Power and Popular Medicine: Illegal Healers in Nineteenth-Century France," *Journal of Social History* 10, no. 4 (1977): 560–87. Bernice Hamilton, "The Medical Professions in the Eighteenth Century," *The Economic History Review* 4, no. 2 (1951): 141–69; and James J. Kerr, "Notes on Pharmacy in Old Dublin," *Dublin Historical Record* 4, no. 4 (1942): 149–59.

[7] I characterize this as relatively laissez faire because America did have many regulations on health and healthcare, including licensing laws and pharmaceutical branding and sales restrictions or price controls at the state and local level. See James Harvey Young, *American Self-Dosage Medicines: An Historical Perspective* (Coronado Press, 1974). chap. 1.

[8] The American and Australian experiences with pharmaceuticals were similar since neither inherited the European guild system and both countries faced problems of medical training and supply as they rapidly expanded. See Judith Raftery, "Keeping Healthy in Nineteenth-Century Australia," *Health and History* 1, no. 4 (December 1, 1999): 274–97, esp. 283. The eighteenth and nineteenth centuries were also relatively laissez faire in Europe, where few limits on consumer choice were enforced. See Terry M. Parssinen, *Secret Passions, Secret Remedies: Narcotic Drugs in British Society, 1820–1930* (Manchester University Press ND, 1983). See also J. L. Montrose, "Contract of Sale in Self-Service Stores," *Northern Ireland Legal Quarterly* 10 (1952): 178.

[9] For example, Thomas Jefferson assumes that self-medication is a fundamental right in arguing for freedom of conscience when he wrote, "Reason and free enquiry are the only effectual agents against error. Give a loose to them; they will support the true religion, by bringing every false one to their tribunal. . . . If it be restrained now, the present corruptions will be protected, and new ones encouraged. Was the government to prescribe to us our medicine and diet, our bodies would be in such keeping as our souls are now." Thomas Jefferson, *Notes on the State of Virginia*, ed. Frank Shuffelton (New York, NY: Penguin Classics, 1998), Query XVII.

included the absolute liberty of the consumer or patient to purchase any and all medications for the amelioration of his or her ailments. Whatever the disease, and whatever the purported cure, the layman should be able to exercise his own scientific judgment in drug purchasing decisions.[10]

Support for self-medication was also tied to a prevalent belief in economic liberties. Martha Mitchell writes, "Any effort to legislate on the subject raised the cry of monopoly and destruction of individual right."[11]

It is unclear whether relatively unfettered access to drugs was good or bad for public health in nineteenth-century America. On one hand, trained physicians were expensive and scarce, so most people lacked reliable access to medical experts. Without rights of self-medication, useful medicines, such as smallpox vaccines and painkillers, would have been inaccessible. By the mid-nineteenth century, pharmacists and druggists were the first-line providers of medical treatment.[12] Druggists bandaged wounds and provided optometry, dentistry, and midwifery. They also examined imported medicines, compounded new drugs, and advised patients about the risk and benefits of new treatments.[13]

On the other hand, medicine was very dangerous at the time. Before the germ theory of disease, even physicians were likely to do more harm than good. Uninformed patients acting alone were especially vulnerable to the dangers of misuse, and of adulterated or ineffective drugs. As the pharmaceutical industry evolved, people developed new drugs to sell and pharmaceutical advertising became more prevalent. Concerns about addiction grew amid widespread opiate and narcotic consumption.[14] In response, physicians' attitudes toward narcotics

[10] Carpenter, *Reputation and Power*, 79.

[11] Martha Carolyn Mitchell, "Health and the Medical Profession in the Lower South, 1845–1860," *The Journal of Southern History* 10, no. 4 (1944): 424–46. esp. 441.

[12] Many trained physicians also acted as druggists, mixing and selling compounds to patients, because the custom at the time (and in some states, the law) forbade physicians from charging fees for service unless medicine was given or a specific invasive procedure was performed. Renate Wilson and Woodrow J. Savacool, "The Theory and Practice of Pharmacy in Pennsylvania: Observations on Two Colonial Country Doctors," *Pennsylvania History: A Journal of Mid-Atlantic Studies* 68, no. 1 (2001): 31–65. David L. Cowen and Donald F. Kent, "Medical and Pharmaceutical Practice in 1854," *Pharmacy in History* 39, no. 3 (January 1, 1997): 91–100; and Joseph I. Waring, "Colonial Medicine in Georgia and South Carolina," *The Georgia Historical Quarterly* 59 (January 1, 1975): 141–53.

[13] Margaret Levenstein, "Mass Production Conquers the Pool: Firm Organization and the Nature of Competition in the Nineteenth Century," *The Journal of Economic History* 55, no. 3 (1995): 575–611. For an account of pharmacists in the 1860s playing this role, see Norman H. Franke, "Pharmaceutical Conditions and Drug Supply in the Confederacy," *The Georgia Historical Quarterly* 37, no. 4 (December 1, 1953): 287–98.

[14] David T. Courtwright, *Dark Paradise: A History of Opiate Addiction in America* (Harvard University Press, 2001), 1–9.

changed, and they began publishing calls for more effective restrictions on the sale of narcotics to children under ten and pregnant women.[15] States passed alcohol and opium prohibitions with varying degrees of success, and physicians stopped recommending narcotics.[16] With these reforms, the typical addict changed from a middle-class woman to a low-status male, and public attitudes toward intoxicants hardened.[17] But it took the Elixir Sulfanilamide tragedy in the early twentieth century to sway public support away from self-medication in favor of federal regulation.[18]

Today, most drugs require a prescription. I have argued that these prescription requirements can be harmful and that they violate patients' rights of self-medication. Specifically, I propose that public officials should not prohibit competent adults from purchasing prescription-grade drugs without authorization from a physician. This is not to say that all pharmacies should provide all forms of drugs on demand. It is only to say that vendors and consumers should not be prohibited from selling and buying drugs. To prevent misuse by minors and incompetent adults, some drugs should be sold behind the counter. In these cases pharmacists should serve as gatekeepers, in the same way that bartenders prohibit minors from purchasing alcohol today.

In this chapter, I develop a further defense of a comparatively laissez-faire approach to prescription drugs. I begin by making the case for the most controversial kinds of prescription drugs—deadly and addictive drugs. If I am correct that prohibitions on these kinds of drugs cannot be justified, then these arguments establish a presumption against prohibitions on non-deadly and non-addictive drugs too. My more general point is that pharmaceutical policy should not discriminate between legitimate and illegitimate drug users. Even if one does not accept my arguments about deadly and addictive drugs, one may accept the more general point that people should at least be permitted to access safe and non-addictive drugs for medical and nonmedical uses.

I then consider which prescription drug policy reforms are most urgent. I argue that the strongest case of reform concerns prescription requirements that violate rights *and* threaten public health. For example, people should be permitted to access drugs that protect them from pregnancy, HIV transmission, or overdose without a prescription. Addiction cessation therapies, insulin, and

[15] Foster, Jeffrey Clayton, "'The rocky road to a 'drug free Tennessee'": a history of the early regulation of cocaine and the opiates, 1897–1913." *Journal of Social History* (1996): 547–64; Joseph Spillane, "The Making of an Underground Market: Drug Selling in Chicago, 1900–1940," *Journal of Social History* 32, no. 1 (October 1, 1998): 27–47. David T. Courtwright, *Dark Paradise: A History of Opiate Addiction in America* (Harvard University Press, 2001), 1–9.

[16] William Novak, *The People's Welfare: Law and Regulation in Nineteenth-Century America* (Chapel Hill: University of North Carolina Press, 1996).

[17] Courtwright, *Dark Paradise.*

[18] Willian J. Novak, *People's Welfare: Law and Regulation in Nineteenth-Century America* (University of North Carolina Press, 1996), 149–234.

asthma inhalers, and other safe and potentially lifesaving drugs should be more broadly accessible as well.

In closing, I argue that there is a role for prescription requirements in limited cases. Dangerous and addictive drugs should remain behind the counter to prevent children and mentally incompetent people from accessing them. For behind-the-counter drugs, people may voluntarily "opt-in" to the prescription system, and employers and insurance companies may require them to do so. And some drugs, such as antibiotics, should be regulated by a prescription system because antibiotics misuse could violate others' rights.

3.1 Deadly Drugs

Consider the following argument against prescription requirements.

> (P1) Competent adults have the right to purchase deadly drugs without a prescription.
>
> (P2) If a person has the right to purchase deadly drugs without a prescription, then she should also have the right to purchase dangerous, harmful, or ineffective drugs without a prescription.
>
> (C) Therefore, competent adults have rights to purchase drugs without a prescription.

In other words, if people in particular circumstances have rights to purchase and use drugs that end their lives, then they have rights to purchase and use less dangerous drugs as well. The first premise states that competent people have the right to purchase and use deadly drugs without a prescription. The argument is not limited to terminally ill people or people with painful chronic diseases.

Arguments against hard paternalism in the previous chapters support the first premise, that competent people have the right to end their lives without prior authorization from a physician or public officials. To further motivate this argument, consider the example of Iris and Don Flounders, an Australian couple who were married for over sixty years. Don had terminal and incurable mesothelioma, a painful form of lung cancer. Iris was not terminally ill, but she had long held that she did not want to live without her husband. As Don's illness progressed, both Don and Iris wanted to die. The Flounders traveled to Mexico to obtain pentobarbital, which is used to euthanize animals and is not available in most developed countries, including their home country of Australia.[19] Before

---

[19] "British Suicide Couple Release Internet Video Calling for Right-to-die Laws," *Daily Mail*, May 1, 2011.

their deaths, Don and Iris recorded a video explaining their choice and arguing for the right to die. In it Don said:

> I knew that I would want to have the choice at the end as to how and when I die. We both very much resented the fact that we had to travel halfway 'round the world just to have the choice. We should have been able to get this drug at our local pharmacy, to be put safely away just in case, for the future.[20]

Iris added, "When we got the drugs I thought I might not want to live on without Don. Three years on, my thinking is the same. We decided this together. No one encouraged us, quite the opposite." [21] The couple was found dead in their home, arm in arm.

On my view, Don Flounders was correct when he claimed that he should have been able to buy pentobarbital at his local pharmacy, just as he should have been able to buy most other drugs. Rights of self-medication entail the right to use deadly drugs just as rights of informed consent entail the right to refuse lifesaving treatment. Moreover, deadly drugs provide benefits to patients who judge that their lives as a whole would be better if their remaining life were shorter and therefore have a legitimate interest in using deadly drugs.[22] For example, patients who suffer from degenerative diseases or debilitating, treatment-resistant depression may choose to use deadly drugs to preserve the dignity of their lives as a whole.[23]

This is not to say that deadly drugs ought to be sold alongside cough syrup and vitamins. Rather, deadly drugs should be sold behind the counter so pharmacists could assess a customer's capacity and enforce age requirements. Against this proposal, one may raise several empirical concerns. First, one may be concerned that deadly drugs will be used in crimes, even if they are sold behind the counter. Though less than 1 percent of all homicides in recent years are due to poison, the possibility of homicidal poisoning is still a legitimate concern, especially because most homicidal poisonings are against socially vulnerable populations, such as infants and the elderly.[24] Second, one may worry about accidental

---

[20] *Don and Iris Goodbye*, 2011, http://www.youtube.com/watch?v=ChKa2b12Yhw&feature=you tube_gdata_player.

[21] Ibid.

[22] Peter Singer, "Voluntary Euthanasia: A Utilitarian Perspective," *Bioethics* 17, nos. 5–6 (2003): 526–41.

[23] J. David Velleman, "A Right of Self-Termination?," *Ethics* 109, no. 3 (April 1, 1999): 606–28, doi:10.1086/et.1999.109.issue-3.

[24] Recent studies of homicidal poisoning found that it is less often used against competent, healthy adults. Greene Shepherd and Brian C. Ferslew, "Homicidal Poisoning Deaths in the United States 1999–2005," *Clinical Toxicology (Philadelphia, Pa.)* 47, no. 4 (April 2009): 342–47, doi:10.1080/15563650902893089.

poisonings. Already, over a quarter of all accidental deaths in the United States are due to drug poisoning, and perhaps the presence of deadly drugs in people's homes could worsen that problem.[25] A third empirical concern about relatively unrestricted access to deadly drugs is that it would increase the rate of successful suicides. Before turning to more principled objections to this proposal, I will address these empirical concerns.

In response to concerns about homicidal and accidental poisonings, I agree that a pharmacist may permissibly treat deadly drugs differently from other drugs but disagree that they may prevent most competent adults from purchasing them. Instead, I propose a regulatory framework similar to the regulation of handguns in countries that permit handgun ownership. For guns, a system of screening, registration, and liability avoids the problems of overcriminalization and black markets, which are associated with a more prohibitive policy.[26] And such a system also does not violate people's rights of self-preservation or prevent legitimate and permissible gun ownership.[27]

Similarly deadly drugs should be sold behind the counter to enable screening for age and capacity, without violating competent adults' rights to die. Some gun-licensing laws require that potential owners submit to a background check and psychiatric evaluation and wait for several weeks before receiving their guns. Similar licensing requirements may be applied to the sale and possession of deadly drugs to mitigate the danger of mentally incompetent people using the drugs to harm themselves or others. Gun registration requirements ensure that guns can be tracked if they are stolen or used in crimes. Registrations for deadly drugs can play a similar role. Standards of strict liability for gun owners ensure that people will store their guns safely to prevent theft, accidental injury, or misuse. Again, standards of strict liability may also apply to the possession of deadly drugs to prevent accidental or non-consensual poisonings.

In response to the concern that the sale of deadly drugs would cause more suicides, we should first question the assumption that it would be a problem if more patients chose to end their lives if given the choice to use deadly drugs. If greater access to deadly drugs caused an increase in suicides, one may infer that people are currently suffering and that demand for deadly drugs exceeds the current level of legal access in most places. But even if we grant that increased suicide rates would on balance be a negative result, there is little empirical evidence

[25] "FastStats," accessed April 11, 2016, http://www.cdc.gov/nchs/fastats/accidental-injury.htm.

[26] Douglas N. Husak, "Guns and Drugs: Case Studies on the Principled Limits of the Criminal Sanction," *Law and Philosophy* 23, no. 5 (2004): 437–93.

[27] Ibid. Michael Huemer, "Is There a Right to Own a Gun?," *Social Theory and Practice* 29.2 (2003): 297–324; Hugh LaFollette, "Gun Control," *Ethics* 110, no. 2 (2000): 263–81; David B. Kopel, "Trust the People: The Case Against Gun Control," *Journal on Firearms & Public Policy* 3 (1990): 77.

to support the claim that more access to deadly drugs on its own would make suicide significantly more prevalent.

In Switzerland, right-to-die organizations are currently permitted to provide and administer deadly drugs and euthanasia to competent adults, even those without medical conditions. A recent study of these organizations found that weariness of life was a prevalent reason for suicide in addition to medical conditions, but very few healthy young people used the clinics' services even though they had the option.[28] In Mexico, patients have de facto access to deadly drugs because pentobarbital is available at veterinary supply stores without a prescription.[29] But Mexico has a suicide rate that is one-third of the suicide rate in the United States. Suicide rates depend far more on cultural factors, such as widespread Catholicism, than on the availability of easy methods of suicide. Countries with comparatively high suicide rates such as South Korea, China, and Japan also have strong norms of social shaming, and suicide is often a response to humiliation. The empirical assumption that access to deadly drugs would substantially increase suicide rates is therefore unwarranted.

Yet few governments explicitly allow the sale of deadly drugs for human use. Most US states and developed countries do not allow patients to purchase deadly drugs. Most countries and states that do permit assisted dying require that a patient have an illness, as well as authorization from a physician or some oversight by a health professional. In Oregon, for example, patients with terminal illnesses are permitted to obtain prescriptions for a lethal dose of medication but they cannot purchase lethal drugs without a prescription. Since competent adults are entitled to end their lives, policies that prohibit people from accessing deadly drugs presumptively violate those rights.

Several philosophers also deny that competent adults are entitled to end their lives and that prohibitive policies therefore violate rights. David Velleman, for example, rejects the first half of this claim. He argues that the general arguments against paternalism do not justify a right to die in most cases. Specifically, Velleman argues that people do not have a right to end their lives in order to prevent suffering.[30] On his view, a person may only end her life in order to preserve the dignity of her life as a whole. Velleman's argument is as follows. First, the reasons we must usually respect people's choices derive from the value of autonomy. When a person's choice would undermine her

---

[28] Severin Fischer et al., "Suicide Assisted by Two Swiss Right-to-Die Organisations," *Journal of Medical Ethics* 34, no. 11 (October 1, 2008): 810–14.

[29] F. Lee Cantrell et al., "Death on the Doorstep of a Border Community—Intentional Self-poisoning with Veterinary Pentobarbital," *Clinical Toxicology* 48, no. 8 (September 2010): 849–50; Marc Lacey, "In Tijuana, a Market for Death in a Bottle," *New York Times*, June 21, 2008, sec. International/Americas, http://www.nytimes.com/2008/07/21/world/americas/21tijuana.html.

[30] J. David Velleman, "A Right of Self-Termination?," *Ethics* 109, no. 3 (April 1, 1999): 606–28, doi:10.1086/233924.

autonomy, though, she cannot appeal to the value of autonomy as a reason to respect that choice because her choice is inconsistent with the value of autonomy. Therefore, someone who asserts that she has a right to end her life to make her life better is committed to a kind of contradiction. On one hand, she holds that her autonomy is so important that it must be respected, even when she is making a very destructive choice. On the other hand, she holds that her autonomy is of so little value that she may destroy her autonomous capacities to avoid further suffering.

Velleman does not conclude that access to deadly drugs ought to be prohibited. But he does conclude that if deadly drugs were prohibited, it would not violate a person's right to die because no such right exists. The rights people have in virtue of the value of their autonomous capacities do not include the right to destroy their autonomous capacities. So when it comes to public policy, a person's *right* to die is not a barrier to permissible prohibition of euthanasia and physician-assisted dying, though it may be wrong to prohibit assisted dying for other reasons.

Yet Velleman's arguments against the right to die rely on the implausible assumption that simply because a person's authority to make decisions is derived from the value of her autonomy, that she is rationally committed to the claim that her autonomy has the kind of value that one cannot permissibly destroy. In this way, Velleman's arguments against the right to die seem to prove too much because the same considerations that Velleman cites in favor of the claim that a person has no right to destroy her autonomous capacities would seem also to support the claim that people have no rights to reduce their capacities. And if so, then this would imply that people had no right to stay up late, ride roller coasters, stand on their heads, watch reality television, or fall in love, because all of these activities reliably hinder one's autonomous capacities. Which, insofar as Velleman's position could be deployed in favor of legal limits on the right to die, would also mean that on this account people's rights were no barrier to regulation or prohibition of these activities either.

Another argument in favor of paternalistic prohibitions of deadly drugs is that some people who attempt suicide are subsequently grateful that they were prevented from succeeding. Danny Scoccia, for example, argues that if a choice is the kind of choice people subsequently regret and if prohibiting it does not limit people's autonomy too much, then paternalistic limits on that choice are permissible.[31] Scoccia's defense of hard paternalism does not consider whether those subject to prohibitive policies are subsequently glad that they were prevented from choosing to die because their preferences changed to adapt to their circumstances, nor does he consider whether people regret attempting suicide because to attempt suicide is stigmatized. If so, then these explanations for

---

[31] Danny Scoccia, "In Defense of Hard Paternalism," *Law and Philosophy* 27, no. 4 (July 1, 2008): 351–81, doi:10.1007/s10982-007-9020-8.

people's preferences for prohibitive policies might undermine Scoccia's argument because those preferences are a product of the very prohibitive policies they are used to justify. For example, if a person were not prevented from choosing to die, he would not subsequently change his mind and regret his choice; so the possibility of regret cannot justify preventing people from successfully choosing to die, even if those who are prevented from choosing to die do regret their choice. And preventing people from using deadly drugs may perpetuate the stigma associated with the choice to use deadly drugs, which could cause people to report a preference for a less stigmatized choice.

Even if people legitimately have a preference to use deadly drugs but change their mind after they were prevented from using deadly drugs and genuinely regret their choice, people would still have a legitimate claim against being prevented from using deadly drugs. As an analogy, imagine a person who loves to eat cheese and ice cream but would benefit if she lost weight. It would be wrong to inject her with a poison that made her lactose intolerant but otherwise did not inhibit her autonomy at all. Even if the poison were administered on the grounds that she would subsequently be happy that she was prevented from eating dairy because it caused her to lose weight, which was a benefit on balance, poisoning would be wrong. Even if she were subsequently grateful that she was prohibited from eating dairy, poisoning would be wrong. Though this case admittedly trivializes the subject matter, it also shows that a person's subsequent endorsement of an intervention is often irrelevant to the ethics of interference.

Scoccia claims that paternalistic policies can be justified insofar as (1) paternalistic policies could be enforced without limiting people's autonomy too much and (2) people would otherwise regret self-destructive choices and (3) people would be grateful for prohibitive policies if they were in effect. But to justify banning deadly drugs, Scoccia would also need to show that (4) public officials are entitled to prevent people from making choices they would regret. Scoccia implicitly assumes that (4) is true, but there is reason to doubt this. We would not accept this treatment from other people in our lives even if their conduct met conditions (1–3). If I sign a mortgage agreement that I cannot afford, I may not value my freedom to take out a mortgage and later regret my choice. If I were prevented from taking out the mortgage, I might be grateful for it. Still, it would be wrong for someone in my life to coercively prevent me from signing the mortgage agreement. For such a defense of hard paternalism to succeed, Scoccia must show why public officials are entitled to paternalistically coerce competent decision-makers where others are not.

Others object that medical professionals should not facilitate patient's deaths because it is wrong for health workers to be complicit in their killing.[32] On my

---

[32] Alec Samuels, "Complicity in Suicide," *Journal of Criminal Law* 69, no. 6 (2005): 535–9.

view, it is morally worse to prevent a patient from choosing to use a deadly drug than to provide her with the drug. But even if we granted that health workers should not be in the business of facilitating people's deaths, this consideration also does not justify a prohibition of deadly drugs. If anything it supports the sale of deadly drugs because patients could purchase drugs directly from willing vendors, unlike some systems that are currently enforced that require supervision and authorization by a physician.

A related empirical argument is that patients would feel pressured to choose death either as a result of explicit or implicit encouragement from their physicians or loved ones.[33] Were patients legally permitted to access suicide drugs, they might feel pressure from people around them (even if no one ever explicitly pressures them) to spare people from the emotional and financial burdens of continuing care. I am sympathetic to the claim that patients should not feel pressured, implicitly or explicitly, to end their lives. But prohibiting the sale of deadly drugs on these grounds would amount to prohibiting the sale of deadly drugs because many of us will disagree with certain people's reasons for ending their lives. It is not our place to decide which reasons should inform patients' life and death decisions, and, in any case, it would be wrong to limit all patients' rights out of concern for this minority of patients.

In a similar vein, some critics of legal euthanasia worry that the quality of medical care would diminish if patients were able to end their lives.[34] Or that if deadly drugs were available, insurance providers would deny disabled and sick patients pain relief and palliative care options.[35] Some critics fear that widespread acceptance of suicide would diminish social support for providing health services to sick and disabled patients. These empirical concerns are controversial. In the United States, the state of Oregon has some of the most extensive hospice services in the country, despite the availability of deadly drugs for terminally ill patients.[36] Even if these concerns are warranted, the objections are

---

[33] J. David Velleman, "Against the Right to Die," *Journal of Medicine and Philosophy* 17, no. 6 (1992): 665–81.

[34] For example, after the Netherlands started allowing euthanasia for terminally ill patients, the quality of palliative care options was worse. S. A. Hurst and A. Mauron, "The Ethics of Palliative Care and Euthanasia: Exploring Common Values," *Palliative Medicine* 20, no. 2 (2006): 107–112; Z. Zylicz and I. G. Finlay, "Euthanasia and Palliative Care: Reflections from The Netherlands and the UK," *Journal of the Royal Society of Medicine* 92, no. 7 (1999): 370; C. Seale and J. Addington-Hall, "Euthanasia: The Role of Good Care," *Social Science & Medicine* 40, no. 5 (1995): 581–7.

[35] D. P. Sulmasy, "Managed Care and Managed Death," *Archives of Internal Medicine* 155, no. 2 (1995): 133; T. D. Watts, "The For-profit Social Welfare Policy Sector and End-of-life Issues: A Troublesome Ethical Mixture," *Catholic Social Science Review* 12 (2007): 351–69.

[36] M. Golden and T. Zoanni, "Killing Us Softly: The Dangers of Legalizing Assisted Suicide," *Disability and Health Journal* 3, no. 1 (2010): 16–30; L. E. Moody, J. Lunney, and P. A. Grady, "Nursing Perspective on End-of-Life Care: Research and Policy Issues, A," *Journal of Health Care Law & Policy* 2 (1998): 243.

addressed not to the use of deadly drugs but to failures of patient care. Sick and disabled patients are entitled to quality medical care *and* the option to use deadly drugs; the right to one is no threat to the other.

Together, these arguments support (P1) that people have rights to purchase and use deadly drugs (subject to some regulation) without authorization from a physician. (P2) states that if a person has the right to purchase deadly drugs without a prescription, then she should also have the right to purchase dangerous, harmful, or ineffective drugs without a prescription. This premise requires a further defense as well.

Bertrand Russell wrote, "Drunkenness ... is temporary suicide. The happiness it brings is merely negative, a momentary cessation of unhappiness."[37] Presumably, the same can be said for intoxication more generally. If suicide is permissible, why should the temporary suicide of intoxication be held to a higher standard? Yet the two are different in one important respect. If a person makes a deadly choice, by necessity she will not live to suffer the consequences. But if a person makes a dangerous and harmful choice, such as misusing a drug for recreational purposes, she will live to suffer the consequences. Therefore one may argue that it doesn't follow from the fact that people have a right to use deadly drugs that they have a right to use dangerous drugs.

Consider for example the thought, originally raised by Derek Parfit, that we may have reason to be paternalistic toward others on behalf of their future selves. This argument arises because Parfit thinks that a person's future self is, to a degree, a different person than her present self. For this reason, it may be rational for a person to act in ways that impose great costs on her future self for the sake of benefits to her present self. But Parfit thinks that imprudence of this sort is immoral, even if it is not irrational, because one's future self is to some extent a different person.[38] So serious imprudence ought to be prohibited because it is immoral to harm one's future self just as it is immoral to harm another person. People who survive their very imprudent choices, as much as survival is possible for anyone, harm other people, and are therefore liable to be interfered with. Parfit writes:

> Since we ought to believe that great imprudence is seriously wrong, we ought to believe that we should prevent such imprudence even if it involves coercion. Autonomy does not include the right to impose upon oneself, for no good reason, great harm. We ought to prevent anyone from doing to his future self what it would be wrong to do to other people.[39]

---

[37] Bertrand Russell, *The Conquest of Happiness* (Lulu Press, 2015), 30.
[38] Derek Parfit, *Reasons and Persons* (Oxford: Oxford University Press, 1986), 318.
[39] Ibid., 321.

For the sake of argument, let's grant the first premise that people have a right to die and grant Parfit's claim that one's future self is in some relevant sense a different person. If so, then Parfit says it is wrong to harm that person through one's imprudence, so the second premise of my argument would be false.

Parfit concedes that there may be instrumental reasons to allow some imprudence. For example, allowing some imprudence helps people learn from their mistakes. Others reject Parfit's case for paternalism on the grounds that each person has a strong interest in living her own life, which she can only do if she is free from paternalistic interference.[40] Yet even if people do not learn from their mistakes or have a particularly strong interest in living their own lives, Parfit's argument still does not support paternalistic interference because were it not for one's imprudent choices, one's future self would not exist at all.

Consider an analogy to procreation. As Parfit famously argued, if a woman has a child at fourteen and as a consequence her child has a very bad start in life, her child still has not been made worse off because had she terminated her pregnancy (assuming that women have rights to do so) or waited to conceive, the child would not have existed at all.[41] Similarly, say a person has a right to die at any point but chooses instead to make a series of imprudent choices that harm his future self. His future self is not worse off, because had he chosen differently, the future self either would not exist or would have been a very different person than the person he is now. Either way, one's past imprudent decisions are a necessary condition for one's present self. So unlike harm to others, harm to one's future self doesn't make people worse off than they otherwise would have been because otherwise they wouldn't have been anyone or they would have been different people.

One may reply that one has a general duty to make one's future as good as it can be, similar to duties of beneficence which we have toward others. But this reply raises the following dilemma. On one hand, if the reason that we have to be beneficent toward our future self is merely that we have reasons to make the world as impersonally good as it can be, then that consideration would not warrant a special concern for oneself or one's future self and would seemingly call for very imprudent decision-making. For example, it would likely make the world impersonally better if any given person either worsened his future self by devoting all future earnings to the betterment of the worst off or ensured his

---

[40] Korsgaard seems to argue something like this, though she writes that a person "will not want others to intervene paternalistically unless it is necessary to prevent me from killing or crippling myself." So it is unclear whether her view would support the first or second premise of this argument. Christine M. Korsgaard, "Personal Identity and the Unity of Agency: A Kantian Response to Parfit," *Philosophy & Public Affairs*, 18, no. 2 (1989): 101–32.

[41] Parfit, *Reasons and Persons*, 351

future self's non-existence by donating his vital and non-vital organs to several people in need.

On the other hand, if the reason we have to be beneficent toward our future self stems from some other consideration, such as the idea that each person has a duty to ensure that her own life includes as many good experiences as possible, such a consideration would undermine the first premise of this argument that people have a right to die, at least in cases where the benefits of future life could plausibly outweigh the burdens.[42]

To review, I have argued that people have a right to die, and that the case in favor of a right to die supports a right to purchase and use deadly drugs without a physician's authorization. And the right to purchase and use deadly drugs without authorization supports the more general right of self-medication, even for patients who use harmful or dangerous drugs, such as recreational drug use or drug use for non-medical purposes. In the next two sections I will provide a further defense of self-medication in these cases.

3.2 Recreational Drugs and Addiction

Drugs that are used to cause death are not the deadliest drugs. The drugs that kill the most people in America are tobacco products, alcohol, and prescription painkillers. The first two are legal, but painkillers are only available with a prescription. The recent escalation of painkiller deaths and addiction is extraordinarily costly and causes a great deal of suffering. In light of this rapid rise in use and addiction, an important objection to rights of self-medication is that unrestricted access to addictive and dangerous pharmaceuticals would increase use—just as alcohol and tobacco use is widespread in part because it is legal. If so, one might worry that self-medication would contribute to a public health crisis and exacerbate the challenges of treating the rapid rise of harmful opioid use. In 1970 the US Congress passed the Controlled Substances Act, which authorized the DEA to enforce prohibitions of non-medical prescription drug use partly for these reasons.

In this section I will respond to three forms of this objection. The first form of the objection states that limits on addictive recreational drugs are justified on soft paternalistic grounds, because addicts are not fully autonomous with respect to their drug of choice. In response, I present empirical evidence that suggests addicts are autonomous with respect to their drug of choice. I also

---

[42] Or even in cases where it doesn't. Elsewhere in *Reasons and Persons*, Parfit considers a couple that commits suicide because they want to die in ecstasy rather than experience a foreseeable natural decline in ecstasy. Parfit writes, "death may be worth desiring" for such a couple and that their suicide would not be irrational, given their values (123).

discuss ways that greater access to pharmaceuticals may, surprisingly, reduce rates of addiction and make opioid use safer for addicts.

The second form of the objection states that limits on addictive recreational drugs are justified on moral grounds, for example, because addicts are unable to participate as equals in a fair society or because people have duties to protect their autonomy. This objection relies on the same false empirical premise about the relationship between addiction and autonomy as the first form of the objection, and also misinterprets the moral value of autonomy in ways that would seemingly license excessive and illiberal interference with people's choices.

The third form of the objection rejects the anti-paternalist framework entirely and states that limits on addictive recreational drugs are justified simply because unrestricted access to them would have terrible public health consequences. Again, I dispute the underlying empirical premise of this objection and argue that even if it were that access to addictive drugs had bad consequences on balance, it would not follow, even within a consequentialist framework, that prohibiting access is the best approach.

Consider first the claim that addicts are not fully autonomous with respect to their drug of choice so they do not have rights of self-medication when it comes to addictive painkiller use. This objection relies on an empirical claim about drug addicts. But empirical studies of drug addicts find that addicts are sufficiently autonomous with respect to the decision to use recreational drugs, even if they are not autonomous while they are intoxicated. For example, neuroscientist Carl Hart finds that among crack cocaine and methamphetamine users, only 10–20 percent become addicted and that those who do become addicted are still able to decide whether to use a drug.[43] Multiple studies have confirmed Hart's findings. When Hart offered addicts the choice of using their drug of choice or receiving cash rewards or merchandise vouchers, addicts' choices were sensitive to incentives. The smaller the dose of a drug or the larger the cash reward, the less likely addicts were to choose to use the drugs. Sociological evidence also shows that addiction is sensitive to incentives.[44] Most drug users are young adults, but people voluntarily quit as they grow older and assume more responsibility or financial commitments. When the price of drugs or penalties associated with drug possession increase, a portion of users quit.[45]

---

[43] John Tierney, "The Rational Choices of Crack Addicts," *New York Times*, September 16, 2013, sec. Science, http://www.nytimes.com/2013/09/17/science/the-rational-choices-of-crack-addicts.html.

[44] For a helpful review of this literature see, for example, Bennett Foddy and Julian Savulescu, "Addiction and Autonomy: Can Addicted People Consent to the Prescription of Their Drug of Addiction?," *Bioethics* 20, no. 1 (February 2006), 1–15. Richard Holton, *Willing, Wanting, Waiting* (Oxford, UK: Oxford University Press, 2009), 70–96.

[45] Gary S. Becker, Michael Grossman, and Kevin M. Murphy, "An Empirical Analysis of Cigarette Addiction," Working Paper (National Bureau of Economic Research, April 1990), http://www.nber.org/papers/w3322.

Other studies of drug users find that even if intoxication or withdrawal symptoms impair drug user's decision-making, regular drug users are rarely intoxicated or withdrawn.[46] Most drug users can't afford to be intoxicated all the time, but they can regularly take maintenance doses of drugs to avoid withdrawal. Even among heroin users who were identified as hard-core addicts, one study found that 43 percent worked full-time jobs.[47] Addictive desires are neurochemically similar to the desire for food or sex.[48] This evidence contradicts the popular perception that drug addicts cannot control their desire to use drugs.

When addicts claim that they cannot control their desire to use drugs, their testimony may not accurately reflect their underlying experiences because the decision to use recreational drugs is stigmatized.[49] And it is true that the desire to use drugs is difficult for addicts to resist, especially when they judge that abstaining from drug use is a worse option. Hart argues that many addicts who use illegal street drugs act rationally in response to circumstances that offer them few other options for temporary pleasure. The same considerations apply to illegal pharmaceutical use. Referring to the recent increases in prescription painkiller use, one physician described opioid users as people with "terribly sad-life syndrome."[50] Another physician noted that opioid abuse is most prominent in poor, rural regions where patients suffer from physical disabilities and depression or anxiety. The problem is compounded because, often in these areas, people are stigmatized for seeking mental health treatment.[51]

On the other hand, many people who are addicted to drugs claim that they would prefer to stop using, and one may worry that rights of self-medication would make drug rehabilitation more difficult. Again, this is an empirical concern, and two kinds of evidence are relevant to answering these worries. First, the effects of street drug decriminalization efforts in Portugal suggest that prohibitive approaches to drug abuse do not necessarily promote rehabilitation better than non-prohibitive approaches.[52] When Portugal decriminalized all

[46] Bennett Foddy and Julian Savulescu, "Addiction and Autonomy: Can Addicted People Consent to the Prescription of Their Drug of Addiction?," *Bioethics* 20, no. 1 (2006): 1–15.

[47] Charles E. Faupel, "Heroin Use, Crime and Employment Status," *Journal of Drug Issues* 18, no. 3 (July 1, 1988): 467–79, doi:10.1177/002204268801800311.

[48] Gianluigi Tanda and Gaetano Di Chiara, "A Dopamine-μ1 Opioid Link in the Rat Ventral Tegmentum Shared by Palatable Food (Fonzies) and Non-Psychostimulant Drugs of Abuse," *European Journal of Neuroscience* 10, no. 3 (1998): 1179–87.

[49] Bennett Foddy and Julian Savulescu, "A Liberal Account of Addiction," *Philosophy, Psychiatry, & Psychology* 17, no. 1 (March 1, 2010): 1–22, doi:10.1353/ppp.0.0282.

[50] Rachel Aviv, "Prescription for Disaster," *New Yorker*, April 28, 2014, http://www.newyorker.com/magazine/2014/05/05/prescription-for-disaster.

[51] Ibid.

[52] Douglas Husak, *Overcriminalization: The Limits of the Criminal Law* (Oxford University Press, 2008).

recreational drugs in 2000, rates of abuse, overdose, and HIV infection fell, and greater numbers of users sought rehabilitation and treatment.[53]

Public health experts generally support Portugal's approach, which devotes resources to risk reduction and rehabilitation instead of punishment and prohibition. In 2014 the World Health Organization expressed support for the decriminalization of recreational drugs as part of a comprehensive approach to reducing rates of HIV infection.[54] The 1988 UN convention against illicit traffic in narcotics and psychotropics allows for non-prohibitive approaches to recreational drugs too, and in 2009 the UN Office of Drugs and Crime issued a discussion paper supporting the treatment and rehabilitation approach to drugs followed by a 2014 statement that favorably discussed decriminalization and the Portuguese approach.[55]

Second, some of the most effective interventions for treating addiction include other pharmaceuticals. Bupropion is an anti-depressant that is an especially effective treatment for nicotine, cocaine, methamphetamine, and even gambling addictions.[56] Other addiction-cessation therapies, such as methadone and narcotic antagonists like naltrexone and acamprosate, can also help people who wish to avoid further drug use. I am not suggesting that greater access

---

[53] Though as Hughes and Stevens argue, the magnitude of the public health benefits of drug decriminalization are potentially overstated by its proponents (such as Greenwald). Glenn Greenwald, "Drug Decriminalization in Portugal: Lessons for Creating Fair and Successful Drug Policies," Cato Institute Whitepaper Series, April 2, 2009, http://papers.ssrn.com/sol3/papers.cfm?abstract_id=1464837; Artur Domoslawski, Hanna Siemaszko, and Helsińska Fundacja Praw Czlowieka, "Drug Policy in Portugal: The Benefits of Decriminalizing Drug Use," Open Society Foundations New York, 2011, https://www.tni.org/en/issues/decriminalization/item/2725-drug-policy-in-portugal; Caitlin Elizabeth Hughes and Alex Stevens, "A Resounding Success or a Disastrous Failure: Re-Examining the Interpretation of Evidence on the Portuguese Decriminalisation of Illicit Drugs," *Drug and Alcohol Review* 31, no. 1 (January 1, 2012): 101–13, doi:10.1111/j.1465-3362.2011.00383.x.

[54] "Illicit Drugs: The WHO Calls for Decriminalisation," *The Economist*, July 17, 2014, http://www.economist.com/blogs/newsbook/2014/07/illicit-drugs.

[55] The 1988 treaty allows that officials may, but are not required to, prohibit recreational drug use, so it allows for non-prohibitive approaches. United Nations Office on Drugs and Crime, "The International Drug Control Conventions," Final Acts and Resolutions (New York, NY: United Nations, 1988 1961), https://www.unodc.org/documents/commissions/CND/Int_Drug_Control_Conventions/Ebook/The_International_Drug_Control_Conventions_E.pdf; United Nations Office on Drugs and Crime, "Discussion Paper: From Coercion to Cohesion: Treating Drug Dependence Through Health Care, Not Punishment," (Vienna: United Nations, 2009), https://www.unodc.org/docs/treatment/Coercion_Ebook.pdf; United Nations Office on Drugs and Crime, "World Drug Report," (Vienna: United Nations, 2014), https://www.unodc.org/documents/data-and-analysis/WDR2014/World_Drug_Report_2014_web.pdf.

[56] Pinhas Dannon et al., "Sustained-Release Bupropion Versus Naltrexone in the Treatment of Pathological Gambling: A Preliminary Blind-Rater Study," *Journal of Clinical Psychopharmacology:* 25, no. 6 (December 2005): 515–653; Heidi Magyar, "Bupropion: Off-Label Treatment for Cocaine and Methamphetamine Addiction," *Current Psychiatry* 9, no. 7 (July 2010), http://www.currentpsychiatry.com/index.php?id=22661&tx_ttnews%5Btt_news%5D=175212.]

to pharmaceuticals would make rehabilitation easier, only that the evidence is mixed at best. Although greater access to pharmaceuticals would mean that some people had greater access to addictive drugs, they would also have more access to drugs that effectively treat addiction and underlying conditions that lead to addiction.

Another way to mitigate the potential harm of addictive pharmaceuticals would be to designate some addictive drugs as behind the counter and enable addicts who do not wish to use addictive pharmaceuticals to commit to not using by enrolling in a voluntary prohibition registry. Casinos have used this strategy to help gambling addicts without withholding access to casinos from customers who endorse their desire to gamble.[57] Such an approach would make all the gatekeeping functions of the prescription drug system available to patients who would prefer not to have legal and easy access to opioids, while allowing other voluntary drug users to purchase and use recreational drugs, a right that is protected by the more general right of self-medication

If soft paternalism cannot justify limits on the sale of addictive painkillers, others have argued that restrictions on access to dangerous and addictive drugs are justified for moral reasons. For example, Samuel Freeman defends paternalistic bans on recreational street drugs that reliably and significantly undermine the moral and rational integrity of users.[58] His argument is that public officials in liberal societies have a moral obligation to secure and protect each citizen's ability to participate as an equal in those communities. His argument is similar to Velleman's argument against the right to die.[59] Freeman claims that liberalism begins with the assumption that autonomy is valuable, so if a public official aims to prevent people from undermining their autonomy by using self-destructive drugs, there is nothing illiberal about doing so.[60] This argument rests on an empirical assumption that some drugs are so damaging that they would render users unable to participate in society. I argued earlier that there is reason to doubt this assumption. As I suggested in the previous section, Freeman's argument that people are not entitled to render themselves unable to participate in society would also seemingly imply that patients do not have the right to die or to refuse lifesaving medical treatment. Therefore, if Freeman interprets the liberal value of autonomy as a capacity that public officials ought to protect, rather than respect, then he is seemingly committed not only to some prohibitions of recreational drug use but a host of other illiberal policies too.

---

[57] Douglas N. Husak, "Paternalism and Consent," *Law and Philosophy* 8, no. 3 (December 1, 1989): 353–81. doi:10.2307/3504593.

[58] Samuel Freeman, "Liberalism, Inalienability, and Rights of Drug Use," in *Drugs and the Limits of Liberalism: Moral and Legal Issues*, ed. Pablo De Greiff (Cornell University Press, 1999), 110–130.

[59] J. David Velleman, "A Right of Self-Termination?," *Ethics* 109, no. 3 (April 1, 1999): 606–28, doi:10.1086/et.1999.109.issue-3.

[60] Freeman, "'Liberalism, Inalienability, and the Rights of Drug Use," esp. 114.

A related objection to permitting people to purchase addictive pharmaceuticals for non-medical use is that drug addicts are more likely than others to do immoral things while intoxicated, such as driving recklessly, committing assault, or neglecting their families. Yet these concerns do not support prohibitions of recreational drug use because it is not in itself wrong to use drugs. As Doug Husak has argued, the law should prohibit immoral conduct, such as driving while intoxicated or child neglect, not permissible conduct such as drug use.[61] Husak's argument that laws should only punish immoral conduct is especially applicable to prohibitive drug policies because the drug war in the United States is one of the greatest policy disasters of the last century, and it would be a grave mistake to continue on this misguided and destructive path. Prohibitive policies can also cause more crime because they bolster black markets, where people depend on private enforcement because they cannot rely on police to enforce property rights in illegal substances.

A final objection to a policy that grants access to addictive painkillers for non-medical purposes is consequentialist. It states that even if the prescription drug system considered as a whole does not promote public health and well-being, prescription requirements for painkillers would promote overall well-being. A consequentialist argument for banning access to addictive pharmaceuticals that are used for recreation might parallel recent arguments for cigarette prohibition. For example, Sarah Conly argues that cigarettes should be banned because the benefits outweigh the costs, especially because if cigarettes were illegal fewer people would be addicted, so fewer people would experience a ban as burdensome.[62] Robert Goodin favors a ban on the grounds that smokers are not reliable judges of their own well-being when it comes to cigarettes because they suffer many cognitive biases such as short-sightedness and an overly optimistic view of their own future as smokers.[63] Kalle Grill and Kristin Voigt argue in favor of a ban on the grounds that the loss of well-being caused by premature death and poor health outweigh the loss of well-being caused by limits on people's choices and lack of access to cigarettes.[64]

These arguments may also justify prescription drug requirements that prevent people from using dangerous and addictive drugs for recreation. Conly supports prescription requirements, and her argument that prohibition can decrease rates of addiction, thus mitigating the loss of well-being associated with a ban can be extended to addictive pharmaceuticals. Similarly, recreational

[61] Husak, "Recreational Drugs and Paternalism."

[62] Conly, Sarah. "The case for banning cigarettes." *Journal of Medical Ethics* 42.5 (2016): 302–3.

[63] Robert E. Goodin, "The Ethics of Smoking," *Ethics* 99, no. 3 (1989): 574–624.

[64] Grill K. and K. Voigt, "The case for banning cigarettes." *Journal of Medical Ethics* 42, no. 5 (2016): 293.

pharmaceutical users potentially suffer from the same cognitive biases that Goodin attributes to smokers. And though not on the scale of tobacco use, recreational pharmaceutical use also causes poor health and early death, which substantially reduces well-being.

However, as in the case of tobacco bans, these considerations also cannot justify prohibiting recreational pharmaceutical use. We can address these proposals from the perspective of ideal theory or non-ideal theory.[65] When we assess a proposal from the perspective of ideal theory, we ask whether it can be justified in light of all relevant moral considerations, but not whether it would be justified in the world as it exists today. When we assess a proposal from the perspective of non-ideal theory, we ask whether the proposal can be justified in light of moral considerations and empirical concerns about the feasibility of the proposal and whether people will generally comply with it. Grill and Voigt and Goodin make their case mainly at the level of ideal theory, whereas Conly makes the case for bans at the level of non-ideal theory.[66]

Within a non-ideal framework, it is clear that while the current restrictions on access to prescription pharmaceuticals are politically feasible, people do not comply with them. Due to the problems associated with compliance, Conly expresses reservations about extending her support for cigarette bans to other drugs on the grounds that "[Alcohol] prohibition seems to have been a consummate waste of money whose only achievement was making criminals rich ... countless people have been killed in drug violence. These are policies that don't work." [67] Painkiller prohibitions are also associated with drug-related violence, such as pharmacy robberies.[68] Since prohibitive painkiller regulations increase the price of black market opioids painkillers, many addicts switch to heroin, which is more dangerous and poses additional public health risks, such as HIV transmission.[69] And black market drug use is associated with incarceration, especially in vulnerable populations, which is harmful to dealers and users, but marginalized communities too.[70] Since the non-ideal approach considers the

[65] Laura Valentini, "Ideal vs. Non-Ideal Theory: A Conceptual Map," *Philosophy Compass* 7, no. 9 (September 1, 2012): 654–64, doi:10.1111/j.1747-9991.2012.00500.x.

[66] I address these arguments for tobacco regulation in more detail in Jessica Flanigan, "Double Standards and Arguments for Tobacco Regulation," *Journal of Medical Ethics*, (April 5, 2016), medethics – 2016-103528, doi:10.1136/medethics-2016-103528.

[67] Conly, *Against Autonomy*, 170.

[68] Chris Hawley and News Services, "'An Epidemic': Pharmacy Robberies Sweeping US," *NBC News*, June 25, 2011, http://www.nbcnews.com/id/43536286/ns/us_news-crime_and_courts/t/epidemic-pharmacy-robberies-sweeping-us/.

[69] Mike Mariani, "Why So Many White American Men Are Dying," *Newsweek*, December 23, 2015, http://www.newsweek.com/2016/01/08/big-pharma-heroin-white-american-mortality-rates-408354.html.

[70] Michelle Alexander *The New Jim Crow: Mass Incarceration in the Age of Colorblindness* (New York: The New Press, 2012).

costs of non-compliance, these considerations undermine the non-ideal theoretical case for the prohibition of recreational pharmaceuticals.

Another reason that recreational pharmaceutical restrictions may cause more harm than good, even if people comply with them and they are effectively enforced, is that effective enforcement could have negative public health effects. For example, when public officials increase monitoring and enforcement of prescription painkillers, they subject physicians to heightened scrutiny of prescribing practices. Physicians who are suspected of prescribing painkillers to recreational users can face criminal penalties for running "pill mills," so they are reluctant to prescribe painkillers. These policies therefore make it more difficult for patients to access painkillers for medical purposes as well.[71]

Additionally, Conly argues that the case for tobacco regulation is especially strong because tobacco is not immediately pleasurable to use, unlike heroin. Conly suggests that the initial unpleasantness of smoking means that tobacco regulations may be more effective at preventing people from becoming addicted in the first place than other regulations. Yet many of the prescription painkillers used recreationally are opioids, which are pleasurable when people use them for the first time. So, recreational pharmaceuticals are more like heroin than tobacco. Therefore, even if Conly's non-ideal argument for tobacco regulation were successful, the argument would clearly not justify the prohibition of recreational painkillers.

Turning to ideal theory, the prohibition of recreational pharmaceuticals is not justified even in principle. If we assume that reform is politically feasible and that people would comply with laws prohibiting recreational use, there are many other potential policies that could also reduce recreational pharmaceutical abuse and misuse without prohibiting it. And since these policies would also not violate people's rights of self-medication, they would have a principled advantage over coercive regulations. For example, instead of prohibiting people from using pharmaceuticals for recreational purposes, public officials could invest in addiction-cessation programs and effective drug rehabilitation and treatment, as well as facilitating access to drugs like naltrexone.

Officials could also provide incentives or subsidies for the development of non-addictive drugs that treat chronic pain. In some cases, expanded rights to use drugs could cause less harmful drug use. For example, some researchers suggest that medical marijuana could treat some of the conditions that are currently treated with opioid painkillers, which could potentially reduce the rates

---

[71] Because non-medical painkiller use is criminally prohibited and enforced by the DEA, a black market for painkillers has become increasingly lucrative, causing armed robberies at pharmacies. In response, some pharmacies have discontinued the sale of painkillers, depriving medical users of easy access to prescribed drugs. See N. R. Kleinfield, "Anxious Days for Long Island Pharmacies," *New York Times*, January 8, 2012.

of accidental poisonings because marijuana is much safer and less addictive than opioids.[72] Non-medical factors seem to increase rates of recreational drug misuse and addiction too. For example, people who are unemployed and socioeconomically disadvantaged are more likely to be dependent on opioid painkillers. If material depravation contributes to self-destructive and addictive behavior and officials hope to prevent harmful drug use, then they should also consider interventions that address poverty, such as a universal basic income or other efforts at promoting social equality.

3.3 Therapeutics

Arguments in favor of paternalistic limits on other forms of pharmaceutical use will fail for many of the same reasons that arguments in favor of restrictions on the right to die or the right to use addictive drugs failed. Yet self-medication for therapeutic purposes may seem importantly different from deadly and addictive drug use because most people who do not use pharmaceuticals for recreation or suicide use them to improve their health. From this observation, one may then argue that therapeutic drug use is different because it is not an end in itself, only a means to an end, health. And it also may seem that paternalistic restrictions on the means to one's ends are easier to justify, because interference with the means to one's ends does not disrespect a person's authority to set goals and pursue them or force her to live in accordance with a controversial theory of the good life that she does not accept.[73]

If there were a moral distinction between choices that are means to an end and one's choices of ends, then that distinction would be relevant to the previous arguments for rights of self-medication. The epistemic argument for self-medication relied on the claim that people are generally in the best position to judge what is good for them. But it could be that people are generally experts about whether certain projects and goals will promote well-being but not experts about how to achieve those projects. If so, a patient may be in the best position to judge her tolerance for side effects and the value of health while a physician is in the best position to judge which drugs will minimize side effects and promote her health. Even if we grant this point and accept that people may require more information about the means to achieve their ends than they require about their ends, a certification system for pharmaceuticals could address concerns about

---

[72] David Powell, Rosalie Liccardo Pacula, and Mireille Jacobson, "Do Medical Marijuana Laws Reduce Addictions and Deaths Related to Pain Killers?," Working Paper, National Bureau of Economic Research, July 2015, http://www.nber.org/papers/w21345.

[73] I am thankful to Sarah Conly for encouraging me to consider this point.

people's qualifications to assess whether a particular drug will ultimately promote their goals, especially if people can consult with physicians as well.

But we should resist attempts to establish a more principled distinction between ends and means. If we accept that people are usually in the best position to judge whether they should pursue a particular goal or project, the same considerations would also support the assumption that people are usually in the best position to choose the means to achieve their goals or projects. Or, one could deny that people are usually in the best position to decide how to achieve their goals. But the denial of this claim invites skepticism against the claim that people are usually in the best position to set their own goals in the first place. And to deny this claim would have a high intuitive price, since it would seemingly justify a paternalistic interference with people's most deeply held projects, including violations of informed consent.

Moreover, the distinction between ends and means is further undermined by the fact that judgments about safety and efficacy are normative judgments about how much risk a person accepts in her life. In this way, choices about therapeutic drugs are not solely instrumental to promoting a person's health. Just as a person may reasonably take up the project of risky recreational drug use, she may also take up the project of risk-minimization by choosing to use safe drugs that cause more discomfort than their riskier alternatives. When making a decision about using a drug as a means to some other goal or as an end in itself then, people often have good reason to expect that other people defer to their judgment while also seeking out information about their choice to ensure that their judgment about whether to use a drug truly reflects their values. A system of certification would enable people who value different ends, for example,. health or recreation, and different considerations related to the means to their ends, for example, risk or cost, to make informed choices that reflected each person's distinctive values.

For these reasons I am skeptical that there is a principled distinction between paternalistic limits on means and paternalistic limits on people's ends. But there may be other reasons to think that unrestricted access to therapeutics is even more problematic than unrestricted access to deadly drugs or addictive recreational drugs. Specifically, when people are sick, they may be particularly bad at assessing risks, ignorant, and extremely vulnerable. These considerations could undermine people's decisional capacity in ways that are especially worrisome. And while public officials have their own biases and are ignorant about each patient's overall interests, they are not as emotionally compromised as patients who encounter an illness for the first time.

On the other hand, a patient's emotional state may also be an asset in overcoming biases and ignorance, since each patient is more motivated to make a qualified decision about her health more than anyone else in her life. Just as insurance salespeople and real estate investors are better at assessing risks than ordinary consumers because they stand to gain more from accurate assessments and lose more from inaccurate judgments, patients bear the costs of their judgments more than anyone else. And if a patient recognizes her own biases and ignorance, she may choose to consult with experts. And while people who face life-threatening illnesses are especially vulnerable and potentially susceptible to manipulation, public officials should address these concerns by protecting patients from fraudulent marketing, certifying drugs, and perhaps subsidizing access to physicians for people who would otherwise lack access to expert advice.

A related concern is that some patients are not only poorly equipped to understand the risks and benefits of treatment, but they also are poorly equipped to recognize that they are poorly equipped to understand their treatment choices. The Dunning-Kruger effect is a cognitive bias in which those who are least qualified to make a judgment mistakenly judge themselves as qualified.[74] The Dunning-Kruger effect is particularly troubling in healthcare contexts because people are unrealistically optimistic when they assess their own health risks relative to other people and confidently misdiagnose themselves on the basis of false beliefs about medicine.[75]

These biases are most prominent in circumstances of pervasive ignorance, when patients know so little about health and medicine that they don't know what they don't know. But we should not assume that the pervasiveness of the Dunning-Kruger effect is a fact of nature, rather than a fact of our environment and the current system. One reason that patients may be so pervasively ignorant about health is that they have had little reason to investigate their treatment options or to learn how to evaluate different drugs. Under the current system of pharmaceutical regulation, patients may not attempt to educate themselves or to investigate their options out of a sense of learned helplessness. In healthcare settings, learned helplessness can be caused by social factors, policies, and stereotypes that undermine patients' sense of responsibility, control, and independence.[76] Prohibitive pharmaceutical policies are policies that reinforce the stereotype that patients are helpless. Existing policies could also lead some patients to quite reasonably conclude that attempts to control their course of treatment are likely to be futile, and patients may therefore refrain from investing resources in educating themselves. But if officials and physicians respected patients' rights of self-medication, then patients may invest more resources in

---

[74] Justin Kruger and David Dunning, "Unskilled and Unaware of It: How Difficulties in Recognizing One's Own Incompetence Lead to Inflated Self-Assessments," *Journal of Personality and Social Psychology* 77, no. 6 (1999): 1121–34, doi:10.1037/0022-3514.77.6.1121.

[75] David Dunning, Chip Heath, and Jerry M. Suls, "Flawed Self-Assessment Implications for Health, Education, and the Workplace," *Psychological Science in the Public Interest* 5, no. 3 (December 1, 2004): 69–106, doi:10.1111/j.1529-1006.2004.00018.x.

[76] Kenneth Solomon, "Social Antecedents of Learned Helplessness in the Health Care Setting," *The Gerontologist* 22, no. 3 (June 1, 1982): 282–87, doi:10.1093/geront/22.3.282.

learning about drugs and health, thereby overcoming the pervasive ignorance about health that causes oblivious and biased decision-making today.

3.4 Antibiotics

If people's rights of self-medication support rights to use deadly drugs and addictive painkillers, then it may seem that patients have rights to unrestricted access to all and any pharmaceuticals. Yet the arguments on behalf of the right to die and rights to use painkillers and other pharmaceuticals relied on the assumption that deadly drug use and painkiller addiction and self-medication did not violate other people's rights. Few pharmaceutical choices do violate rights, but if using a drug does injure other people, physicians and regulators should enforce prescription requirements that limit access.

For example, restrictions on antibiotics are warranted if antibiotic misuse contributes to the development of dangerous antibiotic-resistant bacteria and restrictions can effectively prevent harmful antibiotic misuse. The argument in favor of prescription requirements for antibiotics goes like this:

(P1) If a user violates other people's rights or exposes others to an undue risk of harm by using a drug, then public officials may permissibly limit access to that drug.

(P2) Antibiotic users violate other people's rights against contagious transmission and expose people to an undue risk of harm.

(C) Therefore, public officials may permissibly limit access to antibiotics.

This argument is consistent with the claim that patients' rights of self-medication are analogous rights of informed consent. Neither rights of self-medication nor informed consent are absolute because neither right entitles people to make decisions that violate or significantly risk violating the rights of other people. Just as the right to freedom of movement doesn't entitle a person to ride her bicycle into a crowd, nor do medical rights mean that people are entitled to subject people around them to the risks of being injured by illness.

For example, the doctrine of informed consent does not protect a patients' right to refuse to be vaccinated or to refuse to undergo treatment or quarantine for a contagious disease. As I have argued elsewhere, vaccine refusal decisions can violate others' rights in the same way that drunk drivers violate people's rights by exposing them to an undue risk of harm.[77] Bystanders in public spaces

---

[77] Jessica Flanigan, "A Defense of Compulsory Vaccination," *HEC Forum: An Interdisciplinary Journal on Hospitals' Ethical and Legal Issues* 26, no. 1 (March 2014): 5–25, doi:10.1007/s10730-013-9221-5.

have rights against having their lives endangered by contagious but preventable diseases because they cannot consent to the risks accompanied with associating with an unvaccinated person. If unvaccinated people refrained from using public spaces and those who associated with them were capable of consent, informed of the risks of contagious transmission, and consented to associate with unvaccinated people anyhow, it would not be wrong to refuse vaccination. Yet the risk of non-consensual transmission is morally significant enough to justify compulsory vaccination in most contexts because unvaccinated people use public spaces and put other people at risk.

Similarly, rights of self-medication also are not absolute. Antibiotic overuse is also harmful to innocent bystanders because it increases the severity of some outbreaks of infectious diseases and the probability that antibiotic-resistant bacteria, also known as superbugs, will develop. Antibiotic overuse causes resistance because when people use antibiotics to treat an illness, the antibiotics kill the bacteria causing their illness as well as bacteria protecting their bodies from infection. After treatment, only antibiotic-resistant bacteria remain in the body, so the drug-resistant bacteria multiply. For this reason, exposure to antibiotics increases the amount of antibiotic-resistant bacteria and raises the probability that antibiotic-resistant infections will develop.

As in the case of vaccines, rights of self-medication can reasonably be limited to mitigate the harm that antibiotic-resistant bacteria could cause if transmitted, since contagious transmission would violate other people's bodily rights. The epistemic case for self-medication fails to support a right to access antibiotics too. While it is reasonable to assume that patients usually know whether using a drug, including an antibiotic drug, is good for them, their expertise about the personal benefits of using antibiotics does not entitle them to put others at risk. So when it is clear that limiting access (or requiring vaccination) is necessary to avoid contagious transmission and that it would be effective, public health officials would have the authority to limit access to antibiotics.

Researchers have already documented antibiotic-resistant forms of tuberculosis, syphilis, strep, staph, salmonella, and E. coli. Many antibiotic-resistant infections develop in hospitals, where antibiotics are routinely prescribed. Some experts suggest that hospital-based overuse (along with agricultural antibiotic use) is a primary contributor to antibiotic resistance.[78] Using high doses of antibiotics in hospital settings can increase the probability of bacterial Clostridium difficile (C. diff) infections, which develop when people in hospitals use high doses of antibiotics for a prolonged period, killing the gut bacteria that usually

---

[78] Thomas J. Sandora and Donald A. Goldmann, "Preventing Lethal Hospital Outbreaks of Antibiotic-Resistant Bacteria," *New England Journal of Medicine* 367, no. 23 (December 6, 2012): 2168–70, doi:10.1056/NEJMp1212370.

prevents C. diff infections. In the United States, C. diff sickens more than half a million people each year, and it contributes to tens of thousands of deaths.[79]

If antibiotics were as widely available in consumer markets as they are in hospitals, resistance would be even more likely. In places where pharmaceutical regulations are not enforced and patients can freely access antibiotics, resistance is a greater threat to public health.[80] Therefore, patients' rights of self-medication do not entitle them to purchase and use antibiotics without authorization.

One may reject my analogy between compulsory vaccination and access to antibiotics on the grounds that people who transmit contagious illnesses violate the bodily rights of their victims but people who contribute to antibiotic resistance by using antibiotics do not violate anyone's bodily rights. After all, if a person is infected with measles, it is because she inhaled the virus from someone with measles who spoke or coughed nearby. So, people have a duty to get vaccinated in order to avoid spreading viruses like measles to others. But if a person is infected with antibiotic-resistant syphilis, it is because she touched the active lesions of a sexual partner who was infected with syphilis. It may seem that the person who acted wrongly in such a scenario is her partner, not those who used antibiotics in the past. Likewise, if a person is infected with C. diff, it is because either they touched a surface contaminated with feces and then touched their mouth or a health worker did. It seems that the duty that follows from this wrong is a duty to avoid contaminating surfaces with feces and a duty for health workers to wash their hands thoroughly.

However, compulsory vaccination policies do not prohibit contagious transmission either, such policies prohibit people from creating the conditions where contagious transmission of harmful illnesses is more likely. So too, when people misuse antibiotics, they create the conditions for antibiotic-resistant bacteria to thrive, and therefore subject others to risks of contagious infection. Sick people who use public spaces when they are contagious or health workers who fail to wash their hands may be culpable for contagious transmission, but those who create the conditions for infection to spread are culpable as well because they put people at undue risk of harm.

Prescription requirements for antibiotics and compulsory vaccination are therefore justified policies because public officials may permissibly limit some people's medical autonomy for the sake of public safety and the medical autonomy of third parties. Even though not every unvaccinated person or antibiotics

[79] University of Michigan Health System, "U-M Team Seeks to Outsmart C Difficile with New $92 Million Effort," March 9, 2016, http://www.infectioncontroltoday.com/news/2016/03/um-team-seeks-to-outsmart-c-difficile-with-new-92-million-effort.aspx.

[80] Ramanan Laxminarayan et al., "Drug Resistance," in *Disease Control Priorities in Developing Countries*, ed. Dean T. Jamison et al., 2nd ed. (Washington, DC: World Bank, 2006), http://www.ncbi.nlm.nih.gov/books/NBK11774/.

misuser harms others by creating the conditions for contagious transmission of a harmful and potentially treatment-resistant illness, they do put others at an undue and avoidable risk of being harmed.

Some philosophers endorse even stronger limits on antibiotics than the current prescription system, citing concerns about antibiotic resistance. Jonathan Anomaly argues for a global antibiotics treaty, modeled on the Kyoto protocol, to curb antibiotic overuse.[81] If such a treaty could work, I am also open to the idea that patients, physicians, and public officials should not be permitted to determine the distribution of antibiotics in light of the significant possibility that antibiotic use endangers others. Elsewhere, Anomaly proposes other means to prevent antibiotic resistance, such as bans and taxes on agricultural antibiotic use and funding for antibiotic research, in addition to prescription requirements.[82] This is a case where pharmaceutical regulations pass the regulatory reversal test, and we should infer from the fact that regulations to date have had good effects that further regulations to prevent antibiotic misuse could be justified.

3.5 The Case for OTC Enhancements

Except for antibiotics, the foregoing arguments against prescription requirements call for greater access to most other drugs. Yet some people argue that the same considerations in favor of limiting access to antibiotics can also justify limiting access to drugs that enhance users' capacities. The argument is the same as the argument against antibiotics, except that the second premise is that users of enhancement drugs violate other people's rights to equal opportunity or fair competitive conditions, therefore, public officials may permissibly limit over the counter (OTC) access to enhancements.

One might apply this argument in favor of restrictions on access to steroids for athletic enhancement, stimulants as a form of neuroenhancement, or any other drugs that give users a positional advantage over others but do not treat a disease or disability. For example, Norman Daniels argues that healthcare systems should focus on providing all citizens with equal opportunities for advantage. Diseases and disabilities disadvantage some people, so a just society should provide treatment for people who are sick and disabled for the sake of equality of opportunity. In contrast, enhancements can advantage some people who are not disadvantaged, and may therefore be restricted for the sake of

---

[81] Jonny Anomaly, "Combating Resistance: The Case for a Global Antibiotics Treaty," *Public Health Ethics* 3, no. 1 (April 1, 2010): 13–22, doi:10.1093/phe/phq001.

[82] Jonny Anomaly, "Ethics, Antibiotics, and Public Policy," *Georgetown Journal of Law and Public Policy*, 2017.

equality of opportunity. Similarly, Ori Lev argues that stimulants for the purpose of neuroenhancement should only be available to people who suffer from disadvantages, not to further the opportunities of already advantaged groups.[83]

Unlike antibiotic use however, even if one person's pharmaceutical enhancement makes another person worse off, it would not violate her rights. Arguments against enhancement rely on two assumptions. First, arguments against enhancement rely on the assumption that enhancements give people advantages in the distribution of goods that are mainly positional, and that these positional advantages cannot be justified by the non-positional advantages they also bring. Second, arguments against enhancement assume that people have enforceable entitlements against being made worse off in the distribution of positional goods in the first place.

Both of these assumptions are unfounded. People may legitimately choose enhancements even if they bring no positional advantages because there are other benefits to being enhanced. And in any case, people do not have rights against being made worse off in the distribution of advantages, and even if they did, these rights would not be enforceable. Therefore, restrictions on access to pharmaceutical enhancement cannot be justified on the grounds that people will use enhancements to gain unfair advantages over other people. Moreover, limits on access to enhancement not only violate people's rights of self-medication; pharmaceutical enhancement quotas and bans can also contribute to inequality and prevent patients from accessing treatment.

First consider the claim that access to pharmaceutical enhancements would give people advantages in the distribution of goods that are mainly positional. This claim mirrors Adam Swift's arguments in favor of prohibiting parents from sending their children to private schools on the grounds that education is mainly a positional good and that children who attend private schools will gain unfair advantages over public school students.[84] One might argue that people should not be permitted to access drugs that cognitively enhance their users for the same reason. I am skeptical that Swift's arguments justify abolishing private schools, but even if we grant this claim for the sake of argument, it would not justify restricting access to pharmaceutical enhancements. For one thing, though I have defended pediatric neuroenhancement elsewhere, my argument is focused on adult's enhancement.[85]

Even if it were permissible to restrict children's freedom to access cognitive enhancements, such as private schools or pharmaceutical neuroenhancements,

[83] Ori Lev, "Should Children Have Equal Access to Neuroenhancements?," *AJOB Neuroscience* 1, no. 1 (February 10, 2010): 21–23, doi:10.1080/21507740903504442.

[84] Swift, Adam. *How not to Be a Hypocrite: School Choice for the Morally Perplexed Parent* (Psychology Press, 2003: 23).

[85] Jessica Flanigan, "Adderall for All: A Defense of Pediatric Neuroenhancement," *HEC Forum* 25, no. 4 (August 20, 2013): 325–44, doi:10.1007/s10730-013-9222-4.

restrictions on access to private education or pharmaceuticals for adults are more difficult to justify. Additionally, this argument assumes that enhancements are used mainly to gain advantages over others. But there are many reasons that people may use pharmaceutical enhancements even if they do not give them an advantage over others. Imagine, for example, a mother who works in the home raising children, who feels that access to a cognitive enhancement like Adderall would help her manage her household. Since she is not participating in the labor market, one cannot justify restrictions on her access to pharmaceutical enhancements on the grounds that she would use them to gain advantages over others. Or imagine a person who uses athletic enhancements so he can participate in recreational sports, such as rock climbing and mountain biking. People may legitimately desire to use pharmaceutical enhancements for many reasons that have nothing to do with gaining positional advantages.

In some cases, a person may use enhancements to gain a positional advantage but also for non-positional benefits. These cases may be analogous to parents' practice of reading to their children in order to bond with their children and also to give them educational advantages. In these cases, non-positional benefits of parental closeness can justify contributing to educational inequality. Access to private education may also be justified if it raised the absolute level of educational achievement, even if it also caused greater educational disparity. If the absolute gains in achievement are significant enough, these gains may justify increasing disparity. Similarly, if a person uses pharmaceutical enhancements both because of the intrinsic benefits of better cognition or increased strength and endurance and also for a positional advantage, the non-positional benefits can justify greater inequality, especially if access to pharmaceutical enhancements also improved cognitive and physical abilities within a population overall.

In other cases, a person may use enhancements to gain non-positional benefits that are morally significant, and her use of enhancements could reduce inequalities or the harmful effects of inequality. For example, if more people used cognitive and moral enhancements, then enhancement use could have broad social benefits, including benefits for the worst-off members of society and for people who do not use enhancements.[86] If people used enhancements in ways that increased productivity or peace, for example, then people who do not use enhancements would benefit from others' enhancement use in the same way that societies have benefited from gains in productivity and peace to date.

Even if a person uses pharmaceutical enhancement solely to gain advantages over others, arguments for limiting access to pharmaceutical enhancement

---

[86] Allen Buchanan, *Better than Human: The Promise and Perils of Enhancing Ourselves* (Oxford University Press, 2011).

on these grounds assume that the interests of those who are disadvantaged by other's enhancement use can justify limits on people's rights of self-medication. But even if states ought to promote social and economic equality, public officials are constrained by citizens' rights. For example, few would accept Cecile Fabre's proposal to redistribute people's non-vital organs from the healthy to the unhealthy, even if such a policy would reduce health inequalities, because such a policy would violate rights of informed consent and bodily rights more generally.[87] For the same reason, public officials should not violate rights of self-medication, which are supported by the same normative considerations as informed consent, in order to reduce social, economic, or health inequalities.

Let's grant again for the sake of argument that people have entitlements not to be disadvantaged by other people's enhancement. For such entitlements to justify limits on access to pharmaceutical enhancement, one must show that these entitlements against being disadvantaged are enforceable. Yet, even if access to enhancements could permissibly be limited for the sake of equality, a claim Swift develops in defending the abolition of private schools, it would not justify limiting access to enhancements if public officials could promote social and economic equality in other ways. For example, say the concern is that people would gain economic advantages by using pharmaceutical enhancements. In response, states could either restrict access to pharmaceutical enhancements though a prescription system or allow unrestricted access to pharmaceutical enhancements. The prescription approach would be coercive, it would violate rights of self-medication, and it may not even work if rich and well-connected people were able to navigate the prescription system better than disadvantaged people. The unrestricted access approach would allow people to purchase enhancements to gain advantages over others, but if public officials are concerned that such a system would exacerbate socioeconomic inequality, they may consider subsidizing access to pharmaceutical enhancements for disadvantaged populations instead of implementing a coercive prescription system.

We should also question the assumption that people have entitlements not to be disadvantaged by other people's decision to use pharmaceutical enhancements. Runners who train at high altitudes or spend more time training have greater endurance, but they do not violate the rights of runners who live at low altitudes and have limited time. One may reply that inequality is more troubling when enhancements disadvantage people in more significant ways, such as when people are socially or economically disadvantaged because they could not or would not use enhancements. But people are permitted to enhance themselves in many other ways that translate to social and economic advantages

---

[87] Cécile Fabre, *Whose Body Is It Anyway?: Justice and the Integrity of the Person* (Oxford; New York: Oxford University Press, 2008).

(e.g., reading the newspaper, wearing makeup, saving money, showing up to work early), so why would pharmaceutical enhancements be especially objectionable? One may also reply to the egalitarian assumption behind arguments against enhancement that inequality per se is not objectionable anyhow. Rather, public officials should aim to ensure that people have enough social and economic resources to live a good life, rather than coercing people to better approximate the ideal of social and economic equality.

For these reasons, public officials should not restrict access to pharmaceutical enhancements for the sake of equality, especially if they can address objectionable inequalities without prohibiting people who could benefit from enhancements from accessing them. If anything, policies that limit access to pharmaceutical enhancements may contribute to inequality because, under the current prescription system, only patients who have enough resources to find a physician who will prescribe enhancements are permitted to use them, while those with fewer resources to access prescriptions are excluded from the potential benefits of enhancement even if they may stand to benefit from enhancements the most.[88] In these ways, policies that limit access to pharmaceutical enhancements may further harm the very disadvantaged they aim to benefit.

Some critics of pharmaceutical enhancement use object that permitting enhancement would contribute to an objectionable escalation of competition between students and coworkers.[89] If stimulant use were normalized, people might feel pressured to use stimulants just to keep up. Michael Sandel raises a version of this objection against athletic enhancements, such as steroids, in competitive sports.[90] Bioethicists are also concerned that motivation enhancements could make workers more complacent in lives or jobs that lack meaning, whereas an untreated lack of motivation may encourage the pursuit of more meaningful work.[91] Others worry that enhancement would threaten the value of authentic human achievement. Here the aforementioned response to concerns about inequality is relevant once again. Even if meaningful work and authenticity were genuinely valuable, to justify restrictions on access to prescription enhancement, one would need to show that meaning and authenticity are *more valuable* than bodily autonomy and rights of self-medication. We would not accept a policy that violated people's rights of informed consent so that they could have

[88] I develop a similar point elsewhere with regards to pediatric neuroenhancement. Flanigan, "Adderall for All."

[89] Richard H. Dees, "Better Brains, Better Selves? The Ethics of Neuroenhancements," *Kennedy Institute of Ethics Journal* 17, no. 4 (2007): 371–95, doi:10.1353/ken.2008.0001.

[90] Michael Sandel, "The Case Against Perfection," *Atlantic Monthly* 293, no. 3 (2004): 51–62.

[91] Torben Kjærsgaard, "Enhancing Motivation by Use of Prescription Stimulants: The Ethics of Motivation Enhancement," *AJOB Neuroscience* 6, no. 1 (January 2, 2015): 4–10, doi:10.1080/21507740.2014.990543.

more authentic experiences or laws that banned coffeemakers in offices so that people would feel demotivated and pursue more meaningful work. Nor should we accept limits on self-medication for the sake of these values.

I suspect that much of the resistance to enhancement is not motivated by concerns about equality or meaning but by disapproval of seemingly illegitimate ways of succeeding. Some people perceive pharmaceutical enhancement as a kind of cheating, though they accept other ways of gaining positional advantages. Those who accept limits on access to enhancements for these reasons must then either accept similar limits on dietary, occupational, recreational, and relationship choices that give some people advantages over others or explain why pharmaceutical choices are relevantly different from these other choices such that only pharmaceutical means of gaining advantages should be prohibited.

Policies that limit access to pharmaceutical enhancement can also harm people who are already disadvantaged because of learning disabilities or people with recognized medical reasons to use drugs that can also be used as enhancements. In the United States, for example, the DEA imposes quotas on manufacturers that limit the supply of stimulants that have the potential for abuse. For example, in 2011 a shortage of stimulants was attributed to manufacturing quotas that prevented drug makers from producing enough ADHD drugs to meet the growing demand.[92] These avoidable shortages left those who used the drugs feeling powerless, judged, and stigmatized as they searched for a pharmacy that could fill their prescriptions. One patient described the experience as follows:

> For each new prescription ... I must muster up energy to begin the hunt. Maybe I'll get lucky and my order can be filled on the first try. But most often, it's the start of a very difficult search that can take weeks, and burns precious resources.[93]

In response, the DEA argued that the quotas were appropriate and that any drug shortages were attributable to manufacturers over-manufacturing a greater proportion of expensive versions of drugs, causing an under-supply of generics.[94] Even if this charge is true, quotas ultimately caused the shortages insofar as both versions of drugs would have been produced in the absence of a quota.

Prescription requirements could also stand in the way of normalizing enhancement use, which could contribute to the stigmatization of people who use

---

[92] Lisa Fields, "FDA Says ADHD Drug Shortage to End in April," *Consumer Reports News*, April 5, 2012, http://www.consumerreports.org/cro/news/2012/04/fda-says-adhd-drug-shortage-to-end-in-april/index.htm.

[93] "The Shame of Filling a Prescription."

[94] Gardiner Harris, "F.D.A. Finds Short Supply of Attention Deficit Drugs," *New York Times*, December 31, 2011.

enhancements to treat disabilities and impairments. Nadria Faulmüller, Hannah Maslen and Filippo Santoni de Sio argue that enhancement use is currently stigmatized and that people who use enhancements are seen as intellectual inferiors or cheaters.[95] But as Faulmüller et al. point out, caffeine was stigmatized and prohibited in Sweden in the eighteenth century, and today, Swedes drink more coffee than most. One way to mitigate the indirect psychological costs of using a drug is to allow it; so the fact that using a drug is stigmatized should not be cited as a consideration in favor of restrictions on access.

In sum, while public officials can legitimately limit access to antibiotics to prevent people from harming others, the same strategy cannot justify limits on pharmaceutical enhancement. Though unregulated use of pharmaceutical enhancements may put some people at a disadvantage, these disadvantages cannot justify prohibitive pharmaceutical policies. Furthermore, prohibitive limits on access to enhancements would not only violate rights of self-medication, such policies may also make people worse off on balance and contribute to social and economic inequality.

3.6 Rethinking Non-Medical Use

I argued earlier that a person's medical needs should not dictate whether she has access to drugs. Instead, people have rights to access drugs, which may also promote their overall well-being. Yet, as the examples of deadly drugs, recreational drugs, and enhancements illustrate, prescription drug requirements limit patient's access to pharmaceuticals on the basis of whether a medical professional judges that a person has a legitimate medical need. This practice rules out prescribing pharmaceuticals that can and do improve people's lives in ways that do not address medical needs. Because the prescription drug system forecloses non-medical pharmaceutical uses, prescription requirements not only violate rights of self-medication, they also contribute to the medicalization of normal functioning and potentially deter pharmaceutical innovation.

The first effect of restricting access to medical use is that it encourages patient advocates and pharmaceutical manufacturers to push for the re-classification of seemingly non-medical conditions as medical conditions. There's no intrinsic reason to define concepts of disease and health to include some conditions but not others. Some philosophers argue that concepts like disease and disability are socially constructed. Others say that disease and disability are defined as any

[95] Nadira Faulmüller, Hannah Maslen, and Filippo Santoni de Sio, "The Indirect Psychological Costs of Cognitive Enhancement," *The American Journal of Bioethics* 13, no. 7 (2013): 45–47.

condition that undermines a person's well-being. Another popular definition defines disease and health in contrast to how a normal human would function. All of these definitions of disease, disability, and health tell us something important about what makes disease different from other conditions, but there's no reason to think that each definition cannot be true in its own way. Sometimes people experience the conditions we think of as diseases or disabilities as bad for their welfare, but sometimes they don't. Yet we would still want to characterize those conditions as disabilities. While disability rights advocates often emphasize that many parts of disability are socially constructed, some aspects of disease and disability are not, such as a shorter life-span. And those who define health in terms of normal species functioning capture the idea that it is often a disadvantage to experience impairments that others do not, but what we think of as normal changes as medical technology evolves, so things that were once considered normal may now be seen as diseases.

There are other ways that each model of disease and health fails to capture all of our intuitions about these concepts too, but for now, the important point is that calling a condition a disease or disability, whatever one means by those terms, marks it as different from other conditions in a way that may cause social stigma, loss of well-being, or designation as unnatural or abnormal. Maybe it isn't justified that people with diseases and disabilities are classified this way, maybe this classification is a form of social prejudice against people whose bodies are different. On the other hand, designating a condition as a disease, disorder, or disability can also be useful—insurance providers may use these categories to decide which services and drugs to provide, and they may be used to protect people from discrimination.

Since concepts of disease and health play a role in determining how people are perceived, how they perceive themselves, and whether they receive insurance benefits and legal protection, redefining these concepts is normatively fraught. Yet pharmaceutical companies have incentives to classify a range of conditions as diseases, disorders, and disabilities so that they can market drugs for those conditions. If a condition can be improved with access to drugs, pharmaceutical developers and medical professionals have incentives to try to characterize it as a medical disorder so that they can legally treat it. Ray Moynihan, Iona Heath, and David Henry call this phenomenon "disease mongering."[96] Moynihan et al. argue that disease mongering occurs in five cases.[97] First, ordinary experiences are classified as medical conditions. Second, the risks associated with mild symptoms are overemphasized. Third, "personal or social problems [are] seen as medical ones."[98]

[96] Ray Moynihan, Iona Heath, and David Henry, "Selling Sickness: The Pharmaceutical Industry and Disease Mongering," *British Medical Journal* 324, no. 7342 (April 13, 2002): 886–91.
[97] Ibid.
[98] Ibid.

Fourth, risks are characterized as diseases. And fifth, the prevalence of diseases is exaggerated. Moynihan et al. object to disease mongering on the grounds that it increases healthcare costs and puts patients at risk of iatrogenic effects of using drugs. If patients bear the costs of treatment and consent to the risks, then these complaints seem akin to the complaints that motorcycles increase healthcare costs and put riders at risk. Nevertheless, Moynihan et al. do raise a morally important concern about medicalization because there are other reasons to be wary of disease mongering.

Another concern about medicalizing conditions so that pharmaceuticals that treat them may win approval is that sometimes conditions that are not and should not be considered medical problems may nevertheless merit pharmaceutical treatment, but that they should not be classified as diseases or disorders to justify treatment. This argument relates to a broader point about the appropriate reasons for calling a behavior a medical condition. A danger of characterizing a condition as a disease or disorder is that disease classification can be used to justify medical intervention when a person's conduct is entirely reasonable, or it may characterize reasonable conduct as disordered. The practice of deeming normal behavior or functioning as disordered is especially concerning when vulnerable or marginalized groups are characterized in these ways. Such labels can contribute to existing patterns of stigma and empower people to dismiss groups' legitimate concerns on the grounds that they are abnormal.[99]

Consider, for example, the classification of premenstrual dysphonic disorder (PMDD) as a psychiatric disorder. Many women experience mood changes related to menstruation, either because of hormonal shifts or because of the pain and inconvenience of menstruating. Some of them display the symptoms of a psychiatric disorder during menstruation, and others would greatly benefit from treatment for mood changes related to menstruation, even if they are still able to function. Yet in order for women who suffer from mood changes during menstruation to receive treatment, PMDD must currently be classified as a psychiatric disorder so that pharmaceutical companies can legally develop and market new drugs to treat psychiatric menstrual symptoms.[100] Since it is

[99] For example, during the era of scientific racism, some physicians described a condition called Drapetomania, which caused slaves to attempt to flee captivity. Characterizing the desire to flee slavery as a disease legitimized the provision of "treatments," such as cutting a person's big toes to prevent him from escaping. The medical classification of Drapetomania is the most striking example of how classification of disease can be motivated by the desire to define reasonable behaviors that intellectual elites may disapprove of as abnormal. Similarly, medical elites once characterized homosexuality as a psychiatric disorder to justify treatment (which was really mistreatment) of gay people.

[100] See Natasha Vargas Cooper, "The Billion-Dollar Battle over Premenstrual Disorder: Long-Suffering Women and Big Pharma Make Uneasy Allies as the American Psychiatric Association Nears a Call on PMDD," *Salon.com*, February, 25, 2012.

necessary to characterize PMDD as a psychiatric disorder for manufacturers to research and develop treatments for menstrual mood changes, the medicalization of menstrual mood changes is beneficial for women. But this is not to say calling menstrual mood change a disorder is morally uncomplicated, because there are also costs to characterizing menstrual mood changes in this way. For one thing, calling menstrual mood change a disorder suggests that normal ways of responding to normal bodily functions are inherently problematic.[101] This characterization of PMDD de-normalizes having a female body and mind, which stigmatizes femininity and reinforces existing male normativity. In this way, classifying menstrual mood change as a disorder turns having a normal female body into a pathological condition.[102]

Similar considerations apply to other conditions. Because of existing approval and prescription requirements, for an ailment to be treated with pharmaceuticals, it must be classified as a disease. In theory, there is little reason to oppose expanding existing conceptions of disease and health to include a wider range of conditions. After all, concepts of disease and health are socially constructed concepts that can change as social norms evolve.[103] But in practice, there are risks associated with classifying conditions as diseases. Consider the concept of aging. Though drugs may effectively treat many of the conditions associated with aging, thinking of those conditions as disorders or diseases may contribute to the social marginalization of elderly people and exacerbate discrimination and stigma. These considerations lend support to arguments in favor of reforming prescription drug systems and approval requirements so that patients may use pharmaceuticals to improve their well-being on balance, without requiring a medical diagnosis for access to pharmaceuticals.

There is some precedent for rethinking these standards. Oral contraceptives are not usually used to treat a medical diagnosis (though they were initially approved to treat endometriosis and other gynecological conditions). As in the case of oral contraceptives, manufacturers that develop drugs that can improve people's overall well-being in other ways should not be required to characterize conditions as diseases, disabilities, and disorders. Another benefit of expanding our understanding of which circumstances merit pharmaceutical intervention to include non-medical conditions is that it may address some of the healthcare cost inflation that Moynihan et al. argued were caused by disease mongering. Insurance providers contract with patients to pay for

---

[101] Julie Holland, *Moody Bitches: The Truth About the Drugs You're Taking, the Sleep You're Missing, the Sex You're Not Having, and What's Really Making You Crazy*, reprint edition (Penguin Books, 2016).

[102] Amy Standen, "Should Severe Premenstrual Symptoms Be a Mental Disorder?," *NPR.org*, October 21, 2013, http://www.npr.org/blogs/health/2013/10/22/223805027/should-disabling -premenstrual-symptoms-be-a-mental-disorder.

[103] Peter Conrad and Kristin K. Barker, "The Social Construction of Illness: Key Insights and Policy Implications," *Journal of Health and Social Behavior* 51, no. 1 suppl. (2010): S67–79.

pharmaceuticals that treat medical conditions, but if pharmaceuticals were not generally required to treat medical conditions, then pharmaceuticals may be marketed without characterizing people as diseased or disordered. Expanding pharmaceutical use beyond the realm of healthcare could therefore reduce the costs of services that insurance companies and members of insurance pools are expected to provide.

A final hazard of limiting access to pharmaceuticals only to people with a medical diagnosis is that, in some cases, disease mongering may not succeed. If public officials took a wider view of legitimate pharmaceutical use, then researchers and manufacturers would have greater incentives to develop drugs that treated a wider range of conditions. We can imagine drugs that could improve well-being in a variety of ways that extend beyond the medical context, and some drugs are currently used off-label or illegally for these purposes. In addition to the aforementioned examples of recreational use and enhancement, drugs may also be used to prevent divorce, make people more moral and less violent, and improve people's communication skills.[104]

Going forward, it will become increasingly important to adopt a more flexible understanding of the role that pharmaceuticals can play in people's lives as medicine becomes more personalized and researchers gain a better understanding of the benefits of drugs beyond the treatment of widespread disease. In a world where patients were empowered to decide whether to use drugs based on their assessments of their values and overall well-being, who knows what may develop to improve people's lives?

3.7   Public Health and Preventive Medication

Prescription requirements should not privilege medical reasons for pharmaceutical use over non-medical reasons. One may think that patients with medical reasons to use pharmaceuticals *generally* have more urgent claims to use them than people who would use pharmaceuticals for non-medical reasons. However, existing prescription requirements also prevent patients from accessing pharmaceuticals for medical purposes. So even those who disagree with my claim that non-medical pharmaceutical use ought to be permitted should still rethink the prescription requirements that stand in the way of self-medication that could improve people's health.

---

[104] Thomas Douglas, "Moral Enhancement," *Journal of Applied Philosophy* 25, no. 3 (2008): 228–45; Ingmar Persson and Julian Savulescu, "The Perils of Cognitive Enhancement and the Urgent Imperative to Enhance the Moral Character of Humanity," *Journal of Applied Philosophy* 25, no. 3 (2008): 162–77; Brian D. Earp, "Love and Other Drugs," *Philosophy Now* 91 (2012): 14–17.

One way that prescription requirements stand in the way of self-medication for the purpose of health is that they make drugs more expensive for patients and insurers. To obtain a prescription, a patient must visit a physician first. The sale of prescription-grade drugs subsidizes the cost of employing pharmacists to monitor how the drugs are distributed. It is common in the United States for elderly patients who cannot afford US prescription drug prices to illegally purchase cholesterol and blood pressure medication from Canadian pharmacies. Underground pharmaceutical markets may be relatively more dangerous insofar as patients who make unauthorized pharmaceutical purchases do not have access to expert advice about dosages and interactions and are discouraged from seeking that advice because their choices are illegal. Patients are also subject to criminal sanctions for illegal pharmaceutical use, despite the fact that they are treating a medical condition.

Prescription requirements that prevent patients from purchasing and using relatively safe drugs that provide significant social goods or prevent significant harms also threaten the public's health. The case against prescription requirements is strongest for drugs that protect third parties from medical risks. For example, drugs that prevent unwanted pregnancies, drug overdoses, or HIV transmission, more than other drugs, should not require a prescription. There are also especially strong reasons to allow patients to access relatively safe drugs that prevent death or debilitating diseases, such as asthma inhalers, insulin treatment, and statins.

Today, people can purchase condoms in convenience stores, vending machines, supermarkets, and even online, but oral contraceptives require a prescription in most places.[105] Both forms of contraception have moderate risks. Condoms can trigger a latex allergy that in some cases can cause shortness of breath or hives, and they have a typical use failure rate of 18 percent. Oral contraceptives have risks as well. For some populations contraceptive pills are not recommended because they can increase a person's risk of heart attacks and strokes, some pills can cause weight gain and mood changes, and they have a typical use failure rate of 9 percent.[106] On the other hand, some contraceptive pills can lower the risk of ovarian cancer, pelvic inflammatory disease, uterine cancer, and endometriosis; cause shorter and lighter periods; alleviate acne; and increase bone density before menopause.

---

[105] Pam Belluck, "Birth Control Without Seeing a Doctor: Oregon Now, More States Later," *New York Times*, January 4, 2016, http://www.nytimes.com/interactive/2016/01/04/health/birth-control-oregon-contraception.html.

[106] For this reason, oral contraception is not generally recommended for smokers over thirty-five or women with high blood pressure. Øjvind Lidegaard et al., "Thrombotic Stroke and Myocardial Infarction with Hormonal Contraception," *New England Journal of Medicine* 366, no. 24 (June 14, 2012): 2257–66, doi:10.1056/NEJMoa1111840.

The medical risks of condoms and pills, considered in light of failure rates and potential benefits, highlight an inconsistency in access to contraception. If condoms are safe enough to be sold over the counter to anyone, so are contraceptive pills. In addition, other over-the-counter pills, such as omeprazole, acetaminophen, and aspirin, are much riskier than contraceptive pills. In light of this evidence, public health scholars called for birth control to move over the counter as early as 1993, arguing,

> Prescription status [for contraceptives] entails heavy costs, including the dollar, time, and psychological costs of visiting a physician to obtain a prescription, the financial and human costs of unintended pregnancies that result from the obstacle to access caused by medicalization of oral contraceptives, and administrative costs to the health care system . . . neither safety nor efficacy considerations justify prescription status for oral contraceptives. Revised package design and patient labeling could allow women to screen themselves for contraindications, to educate themselves about danger signs, and to use oral contraceptives safely and successfully.[107]

Unlike other drugs, oral contraception is not designed to treat patients with a specific medical diagnosis, so prescription requirements cannot be justified on the grounds that only patients with a medical need should use the drug. Contraception also has significant social and public health benefits because it prevents abortions and unintended pregnancies. Perhaps for this reason, emergency contraception is available over the counter in some countries. One objection to moving birth control over the counter is that women would not otherwise schedule yearly visits to a gynecologist, but yearly visits are no longer indicated for healthy women, and primary care physicians can still refer women to gynecologists as needed.

For similar reasons, pre-exposure prophylaxis (PrEP), which prevents transmission of HIV, should also be available over the counter. If people who do not have HIV but are at substantial risk take PrEP pills every day, they can prevent HIV infection. PrEP reduces the risk of transmission by up to 92 percent. The prevention of HIV is an important public health goal, and, like condoms, PrEP can be a valuable tool in reducing HIV transmission rates. Just as impediments to condom use set back the cause of HIV prevention, so too do prescription requirements for PrEP, which raise the price of obtaining and using the drug and may prevent consistent use of it, thereby making the prophylaxis less effective.

[107] J. Trussell et al., "Should Oral Contraceptives Be Available Without Prescription?," *American Journal of Public Health* 83, no. 8 (August 1993): 1094–99.

Prescription requirements for PrEP are currently justified on the grounds that users should be re-tested for HIV every three months and receive counseling about HIV risk reduction and safe sex. Yet people do not need to see a physician to test for HIV every three months since in-home HIV tests are available. Patients may find the requirement that they regularly take time out of their schedules and pay to visit a physician to be informed about safe sex and risk reduction patronizing or stigmatizing. Instead, the packaging for PrEP could include information similar to what would be provided by a health worker without requiring a visit to the doctor. In this way prescription requirements for PrEP are not necessary to promote informed use, and they may ultimately deter patients from using a relatively safe drug that would have significant benefits to public health.

Many of the same arguments in favor of allowing patients to access PrEP over the counter also support moving other safe daily preventive medications over the counter. For example, statins are one of the most prescribed drugs. Statins treat high cholesterol and prevent heart attacks for at-risk patients. Some statins are available over the counter in Britain, and manufacturers are pushing for over-the-counter statins in the United States.[108] Yet some physicians are critical of the proposal on the grounds that not all patients understand their cholesterol and some patients would not use the drugs effectively without a physician's supervision. On the other hand, patients can test their cholesterol at a pharmacy instead of visiting a physician, and over-the-counter access would make the lifesaving drugs cheaper and more accessible to patients who do not have reliable access to a physician.

Over-the-counter access to other preventive medicines is justified on similar grounds. Many people with asthma take long-term control medicines on a daily basis, but prescription requirements make them more expensive, putting patients who cannot afford to renew their prescriptions at risk.[109] Similarly, insulin is also among the most prescribed drugs, but prescription requirements prevent diabetic patients from getting the drugs they need.[110] Like asthma, diabetes is a chronic and long-term condition, so diabetics are familiar with how to properly use insulin therapy and monitor their blood sugar. Yet despite their

[108] Peter Loftus, "Lipitor: Pfizer Aims to Sell Over-the-Counter Version," *Wall Street Journal*, March 2, 2014, sec. Business, http://www.wsj.com/articles/SB10001424052702304071004579410930136742414.

[109] Elisabeth Rosenthal, "The Soaring Cost of a Simple Breath," *New York Times*, October 12, 2013, sec. US, http://www.nytimes.com/2013/10/13/us/the-soaring-cost-of-a-simple-breath.html.

[110] Prescription insulin is also prohibitively expensive in part because insurance providers pay for it and most patients do not bear the costs. Some patients without insurance turn to self-medication or black market drugs. Cara Buckley, "For Uninsured Young Adults, Do-It-Yourself Health Care," *New York Times*, February 18, 2009, sec. New York Region, http://www.nytimes.com/2009/02/18/nyregion/18insure.html.

relatively high level of medical knowledge, they can only access the drugs that keep them alive with a physician's authorization. These policies may cost lives in cases where diabetics cannot access the medicine they need. For example, Kevin Houdeshell died when he was thirty-six-years old because he could not obtain a prescription for insulin soon enough. According to his sister, Amy:

> He was young, fit, healthy. The pharmacy told him his script had expired, and "We're sorry, but we can't give you anymore." He tried three times to call his doctor's office, and four days later he passed away from not having his insulin.[111]

Prescription requirements for insulin cannot be justified on the grounds that patients do not understand how to safely use the drugs, especially when the risks of not having access far exceed the risks of use.

In emergency situations like Kevin Houdeshell's, patients are permitted to access emergency doses of insulin. Houndshell's pharmacist was not aware of the emergency exception though, and his family doubts whether an emergency dose would have been enough, but the policy of granting emergency exceptions to prescription requirements highlights another way that prescription requirements can cost lives. Rescue drugs are those that are needed during emergencies rather than for long-term use. In addition to diabetes, rescue drugs can treat drug overdoses, asthma attacks, and allergic reactions. But for rescue drugs to work, they must be accessible not only to patients but also to bystanders who encounter people in need.

Most prescription requirements require patients to receive authorization from a physician to use a drug. But rescue drugs are not generally self-administered, so typical prescription requirements are not well suited to ensure that patients can benefit from drugs during emergencies. For example, naloxone is a drug that can prevent opioid drug users from dying of overdoses. Naloxone requires a prescription, but unlike most prescriptions, it is sometimes prescribed to community health workers or opiate users so they can treat others who are incapacitated after an overdose. Naloxone is safe and easy to administer, and it is not harmful even when given to a person who is not experiencing an overdose. The benefits of naloxone are significant, but prescription requirements may prevent naloxone from helping those who would benefit most. Recreational opioid users may be reluctant to seek a prescription for naloxone, not only because doctor's visits are expensive but also because users may be afraid of judgment from their physicians. In some cases, opioid users may avoid physicians because they are afraid they would then lose their supply of drugs. Even if users do visit a

---

[111] Dawn Kendrick, "Emergency Insulin Could Have Saved Man's Life," *WKYC*, February 12, 2015, http://www.wkyc.com/story/news/health/2015/02/11/emergency-insulin/23276399/.

physician to obtain a naloxone prescription, some doctors do not prescribe naloxone for users because they believe that making opioid use safer will encourage abuse. This belief is mistaken. Naloxone does not encourage drug abuse, but it does effectively prevent deadly overdoses.[112] Like the prevention of unwanted pregnancies and HIV transmission, preventing drug overdoses is an urgent public health priority. Yet prescription requirements stand in the way by blocking access to a safe and beneficial drug.

More generally, relatively safe drugs that can prevent a person from dying during a medical emergency should be available over the counter. For example, asthma inhalers, epinephrine auto injectors, and glucagon should be accessible over the counter so people can use the drugs to provide first aid in the event of asthma attacks, anaphylaxis, or severely low blood sugar. Schools, day cares, workplaces, and gyms are not currently permitted to keep albuterol inhalers on hand to treat asthma attacks, though lay responders may attempt first aid and cardiopulmonary resuscitation (CPR) during emergencies, and businesses may purchase automated external defibrillators to treat life-threatening cardiac events. The same considerations in favor of allowing CPR training and the sale of defibrillators are also reasons to allow greater access to inhalers. Respiratory emergencies can be as dangerous as cardiac emergencies, yet simply because one kind of emergency is treated with a drug and the other is treated with a technique or a device, help is more readily available for cardiac patients.[113]

From a public health perspective, drugs with the potential to save lives during emergencies should be promoted, not restricted. Though rescue drugs do have significant risks if used incorrectly by lay responders, the risks of limiting access to the drugs are much greater because they treat life-threatening emergency conditions. Concerns about misuse could be addressed by better labeling and by selling rescue drugs behind the counter so that patients have an opportunity to discuss proper use with a pharmacist before purchasing them. Or, just as businesses post information about first aid and CPR, they could also post information about how to use rescue drugs.

These examples show the ways that prescription requirements that are ostensibly for the sake of public health can undermine public health in some cases. So even those who are unconvinced by arguments for rights of self-medication

---

[112] Karen H. Seal et al., "Naloxone Distribution and Cardiopulmonary Resuscitation Training for Injection Drug Users to Prevent Heroin Overdose Death: A Pilot Intervention Study," *Journal of Urban Health : Bulletin of the New York Academy of Medicine* 82, no. 2 (June 2005): 303–11, doi:10.1093/jurban/jti053.

[113] In the United States, the FDA recently considered allowing some rescue medications to be available without a prescription after an initial consultation with a physician. US Food and Drug Administration, "Using Innovative Technologies and Other Conditions of Safe Use to Expand Drug Products Considered Nonprescription," FDA, February 28, 2012, http://www.regulations.gov/#!documentDetail;D=FDA-2012-N-0171-0001.

should still favor a less prohibitive prescription drug system that enables people to access drugs in cases where the medical and overall benefits of a drug far outweigh the risks and barriers to access. Preventive medicine is a core component of public health promotion. Policies that stand in the way of preventive medicine may be designed to protect patients, but insofar as regulations prevent people from protecting themselves from overdose, disease transmission, pregnancy, heart disease, or asthma attacks, prescription requirements are themselves a threat to public health.

3.8 Conclusion

I have argued that people are entitled to decide to use pharmaceuticals for medical or non-medical reasons, and prescription requirements paternalistically substitute the judgments of physician and regulators for the consumers' and patients'. The prescription drug system restricts important freedoms, such as the right to die, the right to use recreational drugs, the right to enhance one's cognitive or athletic abilities, and the right to use pharmaceuticals for other non-medical reasons. Even those who reject the claim that patients have the right to use drugs for non-medical reasons should still support prescription drug reform though, because some prescription requirements, by making preventive and emergency treatments inaccessible, curtail the goal of promoting the public's health. In these cases, prescription drug reform is especially urgent.

4

Responsibility and Regulation

Gideon Sofer was diagnosed with Crohn's disease in 1996 when he was twelve years old. At the time he weighed only forty-five pounds and was severely malnourished. Following his diagnosis, he dedicated his life to educating people about the disease, raising money for Crohn's research, and advocating on behalf of patients with inflammatory bowel diseases. Gideon also had other interests as well. He collected stamps, liked Bruce Springsteen, attended UC Berkeley, and hoped to become a lawyer.

By the time Gideon was twenty-two, he weighed one hundred pounds and half of his intestine had been removed. He tried several experimental therapies. One was prohibitively expensive, and his insurance didn't pay for it. Then he enrolled in a clinical trial for an adult stem-cell therapy, but he believes he received the placebo treatment. In an editorial about his experiences accessing unapproved therapies Gideon wrote, "withholding a potential cure is just as bad—if not worse—than the potential death sentence of a serious illness."[1] He was frustrated that the FDA's approval requirements prevented him from using a treatment that had the potential to alleviate his symptoms or extend his life when all other options had failed. Elsewhere, he said, "For people like me, for whom nothing has worked, access to new treatments is absolutely critical . . . it's the only thing that keeps me hopeful, that keeps me living."[2]

Gideon never gained access to the experimental treatment. He died in 2011 when he was twenty-six years old. Thousands of patients like Gideon face similar barriers to access. Yet people generally support the FDA's policy of barring access to investigational drugs. In the previous chapter, I showed that prohibitive testing requirements, especially in their current form, couldn't be justified on the grounds that they promote the public's health. People like Gideon die waiting for approval, and manufacturers are discouraged from investing in new treatments

[1] Gideon J. Sofer, "The FDA Is Killing Crohn's Patients," *Wall Street Journal*, December 30, 2008, sec. Opinion, http://www.wsj.com/articles/SB123059825583441193.

[2] Geeta Anand, "As Costs Rise, New Medicines Face Pushback," *Wall Street Journal*, September 18, 2007, sec. News, http://www.wsj.com/articles/SB119007210553130427.

because the approval process is so expensive. Despite these health effects of pre-market testing requirements, one may still defend testing requirements. Such an argument may go like this. If killing someone is generally morally worse than allowing someone to die, then perhaps approval requirements could be justified on the grounds that they are necessary to prevent manufacturers from killing patients, even if they allow other patients to die.

It may seem that patients like Gideon must bear the costs of approval requirements that benefit all citizens on balance. But, as I argued in the previous chapter, there is substantial evidence that approval requirements do not benefit citizens on balance, because patients are prevented from purchasing and using drugs and also because prohibitive requirements deter innovation.

In this chapter, I argue further that the case against approval requirements is even stronger than the empirical record suggests. When patients die because they knowingly and willingly used a dangerous pharmaceutical, drug manufacturers are not culpable for patients' deaths because patients consent to the risks associated with dangerous drugs. Yet when patients die because they were prohibited from accessing a drug, those who stand in their way are morally responsible for their deaths.

Public officials make many life or death decisions, such as highway construction, airport screening, or the allocation of scarce resources. But there is an important moral distinction between killing and letting die, which marks out particular policies, those that kill people rather than allowing some to die, as especially unjust. If we accept the distinction between killing and letting die, we ought to conclude that public officials kill people by enforcing prescription requirements. This thesis lends further support to rights of self-medication, especially the right to try.

4.1 How Regulation Kills

In some cases public officials may justifiably allow some people to die while preventing the deaths of others. For example by allocating funds to treatment for younger patients, an official may allow older patients to die. Such policy choices may be justified by an appeal to fairness (e.g., younger patients have had fewer years of life already) or overall welfare (e.g., younger patients have more good years ahead of them if they are cured). I have argued that these justifications generally fail to justify approval policies that cause patients to die for the sake of medical research or broader public health goals because patients are relatively worse off than other citizens and because the empirical record suggests that premarket efficacy-testing requirements at least cost more lives than they save by deterring innovation and preventing patients from accessing beneficial therapies. But even if proponents of approval policies could establish that the burdens of premarket testing requirements were fairly distributed and that they promoted overall welfare, they would still be unjust because unlike policies that allow some to die while allocating lifesaving resources to others, public officials kill people when they prohibit the sale of investigational drugs.

The moral distinction between killing and letting die distinguishes prohibitive premarket approval policies as especially unjust—even worse than the empirical record suggests.[3] While it may be acceptable for officials to make life and death decisions when deciding how to allocate resources, officials are not authorized to kill some citizens for the sake of broader public health goals. It would be wrong, for example, for officials to select some citizens by lottery to be killed for the sake of medical research or organ redistribution, even if such a system promoted public health and overall welfare on balance. Public officials who enforced such policies would be morally blameworthy for the death and suffering they caused. For the same reasons, officials who kill patients by enforcing approval requirements are blameworthy for the death and suffering they cause, and would still be blameworthy even if approval requirements did save lives on balance (contrary to available evidence).

I should specify what I mean by "killing" when I say that public officials kill people when they enforce premarket approval requirements. I mean that officials' actions meet the conditions that distinguish other actions that constitute killing from instances of allowing people to die. Though it may appear that public officials merely allow people to die from diseases when they enforce regulations that prevent patients from accessing experimental drugs, when these patients die from diseases, it is because they were killed by pharmaceutical regulators. This argument relies on the moral distinction between killing and letting die, which is grounded in a more fundamental set of moral commitments.[4] It may initially seem that the distinction between killing and letting die is descriptive, that killing simply consists in initiating a deadly sequence of events whereas letting die consists in failing to stop a deadly sequence of events. But a solely descriptive take on the distinction encounters challenging counterexamples, such as cases of killing through inaction. When a nurse deliberately fails to feed the incapacitated patients under his care, he kills them.[5] Nor can a theory of

---

[3] Here I am using the word "kill" in a specific, moralized way, to contrast with "letting die." I am not taking a stand on whether it is wrong to let people die, though I am committed to the claim that killing is more wrong than letting die.

[4] Frances Howard-Snyder, "Doing vs. Allowing Harm," in *The Stanford Encyclopedia of Philosophy*, ed. Edward N. Zalta, Winter 2011, http://plato.stanford.edu/archives/win2011/entries/doing-allowing/.

[5] Defenders of this approach might revise and argue instead that one kills when she is a *but-for* cause of death, whereas she lets die when the death would have happened if she was involved or not. But then consider a case where an assassin shoots his target in the head while the target is in the process of slowly dying from an earlier injury. In this case, the assassin has killed the target even though he was not a *but-for* cause of his death because he would have died from the other

intention or bodily action explain the distinction since a person may intentionally use her body to withdraw aid from another person, thereby letting him die.[6] And sometimes failures to intentionally act are cases of killing. For example, imagine your car is coasting down a hill toward a crosswalk full of people. You do not press the breaks, and several people are run over by your car. In this case, you killed the pedestrians even though you did not intentionally act by steering your car into them.

Descriptive approaches to the distinction between killing and letting die fail because the distinction is based on more fundamental moral distinctions, such as the relative weightiness of negative rights and judgments of responsibility. It is generally worse to kill or harm a person than to allow her to suffer or die because it is worse to violate negative rights than positive rights and because we are generally more responsible for what we do than what we allow. On this reconstruction, seeming instances of killing reliably align with violations of negative rights for which someone is morally responsible, whereas cases of letting die reliably align with failures to satisfy someone's positive rights to assistance.[7]

There are three compelling reasons to accept a moral distinction between killing and letting die. First, negative rights violations are generally morally worse than positive rights violations. Warren Quinn develops this argument on the grounds that to deny a distinction between doing and allowing is to embrace an unacceptable moral theory.[8] Without a distinction between negative rights

injuries. We might revise again to say that the assassin kills because he created a new threat to his target and was therefore a *but-for* cause of his *particular* death. See, e.g., Jeff McMahan, "Killing, Letting Die, and Withdrawing Aid," *Ethics* 103, no. 2 (1993): 250–79. But this revision seems too inclusive because it will characterize cases that are seemingly instances of letting die as killing. For example, imagine that we are rock climbing. You slip, but I catch your rope. Then, seeing that you are too heavy for me to hold, I let you go. Intuitively, I did not kill you in this case. I allowed you to fall, even though I was in some sense a cause of your *particular* death. See, Will Cartwright, "Killing and Letting Die: A Defensible Distinction," *British Medical Bulletin* 52, no. 2 (1996): 354–61. These examples invite skepticism about whether the distinction between doing and allowing is a distinction between what a person causes to happen and what she allows.

[6] Judith Jarvis Thomson, "A Defense of Abortion," *Philosophy & Public Affairs* 1, no.1 (1971): 47–66.

[7] A stronger interpretation of this moralized reconstruction of the distinction is that our intuitions about doing and allowing are moralized because, as Joshua Knobe and other experimentalists have suggested, people's intuitive theory of causation depends largely on their moral appraisals in cases of doing and allowing Joshua Knobe, "Folk Psychology, Folk Morality," (PhD diss., Princeton University, 2006), http://148.216.10.92/archivos%20PDF%20de%20trabajo%20UMSNH/Aphilosofia/folkpsychology.pdf; Craig Roxborough and Jill Cumby, "Folk Psychological Concepts: Causation," *Philosophical Psychology* 22, no. 2 (April 1, 2009): 205–13, doi:10.1080/09515080902802769.

[8] Warren S. Quinn, "Actions, Intentions, and Consequences: The Doctrine of Double Effect," *Philosophy & Public Affairs* 18, no. 4 (October 1, 1989): 334–51.

(against being harmed) and positive rights (against suffering) our bodies and projects would be fully subject to the community's cost-benefit analysis. If harming you led to less suffering overall, then morality would require that you be harmed. At least in principle, act consequentialists believe this. But most of us think that we have a special claim to control our bodies, even if exercising that control is in some sense worse for everyone. Our claims to control our bodies may be justified because each person has a kind of inviolable dignity, or bodily rights could be justified by a more pluralistic commonsense moral theory. In any case, this special claim explains the greater weight of negative rights; they protect our unique entitlement to control our own lives and our own bodies in addition to our entitlement to escape death or suffering, whereas positive rights only protect the latter.

A second reason that denying the distinction between killing and letting die is unsustainable is that our moral concepts, such as our concept of responsibility, presuppose that what people do is morally different from what people allow. For example, Samuel Scheffler argues that if we are going to have a moral theory that assigns responsibility to people *at all*, it must recognize that it is morally worse to do something wrong than to allow something bad to happen.[9] Responsibility is a way of assigning praise or blame to distinctive persons, so we must assume that people are distinctive in their role of making the world better or worse by distinguishing between what people do and what they allow.[10]

A third reason to maintain a distinction between killing and letting die is that denying the distinction would be unfair. A moral theory should give each member of the moral community equal standing. One way to interpret this is that each person should be subject to the same moral requirements and should

---

[9] Scheffler proposes that the very ideas of moral deliberation and choice require that we think of ourselves as more than instruments of impersonal moral requirements. The requirement to prevent death on balance or the requirement to promote happiness does not exhaust the scope of what we should choose to do. Each person is bound by moral requirements, but morality must also make room for self-expression and choice. We must think of ourselves as *agents*, not as cogs in a consequential-ist machine. If we internalized a moral theory that denied the distinction between what people do and what people allow, we could not even see ourselves as distinctive persons because there would be no opportunity to independently decide which reasons to take as relevant for action. Scheffler, therefore, concludes that any plausible moral theory must treat events that result from a person's independent deliberation and agency differently from other events. Namely, when it comes to moral responsibility, people are more culpable for events that are a result of deliberation, what Scheffler calls "primary manifestations of one's agency," than they are for those events that bear no rela-tionship to a person's agency. Samuel Scheffler, "Doing and Allowing," *Ethics* 114, no. 2 (January 1, 2004): 215–39, doi:10.1086/379355.

[10] Bernard Williams similarly argues that a moral theory should not require people to see their most deeply held commitments as so dispensable that they can be abandoned when doing so would promote better consequences. Bernard Williams, "Consequentialism and Integrity," in *Consequentialism and Its Critics*, ed. Samuel Scheffler (Oxford University Press, 1988), 20–50, http://philpapers.org/rec/WILCAI.

have equal rights. But a moral theory that denied the distinction between killing and letting die would disproportionately burden people who were well placed to prevent the deaths of others relative to those who were not well placed to prevent other's deaths.[11] If letting die were as morally serious as killing, then people would be as blameworthy for the deaths that could have been avoided merely due to their circumstances as they would be for deaths that could have been avoided had they not chose to kill.

For these reasons, the distinction between killing and letting die plays two important roles. First, the distinction marks out some actions as especially wrong or unjust because it tracks a more fundamental moral asymmetry between violations of negative rights and positive rights. In this way, the distinction ought to inform our moral assessments of different policy proposals. It may explain, for example, why government policies, such as the Transportation Security Administration's airport checkpoints are less morally objectionable than a policy that confiscated some people's vital organs to save other's lives would be, even if the TSA's policy caused more deaths than they prevented while the organ confiscation program prevented more deaths than it caused. If we accept the distinction between killing and letting die, the TSA would fare better in our moral assessment because even if more people choose to drive to avoid checkpoints, thereby causing more auto fatalities, the victims generally consented to the risks of driving but could not consent to the risks of being killed for the sake of one's organs.

Second, the distinction is important for assigning judgments of culpability, and perhaps blame, sanctioning attitudes, apologies, compensation, or punishment (for those who think that punishment should align with desert or wrongdoing). Those who kill are liable to be sanctioned to a greater extent than those who allow the deaths of others. To see why this is true, consider what it would mean if this idea were false. If killing was not worse than letting die, then failures to provide lifesaving assistance would, in principle (setting aside negative externalities), be as much a blemish on one's character as murder. No one sincerely believes this. As Francis Kamm argues, though philosophers have questioned the distinction between doing and allowing, even those who deny the distinction must acknowledge that we would think very differently of someone who killed a person to save $1,000 and someone who failed to give $1,000 to a charity that saves lives.[12] We are forgiving of people who believe that giving to charities would save lives but fail to do so because they are weak-willed, but we would not be so forgiving of a person who cited his weak will when explaining

---

[11] I defend this claim in more detail in "Duty and Enforcement," which was presented at Oxford Studies in Political Philosophy, 2016.

[12] Alex Voorhoeve, "In Search of the Deep Structure of Morality: An Interview with Frances Kamm," *Imprints* 9, no. 2 (2006): 93–117.

why he killed a person to save $1,000. Instead, killers are usually liable to be punished and may reasonably be expected to apologize and pay compensation to their victims' families.

Turning to approval requirements, when public officials withhold access to potentially lifesaving or therapeutic investigational drugs, they kill those patients who die as a result of premarket approval requirements by the criteria that ground the distinction between killing and letting die. To establish this claim on more solid ground, I will need to show that public officials who enforce premarket approval policies violate rights in ways for which they are morally responsible. To show that officials are responsible, I will need to show that when they violate people's rights not to be killed, it is due to their choices and also that they can and do foresee the deadly consequences of their choices.

Begin with the claim that regulators violate rights by forbidding unauthorized access to investigational drugs. As I previously argued, public officials violate people's rights of self-medication and self-preservation when they prohibit voluntary exchanges between patients and manufacturers in order to enforce premarket approval policies. More generally, public officials violate rights because no one can consent to the approval requirements that prevent them from accessing investigational drugs.

The reasons in favor of respecting people's rights to access investigational drugs are especially strong because patients who seek access are often those with few or no other medical options. Patients with conditions that can be effectively treated with approved therapies are likely to use approved treatments, even if they had access to investigational therapies, because unapproved treatments are risky and potentially ineffective. Patients with treatment-resistant terminal or degenerative medical conditions seek access to investigational drugs when it is more risky to wait for approval than to use an untested drug. In these cases, rights of self-medication are also a species of rights of self-preservation.[13] And even the most Hobbesian proponents of political authority must concede that if people have any rights against public officials, those rights include the right to preserve one's own life.

To illustrate this point as it relates to the distinction between killing and letting die, consider an analogy. If an oppressive government appropriates and rations the food supply in a way that causes mass famine, the government officials kill citizens. Officials are culpable when citizens suffer and ultimately die of starvation, even if the rations were not enforced with the goal of causing starvation, because they violated citizens' rights to purchase food from willing

---

[13] Eugene Volokh develops this argument in more detail with reference to the Abigail Alliance case. Eugene Volokh, "Medical Self-Defense, Prohibited Experimental Therapies, and Payment for Organs," *Harvard Law Review* 120, no.7 (2007):1813–46.

providers. In this case, as in the case of pharmaceutical regulation, prohibiting people from accessing lifesaving goods is best understood as an act of killing, rather than letting die, because prohibitions violate people's rights of self-preservation.

There are countless examples of patients whose rights to preserve their lives were violated because they died waiting for drug approval. Here are two. First, Abigail Burroughs was twenty-one when she died of cancer. In the last stages of treatment, Abigail's oncologist suggested that an unapproved drug, cetuximab, might treat the kind of cancer cells that were killing her. At the time, cetuximab was available only in clinical trials for colon cancer, so only colon cancer patients had access to the drug. Abigail had head and neck cancer. Abigail died in 2001, and in 2006, cetuximab was approved for treating head and neck cancer.[14] Second, seventeen-year-old Adam Askew died of veno-occlusive liver disease in 2008.[15] Before his death, Adam's physician, Dr. Jody Sima, believed that the unapproved drug defibrotide could be used to cure his condition. Dr. Sima based this judgment on published studies of the drug, but FDA regulations did not allow Adam to enter a clinical trial for defibrotide because his symptoms were not severe enough to provide relevant data for the trial. A study released in 2009 confirmed that defibrotide effectively cures 36 percent of younger patients with less severe symptoms—patients like Adam.

Abigail and Adam were denied access to drugs that could have saved or extended their lives. Their stories illustrate how some patients have exceptionally strong rights to access investigational therapies in virtue of their right to preserve their lives through non-lethal means. One may reply that there are other patients who, like Abigail and Adam, suffered from life-threatening illnesses but would have been harmed by using investigational drugs that caused painful side effects or shortened their lives. I grant this point, but it is not as (if at all) wrong for manufacturers to sell dangerous investigational drugs as it is for officials to prohibit people from using dangerous investigational drugs. The following two cases, which are analogous to existing approval policies and a certification system, illustrate this point:

Approval: Patty, Peter, and four others lie in a hospital room dying from a disease. They invite Mark to their room to administer a risky drug. Mark tells them that little is known about the drug, and it is expected to cause one in six patients who use it to die. But the drug is also expected to cure one in six patients who use it. If Mark delivers the drug, it will in fact cause Patty to die and it will cure Peter. While Mark is en route,

---

[14] Ibid.

[15] Hayes Edwards, "Risky Business: How the FDA Overstepped Its Bounds by Limiting Patient Access to Experimental Drugs," *George Mason University Civil Rights Law Journal* 22 (2012 2011): 389.

Gloria intervenes and delays Mark's visit. Patty, Peter, and four others die of their diseases.

Certification: Patty, Peter, and four others lie in a hospital room dying from a disease. They invite Mark to their room to dispense a risky treatment that must be given to all six patients at once. Gloria confirms Mark's claims that little is known about the drug, and it is expected to kill one in six patients who use it and cure one in six patients who use it. Mark delivers the drug to the consenting patients. The drug causes Patty to die and cures Peter. The four others die of their diseases.

These cases illuminate the crucial moral distinction between the actions of manufacturers and regulators. Patients can consent to take a risky drug, but they cannot consent to the risky regulations that endanger their lives.[16] When regulators interfere with transactions between patients and manufacturers, they kill those patients who could benefit. In *Approval*, Gloria kills Peter by preventing him from accessing the cure. She also harms Patty and the others by depriving them of the one in six chance of being cured. In contrast, when manufacturers distribute dangerous and untested drugs that harm patients, as Mark does in *Certification*, their actions do not violate rights because patients like Patty consent to the risks associated with using an investigational drug.

In *Approval*, Gloria also impermissibly interferes with Mark by preventing him from distributing the drugs, because Mark's actions are permissible, and so Mark is not liable to be interfered with. One may question the claim that Mark's actions are permissible and that Mark is not liable to be interfered with on the grounds that consent is not sufficient to establish that a person has assumed certain risks. For example, a person may consent to the risks associated with a mountain biking tour but not consent to the risks associated with the tour company's failure to maintain its equipment. In such a case, the negligent tour company would be liable to be interfered with on behalf of its customers, even if the customers did consent to some of the risks of the tour. But in Mark's case, we are assuming that Mark fully discloses all known risks associated with a drug and that there are not additional risks that are a result of Mark's negligence. So Mark's conduct is more like the conduct of a non-negligent tour company, meaning that the patients are able to give their informed consent.[17]

[16] Consent to pharmaceutical regulations would be possible if patients could opt-in to a regulatory system. Patients could commit to waive their rights of self-medication and consent to regulatory limits. Or, patients could opt-out of the approval system and accept the risks of using dangerous drugs. But, in practice, approval policies prevent manufacturers from selling investigational drugs to patients, and manufacturers and patients are never given the opportunity to consent to these policies.

[17] For those who are skeptical that people can consent to risks of this sort, such skepticism also undermines informed consent because people consent to risks when they consent to surgery or to the use of approved drugs. More generally, if a person can consent to something, then she can consent to a risk of that thing happening. So those who grant that patients are able to consent to use a

Another important feature of these cases is that Gloria actively intervenes with Mark and the patients. This is significant because another reason that killing is generally worse than letting people die is that killing generally involves a knowing decision to cause another person to suffer and die. By preventing manufacturers from providing therapeutic drugs, public officials enforce a policy that they know will cost lives. Every year, patients suffer and die after being denied access to investigational drugs that are subsequently approved to treat their conditions. Whenever a regulatory agency or drug company claims a newly approved drug will save thousands of life-years for each year on the market, they concede that thousands of life-years were lost during the time it took for the drug to win approval. Regulators cannot take credit for their role in facilitating informed access to lifesaving drugs without also taking blame for the lives that were lost because of approval delays.

Pharmaceutical regulators do take some steps to minimize the harm of preventing people from accessing investigational therapies in some cases. For example, clinical trials are governed by the standard of clinical equipoise, which requires that investigators halt a trial or provide the superior treatment to all patients once the trial results pass a threshold of evidence about the relative merits of the control and treatment. The principle of equipoise aims to mitigate the harm of being deprived beneficial treatment for the sake of a clinical investigation. Patients are entitled to treatment that meets standards of equipoise if the patient consented to the risk of receiving the inferior treatment by enrolling in the trial. Yet by this logic, patients who are excluded from trials for investigational drugs have an even stronger claim to receive treatment because they cannot consent to the risks of being denied a superior treatment the way trial participants do. But regulators currently force these patients to accept the standard of care until the drug is approved, even if it is clearly inferior to an investigational drug.

Elsewhere, agencies have taken steps to provide greater incentives to develop drugs for rare diseases and to speed the approval policies, by enforcing policies like the ODA and PDUFA. Their compliance with these policies further suggests that public officials are aware of the deadly effects of enforcing expensive and lengthy approval policies. So regulators recognize that their actions are harmful but nevertheless do not take steps to avoid them.

This is not to suggest that pharmaceutical regulators intend to kill patients by withholding approval for drugs. But whether officials intend to kill patients is extraneous to the permissibility of killing, as it is in other contexts.[18] If a military leader kills dozens of innocent civilians by bombing a bridge that is used by his enemies, he is morally responsible for the civilians' deaths, even

---

deadly drug by allowing that voluntary euthanasia is conceptually possible should also accept that people can consent to use drugs that carry less than a 100 percent risk of death.

[18] T. M. Scanlon, *Moral Dimensions* (Harvard University Press, 2009).

though he did not directly intend to kill them. Assuming that refugees have rights to asylum, if a border patrolman turns away a boat full of refugees and they die in the sea, then the patrolman has killed the refugees, even if he only intended to prevent them from landing on the shores of his country. So too, when regulators prohibit patients from accessing lifesaving therapeutics, they kill patients, even if they intend to minimize the number of dangerous drugs on the market.

In summary, existing pharmaceutical regulations are morally worse than the empirical record suggests. Even if premarket approval policies prevented more deaths than they caused, they still would not be justified because the prohibition of investigational drugs violates patients' fundamental rights and is not necessary to promote informed patient choice. For this reason, premarket approval requirements are not only deadly but also unjust, and insofar as there is a duty to resist injustice and reform institutions, citizens and officials ought to resist and reform pharmaceutical regulations. Since regulators are morally responsible for the deaths they knowingly cause by enforcing approval requirements, they are liable to be blamed and sanctioned when they kill patients. This argument calls for apology, compensation, and reparation in these cases as well.

4.2 Necessity and the Need to Test

Some people think that public officials may justifiably kill people in the service of a just cause, as long as killing is necessary for the cause and would effectively advance the cause. For the sake of argument, say we granted that in principle public officials could sometimes use their power to prevent people from using dangerous drugs for the sake of public health. Even granting this premise, prohibitive approval requirements would be neither necessary nor effective at promoting public health, so they would not be justified in practice. The requirements are unnecessary because public officials could certify drugs and subsidize access to expert advisors instead of prohibiting unapproved drugs. The requirements are ineffective because they likely cause more harm than they prevent by causing drug loss and drug lag.

One may reply that approval requirements are necessary for the promotion of the public's health and safety when we consider health and safety more broadly. Though prohibitive approval requirements are not necessary to protect patients from using dangerous pharmaceuticals, they may be necessary for the sake of broader public health goals if granting patients the rights to use investigational drugs before they were approved would discourage them from participating in clinical trials. If so, rights of self-medication could violate the public health imperative to promote informed self-medication by threatening the clinical trial system.

In the United States, courts have been reluctant to acknowledge that rights of self-preservation require a right to access for this reason.[19] Before Abigail died, she and her father, Frank Burroughs, founded the Abigail Alliance for Better Access to Developmental Drugs. After her death, Frank sued the FDA and the Department of Health and Human Services on her behalf, alleging that the failure to permit terminally ill patients to access experimental drugs violated the fundamental right to preserve one's own life. In 2004 a DC district court ruled against the Abigail Alliance, but in 2006 a three-judge panel of the DC Circuit Court of Appeals overturned the ruling and found that terminally ill patients *do* have a constitutional right to purchase experimental medicines that had successfully passed Phase 1 safety testing.[20] The judges affirmed the argument that public officials violate patients' rights by preventing them from using potentially lifesaving medication. The court wrote that these approval policies "impinge[d] upon an individual liberty deeply rooted in our Nation's history and tradition of self-preservation."[21] The FDA responded to this ruling by petitioning the Court of Appeals to rehear the case *en banc*, meaning that all judges in the DC appellate circuit were asked to rehear the case. There, a divided court denied that access to experimental drugs was a fundamental right and overturned the previous ruling.[22]

In part, the *en banc* court's reversal was justified by the FDA's assertion that greater patient access would undermine the clinical trial system. The claim was that if people could use investigational drugs outside the context of a clinical trial, there would be no incentive for them to enroll in clinical trials and risk receiving the standard of care. Call this the "need to test" argument. This argument relies on two premises. First, it assumes that granting patients access to investigational therapies would necessarily undermine the clinical trial system. Second, the argument assumes that public officials act permissibly when they prevent patients from using investigational drugs out of concern for the clinical trial system.

Would an expansion of access compromise the approval process? Not necessarily. The claim is that public officials and researchers would be unable to use randomized trials to test a drug's effectiveness if patients insisted on using unapproved drugs. But as Eugene Volokh has argued, this argument cannot

[19] Abigail Alliance v. Von Eschenbach, 445 F. 3d 470 (Court of Appeals, Dist. of Columbia Circuit 2006); Rebecca S. Eisenberg, "Role of the FDA in Innovation Policy," *Michigan Telecommunications and Technology Law Review* 13 (2007): 345; Susan Okie, "Access Before Approval—A Right to Take Experimental Drugs?," *New England Journal of Medicine* 355, no. 5 (2006): 437–40.

[20] Abigail Alliance v. Von Eschenbach.

[21] DC Circuit Judge Judith Rogers, as cited in Okie, "Access Before Approval."

[22] The Alliance's legal options were exhausted in 2008 when the Supreme Court declined to accept further appeal.

justify policies that prohibit patients who do not qualify for enrollment in clinical trials from accessing investigational therapies. Volokh writes:

> If the studies require 200 patients, and there are 10,000 who seek the experimental therapy, there is little reason to constrain the self-defense rights of all 10,000. Likewise, if the drug is now being studied only on people who suffer from a particular kind or stage of a disease, the drug should not be legally barred to those who fall outside those studies. If we must strip people of self-defense rights to save many others' lives in the future, we should impose this tragic constraint on as few people as possible and to as small an extent as possible.[23]

The approach to clinical trials that Volokh describes has already been deployed for some drugs. For example, during the AIDS epidemic, patients who did not qualify for enrollment in clinical trials were permitted to access investigational drugs on a parallel track. Manufacturers and public officials may even have reason to favor a system that allows greater access. Manufacturers can monitor patients on parallel tracks to learn about other potential uses of investigational drugs. Public officials can monitor patients on parallel tracks to learn more about the effects of the drugs for different populations.

More generally, although approval requirements may give patients incentives to enroll in clinical trials, they are not *necessary* to encourage enrollment. Patients in clinical trials already receive other benefits by enrolling, such as subsidized medical care and careful monitoring, which go beyond early access to investigational therapies. Nevertheless, a prominent concern about expanding access to investigational drugs is that patients who are not effectively treated by available therapies will access the drugs rather than risk assignment to a control group in a clinical trial.

Insofar as concerns about incentivizing trial participation are valid, it is because some patients will judge that the risk of assignment to a control group is genuinely worse than access to an investigational drug with unknown effects. Yet in these cases, it is not clear that a trial would be ethical in the first place. Reconsider the principle of equipoise, which requires researchers to remain genuinely uncertain about whether the investigational therapy is better than the standard of care as they conduct a trial. As it becomes clear that an investigational therapy is more harmful than the standard of care, researchers are required to move trial participants out of the treatment arm. Or if it becomes clear that an investigational therapy is more effective than the standard of care, researchers are required to move participants into the treatment arm of the trial.

[23] Volokh, "Medical Self-Defense," 1830.

The principle of equipoise is justified because patients do not have a choice about enrolling in a treatment or a control arm of a trial, so researchers have a duty to ensure that patients are not forced to accept worse care because of their participation in the trial. Yet the argument that patients must be prohibited from accessing investigational drugs because otherwise they would do so illustrates that the principle of equipoise is not met in cases where patients judge that the risks of being in the control arm are clearly higher than the risks of an investigational drug. In other words, if patients only participate in a clinical trial because they have no chance of accessing an investigational treatment otherwise, that is a sign that the trial may be violating standards of clinical equipoise.

While I agree that randomized clinical trials are generally the best method for medical research because randomization can mitigate selection bias, it is also important to remember that researchers can learn about the effects of investigational drugs without random assignment. For new drugs being tested against the standard of care, existing patient populations can serve as a control group, even if most patients flock to use an investigational therapy because the effects of the existing standard of care are already known. For example, instead of looking at a particular subset of patients who are randomly assigned to a treatment at a particular time, researchers can treat the advent of availability as an instrumental variable and compare patients who are treated for a condition at a particular time to those who had the condition before the treatment and received the standard of care.

The success of the off-label market provides further reason to think that efficacy-testing requirements are not necessary for researchers to learn about new drugs. Since the need to recruit patients for clinical trials for every particular condition that a drug could treat is not weighty enough to justify prohibiting the off-label prescription of drugs, the need to test also cannot justify prohibitive approval requirements.

Relatedly, many randomized clinical trials today occur *after* approval when patients have access to the drugs being tested.[24] Researchers use post-approval trial data to find new uses for available drugs.[25] Cancer researchers investigate whether available compounds can effectively treat different kinds of cancers.[26] Investigators are also testing whether statins, which are currently approved to prevent heart attacks and strokes for high-risk patients, could also protect low-risk patients.[27] The Women's Health Initiative (WHI) is another example of

[24] I am grateful to Alex Tabarrok for conversations on this topic and for providing some of the following references and examples, which have helpfully informed my response.

[25] See for example, J. E. Calfee and E. DuPre, "The Emerging Market Dynamics of Targeted Therapeutics," *Health Affairs* 25, no. 5 (2006): 1302–08.

[26] For example, Avastan has been tested in post-approval randomized clinical trials for over twenty conditions. M. Flanagan, "Avastin's Progression," *Bio Century* 14, no. 11 (2006): A1–A5.

[27] E. J. Topol, "Intensive Statin Therapy—A Sea Change in Cardiovascular Prevention," *New England Journal of Medicine* 350, no. 15 (2004): 1562–64.

post-market trials that tested the efficacy of an available treatment.[28] Before the WHI, anecdotal evidence strongly suggested that hormone replacement therapy (HRT) could reduce heart attacks for women. But the WHI conducted randomized clinical trials of the therapy. Though HRT was approved and widely available and prescribed off-label, the WHI successfully enrolled patients in the trial. The results showed that HRT actually increased women's risks of heart attack and other ailments, effectively changing the standard of care through post-market testing.

Trials like these include tens of thousands of patients. In each trial, some participants receive the standard of care and some receive an approved drug that may or may not effectively treat their condition. Yet, despite the fact that both the standard of care and the investigational therapy are available, patients enroll in trials to receive other benefits of clinical trials, such as close monitoring and high-quality subsidized medical care. These examples suggest that patients may participate in trials even if they can access investigational therapies.

The argument that approval policies are necessary because patients would otherwise not have sufficient incentives to participate in clinical trials also assumes that the only possible incentive that researchers could offer is access to an investigational drug. Yet researchers are also permitted to pay healthy subjects to participate in clinical trials. Currently, researchers in the United States, Canada, and Europe are discouraged from paying participants, particularly those viewed as especially vulnerable, and it is frowned on to offer large payments to induce participation, as opposed to fairly compensating participants for their time.[29] But policies that prohibit inducement in research out of concern for the poor and vulnerable only further limit the options of those who are already among the worst off.[30]

Some bioethicists object that even if payment is good for individual participants, there is "something repugnant" about normalization of financial inducement insofar as it will effectively mean that the bodies of the poorest and worst off are used for the benefit of the well off.[31] But consider the alternative. Currently, the worst off cannot access investigational drugs, partly out of concern that they lack incentives to participate in the clinical trial system. So their rights of self-medication and self-preservation are violated in order to induce them to participate in research. In light of that practice, it is certainly not worse to induce people to participate in research by paying them, when paying

---

[28] This example was described in an e-mail with Alex Tabarrok.

[29] Trudo Lemmens and Carl Elliott, "Justice for the Professional Guinea Pig," *American Journal of Bioethics* 1, no. 2 (2001): 51–53.

[30] Martin Wilkinson and Andrew Moore, "Inducement in Research," *Bioethics* 11, no. 5 (1997): 373–89, doi:10.1111/1467-8519.00078.

[31] Paul McNeill, "Paying People to Participate in Research: Why Not?," *Bioethics* 11, no. 5 (1997): 390–96.

them does not violate their rights or make individual participants worse off. The fact that more people who are among the economically and medically worst off would bear the risks of medical research is a symptom of socioeconomic inequality, due to the fact that for many people participation in research is a relatively good option even though it is risky. The appropriate response to socioeconomic inequality should not be to mask the symptoms of it by further limiting the options of the worst off. Rather, policymakers and researchers should be encouraged to give patients more incentives to participate in research, thus providing them more choices.

One may object that greater access to experimental drugs would at least make it more difficult to recruit participants for a randomized trial of a drug that treats rare diseases. When there is a small patient population, it is difficult to establish that a drug is effective because all trials are necessarily under-powered. On the other hand, rare-disease communities can also serve as a resource for recruiting trial participants and educating people about the benefits of a clinical trial. In some cases, patients with rare diseases have been given compassionate access to experimental therapies but opted to participate in clinical trials instead so their participation could benefit the broader patient population and to receive better care.[32]

These considerations suggest that it is not necessary to prevent people from accessing drugs outside the context of a clinical trial in order to learn about the effects of investigational therapies. But even if policies that prevented patients from accessing investigational drugs did help researchers learn about the effects of new drugs, it wouldn't justify approval requirements. The costs associated with respecting patients' rights of self-medication and self-preservation do not necessarily justify violations of those rights.

For example, Udo Schuklenk has argued forcefully that terminally ill AIDS patients have rights to access experimental medicines *even if* there are serious costs to third parties.[33] People whose lives are threatened are often permitted to act in ways that impose costs on others if doing so would preserve their own lives.[34] Some philosophers argue that even lethal force is permissible for

---

[32] Amy Dockser Marcus, "Niemann-Pick Type C: A Fight to Save Children with a Drug," *Wall Street Journal*, http://on.wsj.com/1due624.

[33] Udo Schuklenk, *Access to Experimental Drugs in Terminal Illness: Ethical Issues* (Binghamton, NY: Pharmaceutical Products Press/Haworth Press, 1998).

[34] Many philosophers even believe that harmful action is warranted if it is necessary for self-preservation. Judith Thomson has argued that it is permissible to use lethal force against *multiple innocent threats* to preserve one's own life. For example, imagine that a temporarily drugged but non-blameworthy person is driving a truck with a passenger and the truck is about to hit you. You have a gun, and you could shoot the truck in a way that would make the truck explode, thus preserving your own life but killing the two innocent occupants. In this case, Thomson says it is permissible to shoot the truck to protect yourself, even if the driver and passenger are innocent. Judith Jarvis Thomson, "Self-Defense," *Philosophy & Public Affairs* 20, no. 4 (1991): 283–310.

self-preservation, yet patients who want to use investigational drugs are prohibited from self-medicating because it could make it more difficult for researchers to test new drugs. Insofar as people can do much more harmful and morally fraught things out of self-defense, surely they can access investigational drugs. Therefore, the right of self-preservation is so powerful that healthcare providers and citizens might be asked to absorb the costs of allowing people to use investigational drugs, in the same way that society bears the costs of other basic rights.

This argument is further supported by an appeal to the distinction between doing and allowing. Even if rights of self-medication made it more difficult for researchers to conduct clinical trials, public officials are not generally morally permitted to kill some citizens to help researchers gather information that is useful for promoting public health. Abigail and Adam may have been able to save or extend their lives by using investigational drugs, and the FDA stopped them. If this kind of government interference were generally allowed, it would have unacceptable implications elsewhere. For example, it would be wrong for public officials to conduct deadly medical experiments on non-consenting human subjects, even if the experiments only involved blocking access to lifesaving goods, like food or oxygen, and even if the experiments yielded very useful information. Or if rights of self-medication could be suspended to facilitate research, then officials could in principle rescind approval for existing drugs to encourage people to participate in additional trials.

Finally, clinical trials may improve if more people have access to investigational drugs. One explanation for the apparent ineffectiveness of premarket safety testing is that premarket tests only establish safety for a specific population, while in practice the safety of a drug varies substantially between patients. Drugs that are safe in healthy patients may be unsafe in unhealthy patients. Drugs that are safe for younger populations might have unacceptable side effects for older patients. The side effects and benefits of a drug also vary across populations. Even for safe drugs that are never recalled, hundreds of thousands of patients suffer or die each year from adverse reactions or suffer side effects without receiving any benefit. According to one pharmaceutical executive's estimate, as many as 90 percent of drugs are only effective in 50 percent of cases.[35] This is not a failure of safety testing; it is a necessary limitation. As former FDA Commissioner David Kessler said in his testimony to the Congress, premarket clinical trials cannot generate enough data about drugs to anticipate rare but serious adverse reactions or the long-term risks of a drug.[36] Clinical

---

[35] This figure is cited by Allen Roses, who was then a vice president at GlaxoSmithKlein, quoted in Royal Society of Chemistry, "Medicine Gets Personalised," accessed April 12, 2016, http://www.rsc.org/chemistryworld/Issues/2005/July/Medicine_personalised.asp.

[36] Kessler, David. "Statement to the US House Committee on Oversight and Government Reform," 110 Congress, Second Session, May 14, 2008 Serial No. 110–201.

trials are also very different from typical use conditions, and typical use data may be more relevant to patients than the results of a supervised trial. Therefore, insofar as premarket approval requirements are justified for the sake of learning as much as possible about new drugs, expanding the group of users and conducting post-market surveillance for drugs would generate more and better information than a premarket clinical trial that only includes one patient-type using a drug in conditions that are very different from what will be a typical user's experience.

4.3 Non-Ideal and Ideal Theory

At this point, one may object that I am holding my argument for rights of self-medication and certificatory policies to a double standard by comparing an ideal system of self-medication to a clearly flawed status quo. Perhaps there could be a better regulatory middle-ground in theory, and in practice rights of self-medication would be a disaster.[37] To address this objection, I will compare a certificatory system with an approval system in light of non-ideal considerations, and then compare prohibitive approval requirements with a certification system in ideal theory. In doing so, I will demonstrate that the case for rights of self-medication is even stronger than it may initially seem. In light of non-ideal considerations, regulators and citizens face substantial institutional and psychological barriers to addressing the harmful effects of the approval system. In ideal theory, prohibitive approval requirements are unnecessary because public officials could encourage safe and responsible self-medication through certification and incentive programs instead of prohibition.

We can distinguish non-ideal theory from ideal theory in three ways.[38] First, non-ideal theories consider whether making an institution more just is feasible in light of psychological, social, and physical facts. It is also important to clarify which psychological, social, and physical facts are fixed and which are likely to change as a result of institutional changes. So, for example, it may be a psychological fact that patients have poor medical literacy under the current system, but we should not assume that a system that empowered people and gave them greater responsibility for their health would not influence medical literacy. Second, non-ideal theories account for people's likely non-compliance with principles of justice, either due to personal prejudices or institutional incentives. Third, non-ideal theories advocate transitional efforts at making institutions more just rather than exclusively focusing on an ideal or end-state of justice. For example, non-ideal theorists must also consider whether the ideal policy is

---

[37] I am thankful to David Sobel for encouraging me to consider this point.
[38] Valentini, "Ideal vs. Non-Ideal Theory."

morally inaccessible because achieving it would involve unacceptable violations of rights or very bad consequences.

To evaluate the merits of a prohibitive approval system against the merits of a certificatory approach therefore requires comparing certification and approval policies in light of the extent that they can meet their goals considering each institution's feasibility, people's likely non-compliance, and the possibility that officials sometimes face a choice between advocating a more just system by acting unjustly and acting justly while setting back efforts to create a more just system on balance.

Begin by comparing approval policy reforms with certification policies in light of the various ways that a just approval or certificatory may be psychologically infeasible or infeasible in light of social and institutional facts. A more just approval system would have shorter delays, more effective drug screening, expanded access to lifesaving drugs for patients who do not qualify for clinical trials, and ways of promoting innovation despite the risk that a drug will not win approval. But it is not clear that a more just system is psychologically feasible because, in any system of approval, public officials and voters will be influenced by pervasive psychological biases. In particular, officials face institutional incentives to delay the introduction of potentially lifesaving drugs, and voters are biased to punish officials for drug poisonings but not for the deaths that are caused by drug lag and drug loss.

The first psychological barrier to a more just approval system stems from voters' tendency to make judgments based on an availability heuristic, which undermines people's ability to assess risk. And since drug recalls and the dangerous effects of drug use are well publicized, people assume that pharmaceuticals are generally very risky. But the deaths that are caused by approval requirements are rarely publicized, so voters do not recognize the risks of an approval system. The second psychological barrier to a more just approval policy relates to the first. Any approval policy that tasks public officials with certifying drugs as safe and effective will create incentives for officials to enforce deadly delays in order to meet their charge. While manufacturers have enormous self-interested reasons to avoid causing patients' deaths by selling dangerous drugs, the same cannot be said for regulators who enforce prohibitive regulations. For example, in the United States the FDA's regulatory authority derives from the legislature, and legislators are themselves accountable to the public. Political scientists who study the FDA argue that the agency has a great deal of independence and power because it maintains a good reputation with the public.[39] Yet because the FDA is so reliant on legislative and public support, the agency has incentives to craft its approval policies in anticipation of potential public

---

[39] Carpenter, *Reputation and Power*, 2014.

backlash and sanction from elected officials. The seeming independence of regulatory agencies is an illusion insofar as regulators make decisions in order to avoid public criticism.

Because regulators are reliant on public and legislative approval, they are influenced in favor of reducing drug disasters at the expense of overall access. The distinction between Type I errors (false positives) and Type II errors (false negatives) illustrates this point. A Type I error occurs when an agency approves a dangerous drug, and a Type II error occurs when the agency fails to approve a beneficial drug. Since regulators' power relies on their reputation, their incentives are mostly aligned to avoid committing Type I errors because the media and consumer advocates can easily identify the victims of these errors. On the other hand, when regulators fail to approve a safe and beneficial drug it appears that the people who would have been treated or saved die from their diseases. The victims of approval delay go unnoticed. Therefore, regulators have incentives to minimize Type I errors even though a very risk-averse approval strategy is harmful to the public's health on balance.

There is some empirical support for this diagnosis of pharmaceutical regulator's intentions. Henry Miller, a former FDA employee, described a case where his team at the administration was prepared to approve an application for recombinant human insulin after only four months. Yet Miller's supervisor refused to finalize the approval even though he agreed that the data supported the judgment that the drug was safe and effective, because "If anything goes wrong . . . think how bad it will look that we approved the drug so quickly."[40] The institutional context deterred consideration of the patients who could have benefited from faster access to the drug. Rather, his incentive was to adopt extreme caution out of fear that erroneously approving a dangerous drug would threaten the administration.

Even when pharmaceutical regulators approve a drug, if the public and media conclude that an approved drug is unacceptably risky, then approval could weaken the authority of public officials. For example, in the 1970s the FDA approved a vaccine for the swine flu that effectively treated thousands of patients and may have averted a swine flu pandemic. Yet the vaccine caused several hundred cases of death or paralysis from Guillain-Barre Syndrome.[41] Media coverage of the Guillain-Barre deaths shook the public's faith in the FDA and undermined the credibility of subsequent vaccine-based public health campaigns.[42]

---

[40] Henry Miller, *To America's Health: A Proposal to Reform the Food and Drug Administration* (Hoover Institution Press, 2000).

[41] This example is taken from an unpublished amicus brief in the *Abigail Alliance* case, which was submitted by several economists including Alex Tabarrok, Daniel Klein, and Sam Peltzman.

[42] Shari Roan, "Swine Flu 'Debacle' of 1976 Is Recalled," *Los Angeles Times*, April 27, 2009, http://articles.latimes.com/2009/apr/27/science/sci-swine-history27.

A third psychological barrier raises a deeper concern about approval requirements. One of the reasons that the current approval system is especially unjust is that it is not clearly effective at preventing dangerous drugs from reaching the market (since the introduction of efficacy requirements did not reduce the proportion of drug recalls). But regulators have an impossible assignment insofar as they are required to prevent all dangerous drugs from reaching the market. Many of the risks associated with new drugs stem from long-term use, drug interactions, or typical users' errors, which are difficult to pick up from clinical trial data. And clinical trial data is only an imperfect guide to assessing efficacy; some drugs are approved as effective but subsequent studies discredit regulators' earlier judgments.[43] No matter how long a trial continues, it is impossible to catch all possible problems before a drug reaches the market.

In sum, policies that require regulators to prevent people from using dangerous drugs entrench, rather than correct, the public's biases. Because citizens indirectly authorize regulators, their biases cause agency officials to make decisions in light of political considerations rather than purely on the basis of which policy would save the most lives. And since everyone is subject to prohibitive premarket requirements, even unbiased medical experts are subject to prohibitive policies that do not reflect medical expertise.

A certificatory system would also subject officials to reputational influences that could potentially effect which drugs are certified. But if patients and medical experts had access to a drug when they judged that a drug's lack of certification reflected an overly cautious agency's judgment, they could still purchase and use drugs in light of the relevant risks and benefits. A certification system would also partially relieve members of regulatory agencies from responsibility for drug disasters because they would not be charged with keeping dangerous drugs off the market. So while some of the psychological biases associated with an approval system would be repeated in a certification system, to the extent that they persist, citizens could at least avoid their deadly effects.

Another distinguishing feature of non-ideal theoretical arguments is that they consider whether policy reforms are feasible in light of social facts. Compare the political feasibility of reforming an approval process to minimize drug lag and drug loss with the feasibility of a certification system. If existing approval policies prompt regulators to be overly cautious because their authority rests on their agency's reputation, then perhaps insulating regulatory agencies from public influence would solve this problem to an extent. One might think that

---

[43] See, e.g., the FDA's decision to rescind their approval of Avastin as an effective breast cancer treatment. "FDA Commissioner Removes Breast Cancer Indication from Avastin Label," Press Announcements, November 18, 2011, http://www.fda.gov/NewsEvents/Newsroom/PressAnnouncements/ucm279485.htm.

privatization could prevent regulators from acting on the basis of political pressure, but privatizing an agency like the FDA would not solve the problems associated with public influence insofar as officials authorize and empower a private agency to enforce approval requirements, just as they currently authorize public agencies to do so. Yet it is the enforcement and policing functions of the FDA that wrongfully causes patients' deaths and distinguishes approval policies from an alternative certificatory system.

Alternatively, after public officials outside the FDA blocked the agency's approval for Plan B, Dan Carpenter proposed that the FDA be reformed to act more like the Federal Reserve. He writes:

> A cabinet secretary—and by extension, a president—has overruled a drug-approval decision by the Food and Drug Administration. The precedent risks placing the real power for drug approval not just with a cabinet secretary, but also with the White House itself. The only solution, then, is to make the F.D.A. *truly independent*. Americans have already done this, through the Federal Reserve, to protect our money supply from political meddling; it's time to do it for drugs.... We would never allow this sort of second-guessing when it comes to our financial health. We should have the same standards when it comes to our public health.[44]

In other words, to enable the FDA to set pharmaceutical policies in ways that promote public health, Carpenter proposes that the agency's power should be more fully insulated from its reputation. Reforming the FDA to be even further insulated from public influence would not only solve the problem of agency curbing, but it would also free the FDA to make policy that promotes the public health more generally. Without the possibility of agency curbing and the need to bow to public opinion, the FDA would no longer be required to play it safe by deciding strategically; rather, it could issue judgments that were solely made dependent on medical considerations.

If Carpenter's proposal for reform successfully insulated the FDA from public pressure, then perhaps the agency could adopt a less deadly balance between Type I and Type II errors than the current policy. But such a proposal is unlikely to succeed because it would require a broad base of democratic support for ceding authority to a non-democratic institution. Carpenter's proposal is to make the FDA more like the Federal Reserve, which regulates monetary policy in the United States. But the Federal Reserve is very unpopular, and recent legislative reforms have limited the power and independence of the Federal Reserve

---

[44] Emphasis added. Daniel Carpenter, "Free the F.D.A.," *New York Times*, December 13, 2011, sec. Opinion, http://www.nytimes.com/2011/12/14/opinion/free-the-fda.html.

and required more transparency.[45] Some policymakers campaign to abolish the Federal Reserve entirely.

A fully independent agency to approve drugs is even less likely to win the necessary political support, considering that agencies like the Federal Reserve do not even prohibit particular individual choices. Also, when people disagree with the judgments of an agency like the Federal Reserve, the agency's practical authority can still be justified by the fact that the nation needs *some* unified monetary policy to maintain economic growth. No similar public good is served by prohibitive pharmaceutical regulations though because an agency could certify drugs instead and allow patients to make their own choices about pharmaceuticals.

This is not to suggest that a certification system is likely to fare any better in light of the relevant political constraints. The previous discussion of the regulatory reversal test began with the premise that voters frequently favor the status quo without justification, and just as they would likely oppose making pharmaceutical regulators more powerful and independent, they would likely oppose a certificatory system as well. But to the extent that the merits of a proposal for reform depend on political feasibility, reforms in favor or a more just, efficient, and effective approval system face many of the same political hurdles as reforms in favor of a certificatory system.

A better approval system is also unlikely to be feasible in light of physical facts simply because of the nature of its mission. Approval requirements encounter the competing pulls of two goals: improving the effectiveness of drug screening to minimize the number of drug recalls and accidental poisonings, and helping patients access the drugs they need as quickly as possible. These two constraints reflect the physical constraints that challenge hypothetical proposals for reform. Clinical trials provide useful information about drug safety but take years to conduct and interpret, so it is not feasible to implement a system that speeds trials because some of the effects we are interested in don't show up until later. In contrast, a certificatory system would resolve this tension by abandoning the goal of minimizing the number of drug recalls and dangerous drugs on the market and focusing on the informational function. In this way, it would be more feasible for a certification system to meet its goals than an approval system.

In addition to the feasibility of a proposal in light of psychological, social, and physical facts, non-ideal theory is also concerned with people's potential non-compliance with a policy. People generally comply with existing approval

[45] Rasmussen Reports, "74% Want to Audit the Federal Reserve," November 8, 2013, http://www.rasmussenreports.com/public_content/business/general_business/november_2013/74_want_to_audit_the_federal_reserve; Gallup, "CDC Tops Agency Ratings; Federal Reserve Board Lowest," *Gallup.com*, July 10, 2009, http://www.gallup.com/poll/121886/CDC-Tops-Agency-Ratings-Federal-Reserve-Board-Lowest.aspx.

polices (I will discuss exceptions in the next chapter), so compliance is not a significant barrier to reforming an approval system. There is also little reason to think that officials would refuse to comply with a duty to certify drugs in the absence of approval requirements, since they currently comply with their duties to certify drugs.

On the other hand, one may be concerned that a compliance with a certification system would be less likely because manufacturers would be more likely to mislead patients about the nature of their products if they were permitted to sell drugs before the drugs were approved for particular conditions. There are two ways in which a patient may be misled about the nature of a drug. First, a manufacturer may provide her with insufficient information to judge a product, and she may make incorrect inferences about a drug in the absence of information. This failure would not necessarily constitute a failure to comply with a certification system, as long as patients were aware of a drug's uncertified status. Insofar as an approval process is necessary to protect patients from making choices that are so misinformed as to constitute a failure of patients' consent, then public officials should question patients' ability to consent to the drug during clinical trials and to consent to use approved drugs off-label. Though there are legitimate reasons to be concerned about people's ability to make judgments in the absence of information, as long as a person is aware of the potential for ignorance, she may take this form of uncertainty into account as she decides, just as she accounts for the uncertainty associated with taking a drug that has known risks.

Second, in the absence of approval requirements, one may worry that manufacturers would be more likely to commit fraud. If manufacturers could sell drugs without authorization, then a greater number of drugs for which there is no consensus about safety or efficacy would be available to the public.[46] Without a consensus, it would be more difficult for consumers to ascertain the truth or falsity of marketing materials and drug labels and more difficult for people to establish that they were harmed by misleading information.

This is a legitimate concern about the feasibility of fraud regulations and likely non-compliance with fraud regulations under a certification system. However, proponents of a certification system have resources to address likely non-compliance short of enforcing deadly approval requirements. For example,

---

[46] One may also worry about manufactures' influence on the courts that regulate fraud. Yet, as I discuss in a later description of off-label marketing, courts are not generally disposed to rule in favor of manufactures in labeling and marketing cases. Moreover, concerns about institutional corruption would apply with equal force to manufacturers" influence on regulatory agencies as it does regarding the courts, if not more so, because regulators address a more narrow subset of industry. For this reason, to the extent that concerns about institutional corruption raise the possibility that officials will not comply with their duties under a certification system, they apply with equal or greater force to potential approval systems too.

manufacturers should be liable for deceptive and fraudulent marketing under a certification system, just as they are currently responsible for the claims they make in their labeling and marketing materials. If laws that prohibit fraud were reliably enforced and if the penalties were substantial, then public officials could deter firms from making false or deceptive claims about their products even if firms were authorized to sell drugs without premarket approval. To the extent that holding manufacturers responsible for fraud is not a sufficient deterrent, officials could increase the penalties for fraud rather than preemptively requiring an entire industry to seek approval for every label and advertisement.

Pharmaceutical manufacturers, like firms in other industries, also have substantial incentives to seek certification to prove that they have quality products. Investors may reasonably call for certification as a condition of their continued support. This is not to say all firms would have decisive incentives to seek government certification. Already, private companies, such as hospitals, insurers, and managed care organizations, use their own standards to assess the safety and efficacy of approved drugs when they develop drug formularies. This practice of certifying drugs for use by specific hospital patients or insurance plan members would be even more valuable in the absence of approval requirements.

On the other hand, concerns about manufacturers' non-compliance with fraud regulations may persist in light of the fact that some businesses have incentives to prioritize short-term profits over long-term safety and efficacy. Under a certification system, firms would be permitted to sell drugs on the basis of limited, short-term evidence as long as patients were aware of the lack of long-term studies. Under such a system, one may worry that firms would also lead patients to believe that their products did not carry long-term risks and that it would be difficult to seek damages on behalf of patients who were the victims of these false claims. The Vioxx recall illustrates this point: sometimes it's difficult to identify the patients who are harmed through long-term use when the harmful long-term effects of a drug consist in an elevated risk of events that are likely to occur anyhow. Yet this particular worry about fraud and non-compliance applies with equal force to approval and certification requirements, since the concern is that manufacturers may fail to investigate long-term effects, which the approval process is poorly equipped to assess as well.

The final requirement of non-ideal theory is to consider that in some circumstances a policy is justified as the best available option, even if a better option would be available if concerns about feasibility and non-compliance were not in play. Yet in the case of pharmaceutical regulation, concerns about the psychological, social, and physical feasibility of effective reform undermine calls to reform the existing approval system more than they undermine the case for a certification system. And the concern that a certification system would potentially cause less compliance with fraud standards can be addressed by strengthening fraud protections rather than through an approval system.

Those who nevertheless suspect that the effects of a certification system would be awful given the aforementioned non-ideal considerations should consider why they value the current approval system. Do people value approval requirements for their epistemic benefits (informing patients and providers about the nature of new products) or for their prohibitive effects (preventing people from using new products until they are better understood)? If they value the epistemic benefits of an approval system, a certification system can provide the same benefits. Those who also value the prohibitive effects of an approval system can continue to live their lives as if an approval system is still in place by refusing to use uncertified drugs. If all citizens valued the prohibitive effects of an approval system, then, under a certification system, citizens would universally comply with regulators' recommendations, and patterns of pharmaceutical use would look the same as they do under an approval system.

To the extent that the effects of a certification system would differ from the effects of approval requirements, those differences would be explained by the fact that some citizens would choose not to defer to regulators' judgments. In these circumstances, a certification system would allow patients to consent to use risky drugs whereas approval requirements would force all patients to comply with risky and deadly prohibitions. So while considerations of feasibility and compliance are relevant to non-ideal political theory, when we consider the effects of various proposals for pharmaceutical policy reform in non-ideal theory, even if the effects of various proposals are uncertain, we should also bear in mind the clear moral advantage of a certification system. Namely, whatever its failures in implementation, one effect of a certification system is that officials would not be empowered and encouraged to kill patients by withholding access to lifesaving drugs.

Turning to ideal theory, compare a regulatory system where citizens and public officials could overcome psychological and political barriers with a more effective and humane approval process to a certification system. A principled evaluation of an approval policy's merits may proceed by assuming that officials could overcome their biases and fully comply with the law. But such an evaluation should then be compared with the principled evaluation of a certification system, which may proceed with the assumption that patients and providers are also capable of overcoming well-known cognitive biases and that manufacturers fully comply with anti-fraud legislation and good manufacturing practices. Through the lens of ideal theory, the primary reason to favor a certification system over approval requirements in principle is that approval requirements unnecessarily violate patients' rights when officials could ensure safe drug use in other ways.

All approval delays are marked by the *pro tanto* wrongfulness of coercion because they are backed by legal penalties. If a person distributes an unapproved drug, then he is subject to legal penalties such as fines or jail time. These policies violate patients' rights of self-medication. Since it is better if a person suffers drug-related harms because she knowingly chose to use a dangerous drug than if she suffers because a regulator coercively prohibited her from using a potentially therapeutic drug, coercive approval requirements are *pro tanto* worse than a system that relies on coercive threats.[47] Coercion can be justified if it is necessary to prevent wrongdoing or some other justified goal, but coercive approval policies are unnecessary because, as I argued in the previous sections, officials could achieve most of the goals of approval by providing patients and providers with incentives to self-medicate in accordance with recommendations instead of by enforcing prohibitions. For example, officials could pay citizens to comply with a certification agency's recommendations, and insurance providers could provide incentives as well.

Critics of ideal theory may reject the usefulness of assessing policy in light of these assumptions. As Laura Valentini, writes, ideal theoretical arguments are often paradoxically offered as necessary for guiding us in thinking about what we should do and incapable of offering any concrete proposals, and it is difficult to strike a balance between sticking to one's principles while considering the relevant facts.[48] But it is nevertheless important to consider which principles are sensitive to psychological facts and political constraints, even if it is difficult to strike the right balance, because otherwise people may risk letting themselves off the hook for falling short of doing what they ought to do simply because people are not motivated to do it.[49] In the face of non-ideal constraints, it is important to acknowledge that non-ideal proposals do not always reflect our values and that it is valuable in itself to know if a policy can be justified in principle even if the policy would never be achieved in practice. Thinking about which policy would be ideal can also clarify other values, and therefore provide theoretical resources for assessing existing policies.

So even if approval requirements were a decent pragmatic response to concerns about manufacturers' failure to comply with anti-fraud legislation and patients' ignorance about their health and the effects of drugs (a claim that I dispute in the previous section), they would not be justified in principle when compared with a certification system. All else equal, if it were feasible to either educate a patient or to force him or her to comply with medical recommendations, the educative approach would be morally better. This ideal has equal force in clinical and public health contexts.

[47] And there are other reasons to prefer certification to approval as a matter of principle too, such as the expressive harms of paternalism and the inegalitarian effects of a policy that empowers officials to kill some of society's worst-off members ostensibly for the sake of the greater good.

[48] Laura Valentini, "On the Apparent Paradox of Ideal Theory*," *Journal of Political Philosophy* 17, no. 3 (September 1, 2009): 332–55, doi:10.1111/j.1467-9760.2008.00317.x.

[49] Zofia Stemplowska and Department of Philosophy, Florida State University, "What's Ideal About Ideal Theory?:," ed. Margaret Dancy, Victoria Costa, and Joshua Gert, *Social Theory and Practice* 34, no. 3 (2008): 319–40, doi:10.5840/soctheorpract200834320.

In summary, just as officials should not use civilians' bodies and homes as human shields in the service of a just cause, especially when it is unnecessary, officials also should not violate patients' rights to advance scientific knowledge or to discourage wrongdoing when there are other ways to accomplish these goals. So even if there would be some costs to rescinding prohibitive approval policies, these costs could not justify the rights violations that the existing requirements entail.

4.4 The Risks of an Approval System

Even if some approval requirements could be effectively enforced in ways that minimized the severity of rights violations and the loss of life that characterizes the existing system, enforcing premarket approval policies is extremely morally risky, whereas allowing patients to access unapproved drugs is not as morally risky. Second-order considerations of moral risk lend further support to the normative justification of a certification system.

In cases of life and death, the mere risk that an action could be wrong is a reason against doing it if that risk is substantial.[50] First-order moral deliberation about whether killing is justified is insufficient to justify killing because just as a person can be culpably reckless in exposing others to an undue risk of harm, he can also be culpably reckless in deliberating about the wrongfulness of harming others. In both cases, people should be very cautious about killing or risking the lives of others. Dan Moller defends this principle by appealing to the fact that each of us has reason to believe that we are mistaken about moral facts, just as people in the past were mistaken about the ethics of slavery and warfare.[51] And it is especially easy for someone to err in moral reasoning when he is deliberating things that are very complicated, such as things that involve large numbers of people, uncertainty, or probabilistic judgments.

This is not to say that people should never act in ways that could potentially kill or suggest that public officials should be paralyzed by extreme moral caution in all that they do. Officials should only take action that involves killing, such as the enforcement of approval polices, when there are compelling moral reasons in favor of it, taking one's moral uncertainty and awareness of moral uncertainty into account.[52] Moller suggests that the relevant reasons should account for the likelihood that an action involves wrongdoing, the severity of the wrongdoing,

---

[50] Alexander A. Guerrero, "Don't Know, Don't Kill: Moral Ignorance, Culpability, and Caution," *Philosophical Studies* 136, no. 1 (2007): 59–97.

[51] D. Moller, "Abortion and Moral Risk," *Philosophy* 86, no. 3 (July 2011): 425–43, doi:10.1017/S0031819111000222.

[52] Guerrero, "Don't Know, Don't Kill."

the cost of not acting, the agent's level of responsibility for wrongdoing if it turns out that it was wrong to act, and the potential wrongdoing of not acting.[53] He therefore concludes that public officials should avoid enforcing policies that potentially violate rights even if they believe that it is justified. We might add that officials have especially strong reasons to avoid violating rights when it is unnecessary.

Turning to approval policies, public officials should consider the likelihood that delaying access to a drug is wrong even if they are skeptical of the foregoing arguments. If I am right about the wrongness of enforcing approval policies, then public officials kill patients, which is a severe wrongdoing. In contrast, it would be less costly or morally risky to refrain from prohibiting people from accessing unapproved drugs because then patients would have the opportunity to consent to the risks of a drug, which would mitigate officials' responsibility for risky pharmaceutical use. But with approval requirements, officials are responsible for the deaths they cause by enforcing approval policies.

An analogy to just war theory further illustrates my claim that officials should refrain from enforcing approval policies for second-order reasons even if they reject my first-order arguments against approval policies. In warfare, there is a very high burden of justification for killing people who are not liable to be killed, such as civilians. This justificatory burden requires that the killing be both necessary and proportionate to the goods achieved by killing. Yet in the domestic context, public officials do not hold themselves to these same justificatory standards when enforcing policies that cause their own citizens to die. Even if one rejects my previous arguments that citizens have rights of self-medication and that approval requirements kill citizens, the enforcement of deadly approval policies still is neither necessary nor proportionate to the good it achieves since a certification system could achieve most of the benefits of preventing drug poisonings without causing people to die while waiting for approval. So even if regulators reject the foregoing arguments, if domestic policy officials held themselves to the same justificatory standards that soldiers apply to circumstances of warfare, then officials would find that the case for enforcing approval requirements is not strong enough to justify the lives lost.

Of course, it is not always simple for people to know that they are doing something that is morally risky, just as it is not always simple for people to know that they are acting wrongly. Some philosophers suggest that blameless factual and moral ignorance can be an excuse, so we should withhold assessments of moral culpability when people are ignorant of moral requirements.[54] If regulators are

---

[53] Moller, "Abortion and Moral Risk."

[54] Gideon Rosen, "Culpability and Ignorance," *Proceedings of the Aristotelian Society* 103, New Series (January 1, 2003): 61–84.

blamelessly ignorant of the moral wrongness of causing patients to die while waiting for drugs or of the moral wrongness of taking such a risk, assuming they discharged their epistemic duties, then they might be excused from blame for regulation.

This argument is controversial. One may object that blameless moral ignorance is not an excuse, even though blameless factual ignorance is exculpatory.[55] If so, regulators are morally responsible for the deaths they cause through regulation even if they do not know that it is wrong to cause deaths in this way. Yet the actions of regulators are still wrong, even if they are personally excused from responsibility because they are blamelessly ignorant of the fact that it is wrong to kill patients by withholding access to therapeutic medicines or to take such a substantial risk. Consider how manufacturers are rightly held liable when they make misleading claims about dangerous drugs. Those manufacturers are liable because patients could not consent to use drugs without reliable information. Preventing patients from making voluntary choices about their treatment is wrong. Even if a manufacturer's employees mistakenly thought they were not misleading patients, if a drug is fraudulently advertised or mislabeled, then the employees acted wrongly. Similarly, employees at regulatory agencies may not think they act wrongly, but they do insofar as their actions prevent patients from making treatment decisions.

In both cases, organizations that impermissibly violate patients' rights of self-medication should be held liable for the harms they cause and for their lack of caution in morally risky circumstances. Though public officials who enforce approval requirements do not know the identities of those who are harmed, if they know that there is some probability that a portion of people waiting for access will be harmed by a lack of access, they are responsible for the harmful effects of their risky policy just as manufacturers are responsible for the harmful effects of risky drugs when the risks are not disclosed and patients could not consent to the risks. Today, manufacturers who fraudulently market drugs can be legally compelled to pay patients who were harmed. So too, the government should be legally required to compensate patients and their families when patients are harmed by coercive approval policies.

I do not doubt that the employees of regulatory agencies believe they are doing the right thing when they require approval for new drugs, but that belief is not sufficient to justify their lack of caution. Researchers and public officials who prevent manufacturers from selling investigational drugs to patients believe that they are protecting patients from making a harmful and dangerous choice but fail to consider the harms and dangers of their own choices.

---

[55] Elizabeth Harman, "Does Moral Ignorance Exculpate?," *Ratio* 24, no. 4 (November 9, 2011): 443–68.

4.5 The Risks of a Certification System

Do similar considerations about moral risk apply to manufactures that sell potentially harmful drugs? In the previous section, I argued that even those who reject the foregoing arguments against approval requirements should consider that the mere possibility that these arguments succeed is a reason for caution. But similarly, the mere possibility that the foregoing arguments do not succeed may be a reason for manufacturers to exercise caution in the provision of new drugs. It is morally risky to make pharmaceuticals. Manufacturers are not only uncertain about the risks of their products, but they may also be morally uncertain about the permissibility of selling dangerous products to consumers, especially in light of concerns about exploitation. These moral risks should inform manufacturers' conduct. In some cases it may be wrong to provide patients with dangerous drugs or to exploit patients because doing so shows a lack of moral caution. But even if manufacturers should exercise moral caution when developing and selling drugs, the chance that they are acting wrongly does not necessarily tell in favor of policy interventions.

For manufacturers, two kinds of risks are worth considering. First, when manufacturers develop and sell new pharmaceuticals, they risk negligently selling dangerous drugs or misleading patients, even if they do not knowingly act wrongly. I have argued that if a manufacturer takes care to disclose all known and unknown risks, then it is not wrong to sell dangerous drugs. But this is a controversial statement. It may be wrong to sell drugs about which little is known even if that fact is disclosed. I have also defended the controversial claim that it is not wrong to sell investigational drugs to patients with terminal illnesses, but this claim is controversial too. Some philosophers argue that profiting from another's person extreme need or depravation is wrong because it exploitative. These considerations may give manufacturers reason to be exceptionally cautious when providing people with access to investigational drugs, but, even if manufacturers do fail to exercise appropriate moral caution, it does not follow that public officials may permissibly prevent them from selling unapproved therapies.

The first argument against selling investigational drugs because of the moral risks concerns the risks of providing desperate people with products when there is limited information. The possibility that I am wrong about patients' ability to consent to unknown risks of drugs may call for manufacturers to be exceptionally cautious about selling uncertified drugs. They may therefore choose to implement testing requirements for patients or to require authorization from a physician for patients to use their uncertified products. Though I have suggested that such a policy would be unnecessarily paternalistic and would express an offensive judgment about patients' ability to choose their course of treatment, insofar as manufacturers have the right to decline to sell their products at all, they would also be entitled to sell their products only under certain conditions out of a desire to be cautious and to avoid moral risks.

On the other hand, the potential moral risks of selling uncertified drugs would not license an approval system, even if manufacturers do have obligations to exercise caution in distributing their uncertified products. Public officials should exercise caution when considering interference because there are substantial moral risks to preemptively interfering with transactions between patients and manufacturers, even if manufacturers' conduct is also morally risky. If manufacturers do have duties to take extra care to obtain consent when selling investigational drugs, then public officials may at most hold manufacturers liable for failures to disclose the required information.

The second argument against selling investigational drugs for reasons related to moral risk concerns the risks of exploitation. The argument goes like this: Exploitation consists in taking advantage of someone who is badly off. Exploitation is wrong. Selling potentially dangerous and ineffective investigational drugs to dying patients takes advantage of people who are badly off. So selling investigational drugs is wrong. I have suggested that this argument is unsound because exploitation is not immoral, since it does not violate a person's rights when one simply gives her an additional option. The paradigm cases of exploitation are those where a vulnerable person's only reasonable option benefits whoever is providing that option much more than it benefits the vulnerable person. But in these cases, whoever provides a vulnerable person with an additional option still benefits her more than anyone else does.[56] So while desperate and dying patients are vulnerable and, by selling drugs to them, a manufacturer may be accused of profiting from their desperation, it is unclear why manufacturers act more wrongly than people who do nothing for sick patients. As Matt Zwolinski has argued, if it is permissible to decline to interact with people who are badly off, it is also permissible to give them an offer if by refusing that offer they would not be any worse off.[57]

But this argument could be false, and if it is, then manufacturers may wrongfully exploit patients by profiting from the sale of investigational therapies to desperate people. In light of this possibility, manufacturers may have reason to avoid charging exorbitant prices for drugs that are unlikely to work. Concerns about moral risk could theoretically support a more cautious approach to drug prices if it were possible to provide more affordable access without diminishing

---

[56] Alan Wertheimer and Matt Zwolinski, "Exploitation," in *The Stanford Encyclopedia of Philosophy*, ed. Edward N. Zalta, Spring 2013, http://plato.stanford.edu/archives/spr2013/entries/exploitation/.

[57] Matt Zwolinski, "Price Gouging, Non-Worseness, and Distributive Justice," SSRN Scholarly Paper (Rochester, NY: Social Science Research Network, February 4, 2009), http://papers.ssrn.com/abstract=1337654.

incentives to develop new drugs. On the other hand, insofar as one accepts this argument, it would not apply uniquely to investigational therapies but also to all drugs that are marketed to sick and dying patients and other lifesaving products too. For example, if a patient is diagnosed with bacterial meningitis, he must purchase and use an expensive antibiotic to save his life. But whether the antibiotic is an investigational drug or not does not seem relevant when we ask if it is permissible for a manufacturer to sell it to him at a high price. If it were wrongly exploitative to target the worst off when selling drugs, then that argument would seemingly call for a cautious approach to the sale of approved drugs as well. In light of this consideration, it is clear that caution carries its own risks. Manufacturers' voluntarily limiting the prices of lifesaving drugs could deter investment in therapeutics going forward. For this reason, considerations of moral risk may not call for a cautious approach to the sale of investigational drugs on balance even if there are *pro tanto* reasons to account for uncertainty about the wrongfulness of exploitation.

But even if it were wrong to risk exploiting patients by selling unapproved therapies, it still wouldn't follow from that claim that manufacturers ought to be legally prohibited from providing investigational drugs to patients. This is because it would be *more risky* to legally limit the options of the worst off, even if it is also immoral in some way to provide those options. For example, paying low wages might be morally risky. To the extent that it is, potential sweatshop owners have reasons to raise wages in light of their moral uncertainty as long as high wages would not deter employment. But for similar reasons, public officials would also have reason to permit low sweatshop wages, in light of the moral risks associated with coercion.

Furthermore, those who would press the charge of exploitation against manufacturers who would sell unapproved drugs should consider that approval policies that limit patients' options make exploitation more likely, not less. For example, patients are more likely to make imprudent, desperate decisions when more conventional treatments are unavailable.[58] So allowing patients who have no other medical options rights to try investigational therapies could reduce allegations of exploitation on balance if it prevented alternative care centers and supplement manufacturers from profiting from vulnerable patients with few remaining choices.

---

[58] A similar story applies to prescription requirements. According to the US Federal Trade Commission, consumers spend more money on supplements during an economic downturn because it is expensive to visit a doctor in order to gain access to approved therapies. Federal Trade Commission, "Health Claims" Media Resources https://www.ftc.gov/news-events/media-resources/truth-advertising/health-claims, 2009.

4.6 Conclusion

In summary, I have argued that public officials wrongfully kill patients by withholding access to investigational drugs. Public officials' belief that patients ought to be protected from the option to use dangerous drugs, even if some patients will die as a result of these protections, relies on the premise that it is morally worse for patients to be killed than to be allowed to die. I accept this distinction, but a second look at the case reveals that manufacturers do not kill patients by selling potentially dangerous investigational therapies because patients can consent to the risks of the treatment. And a third look reveals that well-intentioned employees at regulatory agencies are culpable for the deaths they cause when they prevent patients from choosing to use investigational therapies.

This killing cannot be excused by the need to test because approval requirements are not necessary to obtain information about new drugs. Nor can worries about manipulative marketing or the exploitation of vulnerable patients justify an approval system. Perhaps, regulators are blamelessly ignorant of the moral facts. This could be the case if regulators believe that drug lag is not morally wrong. Nevertheless, officials are also obligated to exercise caution when coercing people, especially in matters of life and death. So even if officials are not convinced of the wrongfulness of killing people by enforcing approval requirements, the mere risk of wrongful killing calls for a more cautious approach to regulation.

I have also developed a methodological argument in this chapter, which is that assessments of an approval system should be held to the same standards as assessments of a certification system. One may object to calls for a certification system on the grounds that reform is infeasible, but the same can be said of efforts at a more just approval system. Are we then to accept the deadly status quo? Perhaps the status quo approval system will persist, but that doesn't mean it ought to. And as a matter of ideal theory, a certification system is clearly preferable because it avoids the wrongfulness of unnecessarily coercing patients and providers and killing people through approval delays.

5

The Politics of Self-Medication

On October 11, 1988, more than one thousand protesters gathered outside the headquarters of the FDA to protest the FDA's slow approval process and failure to support the development of AIDS treatments. They stopped traffic and blocked entrances. Some protestors held signs saying things like "RIP—Killed by the FDA" and chanted "Hey, Hey FDA—how many people did you kill today?" At least 120 protesters were arrested by police officers who wore surgical gloves and helmets.[1] An organization called AIDS Coalition to Unleash Power (ACT UP) organized the protest, as well as several other activist campaigns on behalf of AIDS patients and AIDS awareness. According to Gregg Bordowitz, who was one of the principal organizers of the FDA protest, the goal of the protests was to "cut through the bureaucratic red tape" of the FDA and also to ensure that people with AIDS were involved in decision-making about research related to treatment and cures.

The ACT UP protests were exceptional in their scope and influence, but political opposition to limits on self-medication is not uncommon. At every stage of drug development, patients and their advocates have asserted their rights of self-medication in institutional contexts that limit medical autonomy. During the early stages of drug development, citizen scientists not only participate in early stage research by funding studies and shaping the design and goals of experiments, but also, in some cases, play a role in developing and testing new treatments. During later stages of development, patients and their families use social media to support calls for compassionate access. As trials continue, patient groups protest and petition for accelerated approval and expanded access to drugs that treat specific conditions, such as muscular dystrophy or ALS (amoyotrophic lateral sclerosis).

---

[1] United Press International, "Police Arrest AIDS Protesters Blocking Access to FDA Offices," *Los Angeles Times*, October 11, 1988, http://articles.latimes.com/1988-10-11/news/mn-3909_1_police-arrest-aids-protesters.

When drugs are not approved, patients and their physicians may engage in civil disobedience. For example, advocates of self-medication have disobeyed laws that prohibit assisted suicide or medical marijuana on the grounds that such prohibitive policies were illegitimate. Patient activism and protest also draws attention to the deaths caused by prohibitive regulations. For example, right to try activists have successfully convinced twenty-four state legislatures in the United States to adopt legislation that would facilitate terminally ill patients' access to unapproved experimental drugs.

In this chapter, I discuss the ethics of patient activism and the political changes that a right of self-medication would require. My argument follows the trajectory of a drug's development. I begin by discussing the ethics of patient-driven drug development. I argue that patients should be included in the drug development process and that they should not be prohibited from developing and testing treatments on their own as well. I also make the case that privately funded medical research by patients and foundations is no more fraught than research funded by universities and governments. Second, I discuss justifications of other forms of patient activism during the approval process, such as social media campaigns for compassionate access and political advocacy for drug approval. Though the language of compassionate access suggests that regulators are benevolent when they grant patients the right to use unapproved therapies, I argue that those who request compassionate access should be seen as victims of political oppression because the state threatens their lives.

Since existing pharmaceutical policies are seriously unjust, I argue in the third section that civil disobedience and illegal distribution of pharmaceuticals is justified. I then present several reasons that those who disobey pharmaceutical policies should not be required to publically disobey for the purpose of drawing attention to an unjust law. Rather, secret disobedience and disobedience that is not politically motivated is morally permissible. Fourth, I consider larger scale efforts at patient activism, such as the ACT UP and right to try movements, and I argue that citizens have duties to support these efforts or at least to not oppose them. Finally, I consider the kinds of political reforms that would be necessary to protect rights of self-medication. I argue that political reforms should proceed by way of constitutional change and judicial bodies should protect rights of self-medication. Limits on self-medication developed through popular calls for greater regulation, but these democratic sentiments are influenced by unjustified cognitive biases, and they support policies that violate people's rights. For these reasons, voters do not have the authority to pass laws that limit self-medication and constitutional measures are preferable to democratic or legislative initiatives.

5.1   Patient-Driven Development

The phrase "nothing about us without us" is popular within the disability rights movement.[2] It is meant to convey the idea that disabled people should be included when medical professionals and public officials make decisions that affect their lives. The same can be said of all people, but especially for patients who are suffering from diseases that pharmaceutical researchers aim to treat. Since patients have rights to pursue treatment options, including access to unapproved drugs, participating in the process of drug development is one way for patients to assert these rights even before a specific treatment exists.

In recent years, patients have claimed a greater role in drug development and treatment within the pharmaceutical industry and throughout the regulatory process. For example, the FDA recently introduced a new initiative for patient-focused drug development, which aims to include patients' perspectives in pharmaceutical research at every stage.[3] Patients will have an opportunity to provide information about their experiences that inform researchers' and regulators' assessments of risks and benefits. Or patients can help researchers develop more efficient ways of communicating about new drugs. And patient-focused development may also empower patients to influence researchers' priorities and the goals of treatment development. Patient-focused drug development is currently limited to meetings with a narrow set of patient populations, but the initiative represents a shift to greater inclusion of patients in pharmaceutical development.[4]

Other forms of patient-driven drug development occur outside of formal research settings and regulatory institutions. Patients fund trials, develop and test pharmaceutical and alternative therapies, and form communities of citizen-scientists that share research and experiences in order to provide better treatment for people within their disease communities. Citizen-science movements are found within rare disease communities where there is little institutional or industry support for research and among large patient populations whose collective voices can be particularly influential. Some companies have recently facilitated greater patient involvement in the development process as well.

The first way that patients can play a greater role in development is by financing trials or paying to participate in trials. Amy Marcus calls these practices "venture philanthropy," which refers to a system where patients can provide support

[2] James Charlton, *Nothing About Us Without Us: Disability Oppression and Empowerment* (Berkeley: University of California Press, 2000).

[3] Eleanor M. Perfetto et al., "Patient-Focused Drug Development: A New Direction for Collaboration," *Medical Care* 53, no. 1 (January 2015): 9–17, doi:10.1097/MLR.0000000000000273.

[4] Ibid.

for early stage research and therefore shift attention to questions that concern their own patient community.[5] In some cases, venture philanthropy can not only finance effective treatments but also generate revenue for future research. For example, the Cystic Fibrosis Foundation recently received a $3.3 billion payout, which was a financial return for its early investment in a drug that was subsequently approved by the FDA as a treatment for the lung disease.[6] Critics alleged that the Cystic Fibrosis Foundation should not have been in a position to profit from the high price of treatment because it would conflict with their interest in advocating low drug prices for people with cystic fibrosis. Yet others reply that it is good that some of the profits from new treatments go toward further improving cystic fibrosis patients' lives and funding new research, which would not be guaranteed if all profits went to a pharmaceutical company.[7]

Alexander Masters describes another model of patient-funded development where clinical trials are funded in part by patients who purchase the chance to receive a potentially effective treatment.[8] As a preliminary test of this system, he describes a new trial, which will allow people who wish to purchase a place in a glioblastoma trial to pay $2 million to secure a spot if they meet the inclusion criteria.[9] As long as the inclusion of wealthy patients does not disadvantage people who cannot pay or hurt their chances of participating in a trial, Masters argues that allowing patients to secure their place in a trial could be a viable way to finance medical research. Of course, such a system would only work if patients were prohibited from purchasing unapproved therapies directly. But in light of prohibitive approval policies, Masters's financing model allows more patients to effectively exercise their rights of self-medication by using unapproved drugs.

Another form of patient-driven drug development is more direct. In some cases, patients or their family members may develop and test therapies on themselves, and share their results and experiences with people who suffer from the same diseases. As an example of this approach, consider Chris and Hugh Hempel's efforts to develop an experimental treatment for their twin daughters, Addi and Cassi. The Hempel twins suffer from Niemann-Pick Type C (NPC), which is a rare and fatal progressive disease that causes degeneration of the nervous system and dementia.[10] Most children with NPC require extensive care

---

[5] Amy Dockser Marcus, "The Loneliness of Fighting a Rare Cancer," *Health Affairs* 29, no. 1 (January 1, 2010): 203–6, doi:10.1377/hlthaff.2009.0470.

[6] Andrew Pollack, "Deal by Cystic Fibrosis Foundation Raises Cash and Some Concern," *New York Times*, November 19, 2014, http://www.nytimes.com/2014/11/19/business/for-cystic-fibrosis-foundation-venture-yields-windfall-in-hope-and-cash.html.

[7] Ibid.

[8] Alexander Masters, "A Plutocratic Proposal," *Mosaic*, April 7, 2015, http://mosaicscience.com/story/plutocratic-proposal.

[9] Ibid.

[10] Marcus, "Niemann-Pick Type C."

as they lose the ability to eat, walk, and talk, then die before reaching adulthood. The disease is generally resistant to treatment, but when Chris Hempel's daughters were diagnosed with NPC, she researched all potential therapies, including animal studies of NPC. She eventually discovered very limited evidence that cyclodextrin, a sugary substance used to dissolve other drugs, extended the lives of mice with NPC. Hempel ordered powdered cyclodextrin and tested the substance on herself for a few weeks before giving it to her twin daughters. Hempel then petitioned the FDA for access to intravenous cyclodextrin and was granted permission for a physician to administer it to the twins. Though it was not a miracle cure, the twins improved after using the drug, and it seemed to slow the progression of their disease. Chris Hempel then shared her experiences with the drug and organized other parents whose children were using experimental cyclodextrin to collect patient data, as the National Institutes of Health (NIH) ran a parallel trial on other children with NPC.

If Chris Hempel had not started the drug development process on her own, cyclodextrin research for children with NPC may never have progressed. NPC is a rare disease, and there are limited resources for research that addresses it. Nevertheless, some parents of children with NPC questioned the Hempels' decision to give their daughters cyclodextrin because it had not been tested or approved as a treatment for NPC and was potentially more risky than allowing the disease to progress.[11] Cassi suffered a blood clot related to the catheter she used to receive cyclodextrin that paralyzed the left side of her body. Subsequent research found that cyclodextrin infusion could cause NPC patients to become deaf, though it may also extend their lives.[12] And for children with NPC, rights of self-medication cannot justify the risks because the children cannot give informed consent to treatment. On the other hand, parents and physicians may reasonably judge that "home remedies" give their children the best chance at managing a rare or terminal illness. Medical professionals agreed with the Hempels that cyclodextrin was a promising treatment and supported their treatment plan.

For adult patients, the case for DIY drug development is even stronger, because patient-driven development may uncover promising new treatment possibilities, but, even if it didn't, adult patients are entitled to make their own treatment decisions and exercise their rights of self-medication. Those who claim that drug development outside institutional or regulatory contexts should be discouraged on the grounds that patients are not qualified to develop drugs without any professional or regulatory oversight must also question whether

---

[11] Ibid.

[12] Amy Dockser Marcus, "Deaf or Death? In Drug Trial, Parents Weigh Life vs. Hearing Loss," *Wall Street Journal*, March 2, 2015, sec. Business, http://www.wsj.com/articles/deaf-or-death-in-drug-trial-parents-weigh-life-vs-hearing-loss-1425267002.

patients are qualified to refuse treatment without professional or regulatory oversight. If so, then the same considerations justify these forms of patient-driven drug development.

Patients may also facilitate pharmaceutical development through communities of citizen-scientists. Consider the story of David deBronkart, who was one of the earlier "e-patients" to advocate patient empowerment through online networks. When deBronkart was diagnosed with stage IV renal-cell carcinoma, he joined an online community of cancer patients where he learned about new treatments that were relatively unknown.[13] DeBronkart attributes his survival partly to the treatment information and support he found in his online community. While physicians and researchers still play an important role, deBronkart argues that other patients know things that are relevant to treatment decisions that medical professionals are unlikely to know, such as new therapies, and things that they cannot know, such as the experience of treatment and potential side effects.

DeBronkart's experience is just one example of a more general phenomenon, where patients are using online networks to gain access to drugs that are newly approved or still in development. Amid calls for greater access to medical research, open data and open science, patients can increasingly play a role not only in choosing treatments but also in developing new ones. Eric Topol also describes how patients can use online communities to influence drug development. For example, ALS patients used publically available information and their own data to test an unapproved therapy:

> Studying [Phase 1 studies] enabled one patient with ALS to conclude that the active drug in one of these early Phase 1 studies was sodium chlorite. Affected patients began treating themselves with this chemical, which is obtained by bleaching paper pulp. Collectively, via the social online health network PatientsLikeMe, a rapid crowdsourced clinical trial took form, albeit without controls.... [The trial showed] no sign of efficacy. In fact, taking sodium chlorite was associated with an adverse effect. Using clever algorithms, PatientsLikeMe can simulate a randomized trial within their database and had already demonstrated that another candidate drug for ALS, lithium bicarbonate was ineffective using this method. That finding was subsequently validated by a traditional, expensive, and time consuming randomized trial.[14]

[13] Dave deBronkart, "How the E-Patient Community Helped Save My Life: An Essay by Dave deBronkart," *BMJ* 346 (April 2, 2013): f1990, doi:10.1136/bmj.f1990.

[14] Eric Topol, *The Patient Will See You Now: The Future of Medicine Is in Your Hands* (New York: Basic Books, 2015), 213.

Topol writes that pharmaceutical companies also use online networks to recruit patients for clinical trials, which could further improve patients' access to unapproved medications.

New businesses and nonprofits have recently emerged to further facilitate this patient-driven approach. MyTomorrows is a patient platform that helps patients find drugs that are in development, navigate early access provisions and clinical trials, and manage regulatory systems across borders. Patients do not pay for these services. Instead, drug developers pay MyTomorrows drug royalties or a commission for connecting patients with development-stage treatments. Sage Bionetworks is a nonprofit that advocates open science as a way of facilitating drug discovery. In 2013 Stephen Friend announced that Sage was developing a cloud-based platform to encourage patients to share their medical data and experiences as a way of including patients in drug development while also facilitating better drug development.[15] In 2015, Sage opened enrollment for two studies as part of this initiative—a Parkinson's study that uses data from mobile apps to study the factors that influence fluctuations in neuromotor development, and a breast cancer survivor study that explores the long-term effects of chemotherapy and the efficacy of behavioral and environmental modifications as a way of managing these effects.[16]

These forms of patient-driven drug development are an example of one of the ways that patients can assert their medical autonomy and rights of self-medication. New technology is empowering people in need to access information, treatment, and support like never before. And just as importantly, these technological innovations are making the political ideal of "nothing about us without us" a real possibility. As with other political movements, as patients gain the capacity to inform themselves and form organized communities, they also gain the ability to resist the traditional, paternalistic norms that have governed medicine for so long.

Patient-driven drug development is also a political act insofar as it challenges existing approval policies by empowering patients to take their medical decisions into their own hands. The medical progress that has been made by patient developers and communities of citizen-scientists also further undermines claims that rights of self-medication for people with terminal and degenerative illnesses are infeasible because patients are incapable of understanding complex medical information and making such serious treatment decisions. Not

[15] Sage Bionetworks, "Press Release: Sage Bionetworks Announces Program to Develop BRIDGE: An IT Platform That Leverages Patient Wisdom and Data for 21st Century Biomedical Research," MarketWatch, accessed March 11, 2016, http://www.marketwatch.com/story/sage-bionetworks-announces-program-to-develop-bridge-an-it-platform-that-leverages-patient-wisdom-and-data-for-21st-century-biomedical-research-2013-09-27.

[16] Sage Bionetworks, "Current Bridge Studies," 2016, http://sagebase.org/bridge/.

only can citizen scientists access and interpret evidence that informs their own treatment decisions, their expert knowledge is also increasingly driving drug development for everyone.

5.2 Disobedience and Distribution

To legally use an unapproved therapy, patients must enlist manufacturers and physicians to assist them as they navigate either a clinical trial or an expanded access program. In some cases, neither of these efforts is successful, and patients cannot access an unapproved therapy. In these circumstances patients historically acted outside the law when regulations gave them few other options. The citizen-scientist movement was initially formed in the 1980s and 1990s at the start of the AIDS epidemic. At the time, scientists did not know a lot about AIDS, there were few available therapies, and patients died quickly after being diagnosed. When experimental drugs and off-label therapies were suggested as potential treatments, patients formed buyers' clubs that imported and distributed unapproved therapies to members.[17] At the time, critics worried that buyers' clubs would harm patients, undermine the testing process, and threaten approval for promising drugs. But people with AIDS had few other options. They could not legally access unapproved therapies, and all approved therapies were ineffective.

In this section, I argue that citizens may permissibly disobey pharmaceutical regulations and drug laws. Especially in the circumstances that AIDS patients faced in the 1980s, illegally importing and distributing pharmaceuticals to willing consumers is not only permissible, it is also praiseworthy. Many discussions of the ethics of disobedience focus on *civil disobedience*, which is disobedience for the sake of a political cause. Philosophers sometimes argue that disobedience is only justified if lawbreakers act publically, so that their conduct calls attention to injustice, and accept punishment for breaking the law.[18] Yet, in some circumstances, civil disobedience is not justified, such as when lawbreakers wrongfully violate a just law. And in other cases, disobedience that does not qualify as civil disobedience is justified, such as when people secretly resist an unjust law to benefit the victims of injustice. So while civil disobedience is distinctive in that it is a form of protest, whereas other acts of disobedience are not, whether an act of disobedience is political does not settle questions about its permissibility. First, I will address the permissibility of disobedience in general. Then, in the

[17] Steven Epstein, *Impure Science: AIDS, Activism, and the Politics of Knowledge* (Berkeley, CA: University of California Press, 1998).

[18] John Rawls, *A Theory of Justice* (Cambridge MA: Harvard University Press, 1971), 363–89.

next section, I will turn to civil disobedience, which I think is closer to freedom of expression or protest because of the normative issues it raises.

Buyers clubs for AIDS patients were politically motivated in a sense. Certainly the members were politically minded and disapproved of the FDA's policies. But their primary purpose was to distribute drugs to AIDS patients. Other examples of unauthorized self-medication or facilitating other people's self-medication when it is against the law illustrate that disobeying drug laws can take many forms. For example, when patients import drugs from other countries to obtain unauthorized drugs, to use drugs without a prescription, or to pay lower prices, they disobey pharmaceutical policy for non-political reasons. Patients who fail to comply with quotas or monitoring of prescription painkillers disobey too. Patients who use medical marijuana in places where it is illegal and those who form medical marijuana buyers' clubs disobey too. Recreational drug users and dealers also disobey drug policy to exercise their rights of self-medication or to facilitate self-medication by others. Whether these forms of disobedience are permissible will depend on whether the laws they break are just laws, and if not just, whether citizens have obligations to obey laws that are unjust. In previous chapters, I argued that laws that prohibit self-medication are unjust laws. I will now argue that citizens do not have obligations to obey them.

My view is that citizens do not have duties to obey unjust laws that violate people's rights.[19] Public officials are entitled to enforce laws that protect people's enforceable rights. But officials may not permissibly coerce or force citizens to comply with laws when citizens lack sufficient moral reasons to obey and may have strong moral reasons to disobey. The mere presence of a legal prohibition is not sufficient to establish that citizens have a duty to obey a law that constrains their choices. Officials must also be morally entitled to enforce the law, for example on the grounds that citizens would lack the moral authority to make those choices in the absence of legal prohibition.

For those who share this view, the conclusion that citizens may permissibly exercise their rights of self-medication even when it is illegal will follow from the preceding argument that limits on self-medication are unjust. But many philosophers do not share this view of obligation and may be unconvinced by my claim that rights of self-medication are generally so strong. For example, many people think that if a state is sufficiently just or legitimate, then citizens can have duties to obey some unjust laws. Yet even those who endorse theories of political obligation think that the duty to obey the law is only a *pro tanto* obligation,

[19] See the work of John Simmons and Michael Huemer for a more thorough defense of this position. Michael Huemer, *The Problem of Political Authority: An Examination of the Right to Coerce and the Duty to Obey* (Houndmills, Basingstoke, Hampshire; New York: Palgrave Macmillan, 2012); A. John Simmons, "Justification and Legitimacy," *Ethics* 109, no. 4 (1999): 739–71, doi:10.1086/233944.

meaning that it can be outweighed if there are stronger moral considerations in favor of breaking it. For example, if obeying an unjust law requires a citizen to violate another person's fundamental rights, such as rights of self-preservation or bodily rights, then the citizen's general duty to obey would be outweighed by the duty to respect people's rights. So even according to this view, disobedience would be permissible when public officials enforced policies that violated rights to make medical decisions or rights of self-preservation. But those who hold this view might reject the claim that disobedience is permissible when officials prohibit recreational drug use.

Others may argue that disobedience is only justified if obeying an unjust law would have terrible consequences—if it caused unnecessary death and suffering for example. According to this view, the *pro tanto* duty to obey the law and the duty to respect rights of self-medication could both be outweighed by a more general duty to avoid bad consequences. For consequentialists, both obligations (to obey law and respect rights of self-medication) would be justified by an appeal to the well-being they promote.[20] Yet on this view, it would be permissible to violate prohibitive pharmaceutical policies whenever violating disobedience would have good consequences. Therefore, even if there were a *pro tanto* obligation to obey the law because obedience generally had good consequences, such an obligation would be outweighed whenever disobeying pharmaceutical regulations to promote well-being on balance would have good consequences.

For other prominent theories of political obligation, the considerations that people generally cite in favor of a duty to obey the law cannot justify a duty to obey unjust pharmaceutical regulations that violate patients' rights.[21] For example, Richard Dagger argues that citizens have duties of fair play to obey laws.[22] On this account, because citizens benefit from the overall legal system, they must bear the burdens of complying with the particular law that they do not support. Yet at least for those patients whose fundamental rights of self-preservation are violated by prohibitive drug policies, the overall legal system does not benefit them on balance because the legal system deprives them of the means to save their own lives. At least for these patients, duties of fair play do not generate any obligation to comply with pharmaceutical policies.

Democratic theories of political obligation also do not support the claim that citizens are obligated to comply with all pharmaceutical regulations. For

[20] This objection relies on a consequentialist assumption about political obligation and an empirical claim about self-medication. I address the consequences of self-medication in chapter 2.

[21] I am grateful to Javier Hidalgo for helpful discussions about the duty to obey unjust laws. My thoughts on this topic are informed by his work on immigration restrictions. Javier Hidalgo, "Resistance to Unjust Immigration Restrictions," *Journal of Political Philosophy* 23, no. 4 (December 1, 2015): 450–70, doi:10.1111/jopp.12051.

[22] Richard Dagger, "Membership, Fair Play, and Political Obligation," *Political Studies* 48, no. 1 (March 1, 2000): 104–17, doi:10.1111/1467-9248.00253.

example, Thomas Christiano argues that people have a duty to obey the law because those laws were a result of fair democratic procedures.[23] Say we grant for the sake of argument that laws that are democratically passed could generate a moral duty for citizens to obey them. Democratically passed laws would presumably have authority because they derive from each person's equal authority to participate in government. In other words, such a duty to obey would be grounded in people's pre-political rights, which would explain why even those who believe that people have duties to obey democratically passed laws deny the claim that people must obey laws that violate the fundamental non-political rights of minorities. But pharmaceutical restrictions violate the fundamental rights of minorities, for example, sick or disabled people, so the claim that citizens have obligations to comply with pharmaceutical regulations in virtue of their role as citizens would not succeed because prohibitive regulations violate the very rights that generally justify participatory rights.

Others argue that people have duties to obey laws in virtue of their associative obligations to fellow citizens. For example, Samuel Scheffler argues that people who are in non-instrumentally valuable relationships can have special obligations to one another even if they did not consent to the obligations, just as people have general moral obligations, even if they do not consent to them.[24] John Horton develops similar arguments in favor of political obligation.[25] These arguments for political obligation draw analogies between citizenship and other relationships that seemingly generate obligations without consent, such as friendship or family relationships.[26] But if these relationships can generate duties between citizens, they would most plausibly generate a duty to assist citizens who are threatened by unjust pharmaceutical regulations. Generally, special obligations are cited as reasons in favor of providing people with assistance, not as license to violate their rights.

Proponents of these arguments on behalf of a duty to obey the law also agree that such duties are infeasible, so even if they did justify a general duty to obey the law, just as obligations between friends can be outweighed by our general moral obligations, compatriot obligations could be outweighed too. And those who argue for associative duties also deny that they generate obligations when a relationship is not valuable, such as friendships that are premised on abuse or

[23] Thomas Christiano, "The Authority of Democracy," *Journal of Political Philosophy* 12, no. 3 (2004): 266–90. For a more comprehensive response to Christiano's argument see Michael Huemer, *The Problem of Political Authority: An Examination of the Right to Coerce and the Duty to Obey*.

[24] Samuel Scheffler, "Relationships and Responsibilities," *Philosophy & Public Affairs* 26, no. 3 (July 1, 1997): 189–209, doi:10.1111/j.1088-4963.1997.tb00053.x.

[25] John Horton, "In Defence of Associative Political Obligations: Part Two," *Political Studies* 55, no. 1 (2007): 1–19; John Horton, "In Defence of Associative Political Obligations: Part One," *Political Studies* 54, no. 3 (October 2006): 427–43.

[26] Bas van der Vossen, "Associative Political Obligations," *Philosophy Compass* 6, no. 7 (2011): 477–87.

injustice. So as above, for these reasons, even if people did have duties to obey laws in virtue of the political relationship, they would not be morally required to comply with harmful pharmaceutical regulations that treat patients and consumers unjustly.

Another theory of political obligation appeals to the idea of natural rights. Rawls, for example, argued that citizens are obligated to obey the law because the law protects their natural rights.[27] Relatedly, Anna Stilz argues that people have duties to obey the law because the law is a necessary condition for the protection of people's freedom from interference.[28] But since pharmaceutical regulations violate people's fundamental non-political rights, such as bodily rights and rights of self-medication, self-preservation, and the rights to die, democratic and natural rights theories of political obligation do not support a duty to obey pharmaceutical regulations. And the same response is apt regarding Christopher Wellman's argument that people have duties to obey the law because they have Samaritan duties to provide assistance, and supporting the law is one way of satisfying these duties.[29] Even if this argument were successful, in cases where laws are harmful and policies prevent people from providing assistance, as is the case for many pharmaceutical regulations, then the Samaritan duties that Wellman cites as a general reason to obey would not only permit but also require that people disobey pharmaceutical policies.[30]

Like Wellman, George Klosko argues that people have duties to contribute to systems that provide people with presumptively beneficial goods.[31] But Klosko clarifies that these duties apply particularly to goods that are non-excludable, such as clean air or national defense.[32] And pharmaceutical regulation is not presumptively beneficial, and it is excludable since knowledge about drugs and certification could theoretically be given to those who pay for it and not to others. Klosko also caveats his argument for political obligation by noting that citizens do not have duties to comply with legal systems that disproportionately benefit some groups more than others, even if all citizens benefit from the system

---

[27] Rawls, *A Theory of Justice*.

[28] Anna Stilz, *Liberal Loyalty: Freedom, Obligation, and the State*, reprint (Princeton, NJ: Princeton University Press, 2011).

[29] Christopher H. Wellman, "Liberalism, Samaritanism, and Political Legitimacy," *Philosophy & Public Affairs* 25, no. 3 (1996): 211–37.

[30] For a similar argument as it relates to immigration restrictions see Hidalgo, Javier "The Duty to Disobey Immigration Law." *Moral Philosophy and Politics* 3, no. 2 (2016): 165–86.

[31] George Klosko, "Presumptive Benefit, Fairness, and Political Obligation," *Philosophy & Public Affairs*, 1987, 241–59.

[32] Citizens may also have duties to contribute to the provision of additional discretionary goods that are not presumptively beneficial on Klosko's account, as long as it is not too burdensome. However, even if information about pharmaceuticals is a presumptively beneficial discretionary good, insofar as laws that provide information also prohibit people from accessing pharmaceuticals, then the system of pharmaceutical regulation as a whole would impose additional burdens on people.

on balance. Pharmaceutical regulations excessively burden sick people who are denied access to beneficial drugs. So on this view, even if citizens benefit from the information provided by regulatory agencies, they are not obligated to obey the overall system of pharmaceutical regulations, even if such an argument could justify political obligation in other cases.

This overview of theories of political obligation is meant to show one does-n't need to be an anarchist to think that citizens do not have duties to comply with pharmaceutical regulations. In general, arguments for the claim that there is a duty to obey the law focus on duties to comply with redistributive property rules or to support policies that are not otherwise required by moral obligations. However, most people who support a duty to obey the law would deny the claim that it can generate a duty to obey an unjust law that violates people's most fun-damental rights, so political obligations are limited. Many theories of political obligation are justified by an appeal to fundamental rights or a general duty to promote well-being, and in these cases the very reasons that are cited in favor of political obligations can also be cited in favor of disobeying some pharmaceu-tical regulations. Therefore, even if people did have duties to obey the law, the most prominent justifications for such duties would not support duties to obey pharmaceutical regulations.

5.3 Civil Disobedience

Some forms of disobedience go beyond lawbreaking for the sake of self-medication and also function as acts of protest against policies that prohibit self-medication. Civil disobedience is a form of political expression where a cit-izen breaks an unjust law in order to draw attention to the injustice of the law. Patients and their advocates can violate pharmaceutical regulations in this way when they publically assert the right to die or when they grow and distribute medical marijuana. We can imagine other forms of civil disobedience on behalf of rights of self-medication as well, such physicians publically providing patients with unauthorized or unapproved drugs.

In this section I will develop a qualified defense of civil disobedience and lawbreaking for the sake of rights of self-medication. Since I have argued that patients are not obligated to obey pharmaceutical regulations that violate rights of self-medication anyhow, their conduct needn't meet the usual criteria for civil disobedience to be permissible. And there are also good reasons for patients and their advocates to refrain from characterizing their decision to violate pharma-ceutical regulations as civil disobedience since publically violating such laws for political reasons and submitting to punishment could in some cases undermine the cause of self-medication rather than drawing attention to the injustices of pharmaceutical regulations.

Consider two forms of civil disobedience currently practiced by advocates of self-medication. First, in 1998 Dr. Jack Kevorkian famously assisted in the voluntary euthanasia of Thomas Youk on national television. Youk suffered from ALS and consented to euthanasia. He and Kevorkian chose to televise the procedure as a way of drawing attention to the injustice of laws that prohibit euthanasia. Kevorkian was then convicted of second-degree murder and served eight years in prison. In Australia, Dr. Philip Nitschke and Dr. Fiona Stewart distribute information about how to illegally obtain drugs for the purpose of euthanasia. In *The Peaceful Pill Handbook,* Nitschke and Stewart describe a group of elderly patients who illegally manufactured deadly barbiturates as an act of mass civil disobedience against the prohibition of voluntary euthanasia.

Second, some citizens engage in civil disobedience in protest of medical marijuana policy too. For example, in 1998 Cheryl Miller suffered from multiple sclerosis, and illegal medical marijuana effectively treated her symptoms. As a medical marijuana advocate, she used marijuana in a congressman's office to protest federal marijuana regulations. Gustin Reichbach was a judge who wrote a letter to the *New York Times* in 2012 describing his medical marijuana use in an effort to give voice to the concerns of other patients who were unable to publically protest prohibitions. Reichbach wrote:

> This is not a law-and-order issue; it is a medical and a human rights issue.... Doctors cannot be expected to do what the law prohibits, even when they know it is in the best interests of their patients. When palliative care is understood as a fundamental human and medical right, marijuana for medical use should be beyond controversy.... Because criminalizing an effective medical technique affects the fair administration of justice, I feel obliged to speak out as both a judge and a cancer patient suffering with a fatal disease.[33]

In 2016, Allen Peake, a Georgia state representative, committed civil disobedience by publically defending his decision to transport medical marijuana from Colorado, which permits marijuana use, to patients in Georgia, where medical marijuana is prohibited. Peake told a reporter, "I made a commitment to these families when I got involved.... If it involved civil disobedience, it's been absolutely worth it."[34]

---

[33] Gustin L. Reichbach, "A Judge's Plea for Medical Marijuana," *The New York Times*, May 16, 2012, http://www.nytimes.com/2012/05/17/opinion/a-judges-plea-for-medical-marijuana.html.

[34] Jim Galloway, "The Next Stage of Medical Marijuana Debate: Civil Disobedience," Political Insider Blog, 2016, http://politics.blog.ajc.com/2016/01/20/the-next-stage-of-medical-marijuana-debate-civil-disobedience/.

The examples of voluntary euthanasia advocacy and medical marijuana protests show that civil disobedience can be an effective way to draw attention to unjust policies that violate patients' rights of self-medication. And since it is permissible to disobey pharmaceutical regulations that prohibit self-medication for non-political reasons, it is also permissible to violate them as a form of political protest. On the other hand, patients and their advocates are not obligated to publically disobey pharmaceutical regulations to draw attention to the law, and, in some cases, there are good reasons to disobey secretly, for non-political purposes and to attempt to evade punishment.

One good reason to secretly disobey pharmaceutical regulations is if the purpose of disobedience is to provide treatment to someone in need. So while Rep. Peake publically admitted to bringing marijuana from Colorado to Georgia, he did not disclose the identities of the families he was assisting because doing so could have endangered them. Typically, people who use pharmaceuticals without authorization intend primarily to treat their symptoms and not make a political point. In these cases publicity for the sake of rights to self-medication could undermine people's exercise of their rights of self-medication.

Public disobedience can also harm other patients. For example, it is currently extremely difficult to legally access unapproved therapies outside the context of an expanded use program, and manufacturers are sometimes reluctant to provide therapies outside the context of a trial because they are concerned that adverse reactions would expose them to liability and public backlash. Adverse reactions are also more likely for patients who suffer from terminal and degenerative conditions because those patients are already in poor health and typically take many other drugs, even though they are the patients who stand to benefit most from new therapies. So if a patient were able to access an unapproved drug (which is unlikely) and she experienced an adverse reaction, then she could potentially undermine the prospects of approval for a drug, cause manufacturers to halt a trial, and harm other patients who would potentially benefit from approval. This concern is not unfounded. In 2014 the FDA halted a clinical trial of the cancer drug CytRx after a patient who was using the drug through an expanded use program died.[35]

Or if physicians publically disobeyed pharmaceutical regulations, they could lose their prescribing power, which would thereby undermine their ability to facilitate informed self-medication long-term. Similarly, cannabis buyers' clubs and dispensaries that operate in violation of federal law may reasonably operate in secrecy because otherwise they would be punished for providing valuable

---

[35] John Carroll, "FDA Orders CytRx to Halt Patient Enrollment after Death of a Cancer Patient," *FierceBiotech*, November 18, 2014, http://www.fiercebiotech.com/story/fda-orders-cytrx-halt-patient-enrollment-after-death-cancer-patient/2014-11-18.

services to patients in need.[36] Health workers should not concern themselves with drawing attention to the injustice of approval policies when they encounter dying patients and judge that the best way to remedy the injustices that individual patients face is to secretly provide unapproved drugs. Their first priority physicians should be helping their patients in ways that do not set back the potential for other patients to benefit from a drug.

Disobedience also need not be motivated by conscientious reasons. Though people who illegally facilitate access to pharmaceuticals often are altruistically motivated, they are not motivated by the conviction that pharmaceutical regulations are unjust. For example, some physicians who illegally distribute opioids to patients sincerely believe they are helping their patients. Stephen Schneider is a physician who is currently in prison for unlawful distribution of controlled substances:

> He almost always took his patients' side when they complained about doctors who had "discriminated" against them for needing opioids. Schneider [said], "I don't even know the actual quote for the Hippocratic Oath, but aren't you doing harm if there's a treatment for something and you refuse to use it?"[37]

Schneider argued that no one else in his community was willing to provide healthcare to low-income patients who suffered from chronic pain. He believed he was doing the right thing, even though many of his patients used opioids in ways that were not medically indicated. Though Schneider did not disobey opioid policy for political reasons, he was still motivated to disobey.

Even purely self-interested motives would not render disobedience impermissible. Health workers who illegally sold unapproved drugs to AIDS buyers' clubs or Canadian pharmacists who ship low-cost pharmaceuticals to patients in the United States may be motivated by the desire to profit. But they still do more for patients in need than an altruistic health worker who refuses to take professional risks for the sake of her patients. The intention behind disobedience does not bear on its permissibility.[38]

---

[36] The Department of Justice no longer actively prosecutes dispensaries in states where medical marijuana use is permitted. It is still illegal to manufacture unapproved medicines, and it is illegal to sell prescription drugs to patients without authorization to do so. United States v. Oakland Cannabis Buyers' Cooperative, 532 US 483 (Supreme Court 2001).

[37] Rachel Aviv, "Prescription for Disaster," *The New Yorker*, April 28, 2014, http://www.newyorker.com/magazine/2014/05/05/prescription-for-disaster.

[38] Tim Scanlon, Judith Thomson, and others argue that intention doesn't bear on the permissibility of an act, though this idea is controversial. Matthew Liao argues that our intuitions about cases where intention wouldn't matter for permissibility are unreliable and that intention plausibly does matter for the permissibility of an act. T. M. Scanlon and Jonathan Dancy, "Intention

Physicians like Stephen Schneider and those who violate approval requirements also should not be expected to submit to punishment because it is not
morally wrong to provide pharmaceuticals to informed and consenting patients.
The main justification for a requirement that lawbreakers submit to punishment is the idea that lawbreakers should acknowledge the overall legitimacy
of the state when drawing attention to an unjust law. But even if states were
legitimate on balance, it would still be wrong for states to punish those who are
not liable to be punished. Since people who illegally provide and use pharmaceuticals act permissibly, they are not liable, so the state would act wrongly by
punishing them.

So when Don and Iris Flounders engaged in civil disobedience by speak-
ing publicly about their decision to obtain deadly amounts of Nembutal from
Mexico, they were not under a duty to submit to punishment for illegally importing deadly drugs. Don Flounders was therefore justified in hiding the drugs from
the Australian government, who raided the Flounders' home after they publicized their choice. As Don commented in a video that he recorded before his
death, "luckily I'd hidden the drugs well . . . there's a lot of rabbit burrows down
here at Warragul [Austrailia]." If Don and Iris had not tried to evade punishment for importing illegal drugs, the Australian government would have frustrated the couple's efforts to choose the time and manner of their deaths. If the
Flounders complied with the law they would have implicitly validated the state's
authority to enforce laws that violate patients' rights and cause needless suffering. Patients like Don and Iris are under no obligation to acknowledge the legitimacy of unjust laws that violate their rights, even if their governments were
more broadly legitimate.

At this point a caveat is in order. These arguments are not meant to suggest
that all acts of legal disobedience are justified when it comes to pharmaceuticals. In particular, the wrongfulness of prescription and approval requirements
would not necessarily permit stealing drugs from pharmacies and manufacturers. This is more than a theoretical concern since hundreds of pharmacies are
robbed every year in America alone. Yet pharmacy robberies not only consist
in disobeying approval and prescription requirements (which I have argued are
illegitimate laws), they also violate people's property rights and often involve
threats of violence against pharmacy employees. In most cases at least, pharmacy employees do not forfeit their rights against violence by participating
in the prescription drug system. Whether non-violent pharmaceutical theft is
morally wrong would depend on more general questions about the justice of
the property system, especially in light of the urgent needs of others. Assuming

and Permissibility," *Proceedings of the Aristotelian Society, Supplementary Volumes* 74 (January 1,
2000): 301–38; S. Matthew Liao, "Intentions and Moral Permissibility: The Case of Acting Permissibly
with Bad Intentions," *Law and Philosophy* 31, no. 6 (2012): 703–24.

that manufacturers and pharmacists have legitimate property rights over pharmaceuticals, then pharmacy robberies are unlikely to qualify as permissible disobedience.

5.4 Protest and Activism

The tension between disobeying in order to exercise one's rights and disobeying in order to draw attention to rights violations is not unique to rights of self-medication. Henry David Thoreau secretly harbored slaves in violation of the Fugitive Slave Act, and by concealing his actions, he was able to help more people than he would have if he had publically harbored slaves.[39] Fredrick Douglass also opposed public disobedience on the grounds that it would make slave owners more watchful, and therefore more effective at continuing to enslave people.[40] So while secret disobedience is sometimes criticized on the grounds that it prevents other citizens from judging whether disobedience is permissible, when the public is blind to the injustice of the current system, disobedience may not be the best way to draw attention to injustice.

This is not to suggest that people should not advocate rights of self-medication in other ways. As Thomas Hill argues, everyone who is a bystander to an unjust law has a duty to oppose or resist it.[41] The paradigmatic examples of bystanders to injustice are ordinary Germans during World War II who did not support or oppose Nazism and southerners who recognized the injustice of Jim Crow and segregation but did not do anything to change it. Some scholars have argued that the criminalization of recreational drugs is akin to these policies because the drug war is instrumental to the oppression of black Americans. Insofar as the drug war is the new Jim Crow, ordinary Americans remain bystanders to oppression if they do not resist unjust drug policy. And as I have argued, prohibitive pharmaceutical regulations are a form of oppression too. Patients are vulnerable groups. People who are sick have a difficult time asserting their rights. Patients are politically and economically disenfranchised, and the patient rights movement is spread thin across many disease-specific advocacy groups. Yet patients' rights are a species of human rights. People are entitled to make decisions about

---

[39] Henry David Thoreau, *Civil Disobedience and Other Essays* (Courier Corporation, 2012).

[40] This concern about the negative effects of publicity was the basis of Fredrick Douglass's criticism of the Underground Railroad. In his autobiography, Douglas worried that publically violating the Fugitive Slave Act made slave owners more watchful and could have therefore undermined individual slave's ability to escape. Frederick Douglass, *Narrative of the Life of Frederick Douglass*, unabridged edition (New York: Dover, 1995).

[41] Thomas E. Hill Jr, "Moral Responsibilities of Bystanders," *Journal of Social Philosophy* 41, no. 1 (2010): 28–39.

their own bodies. Policies that violate patients' rights of self-medication are therefore oppressive policies that mistreat vulnerable groups.

The primary agents of injustice, such as the public officials who enforce prohibitive drug regulations, are the most morally culpable for oppressive policies. But all citizens in states that enforce unjust pharmaceutical laws have duties to critically examine current laws and to ask themselves whether they are justified in remaining passive. Hill argues that each citizen should cultivate a character that enables him or her to resist an unjust law if given the chance. By tolerating injustice, people contribute to the ongoing oppression of patients through negligence. Even if bystanders to oppressive drug regulations do not intend to violate patients' rights, even if they are ignorant of the harm that is caused by the policies, and even if they are basically good people who want to help patients, all citizens who accept unjust pharmaceutical policies are involved in a system of oppression in some way. Those who are more closely involved in patient care, such as manufacturers and physicians, are more culpable for their complicity in these injustices. Hill writes:

> Bystanders . . . can be enablers of oppression in ways that amount to complicity. They may be regarded as oppressing or adding to the oppression of the victims through their omissions and passivity.[42]

Citizens should therefore consider how they could oppose and resist policies that violate patients' rights of self-medication, even if it requires them to take some professional risks or to bear some personal sacrifices.

Advocates of self-medication have historically approached the cause in three ways—protest, direct advocacy, and political lobbying. In addition to the ACT UP protests of the 1980s, patient groups have organized rallies and protests outside the offices of public officials and regulatory agencies in order to get better access to drugs that treat ALS, and obtain emergency contraception, medical marijuana, and cancer treatments.[43] On the other hand, people have

[42] Ibid., 31.

[43] Amy Ellis Nutt and Dennis, "ALS Patients Press FDA for Quick Access to Controversial Biotech Drug," *Washington Post*, April 3, 2015, sec. Health and Science, https://www.washingtonpost.com/national/health-science/als-patients-press-fda-for-quick-access-to-controversial-biotech-drug/2015/04/03/fb954618-d220-11e4-a62f-ee745911a4ff_story.html; Marc Kaufman, "9 Arrested Protesting Morning-After Pill Plan," *Washington Post*, January 8, 2005, sec. Nation, http://www.washingtonpost.com/wp-dyn/articles/A57879-2005Jan7.html; Eliana Dockterman, "People Want DEA Chief to Resign for Calling Medical Marijuana 'A Joke,'" *Time*, November 10, 2015, http://time.com/4107603/dea-medical-marijuana-joke-2/; James Oliphant, "Activist Takes on FDA for Experimental Drugs," *Chicago Tribune*, August 21, 2007, http://www.montereyherald.com/article/ZZ/20070821/NEWS/708219923; Ángel González, "Protesters Demand New Cancer Drugs," *Seattle Times*, September 19, 2007, http://www.seattletimes.com/business/protesters-demand-new-cancer-drugs/; United Press International, "Police Arrest AIDS Protesters Blocking Access to FDA Offices," *Los Angeles Times*, October 11, 1988, http://articles.latimes.com/1988-10-11/news/mn-3909_1_police-arrest-aids-protesters.

also protested policies that gave people more access to pharmaceuticals, such as approval of opioid painkillers and Truvada for pre-exposure prophylaxis.[44] Though both forms of protest should be protected as acts of political speech, only the protests in favor of self-medication are praiseworthy because they are advocating for more just pharmaceutical policies.

Another way to advocate for rights of self-medication is through direct advocacy, such as social media campaigns on behalf of patients who seek access to potentially lifesaving therapeutics. For example, when a pediatric patient named Josh Hardy suffered from a life-threatening adenovirus infection in 2014, his physicians at St. Jude Hospital were initially denied access to Brincidofovir, an experimental drug that was being tested as a treatment for a different virus in immunocompromised adults. Even though Brincidofovir showed promise as a treatment for adenovirus as well, the manufacturer, Chimerix, was initially reluctant to provide the drug presumably out of concerns that it could potentially harm Josh and undermine the drug's chances of approval. Josh's family then launched an extensive social media campaign on Hardy's behalf, which compelled Chimerix to establish a new clinical trial for adenovirus that included Hardy as the first patient.[45] Hardy recovered from the infection. Hardy's story is just one among an increasing number of accounts of patients who use social media to directly advocate greater access to pharmaceuticals.[46]

Citizens may also advocate rights of self-medication through political speech such as lobbying. For example, the Goldwater Institute has followed ACT UP's lead in framing self-medication as a political cause.[47] Whereas ACT UP focused on access to AIDS treatment, the Goldwater Institute advocates for right to try policies that would give patients with treatment-resistant degenerative and terminal diseases earlier access to unapproved drugs. The Abigail Alliance also advocates for better access to experimental drugs. Drug policy reform groups such as NORML and the Drug Policy Alliance and Students for a Sensible Drug Policy and Americans for Safe Access also advocate the decriminalization of recreational drugs and the legalization of medical marijuana. Non-governmental organizations such as the World Health Organization, International Red Cross,

[44] Chris Good, "White House Protesters Blast Prescription Drug Policy," *ABC News*, September 28, 2014, http://abcnews.go.com/blogs/politics/2014/09/at-white-house-prescription-drug-protesters-call-for-new-fda-chief/; AIDS Healthcare Foundation, "FDA AIDS Protest Targets Approval of Gilead's Prevention Pill," | January 23, 2012, http://www.aidshealth.org/#/archives/6488.

[45] K. John Morrow, "Drug Development in the Age of Social Media," *Life Science Leader*, April 25, 2015.

[46] Tim K. Mackey and Virginia J. Schoenfeld, "Going 'social' to Access Experimental and Potentially Life-Saving Treatment: An Assessment of the Policy and Online Patient Advocacy Environment for Expanded Access," *BMC Medicine* 14 (February 2, 2016), doi:10.1186/s12916-016-0568-8.

[47] Darcy Olsen, *The Right to Try: How the Federal Government Prevents Americans from Getting the Lifesaving Treatments They Need*, 1 edition (New York, NY: Harper, 2015).

and the UN Commission on Drugs and Crime also advocate the decriminalization of recreational drugs.

These organizations develop legislation, publicize research about the harmful effects of policies that violate patients' rights of self-medication, and organize citizens to lobby public officials on behalf of patients and consumers. These forms of political advocacy may ultimately be the most effective way of achieving large-scale pharmaceutical policy reform since they do not compromise individual efforts at accessing unapproved drugs and, unlike social media advocacy, proposals for reform are not specific to individual patients.

Though all forms of advocacy in favor of a more just system of drug regulation are laudable, not everyone who is a bystander to oppression has a duty to oppose it. When opposing oppression requires that one makes oneself a victim of that oppression, people do not have a duty to submit to an oppressive policy out of solidarity with the oppressed. In other cases, opposing oppression would cause greater injustice on balance. These considerations weigh against civil disobedience and in favor of other forms of activism. But as long as the costs are not so high that opposition to an unjust policy would only make more people victims of the policy, people should resist oppressive policies through civil disobedience, direct advocacy, or political expression.

5.5 Democratic Authority and Self-Medication

In 2011 the FDA determined that emergency contraception (Plan B One-Step) could be safely sold over the counter without age restrictions. Kathleen Sebelius, then the secretary of human services, overturned the FDA's judgment and instructed the agency to maintain age restrictions on Plan B on the grounds that there was insufficient evidence to justify the agency's decision. President Barak Obama publically supported Sebelius's decision, and the FDA ultimately rejected an application to sell Plan B over the counter without age restrictions. This reversal prompted the Center for Reproductive Rights to initiate a citizen's petition and lawsuit against the FDA and Sebelius asserting that the failure to approve Plan B was not justified in light of the medical evidence. In 2013 a judge overturned Sebelius and the FDA's decision on the grounds that it was made on the basis of "bad faith and improper political influence."[48] After a series of appeals, the FDA approved Plan B for over the counter use by all women of childbearing potential.[49]

---

[48] "Timeline: The Battle for Plan B," *Time*, June 11, 2013, http://healthland.time.com/2013/06/11/timeline-the-battle-for-plan-b/.

[49] Erica Jefferson, "FDA Approves Plan B One-Step Emergency Contraceptive for Use without a Prescription for All Women of Child-Bearing Potential," Press Announcements, June 20, 2013, http://www.fda.gov/NewsEvents/Newsroom/PressAnnouncements/ucm358082.htm.

One might think that people who advocate rights of self-medication and patient-driven development ought to favor political reforms via democratic institutions rather than via non-democratic institutions. But the history of drug regulation, from the early calls to regulate pharmaceuticals after the Elixir Sulfanilamide disaster to the Obama administration's politically motivated opposition to Plan B approval, is marked by a series of democratic impediments to self-medication. Just as the doctrine of informed consent evolved through judicial institutions and interpretations of constitutional law, rights of self-medication should also be insulated from democratic encroachment and protected by constitutional courts. Voters are not reliable judges of whether patients should have rights of self-medication because they suffer from several cognitive biases that blind them to the injustices of regulations and overemphasize the benefits of regulation. To the extent that regulatory agencies are accountable to democratic branches of government, their policies will be informed by voters' misguided beliefs. Therefore, pharmaceutical policy should be shielded from democratic pressures, like other policies that affect fundamental rights.

The argument in favor of protecting people's rights of self-medication from democratic pressures goes like this:

(P1) Voters are biased against rights of self-medication.

(P2) If voters are biased, democratic institutions are systematically unreliable at producing just or effective policies.

(P3) If democratic institutions are systematically unreliable, public officials should not rely on democratic mechanisms to regulate access to pharmaceuticals.

(C1) Public officials should not rely on democratic mechanisms to regulate access to pharmaceuticals.

(P4) Public officials must use some mechanism to regulate access to pharmaceuticals.

(C2) Public officials should use non-democratic mechanisms to regulate citizens' access to pharmaceuticals.

In other words, self-medication should be protected in the ways that other politically vulnerable rights (e.g., freedom of speech and association) are protected from popular efforts to restrict the freedom of vulnerable groups. Public officials should adopt institutional reforms that protect patients' rights through constitutional provisions, international institutions, and independent agencies.

The first premise of the argument states that voters are systematically biased against rights of self-medication. In addition to regulators' aforementioned biases in favor of committing Type II errors in order to avoid committing Type I errors, the voters whose preferences influence regulators are also subject to various cognitive biases. For example, people are generally optimistic that they will not become the victims of prohibitive pharmaceutical regulations that prevent them from accessing therapeutic medicines because people systematically overestimate the degree of control they have over their lives and health and underestimate the probability of negative events.[50] At the same time, people are also influenced by availability bias. So when there is an unusual negative event, such as a drug disaster, it more readily comes to mind when considering the benefits and drawbacks of drug regulation; whereas people are less likely to consider less visible harms, such as people dying of diseases.[51] People are also biased in favor of the status quo, so it generally is difficult to convince them of the merits of reform.[52] And terror management theory predicts that thinking about death or mortality makes people more supportive of authority and the perpetuation of current cultural norms and values.[53] Add to that people's systematically less permissive attitudes toward bodily choices and choices regarding health and drugs, and there is further reason to suspect voters of bias. Additionally, drug use is stigmatized, especially insofar as it is associated with disadvantaged populations. And prejudices against chronically ill and disabled people are common too. So it is not clear that citizens are generally well equipped to judge the merits of self-medication in their capacities as voters.

In light of these biases, democratic institutions are unlikely to assess the merits of proposals for patients' rights of self-medication. Political scientists and economists have established that voters who are biased influence policy in ways that comport with their biases.[54] And there is historical evidence of the hazards of systematically biased democratic decision-making as well—democratic majorities often support policies that discriminate against marginalized groups

[50] David M. DeJoy, "The Optimism Bias and Traffic Accident Risk Perception," *Accident Analysis & Prevention* 21, no. 4 (1989): 333–40; Tali Sharot, "The Optimism Bias," *Current Biology* 21, no. 23 (2011): R941–45.

[51] Amos Tversky and Daniel Kahneman, "Availability: A Heuristic for Judging Frequency and Probability," *Cognitive Psychology* 5, no. 2 (September 1973): 207–32, doi:10.1016/0010-0285(73)90033-9.

[52] Bostrom and Ord, "The Reversal Test."

[53] Jeff Greenberg et al., "Evidence for Terror Management Theory II: The Effects of Mortality Salience on Reactions to Those Who Threaten or Bolster the Cultural Worldview," *Journal of Personality and Social Psychology* 58, no. 2 (1990): 308.

[54] Scott L. Althaus, *Collective Preferences in Democratic Politics: Opinion Surveys and the Will of the People* (Cambridge; New York: Cambridge University Press, 2003); Scott Althaus, "Opinion Polls, Information Effects, and Political Equality: Exploring Ideological Biases in Collective Opinion," *Political Communication* 13, no. 1 (1996): 3–21; Bryan Caplan, *The Myth of the Rational Voter: Why Democracies Choose Bad Policies*, new edition with a new preface by the author (Princeton, NJ: Princeton University Press, 2008).

out of an (often unjustified) fear that they will be harmed if marginalized groups benefit.[55]

In these cases, even if epistemic or instrumentalist arguments on behalf of democratic institutions succeeded as a general matter, they would fail to justify democratic decision-making in cases where voters are poorly equipped to evaluate evidence and make moral judgments because uninformed and biased decision-making leads to worse outcomes. And non-instrumental rights-based arguments cannot justify giving uninformed and potentially prejudiced voters the authority to enforce policies that violate important rights. Citizens are not entitled to use their power to harm less powerful groups.[56]

Therefore, public officials should be wary of democratic mechanisms when evaluating the merits of self-medication or pharmaceutical regulations more generally. Instead, they should look to the same non-democratic mechanisms that states use to protect other rights from threats from popular opinion. First, constitutional protections and judicial institutions may prove to be a productive path to securing rights of self-medication, just as the doctrine of informed consent evolved through the judiciary in the United States. Second, international organizations may affirm rights of self-medication within human rights doctrines to further support constitutional and judicial efforts on behalf of patients' rights.

5.6 Conclusion

Self-medication is a political cause. Patients should feel empowered to take drug development and distribution into their own hands. In the absence of political reforms that protect patients' rights of self-medication, patients may justifiably develop drugs outside the formal mechanisms of the approval process, disobey pharmaceutical regulations, and protest existing policies. I also suggested that patients and their advocates are not morally required to seek the approval of voters and political reform needn't be backed by democratic support because voters are potentially biased against rights of self-medication. For this reason, constitutional and judicial reforms may be necessary to secure rights of self-medication, just as rights of informed consent emerged through a series of judicial decisions.

---

[55] Javier Hidalgo, "The Case for the International Governance of Immigration," *International Theory* 8, no. 1 (March 2016): 140–70, doi:10.1017/S1752971915000226.

[56] Jason Brennan, *The Ethics of Voting*, new edition with a new afterword by the author (Princeton, NJ: Princeton University Press, 2012).

6

The Business of Medicine

Though every human life is beyond price, lifesaving drugs are not. New pharmaceuticals are prohibitively expensive for many patients, and in many countries, public officials not only regulate which drugs are available, they also regulate drug prices and intellectual property rights. Where there are relatively fewer regulations of drug prices, critics of the industry decry high prices. For example, in 2015 the *New York Times* editorial board condemned the pharmaceutical industry for charging "astronomical" drug prices "for no reason other than the desire of drug makers to maximize profits."[1]

The editorial was prompted by Turing Pharmaceuticals's recent increase in the price of Daraprim, a sixty-two-year-old drug used to treat parasitic infections, from $13.50 per pill to $750 per pill after the company purchased the rights to produce it. In the same editorial, the editors also cited Valeant Pharmaceuticals's decision to steeply raise the price of two drugs that are used to treat heart conditions, Eli Lilly's decision to charge patients in the United States more than $11,000 a month for its new lung cancer drug, and Pfizer's decision to charge almost $10,000 for a drug that treats advanced breast cancer. Philosophers echoed the *New York Times* editorial board's condemnation of pharmaceutical companies that charge high prices.[2]

Elsewhere, public officials regulate the pharmaceutical industry to limit price inflation and make drugs more affordable. Yet industry advocates argue that regulation stifles innovation and delays access to potentially lifesaving drugs. Arguments on behalf of patients' rights of self-medication and manufacturers' economic freedom also undermine calls for regulations that ensure affordability since patients and manufacturers may voluntarily agree to pay and charge high prices for drugs.

[1] The Editorial Board, "No Justification for High Drug Prices," *New York Times*, December 19, 2015, http://www.nytimes.com/2015/12/20/opinion/sunday/no-justification-for-high-drug-prices.html.

[2] Justin W., "Philosophers on Drug Prices," *Daily Nous*, September 28, 2015, http://dailynous.com/2015/09/28/philosophers-on-drug-prices/.

If patients' physical well-being and public health cannot justify government interference, can patients' financial well-being and public budgets justify interference? In this chapter, I argue that rights of self-medication require that patients not only be permitted to purchase and use pharmaceuticals, they also support a more general presumption against interfering with transactions between patients and pharmaceutical manufacturers. Not only do policies that prohibit manufacturers from charging high prices for drugs potentially hinder patients' access to drugs, they also violate producers' rights. To make this case, I consider three justifications for enforcing prohibitive pharmaceutical regulations that do not appeal to matters of health but rather relate to the business of medicine. Can financial considerations justify policies that interfere with voluntary exchanges between patients and pharmaceutical manufacturers?

First, I ask whether the pharmaceutical industry is normatively different from other industries because drug manufacturers have special duties to patients and citizens. In response, I argue that the pharmaceutical industry is not normatively different from other industries, and that even if it were, it would not justify policies that prohibited producers from charging high prices for drugs because, in general, people do not forfeit their entitlement to set prices when selling their property even if they are in industries that provide lifesaving products.

Second, I consider whether public officials may prohibit manufacturers from charging high drug prices on the grounds that patients do not voluntarily pay high prices for lifesaving drugs. I dispute the claim that patients' decisions to pay high prices are not voluntary, and I argue against price caps for pharmaceuticals. However, public officials can and should take non-prohibitive steps to reduce the cost of new drugs. For example, officials may address high drug prices by adopting a certification system that would lower the cost of drug development.

Third, intellectual property protections also consist in government interference with voluntary transactions between patients and manufacturers. After all, if a patient wants to purchase a drug from a generics manufacturer while another manufacturer holds the intellectual property rights to produce and sell the drug, public officials are empowered to interfere with their transaction for the sake of the intellectual property owners. Whether this form of interference is justified will depend on whether a system of pharmaceutical patents is defensible. This depends on whether intellectual property laws are warranted by an appeal to the good they do or by an appeal to people's rights.

If pharmaceutical patents are justified on the grounds that they benefit patients and consumers on balance, then the burden of proof lies with manufacturers to show that patents do promote well-being on balance. If pharmaceutical patents are justified on the grounds that producers have the right to profit from what they create, then it is a separate question whether a twenty-year period of patent exclusivity would achieve this goal. Public officials may respect producers' entitlements either by upholding patents *or* by providing prizes for pharmaceutical innovations.

But before we address the patent system, we should first consider safer ways that public officials and the industry may expand access to lifesaving drugs while also respecting patients' rights. These reforms include policies that hold the pharmaceutical industry to the same moral standards of other industries, though public officials may also use their purchasing power to negotiate for lower drug prices as long as they also allow access to private prescription drug plans and a global pharmaceutical marketplace. A certification, or at least a system of regulatory reciprocity, would also address high drug prices while respecting patients' rights of self-medication more than existing approval policies.

6.1 Single Standards for Industry

When business ethicists and commentators call for greater regulation of the pharmaceutical industry, they often appeal to the idea that manufacturers have special duties to promote public health. On the basis of this premise, some call for voluntary self-regulation by the industry. Insofar as these arguments are used to justify policies that are coercively enforced by public officials, proponents of this view implicitly assume that the industry not only has special duties but that their duties are so weighty or urgent that they are enforceable.

People may claim that people who work in the pharmaceutical industry have special obligations to ensure widespread access to affordable drugs because drugs are morally different from other products, since people need some drugs to live. Others suggest that people who work in the pharmaceutical industry have special role obligations as health professionals, based on the idea that businesses have a duty to benefit all stakeholders. Or people claim that people in the pharmaceutical industry have duties of fairness to reciprocate for the benefits that taxpayers and public officials have provided them by providing citizens with affordable access to drugs. In this section, I argue that these attempts to hold the pharmaceutical industry to higher moral standards do not succeed in general, and they certainly cannot justify a duty to provide widespread access to affordable drugs. Instead, I suspect that many of these intuitions about the special status of the pharmaceutical industry are better understood as the product of widespread psychological biases related to ideas about sacredness or betrayal aversion.

Consider first the idea that drugs are morally different from other products because they save and preserve people's lives. This is a common argument in favor of the claim that drug companies have special duties. As Richard Spinello writes:

> Few are concerned about the ethics of pricing a BMW or a waterfront condo in Florida. But the matter is quite different when dealing with vital commodities like food, medicine, clothing, housing, and education. Each of these goods has a major impact on our basic wellbeing and our ability to achieve any genuine self-fulfillment.[3]

Critics of the pharmaceutical industry echo this point when they argue, "this is not like lipstick or perfume, these are drugs that people need to live."[4] For the sake of argument, let's grant that drugs are morally different from other products, at least when they are used to save and sustain lives or promote people's most urgent and weighty interests. In this way, drugs are like food. People do not need access to all kinds of food, but they need affordable access to a sufficient amount of food, and, depending on one's theory of well-being, the relationship between food and people's important interests may justify treating food differently from other goods.[5] Specifically, it would support policies that provided people a sufficient income to purchase food or policies that provided food directly to ensure that people had the basic capability to survive and pursue other projects. Similarly, if drugs are different in this way, perhaps public officials should provide people who cannot afford necessary medicines with drugs. But just as it would be a mistake to impose universal limits on the price of food or for public officials to regulate the prices of all foods in virtue of its importance for people's overall well-being, it is also a mistake for officials to control or cap the price of all drugs to ensure that people in need have access to drugs.

Another reason that the pharmaceutical industry may be held to higher standards than other industries is the industry itself is intrinsically different from other industries. For example, some people argue that health professionals have special obligations to promote public health, that businesses have responsibilities that correspond to their social role, or that industries that benefit from public subsidies have heightened duties to contribute to citizens' well-being.

---

[3] Richard A. Spinello, "Ethics, Pricing and the Pharmaceutical Industry," *Journal of Business Ethics* 11, no. 8 (August 1992): 617–26, doi:10.1007/BF00872273.

[4] Neil A. Lewis with Robert Pear, "U.S. Drug Industry Fights Reputation for Price Gouging," *New York Times*, March 7, 1994, sec. U.S., http://www.nytimes.com/1994/03/07/us/us-drug-industry-fights-reputation-for-price-gouging.html.

[5] This claim depends on one's theory of well-being to some extent. Hedonists and objective list theorists may hold that food is especially important for well-being either because of its relative pleasurableness or because at least some quality food is part of a flourishing life. Desire satisfaction theories would also hold that lifesaving goods are importantly related to a person's well-being, though the relationship would be more contingent.

Consider first the claim that pharmaceutical companies have special obligations in virtue of their role obligations as members of the healthcare industry. In general, role obligations refer to the duties that people have in virtue of an "institutionally specified social function," such as an occupation, which is important either to the furtherance of a community's values or as an independently good cause.[6] Since health is generally seen as a good cause and valued by the community, people attribute special role obligations to health professionals and hold them to higher standards of praise and blame. On these grounds, some argue that the pharmaceutical industry has special obligations in virtue of their membership in the health profession.[7]

The claim that health professionals have special role obligations does not imply that they must be entirely altruistic in their devotion to healthcare, but that they have duties to promote health that people in ways that other industries do not. We may think of this as a kind of moral division of labor, where members of the health professions take on a greater share of responsibility for citizens' health. Dan Brock and Allen Buchanan write that it is "stubbornly one-sided" to view physicians either as "self-interested economic accumulators or as devoted altruists," but that physicians can adopt both perspectives and ought to balance their public spirit against their private motives.[8] For this reason, physicians may have a duty not to encourage patients to use unnecessary medicines, even if they could profit by prescribing them.[9] These duties may be especially salient to physicians, especially when they pledge to protect patients' health and thereby consent to take on special duties, but they may apply to other members of the health professions too.

One response to this argument is to deny that, as a conceptual matter, being in the health professions gives a person special duties to promote health. People in the apparel industry do not have special obligations to balance people's interest in being stylish against their interest in selling clothes. Bankers do not have a duty to ensure that everyone receives the lowest possible interest rates on loans rather than to try secure the best rates they can. One might reply that members of the healthcare industry are different because they provide vital services. But people are also in need of food and housing and cannot afford them, and few think that grocers and builders have special duties that other citizens lack to provide affordable access. If anyone has a duty to provide food and housing, it is taxpayers and members of the political community, not builders and grocers. Even if many health professionals thought of themselves as having special duties and

[6] Michael O. Hardimon, "Role Obligations," *Journal of Philosophy* 91, no. 7 (1994): 333–63.

[7] Richard T. De George, "Intellectual Property and Pharmaceutical Drugs: An Ethical Analysis," *Business Ethics Quarterly* 15, no. 4 (2005): 549–75.

[8] Dan W. Brock and Allen E. Buchanan, "The Profit Motive in Medicine," *The Journal of Medicine and Philosophy* 12 (February 1987): 1–35. doi:10.1093/jmp/12.1.1.

[9] William C. Hsiao, "When Incentives and Professionalism Collide," *Health Affairs* 27, no. 4 (2008): 949–51.

consented to acquire such duties, one may simply disavow his or her membership in the profession and redefine her role as a "lifestyle professional" or a researcher, thereby disavowing the special duties of health professionals as well.

But say we grant that people in health industries had special duties in virtue of their role. Perhaps drug companies would therefore have special duties to promote patients' health too. Nevertheless, such an argument would not necessarily justify special duties for pharmaceutical companies to change their behavior or special regulations of the industry, for three reasons.

First, the pharmaceutical industry already promotes people's health more than other industries (including many parts of medicine), so it seems that insofar as they have duties to promote health they already satisfy them. For example, Frank Lichtenberg finds that drugs increased life expectancy (and lifetime income) in the late twentieth century by 0.75–1.0 percent per year in the United States.[10] Unless other health industries were expected to increase life expectancy by as much or more, it would be disproportionate to claim that pharmaceutical companies were required to promote health even more by providing affordable access to their products when other health industries do not promote health as well as the pharmaceutical industry already does.

Second, even if people in the pharmaceutical industry did have special obligations in virtue of their role as health professionals, such an argument would not necessarily justify policies or regulation that required drug companies to promote public health or to provide affordable access to drugs. In order for special obligations to justify public policies, one would need to show not only that they had such obligations but also that their obligations were enforceable. That is, public officials would need to show that manufacturers were liable to be interfered with in virtue of their professional role. Here again, attempts to justify regulations by an appeal to special obligations would not only require holding the pharmaceutical industry to higher standards than others, it would also require that health professionals were more liable to be interfered with relative to people in other industries in virtue of their professional role. Even if we granted that the health industry had special obligations, it would not follow that public officials should disproportionately limit the freedom of those who chose a socially useful profession by becoming health workers.

Third, if it were true that people in the pharmaceutical industry had special duties to limit their profits for the sake of public health, such a principle would also justify the claim that physicians are obligated to provide their services at an affordable rate or to serve low-income communities, rather than charging

[10] Frank R. Lichtenberg, "Pharmaceutical Innovation, Mortality Reduction, and Economic Growth" (Working Paper, National Bureau of Economic Research, May 1998), http://www.nber.org/papers/w6569.

market prices to patients. Some political philosophers, such as Norman Daniels and Gillian Brock accept this conclusion.[11] Arnold Relman argues in favor of reducing the profit motive in healthcare by controlling the growth of specialty practices.[12] But this point illustrates that the price of crafting policy to reflect the pharmaceutical industry's seeming obligations to limit profits is higher than it may appear because to justify limits on pharmaceutical pricing, such an argument would also have revisionary implications for physicians' occupational freedom.

Relatedly, some business ethicists may argue that all businesses have special obligations not because they provide vital services but because their actions affect people who have a stake in the outcome of a business's choice. For example, Jeffery Moriarty argues that CEOs and other employees with fiduciary duties to shareholders have a moral obligation to decline excessive compensation, but while such an argument may justify limits on executive pay in the drug industry, it would weigh in favor of profit-seeking business practices.[13] In contrast, proponents of "corporate social responsibility" advance this argument when they argue that the pharmaceutical industry is not socially responsible insofar as they charge prices for drugs that severely limit consumers' access to drugs. They therefore conclude that manufacturers should provide assistance to low-income consumers to avoid public outcry and accusations of price gouging.[14] Other business ethicists think that corporations have special duties to promote the well-being of all stakeholders in addition to their general moral obligations and contractual duties to shareholders and customers, which would require that they consider the interests of whomever could benefit from using their products.[15]

These calls for corporate accountability and deference to stakeholders often appeal to the negative publicity that is associated with charging high drug prices

[11] Norman Daniels, "Health-Care Needs and Distributive Justice," *Philosophy & Public Affairs* 10, no. 2 (1981): 146–79; Gillian Brock, "Is Active Recruitment of Health Workers Really Not Guilty of Enabling Harm or Facilitating Wrongdoing?," *Journal of Medical Ethics* 39, no. 10 (2013): 612–14.

[12] Arnold S. Relman, "Eliminate the Profit Motive in Health Care," Physicians for a National Health Program. September 28, 2011. http://www.pnhp.org/news/2011/september/eliminate-the-profit-motive-in-health-care.

[13] Jeffrey Moriarty, "How Much Compensation Can CEOs Permissibly Accept?," *Business Ethics Quarterly* 19, no. 2 (2009): 235–50.

[14] Thomas A. Hemphill, "Extraordinary Pricing of Orphan Drugs: Is It a Socially Responsible Strategy for the U.S. Pharmaceutical Industry?," *Journal of Business Ethics* 94, no. 2 (November 18, 2009): 225–42, doi:10.1007/s10551-009-0259-x.

[15] R. Edward Freeman, *Strategic Management: A Stakeholder Approach* (Cambridge University Press, 2010); Andrew L. Friedman and Samantha Miles, "Developing Stakeholder Theory," *Journal of Management Studies* 39, no. 1 (January 1, 2002): 1–21, doi:10.1111/1467-6486.00280; Kevin Gibson, "The Moral Basis of Stakeholder Theory," *Journal of Business Ethics* 26, no. 3 (August 2000): 245–57, doi:10.1023/A:1006110106408.

or the potential for regulatory intervention.[16] But while it may be strategically useful for members of the pharmaceutical industry to voluntarily self-regulate and to act as socially responsible corporations that consider the interests of all stakeholders, these considerations would not establish that such corporations actually have special responsibilities from a moral perspective. I grant that it may be useful for corporations to act as if they have special responsibilities, but establishing that they actually have special responsibilities would require further argument. For example, it may be true that manufacturers face public criticism when they sell expensive drugs, but it would not follow that criticism was *warranted* unless it were unfair to charge high prices for drugs.

Here again, critics of the pharmaceutical industry hold it to higher standards than other industries. Classic examples of unethical businesses include banks that fraudulently sold financial instruments, energy companies that used accounting methods that misrepresented their profits, mortgage lenders that discriminated against racial minorities, automakers that concealed deadly manufacturing defects, factories that polluted their communities and caused people to get sick, and pharmaceutical manufacturers that developed expensive drugs that treat small populations while neglecting to develop affordable drugs for larger populations with more urgent needs. One of these industries is not like other. With the exception of the drug industry, classic examples of businesses that neglect to consider stakeholders or fail to act in a socially responsible way either committed fraud or violated people's rights. For example, it is fraudulent to construct financial instruments that carry high risks but to tell consumers and regulators they are safe investments. It violates people's rights against being poisoned to pollute their water supply and make them sick. Yet the drug industry encounters moral criticism on the grounds that it doesn't benefit as many people as much as it theoretically could.

Perhaps the pharmaceutical industry is different because many pharmaceutical innovations begin in publically financed institutions, such as nonprofit organizations, universities, or research institutes. Early research often relies on public grants. And many people in the pharmaceutical industry also rely on their publicly subsidized education to develop new drugs. And drug development relies on the cooperation of public hospitals and patients with publically provided health insurance. Finally, public officials enforce intellectual property laws that make it possible for manufacturers to profit by selling drugs. As President Barack Obama argued in 2012, profitable companies are profitable because of the efforts of taxpayers and public officials, so taxpayers and officials are therefore entitled to tax profitable companies to further develop public goods.[17]

---

[16] Lee Burke and Jeanne M. Logsdon, "How Corporate Social Responsibility Pays Off," *Long Range Planning* 29, no. 4 (August 1996): 495–502, doi:10.1016/0024-6301(96)00041-6.

[17] Obama said, "If you were successful, somebody along the line gave you some help. There was a great teacher somewhere in your life. Somebody helped to create this unbelievable American system that we have that allowed you to thrive. Somebody invested in roads and bridges. If you've got a business—you didn't

In this spirit, we might reconstruct an argument that pharmaceutical companies are especially indebted to the public good because they have greatly benefited from public institutions. Fair play theorists argue that a citizen could have duties of fairness to provide benefits if he accepted benefits, even if he did not consent to acquire those duties by accepting the benefits.[18] I do not think that people can acquire special obligations in this way, but some people make an argument like this when they argue that the pharmaceutical industry has special duties to assist people because they accept the benefits of intellectual property protection and public subsidies for research.[19] But fair play arguments are usually limited to contexts where the benefits are non-excludable because otherwise the beneficiary could refuse the benefit and any accompanying obligations. So the fair play argument could not support the claim that pharmaceutical companies have special duties simply because they accept public benefits, like intellectual property protection, because public officials could feasibly exclude them from receiving those benefits. Instead, officials may give drug companies the opportunity to accept benefits, such as patent protections, only if they consent to take on further obligations to benefit the political community (more on this in a bit).

On the other hand, one might think of publically financed research as a non-excludable benefit that drug companies accept, which gives them special duties to the taxpayers who finance public research. If publically funded research must remain nonexcludable and publically accessible to all under current conditions, then fair play arguments, if successful, would be valid justifications for the claim that the pharmaceutical industry has special duties. But research needn't be public; it is only that researchers judge that the benefits of publicizing their publically subsidized research likely outweigh the costs. But say drug companies did accept nonexcludable benefits from the public. It still wouldn't follow that they had special duties of fairness to promote the health of patients in particular, since they would not be free riding on their efforts but rather the efforts of taxpayers and researchers. So even if people could acquire duties by accepting benefits, in these circumstances companies would have duties to taxpayers and researchers, not particular patients. And their duty would be to fairly contribute to research, not to provide affordable drugs.

build that. Somebody else made that happen. The Internet didn't get invented on its own. Government research created the Internet so that all companies could make money off the Internet." Remarks by the president at a campaign event in Roanoke, Virginia, *Whitehouse.gov*, July 13, 2012, https://www.whitehouse.gov/the-press-office/2012/07/13/remarks-president-campaign-event-roanoke-virginia.

[18] Klosko, "Presumptive Benefit, Fairness, and Political Obligation"; Dagger, "Membership, Fair Play, and Political Obligation."

[19] Marcia Angell, *The Truth About the Drug Companies: How They Deceive Us and What to Do About It* (New York: Random House Trade Paperbacks, 2005).

Another drawback of arguments that ground an industry's special duties in duties of fairness is that often the people who are most in need of the benefits that the pharmaceutical industry can provide are also the least likely to contribute to drug development by participating in public institutions. Specifically, people who live in poor countries that do not subsidize drug development or effectively enforce intellectual property rules may have especially urgent need for access to drugs and pressing health problems, but they do not contribute to public schemes that benefit the pharmaceutical industry. Similarly, people with severe disabilities and children do not contribute to the kinds of public goods that make pharmaceutical research possible, but they can often benefit the most from the kinds of goods that the drug industry provides. Paradoxically, if we accepted the claim that the pharmaceutical industry had special duties of fairness to promote people's health or to provide affordable access to drugs, fulfilling those duties may benefit those who are least in need of the benefits.

For these reasons, the kinds of arguments that are generally deployed to justify special duties for people in certain industries do not support the claim that the pharmaceutical industry has special obligations. So why do people think that drug companies have special duties to promote people's health and provide affordable access to drugs? James Huebner presents several psychological explanations for the widespread intuition that pharmaceutical companies have special duties to patients. He first argues that the intuition that pharmaceutical companies have special duties to provide lifesaving drugs is an expression of more general intuitions about sacredness or the idea that some things are valuable in a way that should be insulated from market forces.[20] For example, researchers find that consumers reject arguments in favor of market-pricing systems for pharmaceuticals (e.g., the argument that high prices are necessary to fund further research and development) but accept the same arguments in favor of market pricing for computer software.[21] The taboo against selling things that are seen as sacred is not unique to pharmaceuticals. People also oppose markets in sexual services, non-vital organs, votes, citizenship, and gestational surrogacy, often out of concerns about sacredness. Yet we should be wary of arguments from intuitions that are grounded in taboos related to bodies, feelings of disgust, or thoughts about impropriety, since these intuitions often do not withstand further scrutiny.[22] Furthermore, as Martha Nussbaum argues, judgments

[20] James M. Huebner, "Moral Psychology and the Intuition That Pharmaceutical Companies Have a 'Special' Obligation to Society," *Journal of Business Ethics* 122, no. 3 (June 15, 2013): 501–10, doi:10.1007/s10551-013-1773-4.

[21] A. Peter McGraw, Janet A. Schwartz, and Philip E. Tetlock, "From the Commercial to the Communal: Reframing Taboo Trade-Offs in Religious and Pharmaceutical Marketing," *Journal of Consumer Research* 39, no. 1 (June 1, 2012): 157–73, doi:10.1086/662070.

[22] Haidt's work, for example, demonstrates that feelings of disgust can influence people's moral judgments even when the considerations that induced feelings of disgust are not directly relevant

that are grounded in feelings of disgust or taboo often reflect harmful prejudices and can be used to justify discriminatory policies.[23]

Huebner also argues that people distrust the pharmaceutical industry in light of public instances of corporate misconduct, but they also expect the pharmaceutical industry to promote health because of the nature of their products.[24] These circumstances induce feelings of betrayal aversion—a psychological phenomenon where people hold people or companies that are entrusted to protect them to higher moral standards than people or companies that are not explicitly charged with a protective role.[25] Huebner speculates that this impulse is sometimes expressed as the view that pharmaceutical companies have special duties, whereas people would not attribute special duties to industries that do not sell products related to health or safety. Betrayal aversion may be rational. If people do not feel qualified to evaluate the safety of drugs, they may instead express high expectations for manufacturers in order to establish the expectation that pharmaceutical companies will primarily aim to promote health. Yet even though it may be rational to act as if pharmaceutical companies have special duties, it doesn't follow that they in fact have special duties.

So people's tendency to think that drug companies have special duties to protect people does not establish that those duties exist. Further argument is necessary. And when we consider the arguments for the claim that pharmaceutical companies have special duties to promote people's health or to provide affordable drugs, we find that more general arguments on behalf of special

---

to moral considerations in a particular circumstance. On the other hand, one may reply that the foregoing arguments in favor of rights of self-medication, insofar as they appeal to intuitions about self-ownership, are also grounded in intuitions related to disgust. Christopher Freiman and Adam Lerner developed an argument like this. I am not convinced that self-ownership intuitions are best explained by disgust as they are by a more general commitment to the value of autonomy. Moreover, a principle of self-ownership may be intuitive to some because of intuitions about disgust, which we ought to discount, but the principle may nevertheless be justified for other reasons. But in any case, arguments in favor of rights of self-medication do not rely on a self-ownership premise. Christopher Freiman and Adam Lerner, "Self-Ownership and Disgust: Why Compulsory Body Part Redistribution Gets Under Our Skin," *Philosophical Studies* 172, no. 12 (March 11, 2015): 3167–90, doi:10.1007/s11098-015-0463-8; Jonathan Haidt, Clark McCauley, and Paul Rozin, "Individual Differences in Sensitivity to Disgust: A Scale Sampling Seven Domains of Disgust Elicitors," *Personality and Individual Differences* 16, no. 5 (May 1, 1994): 701–13, doi:10.1016/0191-8869(94)90212-7; Simone Schnall et al., "Disgust as Embodied Moral Judgment," *Personality and Social Psychology Bulletin*, May 27, 2008, doi:10.1177/0146167208317771.

[23] Martha C. Nussbaum, "Danger to Human Dignity: The Revival of Disgust and Shame in the Law," *Chronicle of Higher Education*, August 6, 2004.

[24] Huebner, "Moral Psychology and the Intuition That Pharmaceutical Companies Have a 'Special' Obligation to Society."

[25] Jonathan J. Koehler and Andrew D. Gershoff, "Betrayal Aversion: When Agents of Protection Become Agents of Harm," *Organizational Behavior and Human Decision Processes* 90, no. 2 (2003): 244–61.

duties cannot justify special duties in these cases. Specifically, even if people did acquire special duties when they consented to them, accepted benefits, or took on a professional role, these considerations would not support the claim that drug companies currently have special duties to promote patients' well-being by providing affordable drugs.

6.2 Private Options and the Global Marketplace

Despite people's discomfort with placing a price on lifesaving drugs, people pay for pharmaceuticals in every country, either as taxpayers or as consumers. Prices are determined in different ways and vary worldwide. In some countries, such as Switzerland, Canada, and India, public officials enforce caps on the price of pharmaceuticals to ensure affordable access.[26] In other countries, such as Australia, the United Kingdom, and Japan, drugs are provided through a national insurance program or pharmaceutical benefit scheme that directly negotiates the prices of drugs on behalf of all citizens so that manufacturers must provide drugs at a low price to access the national market.[27] In Germany,

---

[26] In Switzerland, manufacturers are only permitted to sell drugs that are deemed both effective and cost-effective, and the Swiss government sets maximum price limits for each drug. In Canada, the Patented Medicine Prices Review Board (PMPRB) regulates the prices of new drugs and prohibits manufacturers from charging "excessive" wholesale prices. Pharmaceuticals are then provided through the federal health system for in-hospital drug use, each province offers public drug plans for outpatient pharmaceuticals, and citizens can also purchase private prescription drug plans. Each drug plan negotiates the retail price of drugs for its members. Public plans are less expensive, but more drugs are eligible for reimbursement under private plans. The Indian government also enforces price caps for essential drugs that treat common conditions. "Pharmaceutical HTA and Reimbursement Processes—Switzerland," April 2011, https://www.ispor.org/HTARoadMaps/SwitzerlandPH.asp; Akane Takayama and Mamoru Narukawa, "Pharmaceutical Pricing and Reimbursement in Japan for Faster, More Complete Access to New Drugs," *Therapeutic Innovation & Regulatory Science*, December 23, 2015, doi:10.1177/2168479015619202; PTI, "39 More Drugs to Become Affordable; Diabetes, Digestive Disorder Medicines in Price Control List," *The Times of India*, July 16, 2015, http://timesofindia.indiatimes.com/india/39-more-drugs-to-become-affordable-diabetes-digestive-disorder-medicines-in-price-control-list/articleshow/48097256.cms.

[27] In Australia, most drug prices are set by the Pharmaceutical Benefits Scheme (PBS), which negotiates with drug companies to provide drugs at fixed prices. For drugs that are not covered by the PBS, patients must either pay a market price or use private insurance to pay for them. Similarly, in the United Kingdom, the National Institute for Health and Care Excellence (NICE) typically recommends drugs for use by the National Health Service (NHS) only if they cost less than £30,000 per quality adjusted life year (QALY) saved. This means that if a £35,000 drug would extend a person's life by one year of good health, it is unlikely that patients in the UK would receive the drug. Japan has a similar system, where Japan's public National Health Insurance (NHI) agency maintains a price list for new drugs. Sir Andrew Dillon, "Carrying NICE over the Threshold," | *NICE Blog*, February 19, 2015, https://www.nice.org.uk/news/blog/carrying-nice-over-the-threshold; Takayama and Narukawa, "Pharmaceutical Pricing and Reimbursement in Japan."

a set of statutory nonprofit insurance collectives pool their bargaining power to negotiate with manufacturers for low drug prices.[28]

Some drug prices in the United States are notoriously high, and prices vary between patients in the United States more than other countries. Usually, pharmaceuticals are initially more expensive in the United States than in other countries, but generic drugs are less expensive.[29] Some citizens receive publically provided health insurance, and the US government controls the price of drugs for low-income Medicaid patients and veterans, but not for senior citizens and disabled people who access drugs through Medicare.[30] For patients with private insurance plans, insurance benefit managers, HMOs, and hospital formularies independently negotiate with manufacturers for lower prices, which causes people with different private insurance plans to pay different prices for the same drugs. Uninsured patients are generally charged the highest prices for drugs.

Debates about pharmaceutical pricing are sometimes characterized as debates about the merits of a regulatory approach like the European model versus a more market-based approach to pricing like the United States' system.[31] We should be careful, however, in accepting this characterization because it is somewhat misleading. Drugs may seem more expensive in the United States simply because the United States is often among the richest countries included in most surveys of drug prices, and prices reflect each nation's income level rather than particular

---

[28] If a new drug is not clearly more effective than previous treatments, then the insurance collectives will only reimburse patients for the cost of the previous treatment, and patients who want to use the new drugs must pay the price differential. Ludwig Burger and Torsten Severin, "Germany's Stance on Pricing Threatens Drug Firm Profits," *Reuters*, February 18, 2014, http://www.reuters.com/article/us-germany-drugs-analysis-idUSBREA1H09E20140218. Olga Khazan, "Why Medicine Is Cheaper in Germany," *The Atlantic*, May 22, 2014, http://www.theatlantic.com/health/archive/2014/05/why-medicine-is-cheaper-in-germany/371418/.

[29] Drugs are more expensive in Japan. Generic drugs are less expensive in the United States where the generic market is more competitive. Patricia M. Danzon and Li-Wei Chao, "Cross-National Price Differences for Pharmaceuticals: How Large, and Why?," *Journal of Health Economics* 19, no. 2 (March 2000): 159–95, doi:10.1016/S0167-6296(99)00039-9; Patricia M. Danzon and Michael F. Furukawa, "Prices and Availability of Pharmaceuticals: Evidence from Nine Countries," *Health Affairs*, 2003, W3, 521–26.

[30] Prices are controlled for Medicaid patients because the government requires drug companies to pay rebates to Medicaid patients when the price of drugs rises faster than inflation. Veterans' drug prices are also fixed by a federal formulary that provides a limited number of discounted drugs. In contrast, the US government does not directly negotiate drug prices for citizens covered by Medicare, the public insurance option for senior citizens and people with disabilities. Instead, outpatient drug coverage is paid for by private insurers that are under contract with Medicare. Robert Pear, "Medicaid Pays Less Than Medicare for Many Prescription Drugs, U.S. Report Finds," *New York Times*, August 15, 2011, http://www.nytimes.com/2011/08/16/us/16drug.html.

[31] Ian Maitland, "Priceless Goods: How Should Life-Saving Drugs Be Priced?," *Business Ethics Quarterly* 12, no. 4 (October 2002): 451–80, doi:10.2307/3857995.

policy choices or regulations.[32] And even in countries that directly limit the price of drugs, providers negotiate prices within a global marketplace and pay manufacturers for their products. And even in the United States, intellectual property requirements and healthcare policy affect drug prices. The question is not whether the pharmaceutical industry should be a fully socialized industry or an anarchic free market (though both of these options have a few proponents) but whether policies such as price caps and price controls should limit pharmaceutical prices.

Public officials can directly control the price of drugs in their countries in two ways. First, they may directly prohibit manufacturers from charging high prices for drugs. Or they may use their purchasing power to negotiate for lower prices. In this section, I develop an argument against price caps and price controls on the grounds that they would unduly limit peoples' rights of self-medication and economic freedom. However, if people voluntarily joined insurance collectives to negotiate lower drug prices, it would not violate people's rights of self-medication or anyone's economic freedom. And insofar as public officials may permissibly provide publically funded healthcare to citizens, they too may permissibly negotiate with drug companies to purchase drugs for lower prices.

Ian Maitland's thorough and compelling case against price controls and price caps in the pharmaceutical industry serves as the foundation of my argument. Maitland argues that "other things equal, whatever [pharmaceutical pricing] regime saves the most lives, relieves the most suffering, and brings the greatest improvement in the quality of our lives is the morally superior one."[33] Maitland then makes the case that a market-based approach to prices is morally superior because price controls create shortages and discourage pharmaceutical companies from investing in drug development. Since drug development can potentially save so many lives, even if price controls or caps did expand access in ways that enabled more people to use therapeutic or lifesaving drugs, if limits on pricing deterred investment, Maitland suggests that they would do more harm than good.

At this point it may be helpful to revisit an argument from a previous chapter, where I drew an analogy between cases of exploitation and circumstances where desperate patients are granted access to unapproved drugs. Zwolinski's defense of practices that seem like impermissible forms of exploitation is relevant to this discussion too. Zwolinski describes a paradigmatic case of price gouging—after a hurricane people transport ice to an area that has lost power and charge $12

---

[32] Antonio Cabrales and Sergi Jimenez-Martin, "The Determinants of Pricing in Pharmaceuticals: Are U.S. Prices Really Higher than Those of Canada?," SSRN Scholarly Paper, Rochester, NY: Social Science Research Network, April 1, 2007, http://papers.ssrn.com/abstract=1003132.

[33] Maitland, "Priceless Goods."

for each bag of ice that usually costs less than $2.[34] But as Zwolinski argues, laws that prohibit price gouging effectively punish the only people who are willing to assist those who are stranded without power. By arresting the alleged price gougers, no one has incentive to bring ice to people in need, and those who are willing to pay $12 for a bag of ice (e.g., so they can refrigerate insulin) are left without any means of purchasing ice. If people were allowed to charge high prices for ice, more people would enter the market and the prices of ice would fall in response to increased demand. Zwolinski develops a similar argument against usury caps on lending terms.[35] Zwolinski's case for price gouging does not neatly translate to the case of pharmaceutical pricing because public officials prevent competition by upholding patents for new drugs. But the case against prohibiting people from charging high prices does apply to the pharmaceutical industry insofar as limits on prices deter drug development.

Maitland also considers that market pricing for drugs could prevent some people from accessing drugs at an affordable price, but he replies that even if the sick have a right to access affordable pharmaceuticals, it is not drug makers' responsibility to provide it.[36] One may argue that the drug industry does have a responsibility to provide affordable pharmaceuticals to people in need because they are well placed to do so. But manufacturers are only well placed to provide affordable drugs because they have invested in developing the drugs in the first place. To claim that they are responsible for providing affordable drugs because they are able to provide the drugs violates the arguments for single standards of industry obligation, which I developed in the previous section, since other industries that create useful or even lifesaving products do not incur duties to provide them at low prices in virtue of creating the products in the first place.

And as Maitland points out, to say otherwise could potentially encourage people not to pursue drug development so that they can avoid unwanted obligations to forgo profits in order to provide people with affordable drugs.[37] So while it may seem exploitative to charge high prices for lifesaving drugs, it is not necessarily *wrongful* exploitation since providing patients with the opportunity to purchase lifesaving drugs does not make them worse off than they would have been without the option to purchase the drugs.[38] Instead of relying on drug companies to provide affordable access, public officials could alternatively subsidize pharmaceuticals (as most public insurance options do) or provide prescription drug vouchers for low-income patients to purchase drugs that

---

[34] Matt Zwolinski, "The Ethics of Price Gouging," SSRN Scholarly Paper (Rochester, NY: Social Science Research Network, March 3, 2008), http://papers.ssrn.com/abstract=1099567.

[35] Matt Zwolinski, "Are Usurious? Another New Argument for the Prohibition of High Interest Loans?," *Business Ethics Journal Review* 1, no. 4 (2013): 22–27.

[36] Maitland, "Priceless Goods."

[37] Ibid.

[38] Wertheimer and Zwolinski, "Exploitation."

treat life-threatening conditions and subsidies for manufacturers to produce low-cost drugs. Such a political intervention to address unaffordable drug prices could preserve some of the benefits of a pharmaceutical market while improving access for economically disadvantaged patients. The same considerations apply in the global context as well. If people have general humanitarian duties to promote global health, then everyone in the global community has these duties, not just the manufacturers of drugs that can improve global health.[39]

Another concern regarding price caps or price controls for drugs is that there is no principled way to determine whether a drug is appropriately priced besides considering whether people will pay for it. If the just price of a drug is not the price that people are willing to pay, then what is it? The very same people who claim that a human life is priceless, also claim that $51,000 is too much to charge for cancer treatments. If manufacturers do not set a price on these drugs, public officials will. And if public officials prohibit manufacturers from selling an expensive drug and also refuse to provide it, then they place a price tag on a person's life at whatever cost savings they achieve by negotiating low drug prices in exchange for market exclusivity.

Since there is not a clear "just price" for lifesaving drugs, and since those who provide lifesaving drugs generally benefit patients more than most other people, even if they do charge high prices, there is a strong moral presumption against policies that impose price regulations on drugs as a condition of sale. On the other hand, philosophers raise three objections to market pricing for lifesaving goods that are worth considering before we address collective negotiations. These objections are generally framed in the context of labor and lending regulations, but they would apply with equal force to arguments against price regulations for drugs. First, some may argue that the decision to pay high prices for drugs is not voluntary if patients lack acceptable alternatives. Second, one may argue that it is wrong for drug companies to exploit patients by charging high prices for drugs when patients depend on drugs to survive. Third, others may argue that market pricing in lifesaving goods is often incompatible with a commitment to human dignity.

Serena Olsaretti argues a person cannot voluntarily agree to an exchange if she lacks acceptable alternatives. In response to Robert Nozick's defense of a broadly laissez-faire system of labor regulation, Olsaretti argues that people do not voluntarily choose undesirable outcomes when the only reason that they are making an undesirable decision is because all the alternatives are worse.[40] One

[39] Allen Buchanan and Matthew DeCamp, "Responsibility for Global Health," *Theoretical Medicine and Bioethics* 27, no. 1 (2006): 95–114, doi:10.1007/s11017-005-5755-0.

[40] Robert Nozick, *Anarchy, State, and Utopia*, 2nd ed. (New York: Basic Books, 2013); Serena Olsaretti, "Freedom, Force and Choice: Against the Rights-Based Definition of Voluntariness," *Journal of Political Philosophy* 6, no. 1 (March 1, 1998): 53–78, doi:10.1111/1467-9760.00046.

could apply Olsaretti's general argument against unregulated pricing to pharmaceutical pricing on the grounds that people in need do not voluntarily choose to purchase extraordinarily expensive drugs when their lives depend on using the drug. Yet while Olsaretti takes this insight to justify policies that limit systems of market pricing on the grounds that capitalism is often the reason a person must engage in a market transaction or suffer unacceptable consequences. For pharmaceuticals though, people's lack of acceptable alternatives to high drug prices is not a result of laissez-faire economic policy, it is a result of disease. So even if patients do not voluntarily pay high prices for drugs, it is not clear that the remedy in this case is to prevent them from paying high prices for drugs because doing so would not address the underlying reason that their alternatives to high prices were unacceptable.

Another argument in favor of regulating prices is that some markets are wrongfully exploitative even though they do not make patients worse off. Consider for example Jeremy Snyder's claim that employers can have duties to refrain from paying low wages to employees who rely on a job to meet their basic needs because relationships of dependency generate special duties to refrain from sacrificing dependents' basic well-being for the sake of profit.[41] We may extend this argument against the practice of charging high prices for drugs in the following way. Patients rely on drug companies to meet their basic needs, so drug companies have special duties to ensure that patients' needs are met foremost before they consider their own bottom line.

On Snyder's account, the failure to consider a dependent's basic need expresses an unacceptable level of disregard that is morally worse than the disregard people express toward non-dependents.[42] However, at the point that a patient initially encounters an expensive drug, she is not in a relationship of dependence with the manufacturer just as an employee is not in a relationship of dependence with her employer before she is hired. Moreover, even if drug companies were required to put their patients' needs before their bottom lines, lest they express an offensive attitude toward them, such an argument could not straightforwardly justify price controls or caps. To establish this, one would need to show not only that people should consider the basic needs of dependents but also that public officials were entitled to limit patients' and providers' options to ensure that people express appropriate regard for each other by considering the needs of their dependents.

A final objection to Maitland's defense of market pricing appeals to a Kantian ideal of treating people as ends in themselves and not merely as means to profit. For example, Norman Bowie defends a more general Kantian approach

---

[41] Jeremy Snyder, "Needs Exploitation," *Ethical Theory and Moral Practice* 11, no. 4 (2008): 389–405.

[42] Jeremy Snyder, "Disregard and Dependency," *Business Ethics Journal Review* 1, no. 13 (May 20, 2013): 82–85.

to business ethics that appeals to this principle.[43] Elsewhere Bowie argues that transactions are unfair when sellers and consumers have unequal bargaining power and that "the obligations of manufacturers rest upon the demands of social justice."[44] Bowie may therefore conclude that it is wrong for drug companies to charge high prices because in doing so they treat patients as means and flout the demands of social justice by making people who are already disadvantaged by illness even more disadvantaged by causing material depravation. On this account, manufacturers would not be entitled to charge high prices if their prices were only possible because consumers lacked the power to negotiate for lower prices due to their unequal circumstances.

Yet Bowie's approach to markets rules out many markets that are mutually beneficial but also inherently unequal. For example, markets in services that rely on expertise, such as tax preparation or preparing a mortgage, are premised on the assumption that consumers are less knowledgeable about the thing they are purchasing than the providers, yet they do not treat consumers unfairly in virtue of this fact. Similarly, markets in lifesaving therapies, including certain pharmaceuticals, are necessarily unequal because only the consumer's life is at stake, but the presence of unequal bargaining power is insufficient to establish that a market treats people unfairly. Moreover, even if a broadly Kantian approach could establish that it is wrong to treat a person as a mere means, it is not always wrong to treat people as means, as long as they are also respected as ends in themselves. One way to treat a person as an end in herself is to respect her choices rather than seeing her as an instrument for the furtherance of overall well-being. In this way, Kantian considerations would support policies that permitted manufacturers and consumers to freely negotiate the prices of drugs, not restrictions on drug prices.

There are also ways of responding to Bowie's concern about unequal bargaining power that do not require price controls or caps. For example, patients increase their power to negotiate by purchasing prescription drug plans that collectively negotiate for lower drug prices on behalf of their members. Collective negotiation is not incompatible with Maitland's argument against price controls or caps. Patients are not obligated to disadvantage themselves in the market so that manufacturers have incentives to develop new drugs. Insofar as public officials may permissibly tax citizens to provide people with public healthcare services, they may also collectively bargain to provide members with lower prices.[45]

---

[43] Norman E. Bowie, "Fair Markets," *Journal of Business Ethics* 7, no. 1/2 (1988): 89–98; Norman E. Bowie and Thomas W. Dunfee, "Confronting Morality in Markets," *Journal of Business Ethics* 38, no. 4 (July 2002): 381–93, doi:10.1023/A:1016080107462.

[44] Bowie, "Fair Markets."

[45] These policies are more fraught than private insurance because people do not consent to pay taxes in exchange for public healthcare. But citizens' lack of consent would not undermine public officials' standing to negotiate lower prices on behalf of citizens.

More inclusive and generous public health systems would have more power to negotiate for lower prices to the extent that they provided access to a greater number of patients.[46]

On the other hand, public officials may not use their power to prohibit the sale of expensive drugs or unapproved drugs outside the context of a national health plan in order to achieve lower drug prices. In these cases, they would violate citizens' rights of self-medication, which include the right to purchase any drugs without government interference. Just as public officials are not entitled to paternalistically prohibit people from accessing dangerous drugs on the grounds that they have negative side effects, public officials also are not entitled to prohibit people from purchasing drugs out of concerns about negative financial side effects either. This argument supports policies that would promote greater access to drugs within and across borders, such as recent proposals that would allow American consumers to legally import drugs from Canadian pharmacies.[47]

6.3 Drug Prices and Deregulation

Though the pharmaceutical industry does not have special duties to promote public health, and it is not wrong to charge high prices for lifesaving drugs, it is also not wrong for public officials and insurance providers to negotiate for lower drug prices, as long as those policies do not violate the rights of consumers or manufacturers. In addition to removing price regulations that prevent consumers from purchasing drugs that are not provided by their healthcare plans, public officials and insurance providers may also take steps to provide affordable access to drugs by removing regulations that not only violate rights of self-medication but also make drugs more expensive.

Existing limits on patients' rights of self-medication potentially inflate the cost of drugs in five ways. First, premarket approval policies increase the fixed cost associated with drug development. Second, approval requirements prevent manufacturers from developing affordable drugs. Third, prescription requirements make drugs more expensive for consumers. Fourth, existing standards of liability prevent patients from waiving their rights to seek damages in case they are injured by using a drug, even if they were informed of the risks and consented to use the drug. Fifth, manufacturing regulations potentially prevent consumers

[46] L. W. Cleland, "Modern Bootlegging and the Prohibition on Fair Prices: Last Call for the Repeal of Pharmaceutical Price Gouging," *Bepress Legal Series*, 2004, 264.

[47] Patrick Healy and Margot Sanger-katz, "Hillary Clinton Proposes Cap on Patients' Drug Costs as Bernie Sanders Pushes His Plan," *New York Times*, September 22, 2015, http://www.nytimes.com/2015/09/23/us/politics/hillary-rodham-clinton-proposes-cap-on-patients-drug-costs-as-sanders-pushes-his-plan.html. For context, see Bhosle M. J. and R. Balkrishnan, "Drug Reimportation Practices in the United States." *Therapeutics and Clinical Risk Management* 3, no. 1 (2007): 41.

from purchasing drugs from low-cost providers and maintain monopolies that empower manufacturers to charge high prices for a drug even after its patent expires.

Manufacturers often cite the high cost of premarket approval policies as an explanation for the high cost of drugs. It is costly to conduct the required safety and efficacy tests and to navigate the approval process, which can cost up to $2 billion. So in addition to concerns about drug loss and drug lag, the approval process also limits access to drugs insofar as manufacturers pass the costs to consumers.[48] The high cost of development contributes to the overall cost of drugs because the cost of developing any particular drug does not correlate with the market price of that drug; rather, more profitable drugs subsidize the development of less profitable treatments that could nevertheless provide a greater therapeutic benefit and investment in the development of drugs that may either fail to gain approval or be unprofitable. For this reason, it would be a mistake to focus exclusively on the development costs for a particular drug when evaluating whether the price of that drug is reasonable.

Regulatory agencies also withhold approval for drugs that are less effective (but cheaper) than existing drugs. This means that consumers who are willing to compromise effectiveness for cheaper drugs never get the chance to access those drugs.[49] This standard discourages companies from developing cheaper drugs where expensive drugs already treat a condition. In this way approval requirements also contribute to high drug prices because they do not consider the financial benefits of a drug when weighing the costs and benefits of approval. Such policies also violate rights of self-medication and potentially have negative health effects since patients who cannot afford expensive drugs are prevented from using less effective but cheaper drugs, so they are left without options. In other words, poor patients are left without treatment because they cannot afford the *most effective* treatment

Short of full rights of self-medication, officials could address the high costs and negative health effects of the approval process by adopting a policy of

---

[48] Though other estimates place the average cost of drugs around $800 million. Christopher P. Adams and Van V. Brantner, "Estimating the Cost of New Drug Development: Is It Really $802 Million?," *Health Affairs* 25, no. 2 (March 1, 2006): 420–28, doi:10.1377/hlthaff.25.2.420. As Brian Palmer writes, "It costs around $1.75 billion to develop the average cancer medicine. Only drugs for respiratory disorders, at $2 billion, can top that total. (AIDS drugs and anti-parasitic are the real bargains, at between $500 million and $700 million.)" Brian Palmer, "The $8,000 Pill," *Slate*, August 16, 2010, http://www.slate.com/articles/news_and_politics/explainer/2010/08/the_8000_pill.html. See also "'Big Ideas,' by Gary S. Becker," *The Milken Institute Review*, June 2004, 93–94," *UNZ.org*, n.d., http://www.UNZ.org/Pub/MilkenInstituteRev-2004q2-00093.and also Sam Peltzman, "An Evaluation of Consumer Protection Legislation: The 1962 Drug Amendments," *Journal of Political Economy* 81, no. 5 (1973): 1049–1091.

[49] Michael Mandel, "How the FDA Impedes Innovation: A Case Study in Overregulation," Policy Brief, Progressive Policy Institute, June 2011.

regulatory reciprocity, where drugs that are approved in one jurisdiction can be sold across borders.[50] Such a policy would permit greater price competition and expand access for low-income consumers.[51] A policy that only granted FDA approval to drugs approved by EMA or the FDA, and vice versa, could save the pharmaceutical industry as much as $672 million per year.[52] Some public officials have recently taken up the cause of reciprocity explicitly in an effort to expand affordable access to pharmaceuticals for American consumers.[53]

Prescription drug requirements also potentially make pharmaceuticals more expensive. When consumers are required to obtain prescriptions to use a drug, they must not only pay for the drug but also the doctor's visit required to get a prescription. Especially for uninsured patients, the additional cost of obtaining a prescription can be prohibitive.[54] But even patients with insurance must pay a price to obtain a prescription to use a drug since doctor's visits often require patients to leave work and pay copays for the visit and prescription.

Prescription requirements can also contribute to higher drug prices because they reduce demand. This may seem counterintuitive at first. The primary predictor of drug price is whether there is a specific demand; the most expensive drugs are those that treat chronic or fatal conditions, with high demand and low competition.[55] If demand for drugs decreased, one might expect the price to fall as well. But pharmaceutical prices are not sensitive to demand in this way. Limited demand usually leads to lower prices because vendors use lower prices to increase demand. But when the supply of consumers is limited by prescription

[50] Daniel Klein and Alexander Tabarrok, "FDA Review," The Independent Institute, 2016, http://www.fdareview.org/09_reform.php#3.

[51] Although, this solution would also potentially violate existing intellectual property protections. For an example, consider the 2001 controversy regarding generic HIV/AIDS drug imports to South Africa. William W. Fisher III and Cyril P. Rigamonti, "The South Africa AIDS Controversy: A Case Study in Patent Law and Policy," Documento de Trabajo, Facultad de Derecho de Harvard, 2005, http://boris.unibe.ch/69881/1/South%20Africa.pdf.

[52] "If A Drug Is Good Enough for Europeans, It's Good Enough For Us," Health Affairs, http://healthaffairs.org/blog/2014/02/14/if-a-drug-is-good-enough-for-europeans-its-good-enough-for-us/.

[53] Conor Friedersdorf, "Ted Cruz's Best Idea for Overhauling the FDA," The Atlantic, December 18, 2015, http://www.theatlantic.com/politics/archive/2015/12/ted-cruzs-best-idea-for-overhauling-the-fda/421158/.

[54] For example, Cara Buckley describes uninsured Americans who could not afford to obtain drugs for conditions like asthma and diabetes because it was prohibitively expensive to see a physician to obtain a prescription. The Affordable Care Act increased the number of insured Americans, but the remaining uninsured Americans still face these barriers to access. In places without universal health coverage, prescription requirements can also contribute to higher drug prices when insurance providers reimburse patients for the cost of prescriptions, so patients and physicians are less sensitive to the cost of pharmaceuticals, making prescriptions more expensive for the uninsured whose drug costs are not reimbursed. Insured patients bear these costs as well because high drug prices and costly doctors' visits also cause higher insurance premiums. Cara Buckley, "For Uninsured Young Adults, Do-It-Yourself Health Care," The New York Times, February 18, 2009.

[55] Palmer, "The $8,000 Pill."

requirements, drug manufacturers cannot lower the price to increase demand. So since they cannot lower the price and profit from more widespread use, they respond by charging more for the drug to compensate for the artificially limited demand. There is some evidence that the cost of prescription requirements is substantial. For example, Peter Temin estimates that switching powerful cold medicines from prescription only to over-the-counter status saved consumers over $70 million per year, and estimates the consumer surplus to be over $770 million per year.[56]

Another domestic reform that could potentially reduce drug prices would be to permit manufacturers to limit their liability for adverse drug reactions. For example, Richard Epstein proposes a contractual model of medical liability where physicians might be permitted to provide risky medical services to patients who waive their right to hold the physician accountable for adverse effects.[57] To the extent that malpractice insurance and legal costs contribute to rising healthcare costs, such contracts might reduce these costs. Similarly, if legal costs contribute to the cost of certain drugs, permitting patients to absolve manufacturers of liability could address such costs. These reforms might be especially attractive if patients were permitted to access any drug without authorization.

Finally, manufacturing regulations also contribute to high drug prices. Not only do regulatory agencies prohibit pharmaceutical companies from selling unapproved drugs, they also prohibit unauthorized manufacturers from selling drugs. Open manufacturing within states and across borders would enable greater price competition. Specifically, as long as manufacturers do not fraudulently represent their process or products, they should not require an expensive license or approval to manufacture pharmaceuticals. Rather than preemptively limiting the production of drugs, regulators should instead monitor drug manufacturing to ensure that producers accurately depict their products and provide certification for producers that adhere to industry standards. However, manufactures should not be disqualified from producing pharmaceuticals on the grounds that they are in a foreign country or because they are compounding pharmacies.

The example of 17P, a drug that prevents premature labor, illustrates how pharmaceutical regulation can exponentially increase the cost of a drug.[58] In 2003 a study conducted by the National Institute of Health found that

---

[56] Temin, "Realized Benefits from Switching Drugs."

[57] Richard A. Epstein, "Medical Malpractice: The Case for Contract," *American Bar Foundation Research Journal* 1, no. 1 (January 1, 1976): 87–149.

[58] Arthur Allen chronicles several similar examples of this phenomenon. Arthur Allen, "A Giant Pain in the Wallet," *Slate*, March 29, 2011, http://www.slate.com/articles/health_and_science/medical_examiner/2011/03/a_giant_pain_in_the_wallet.html.

prescribing a form of progesterone called 17P early in pregnancy could significantly reduce women's risk of preterm birth.[59] Unfortunately, 17P was no longer manufactured because better drugs had been developed for the conditions it was originally designed to treat (uterine cancer and hormonal problems), and 17P remained off-label for prematurity. Fortunately, physicians could still prescribe the drug to be made by individual compounding pharmacies rather than by drug manufacturers. Sold in this form, 17P cost $10 per shot, and pregnant woman received weekly shots of 17P for four months during pregnancy if they were at risk of premature labor. As evidence grew that 17P was an extremely effective prematurity treatment, the FDA encouraged drug companies to develop and manufacture a prematurity drug under the ODA. The agency then granted KV Pharmaceuticals approval and orphan drug status for their manufactured version of 17P, which is called Makena.

Once approved, KV Pharmaceuticals received exclusive rights to manufacture and market all drugs treating prematurity for seven years and immediately sent letters to compounding pharmacies threatening FDA censure for independently compounding the drug.[60] Moreover, KV Pharmaceuticals charged $1,500 per weekly shot, instead of $10. KV Pharmaceuticals explained that the 150x cost increase was justified because of the cost of drug development, testing, and post-market monitoring, as well as the expected benefits.[61] Joanne Armstrong, writing for the *New England Journal of Medicine*, estimated that "the cost of treating all 139,000 patients who could benefit from (17P) . . . is $41.7 million. Substituting Makena . . . would bring the estimated cost to $4.0 billion."[62]

This example is not unusual. The aforementioned objections to Turing Pharmaceuticals' and Valeant Pharmaceuticals' pricing policies also demonstrate how manufacturing licenses can increase the cost of *existing* drugs. The manufacturers of Makena claimed they expected to spend $200 million developing 17P for sale and bringing it through the approval process, and that these development costs explained the high price. By approving Makena, regulators granted exclusive manufacturing rights to KV Pharmaceuticals, thus protecting KV Pharmaceuticals

[59] P. J. Meis et al., "Prevention of Recurrent Preterm Delivery by 17 Alpha-hydroxyprogesterone Caproate," *New England Journal of Medicine* 348, no. 24 (2003): 2379–85.

[60] The letters said, "Continuing to compound this product after FDA approval of Makena renders the compounded product subject to FDA enforcement for violating certain provisions of the Federal Food, Drug and Cosmetic Act, as well as FDA guidance." See Lisa Belkin, "Prematurity Drug Price Jumps Wildly," *New York Times*, April 1, 2011.

[61] Rob Stein, "Critics Slam Cost of FDA-approved Drug to Prevent Preterm Births," *Washington Post*, April 1, 2011.

[62] Joanne Armstrong, "Unintended Consequences—The Cost of Preventing Preterm Births After FDA Approval of a Branded Version of 17OHP," *New England Journal of Medicine* 364, no. 18 (May 5, 2011): 1689–91.

from competition. Even if having a uniform manufacturing process for drugs like Makena would promote safety (there is no evidence to suggest that 17P was unsafe), the benefit of uniformity comes at a high financial price for patients and society. But there is another price as well. If the high cost of drugs like Makena discourages some patients from using it, then more high-risk pregnancies might result in premature births. Premature infants are more likely to die in their first year of life, be severely disabled, or suffer from conditions such as autism. In this way, the financial price translates into a devastating human price as well.

Makena's price increase was so egregious that KV Pharmaceuticals eventually lowered the price in response to criticism, and the FDA stated that it would not enforce restrictions on 17P manufacturing by compounding pharmacies. The agencies' reversal demonstrated that manufacturing restrictions were unnecessary after all and that compounding pharmacies could effectively provide treatment. Similar cases continued to provoke public outcry for the next ten years. Then Turing Pharmaceuticals CEO, Martin Shkreli, purchased the rights to manufacture Daraprim, a drug that treats parasitic infections, and increased the price more than fifty-fold overnight.[63] Again, the price increase was met with near universal public outcry. But as Alex Tabarrok noted at the time, Daraprim was widely available in Europe and India. If the FDA permitted foreign manufacturers to export approved drugs to the United States, then it would not have been rational to raise the price of Daraprim.[64]

Rather than adopting a policy of reciprocity, the FDA decided instead to grant expedited review status to generic drug manufacturing applications, which will hopefully go some way toward reducing drug prices.[65] But compared with policies like legal compounding and regulatory reciprocity, expedited approval alone is likely to fall short of the goals of affordable access and self-medication. More generally, steep increases in the cost of generic drugs illustrate that intellectual property law is not the only cause of high drug prices.[66] Stories like these also show there are other regulatory burdens that make even generic drugs expensive and remedies that could expand access in addition to intellectual property reform.

[63] Andrew Pollack, "Drug Goes From $13.50 a Tablet to $750, Overnight," *New York Times*, September 20, 2015, http://www.nytimes.com/2015/09/21/business/a-huge-overnight-increase-in-a-drugs-price-raises-protests.html.

[64] "Generic Drug Regulation and Pharmaceutical Price-Jacking," *Marginal REVOLUTION*, September 24, 2015, http://marginalrevolution.com/marginalrevolution/2015/09/generic-drug-regulation.html.

[65] Anna Edney, "Shkreli's Strategy to Jack up Drug Prices May Be Curbed by FDA," *Bloomberg.com*, accessed April 7, 2016, http://www.bloomberg.com/news/articles/2016-03-14/shkreli-s-strategy-to-jack-up-drug-prices-may-be-curbed-by-fda.

[66] Elisabeth Rosenthal, "Officials Question the Rising Costs of Generic Drugs," *New York Times*, October 7, 2014, http://www.nytimes.com/2014/10/08/business/officials-question-the-rising-costs-of-generic-drugs.html.

These proposals are speculative. The removal of administrative barriers to access may not effectively lower drug prices. But there are other reasons to support these proposals as well. In addition to approval requirements and prescription requirements that violate patients' rights of self-medication, other regulations violate manufacturers' and consumers' rights to sell and buy pharmaceuticals across borders.

6.4 Lifesaving Innovation and Patents

The pharmaceutical industry is very profitable compared with other industries. For example, Pfizer, the world's largest drug company, reported a 42 percent profit margin in 2013.[67] I have argued that public officials can address high drug prices in part by expanding access to drugs and reducing regulatory barriers to self-medication while still preserving many of the benefits of a competitive pricing system. Yet these proposals will not address the most significant cause of high drug prices—intellectual property law.

Governments currently enforce intellectual property laws that protect manufacturers' rights to create the products they invented for twenty years. Most pharmaceuticals are patented.[68] For many of the years between the date a patent is filed and when a drug is approved, the drug cannot be sold, so manufacturers have only a limited period of time to profit from the drugs they develop that are eventually approved and sold to a large number of patients.

Governments enforce protections for patents to promote innovation, and there is good evidence that patents do promote innovation. For example, in Norway, researchers previously were granted patents on their own research known as "the professors' privilege." Then Norway changed its patent policy to be more like the patent rules of American universities, where patents were granted to institutions instead of individual researchers. Economists noted a 50 percent decline in entrepreneurship and patenting rates and patents for university researchers.[69] On the other hand, patents can also hinder basic research by preventing people from researching an idea, hindering follow-on research and more diverse applications of research into new compounds or technologies.[70]

---

[67] "Best of the Biggest: How Profitable Are the World's Largest Companies?," *Forbes*, May 12, 2014, http://www.forbes.com/sites/liyanchen/2014/05/13/best-of-the-biggest-how-profitable-are-the-worlds-largest-companies/#1a3f0dd14c33.

[68] Anthony Arundel and Isabelle Kabla, "What Percentage of Innovations Are Patented? Empirical Estimates for European Firms," *Research Policy* 27, no. 2 (1998): 127–41.

[69] Hans K. Hvide and Benjamin F. Jones, "University Innovation and the Professor's Privilege" (Working Paper, National Bureau of Economic Research, March 2016), http://www.nber.org/papers/w22057.

[70] Fiona Murray et al., "Of Mice and Academics: Examining the Effect of Openness on Innovation" (Working Paper, National Bureau of Economic Research, March 2009), http://www.nber.org/papers/w14819.

Though researchers do suggest that patents do not meaningfully deter cumulative innovation for drugs, these results only dispute the claim that patents deter follow-on innovation, not that innovation in the drug industry is on balance optimized by the current patent system.[71]

Other research that is focused on the pharmaceutical industry suggests patents at least distort pharmaceutical innovation. For example, part of the success of ODA was that it used patent protections to promote more innovation for drugs that treat rare diseases.[72] Patent protections also direct researchers to focus on developing cancer drugs that treat later stages of the disease since they have a shorter trial and approval process and hence a longer patent life.[73] More generally, less regulated drug classes are less innovative in part because researchers can enjoy a longer period of intellectual property protection once their drugs are on the market.

Yet arguments in favor of a patent system seem contrary to the ideals of self-medication and free exchange between patients and providers. By enforcing patents, public officials prohibit people from selling drugs to willing patients. There are four potential responses to this seeming tension between intellectual property and the ideals of self-medication:

1. Public officials do not have the authority to enforce pharmaceutical patents, and anyone should be permitted to manufacture and sell any drug.
2. Public officials should enforce pharmaceutical patents in ways that promote innovation on balance.
3. Public officials should enforce pharmaceutical patents in ways that promote widespread access to drugs.
4. Public officials should enforce pharmaceutical patents in ways that respect the intellectual property rights of researchers and manufacturers.

The first solution acknowledges that there is a genuine tension between patents and pharmaceutical freedom and resolves the tension on the side of self-medication. This solution would entail a radical revision of our current approach to intellectual property more generally. And as I will argue, the best case for intellectual property enforcement is patents for pharmaceuticals, in light of the enormous benefits associated with innovation. If public officials rethink their

[71] Alberto Galasso and Mark Schankerman, "Patents and Cumulative Innovation: Causal Evidence from the Courts" (Working Paper, National Bureau of Economic Research, July 2014), http://www.nber.org/papers/w20269.

[72] James H. Flory and Philip Kitcher, "Global Health and the Scientific Research Agenda," *Philosophy & Public Affairs* 32, no. 1 (January 1, 2004): 36–65, doi:10.1111/j.1467-6486.2004.00004.x.

[73] Eric B. Budish, Benjamin N. Roin, and Heidi L. Williams, "Do Fixed Patent Terms Distort Innovation?: Evidence from Cancer Clinical Trials," SSRN Scholarly Paper, Rochester, NY: Social Science Research Network, September 5, 2013, http://papers.ssrn.com/abstract=2353471.

role in enforcing intellectual property law, drug patents should be the last form of intellectual property that merits reconsideration.

The second solution acknowledges that there is a real tension between intellectual property and the ideals of self-medication but holds that existing policies are justified because they promote innovation. I am sympathetic to this solution. The third solution also acknowledges a real tension between intellectual property and self-medication but proposes reforms that would better balance the need for innovation against patients' interests in purchasing generic medicines through prizes and patent buyouts. These second two options are broadly consequentialist. They rely on the assumption that public officials are justified in enforcing some intellectual property requirements but also that manufacturers do not have particularly weighty rights to prevent other people from manufacturing products that they invented.

The fourth solution resolves the tension in favor of intellectual property rights. On this view, manufacturers have weighty rights to prevent people from manufacturing products they invented. It is unclear, however, that this system can be justified because unlike people's natural rights, intellectual property rights may quite plausibly be limited.

First consider whether public officials are entitled to enforce intellectual property law in the first place. Unlike other forms of property, it is unclear whether people have pre-political rights to intellectual property.[74] It would clearly be immoral to assault, deceive, or murder someone in the absence of laws against assault, fraud, and murder. It would also be wrong, quite plausibly, to steal someone's physical possessions or to prevent him from carrying out financial contracts with others. But unlike the right to control one's body or labor, using another person's idea need not involve interference with anyone at all. For example, many scientific discoveries are roughly simultaneous, so a producer may develop a patented therapy without ever interacting with the people who initially patented the therapy, but patents will prevent him from selling it to consumers.[75]

If people do not have pre-political intellectual property rights, then either public officials may not permissibly interfere with the pre-political rights people do to enforce patents or public officials may use whatever legitimate power they have to interfere with people's choices to enforce patents that promote innovation or access. Some philosophers argue that public officials may not prevent people from exercising their property rights, freedom of expression, or economic freedom to protect an intellectual monopoly even if having patents do

---

[74] Seana Shiffrin, "Intellectual Property," SSRN Scholarly Paper, Rochester, NY: Social Science Research Network, 2007, http://papers.ssrn.com/abstract=2679176.

[75] James Bessen and Michael James Meurer, *Patent Failure: How Judges, Bureaucrats, and Lawyers Put Innovators at Risk* (Princeton, NJ: Princeton University Press, 2008), 251.

promote well-being on balance.[76] Michele Boldrin and David Levine explicitly extend this argument to the pharmaceutical industry and make the economic case against the current system of patents.[77] Consider an analogy to illustrate the moral argument for this point. If a wealthy person injures his victim by dropping a large gold brick on his arm in order to give him the brick as a gift, the wealthy person has violated his victim's rights, even if he benefited the victim on balance.[78] So even if the victim accepts the benefits of the gold brick, the wealthy person still acted wrongly and would owe compensation and apology to his victim. Similarly, if public officials violate people's rights to manufacture drugs and sell them to customers and consumers' rights to purchase and use drugs from any manufacturers, and these are pre-political rights, then even if such a system of rights violations benefited people on balance, it would not be justified and public officials would owe people compensation for the rights violation that a patent system entails.

If we accept the claim that public officials do not have the authority to violate people's rights to benefit people on balance—for example, by promoting pharmaceutical innovation—then public officials either must refrain from enforcing patents or compensate those whom they harm. Officials could refrain from enforcing patents by adopting a system of open licensing, where anyone can manufacture a patented drug. Open licensing may be particularly beneficial in developing countries where the patent system effectively prevents large numbers of people from using therapeutics.[79] And patents do not always drive innovation in fast-paced, technical fields, nor is it clear that they promote productivity on balance.[80] Patent holders can gain a competitive advantage by impeding others' innovation rather than developing innovative technologies themselves.[81]

On the other hand, officials' refusal to enforce patents for drugs would prevent people from developing innovative, lifesaving therapies and very likely cost

---

[76] Stephan Kinsella, "The Case Against Intellectual Property," in *Handbook of the Philosophical Foundations of Business Ethics* (Netherlands: Springer, 2013), 1325–57, http://link.springer.com/10.1007/978-94-007-1494-6_99; Gary Chartier, "Intellectual Property and Natural Law," *Australian Journal of Legal Philosophy* 36 (2011): 58.

[77] Michele Boldrin and David K. Levine, *Against Intellectual Monopoly* (New York: Cambridge University Press, 2010).

[78] Seana Valentine Shiffrin, "Wrongful Life, Procreative Responsibility, and the Significance of Harm," *Legal Theory* 5, no. 2 (1999): 117–48.

[79] Sean Flynn, Aidan Hollis, and Mike Palmedo, "An Economic Justification for Open Access to Essential Medicine Patents in Developing Countries," *The Journal of Law, Medicine & Ethics* 37, no. 2 (June 1, 2009): 184–208, doi:10.1111/j.1748-720X.2009.00365.x.

[80] Nathan Musick and Phillip Webre, "Federal Policies and Innovation," Congressional Budget Office, November 17, 2014, https://www.cbo.gov/publication/49487.

[81] Alex Tabarrok, *Launching The Innovation Renaissance: A New Path to Bring Smart Ideas to Market Fast* (TED Books, 2011).

lives on balance. Whatever health gains open licensing could bring would be small compared with the losses of abandoning a system of patents. Recall Frank Lichtenberg's research that found drugs substantially increased life expectancy and lifetime income in the late twentieth in the United States.[82] Lichtenberg also finds that pharmaceutical innovation is a primary cause of increased longevity in the twenty-first century, accounting for almost three-fourths of the gains in life expectancy from 2000 to 2009.[83] And elsewhere, Lichtenberg finds, predictably, that factors that decrease expected drug prices also decrease innovation, such that "a 10 percent decline in drug prices would ... be likely to cause at least a 5–6 percent decline in pharmaceutical innovation."[84] Patents maintain high drug prices, and, in so doing, they also preserve incentives to create innovative, lifesaving therapies that substantially promote longevity and income.

For this reason, one may acknowledge the tension between rights of self-medication and free exchange on one hand, and patents on the other, while accepting that the rights violation entailed by intellectual property protections are justified. If so, then public officials may have most moral reason to enforce some intellectual property protections. This is not to say, however, that the existing system of patents and prizes is optimal or that officials should not also consider other ways of promoting innovation, such as prizes.

6.5 Patents and Prizes

If public officials enforce patents for pharmaceuticals, a patent system may aim either to promote long-term innovation and well-being on balance or to ensure greater access to beneficial therapeutics for the worst off. If the goal of a patent system is to promote medical innovation and overall health, there is no principled reason to believe that the current twenty-year system is optimal. The benefits of the current patent system are clear—manufacturers have huge incentives to create new drugs because if they are approved, the manufacturer can sell it without competing with other manufacturers, and the government will protect their monopoly by enforcing their intellectual property rights.[85] Furthermore,

[82] Lichtenberg, "Pharmaceutical Innovation, Mortality Reduction, and Economic Growth."

[83] Frank R. Lichtenberg, "Pharmaceutical Innovation and Longevity Growth in 30 Developing and High-Income Countries, 2000–2009," *Health Policy and Technology* 3, no. 1 (2014): 36–58.

[84] Frank R. Lichtenberg, "Importation and Innovation" (Working Paper, National Bureau of Economic Research, September 2006), http://www.nber.org/papers/w12539.

[85] Henry Grabowski, "Patents, Innovation and Access to New Pharmaceuticals," *Journal of International Economic Law* 5, no. 4 (2002): 849–60; H. G. Grabowski, "Increasing R&D Incentives for Neglected Diseases: Lessons from the Orphan Drug Act," in *Increasing R&D Incentives for Neglected Diseases: Lessons from the Orphan Drug Act*, ed. Keith Maskus and Jerome Reichman (Cambridge University Press, 2005), http://dukespace.lib.duke.edu/dspace/handle/10161/7359; Joseph A.

intellectual property protections empower manufacturers to profit from their products, and manufacturers are more likely to develop drugs that are likely to be profitable.[86]

But as I suggested above, patents can also prevent innovation to the extent that manufacturers divert resources from development to marketing to maximize the value of a licensed product. The costs of litigation and patent enforcement, which are associated with preventing generic manufacturers from selling drugs at lower prices, may also divert resources from further drug development.[87] More worryingly, like the approval process, the patent system also deters small firms and researchers from developing innovative therapies because the legal costs of maintaining a patent can be prohibitively expensive, and new entrants to the pharmaceutical markets face costly legal challenges to their own patents as well.[88] Pharmaceutical "patent trolls" may profit from the system of patents rather than developing new drugs, thereby contributing to the price of drugs without expanding the range of options for consumers.[89] These considerations suggest that the current patent system likely does not promote innovation as well as a system of intellectual property protections could.[90]

Against this backdrop, some researchers wonder whether patents really do promote innovation relative to alternative systems of intellectual property protection.[91] There are few circumstances where public officials intervening in a market to deter competition is the recipe for innovation. Proponents of the current system say that drugs are different because they are easy to manufacture, but the fixed costs of development are high. However, this consideration is an

---

DiMasi, Ronald W. Hansen, and Henry G. Grabowski, "The Price of Innovation: New Estimates of Drug Development Costs," *Journal of Health Economics* 22, no. 2 (2003): 151–85.

[86] Amy Finkelstein, "Static and Dynamic Effects of Health Policy: Evidence from the Vaccine Industry," *The Quarterly Journal of Economics* 119, no. 2 (May 1, 2004): 527–64, doi:10.1162/0033553041382166; David Dranove, Craig Garthwaite, and Manuel Hermosilla, "Pharmaceutical Profits and the Social Value of Innovation" (Working Paper, National Bureau of Economic Research, 2014), http://www.nber.org/papers/w20212.

[87] Jean O. Lanjouw and Mark Schankerman, "Characteristics of Patent Litigation: A Window on Competition," *The RAND Journal of Economics* 32, no. 1 (2001): 129–51, doi:10.2307/2696401.

[88] Ibid.

[89] Robin Feldman and W. Nicholson Price, "Patent Trolling—Why Bio & Pharmaceuticals Are at Risk," *UC Hastings Research Paper*, no. 93 (2014), http://papers.ssrn.com/sol3/Papers.cfm?abstract_id=2395987.

[90] Furthermore, there is reason to believe that insofar as efforts to expand patents have succeeded (such as the ODA) or failed to promote innovation (e.g., arguably Hatch-Waxman), it is unclear what an ideal patent system for promoting innovation would look like.

[91] Michael A. Heller and Rebecca S. Eisenberg, "Can Patents Deter Innovation? The Anticommons in Biomedical Research," *Science* 280, no. 5364 (May 1, 1998): 698–701, doi:10.1126/science.280.5364.698; Fiona Murray and Scott Stern, "Do Formal Intellectual Property Rights Hinder the Free Flow of Scientific Knowledge?: An Empirical Test of the Anti-Commons Hypothesis," *Journal of Economic Behavior & Organization* 63, no. 4 (2007): 648–87.

argument for lowering the fixed cost of development, such as costs associated with the approval process, not an argument for further deterring competition within pharmaceutical markets.[92] Public officials and manufacturers are not required to show that a patent is necessary for innovative research to occur. We might imagine a system that requires evidence of innovation for a patent to be approved, but the existing system only requires novelty. The consequence of the current system is a proliferation of patents that do not necessarily reflect greater medical innovation.[93]

Another critique of innovation-based justifications for pharmaceutical patents is that even if patents promote innovation, the law is not crafted in a way that benefits people on balance. For example, despite efforts such as the ODA to focus attention on rare diseases, the current system nevertheless creates incentives to develop drugs that will treat high-income people or large groups of people. So researchers and manufacturers are unlikely to develop therapies that treat people who are unable to pay for medicine in the present regulatory climate.[94]

And currently, patent law is not crafted in a way that benefits those who have the most to gain from access to drugs. For example, trade agreements such as the General Agreement on Tariffs and Trade and proposals such as the Trans-Pacific Partnership aim to extend many of the intellectual property rules enforced in the United States to developing countries.[95] And while there is some evidence that these international agreements may be necessary to encourage manufacturers to develop drugs for a global marketplace, it can also be counterproductive insofar as navigating cumbersome legal requirements discourages drug development.[96] On the other hand, it is not clear that international patent agreements made the global poor worse off by making drugs more expensive. Evidence from

[92] Richard Posner cited this argument in favor of drug regulation while acknowledging "it's not clear that we really need patents in most industries." "Judge Who Shelved Apple Trial Says Patent System out of Sync," *Reuters*, July 5, 2012, http://www.reuters.com/article/us-apple-google-judge-idUSBRE8640IQ20120705.

[93] Especially in light of me-too drugs—pharmaceuticals that function in the same way and for the same purpose as other drugs but are developed simply to give firms access to markets that are otherwise protected by patents. Me-too drugs do not improve well-being relative to the status quo but can contribute to rising drug prices. Angell, *The Truth About the Drug Companies*.

[94] David B. Resnik, *The Price of Truth: How Money Affects the Norms of Science* (Oxford University Press, 2006); Christopher McCabe, Richard Edlin, and Jeff Round, "Economic Considerations in the Provision of Treatments for Rare Diseases," in *Rare Diseases Epidemiology* (Springer, 2010), 211–22, http://link.springer.com/chapter/10.1007/978-90-481-9485-8_13.

[95] Jean O. Lanjouw, "Intellectual Property and the Availability of Pharmaceuticals in Poor Countries" (NBER Chapters, National Bureau of Economic Research, 2003), https://ideas.repec.org/h/nbr/nberch/10794.html.

[96] Yi Qian, "Do National Patent Laws Stimulate Domestic Innovation in a Global Patenting Environment? A Cross-Country Analysis of Pharmaceutical Patent Protection, 1978–2002," *The Review of Economics and Statistics* 89, no. 3 (2007): 436–53.

India suggests that prices remained low despite patents.[97] Another analysis suggests that Indian patients were not made worse off by new patent laws, because pharmaceuticals were generally unaffordable even in the absence of a patent system.[98]

Alternatively, a prize model may benefit patients more than a patent system in some contexts. One prize model consists of awarding large sums of money to those who create new treatments for pressing medical problems. The treatments are then sold and priced by public officials. For example, Thomas Pogge and Aidan Hollis propose a Health Impact Fund to finance drug innovation for rare diseases that primarily affect low-income populations.[99] The Health Impact Fund is designed to encourage development for neglected diseases by providing patent holders with upfront rewards in exchange for open licensing of their new patents. Essentially, it enables manufacturers to trade their patent protections for up to ten years of annual rewards based on whether their drug effectively treats neglected diseases for needy populations.

One benefit of a prize model like the Health Impact Fund is that it can address more urgent needs, and once the initial innovators are paid, it allows people to access drugs in ways that are insulated from market forces that could make beneficial therapies unaffordable for poor populations. A drawback of the prize model is it relies on a predetermined specification of the value of a new therapy; whereas market-based pricing mechanisms may better reflect how people value having additional access to new drugs. Another drawback is that in order to promote innovation, drug manufacturers must trust that prizes for innovation commensurate with the lifesaving effects of a new drug will be available years in the future. In light of these concerns, Allen Buchanan, Tony Cole, and Robert Keohane propose a Global Institute for Justice in Innovation, which would be established by multilateral treaties and granted legal authority, as a more credible institutional mechanism for encouraging innovation in the treatment of neglected diseases.[100]

[97] Mark Duggan, Craig Garthwaite, and Aparajita Goyal, "The Market Impacts of Pharmaceutical Product Patents in Developing Countries: Evidence from India" (Working Paper, National Bureau of Economic Research, 2014), http://www.nber.org/papers/w20548.

[98] Jean O. Lanjouw, "The Introduction of Pharmaceutical Product Patents in India" (Working Paper, National Bureau of Economic Research, January 1998), http://www.nber.org/papers/w6366.

[99] Thomas Pogge, "The Health Impact Fund: Enhancing Justice and Efficiency in Global Health," *Journal of Human Development and Capabilities* 13, no. 4 (2012): 537–59; Aidan Hollis, "An Efficient Reward System for Pharmaceutical Innovation," (Draft, University of Calgary, June 10, 2004), http://cdrwww.who.int/entity/intellectualproperty/news/Submission-Hollis6-Oct.pdf; Aidan Hollis and Thomas Pogge, "The Health Impact Fund: Making New Medicines Accessible for All," 2008, http://www.popline.org/node/210204.

[100] Allen Buchanan, Tony Cole, and Robert O. Keohane, "Justice in the Diffusion of Innovation," *Journal of Political Philosophy* 19, no. 3 (September 1, 2011): 306–32, doi:10.1111/j.1467-9760.2009.00348.x.

Other solutions are available as well. Some propose using advanced market commitments to incentivize drug development by guaranteeing manufacturers that they will have access to a market if they develop drugs for it.[101] Officials may also address affordability if they subsidize affordable access to pharmaceuticals directly without changing patent law and also subsidized translational and basic research for drugs.[102] James Wilson proposes that public officials should refuse to pay for drugs that are patented because money spent on paying for drugs that are protected by a monopoly could be better spent assisting patients in need, and future patients can still benefit from drugs when they are available without a patent.[103] Nicole Hassoun suggests a rating system that evaluates companies' effects on poor populations in order to encourage them to extend drug access to the world's worst off.[104]

Patent buyouts may also address high drug prices. If patent holders could choose whether to sell their patents to governments, then a patent buyout system could preserve existing incentives to innovate while enabling public officials to expand access to lifesaving medicines sooner than a patent would allow. Michael Kremer argues that officials could use auctions to determine market prices for patents.[105] Kremer notes that buyouts are especially desirable in the pharmaceutical buyouts because patents substantially contribute to the high price of drugs relative to other industries where manufacturing is more expensive and also because pharmaceuticals have a high social value.

For any of these proposals, including the patent system, considerations of moral risk and the relative moral wrongness of causing versus allowing harm should remain at the forefront of debates about pharmaceutical innovation. Intellectual property systems require public officials to violate producers' and consumers' rights to make and purchase potentially therapeutic drugs in order

[101] Owen Barder, Michael Kremer, and Heidi Williams, "Advance Market Commitments: A Policy to Stimulate Investment in Vaccines for Neglected Diseases," *The Economists' Voice* 3, no. 3 (2006), http://www.degruyter.com/dg/viewarticle.fullcontentlink:pdfeventlink/$002fj$002fev.2006.3.3 $002fev.2006.3.3.1144$002fev.2006.3.3.1144.pdf?t:ac=j$002fev.2006.3.3$002fev.2006.3.3.114 4$002fev.2006.3.3.1144.xml; Rachel Glennerster, Michael Kremer, and Heidi Williams, "Creating Markets for Vaccines," *Innovations* 1, no. 1 (2006): 67–79; Ernst R. Berndt et al., "Advanced Purchase Commitments for a Malaria Vaccine: Estimating Costs and Effectiveness" (Working Paper, National Bureau of Economic Research, 2005), http://www.nber.org/papers/w11288.

[102] P. V. Grootendorst and A. Edwards, "Patents and Other Incentives for Pharmaceutical Innovation," *Encyclopedia of Health Economics* 2 (2014): 434–42.

[103] James Wilson, "Paying for Patented Drugs Is Hard to Justify: An Argument About Time Discounting and Medical Need," *Journal of Applied Philosophy*, 2012, http://onlinelibrary.wiley.com/doi/10.1111/j.1468-5930.2012.00567.x/full.

[104] Nicole Hassoun, "Global Health Impact: A Basis for Labeling and Licensing Campaigns?," *Developing World Bioethics* 12, no. 3 (December 1, 2012): 121–34, doi:10.1111/j.1471-8847.2011.00314.x.

[105] Michael Kremer, "Patent Buyouts: A Mechanism for Encouraging Innovation," *The Quarterly Journal of Economics* 113, no. 4 (November 1, 1998): 1137–67, doi:10.1162/003355398555865.

to promote innovation. These rights violations are difficult to justify, so there should be a presumption against any policy that interferes with patients and consumers to produce better health effects on balance. For this reason, the enforcement of any intellectual property system is morally risky, and the moral risks are compounded by the enormous effects that the global system of intellectual property rules have on all patients, including economically disadvantaged people in developing countries. The stakes are so high that public officials should be extremely reluctant to interfere with producers of generic drugs in developing countries in order to protect the intellectual property claims of producers who refuse to sell drugs in those markets at prices that would enable people to use their products.

To the extent that policies that interfere with producers' and consumers' choices to promote innovation are justified, it would be by an appeal to the enormous good that they produce for all people. But if public officials persist in upholding an intellectual property system, they must compensate the producers and consumers whose rights are violated by intellectual monopolies. Producers can be compensated by having access to patent protections within the same system of intellectual monopoly that prevents them from producing patented drugs. However, officials should also compensate consumers for the harms of the patent system, even if consumers and patients benefit on balance. For example, one way public officials could compensate consumers for the ways that the patent system violates their rights to purchase and use drugs would be by providing subsidies for using expensive patented drugs, thereby offsetting some of the harms of a system of intellectual monopoly. Depending on whether enforcing a system of intellectual property genuinely promotes innovation, access, and well-being, public officials may judge that, all things considered, they ought to violate people's rights by enforcing a system of intellectual property and compensate people rather than refraining from enforcing patents altogether.

If policies that interfere with patients and manufacturers rights for the sake of the greater good are justified in theory, it is still clear that the existing system of pharmaceutical patents promotes the goals of innovation and expanded access as well as alternative systems might. That said, I'm unsure about the best solution in light of the available evidence. Whatever the solution to problems of affordability and innovation though, it should be justified on the grounds that it works, not on the grounds that industry professionals support it or that it has been the status quo policy for so long. When lives are at stake, public officials should be open to revisionary solutions. These solutions include a non-prohibitive approval system, fewer burdensome regulations, and rights of self-medication, which would reduce public officials' ability to restrict access to lifesaving therapeutics. And for the same reasons, public officials should also rethink intellectual property laws that empower manufacturers to use the legal system to restrict effective access to lifesaving therapeutics. Though high drug prices do not violate patients' rights in the way that approval and prescription requirements do, policies that prevent manufacturers from selling generic drugs to willing consumers can violate rights if existing intellectual property regulations for drugs are unjust.

At this point one may wonder if I am holding the pharmaceutical industry to double standards when it comes to intellectual property while rejecting double standards for the industry elsewhere. However, the foregoing proposals for patent reform proceed from the assumption that neither manufacturers nor consumers have pre-political rights to publically enforced and regulated intellectual property protections. Unlike other circumstances, where people's bodily rights and freedom of contract should in principle extend to their rights of self-medication and freedom to sell drugs, so far, I have assumed that public officials would not violate more general rights by enforcing a patent system or by financing a prize model for drugs. Furthermore, it is not as if the current system of intellectual property holds the drug industry to the same standards as other industries since the norms of patent enforcement tends to vary between industries. For these reasons, if people do not have pre-political claims to intellectual property enforcement, different standards for different industries would not be objectionable as long as treating different industries in different ways promoted greater innovation and/or access for consumers.

6.6 Patents and the Rights of Producers

So far I have assumed that manufacturers do not have pre-political rights to prevent other people from copying their inventions. But some philosophers argue producers do have pre-political claims to receive compensation for their investment in the initial idea and that public officials ought to respect their claims by upholding intellectual property rules. There are three arguments in behalf of the claim that pharmaceutical manufacturers deserve compensation for innovation. First, personality theorists argue that intellectual property protections are justified as a way of respecting each person's entitlement to control his own life and to develop long-term projects without interference. Second, Lockeans argue that producers have a claim to control their ideas and to profit from their ideas because they mixed their labor with the ideas. And Ian Maitland argues that even if there are not pre-political property rights, manufacturers do have pre-political rights against deception, and changing patent laws would constitute a form of deception by public officials against manufacturers.

Personality-based justifications for intellectual property protections are not well suited to justify property protections for pharmaceuticals. According to this account, intellectual property protections enable individuals to develop long-term plans and creative projects, and to protect author's reputations and freedom of expression.[106] For example, Seana Shiffrin describes the possibility that an artist's creation could reflect poorly on the artist if other people reproduce it in an unauthorized way.[107] Though as Shiffrin notes, concerns about a creators' interest in expression could be addressed by requiring that unauthorized works be labeled as such. And Shiffrin also notes that personality theorists also must explain why a creator's interest in self-expression is so strong that it outweighs others' interest in use. In any case, even if concerns about freedom of expression and personal development could justify some forms of intellectual property protection, they are unlikely to justify unrestricted pharmaceutical patents for decades. And even if creators were entitled to maintain the rights to control their creations, they would also be entitled to alienate those rights. So individual researchers who would have a personality-based claim on intellectual property protection could also be required to alienate their claim to control their intellectual property as a condition of working for a pharmaceutical company or receiving financial support for their research.

A more promising justification for patents is the Lockean approach. On this view, each creator is entitled to receive some of the value of his or her creation.[108] The thought is that just as people's rights over physical creations can be justified when people use their labor to improve on what is available in the state of nature (or in the absence of a property system), so too may people have rights to some of the value that they produce through intellectual labor. For example, Lockeans argue that people who mix their intellectual labor with the world to create value have a claim on it or that property rights are an extension of the rights that people have to their own labor.[109] Critics reply that unlike physical property, intellectual property is non-rivalrous; each person can effectively use and benefit from the use of an idea without hindering another's ability to use it, so insofar as property rights are justified on the grounds that they promote effective use of the commons, such a justification cannot support intellectual property regulations.[110]

---

[106] Charles R. Beitz, "The Moral Rights of Creators of Artistic and Literary Works," *Journal of Political Philosophy* 13, no. 3 (September 1, 2005): 330–58, doi:10.1111/j.1467-9760.2005.00226.x.

[107] Shiffrin, "Intellectual Property," 660

[108] Adam D. Moore, "Lockean Theory of Intellectual Property," *Hamline Law Review* 21 (1997): 65; Adam Moore and Ken Himma, "Intellectual Property," in *The Stanford Encyclopedia of Philosophy*, ed. Edward N. Zalta, Winter 2014, http://plato.stanford.edu/archives/win2014/entries/intellectual-property/.

[109] Wendy J. Gordon, "A Property Right in Self-Expression: Equality and Individualism in the Natural Law of Intellectual Property," *The Yale Law Journal* 102, no. 7 (1993): 1533–1609; Alfred C. Yen, "Restoring the Natural Law: Copyright as Labor and Possession," *Ohio State Law Journal* 51 (1990): 517–59.

[110] Shiffrin, "Intellectual Property."

Bryan Cwik develops an alternative Lockean account of intellectual property rights that captures some of the appeal of the personality theory and does not rely on the assumption that creators are entitled to the value that they produce relative to a baseline state of nature.[111] Cwik's argument goes like this. Each creator uses her intentional capacities as productive capacities to produce goods. In this way, creations are the expressions of a creator's decisions to use her time and resources and skills to achieve a particular goal. On his account, all property systems are grounded in the value of giving people the ability to control and exercise their productive capacities to create something of value. Public officials should require that creators give their consent for the use of their labor, and property rights are a way of protecting a creator's ability to set the terms of their labor. The primary way to do this is to protect people's ability to trade, which enables each person to use her productive capacities to meet other goals beyond her own abilities. So too, Cwik concludes, intellectual property rights give people greater control over the use of their labor by enabling them to control their (on his account, inalienable) rights their lives through the use of their productive capacities.

If intellectual property rights for pharmaceuticals could be justified, the autonomy-oriented arguments that Cwik develops are the most promising. Pharmaceutical companies employ many people and each one uses her capacities to manage her time and skills and communal resources to create drugs. So insofar as people are entitled to control their lives by making long-term plans that enable them to invest time, skills, and resources for an extended period of time (e.g., works in progress), perhaps a similar justification could support some intellectual property protections for manufacturers as well. But even if we granted Cwik's argument in favor of intellectual property rights for creators who use their productive capacities to create something of value, it is a separate question whether existing intellectual property protections could be supported by Cwik's argument. As he notes, his account is

> [a] highly idealized picture [that] ignores all the ugly parts involved. A perhaps glaringly obvious rejoinder to all of this is that the picture . . . is so far from the reality of [intellectual property] as to be farcical. In the real world, IP is the special province of giant, multinational media companies and pharmaceutical corporations. IP institutions primarily function to protect their interests not the interests of small inventors and artists.[112]

---

[111] Bryan Cwik, "Labor as the Basis for Intellectual Property Rights," *Ethical Theory and Moral Practice* 17, no. 4 (September 26, 2013): 681–95, doi:10.1007/s10677-013-9471-y.

[112] Ibid., 694

And while Cwik is then quick to point out that small firms and individuals do hold a great deal of intellectual property rights, insofar as his argument in behalf of intellectual property rights is grounded in the interests of individuals, it is less clear that these considerations could justify strong protections for corporations or how those protections should be enforced even if it could. Again, even if intellectual property rights were justified in principle, current intellectual property laws are unlikely to reflect whatever pre-political property claims people would have according to Cwik's argument.

Finally, Ian Maitland briefly presents an argument that even if people do not have pre-political intellectual property rights, manufacturers do have intellectual property rights because public officials would break their promises to pharmaceutical manufacturers if they changed existing patent laws in an effort to promote greater innovation or expanded access.[113] Two responses are in order to this justification for intellectual property. First, public officials could introduce intellectual property reforms for new patents that did not break their promises to existing patent holders, so Maitland's argument would not preclude patent reform. Second, Maitland's justification assumes that public officials are entitled to enforce existing patents. But if public officials are not entitled to enforce existing intellectual property laws, then by issuing patents, they were making promises they had no entitlement to carry out. In this way, public officials may be required to break their promises to manufacturers, which would violate the letter of the law to promote a more just legal system on balance.[114]

6.7 Conclusion

Drug companies are not especially obligated to provide affordable drugs to people in need. On the other hand, they are also not especially entitled to public protections of monopolies that enable them to collect enormous profits by charging high prices for lifesaving drugs in some cases. Insofar as public officials aim to address high drug prices, they should first consider the removal of regulatory barriers, such as approval requirements and manufacturing restrictions, rather than price controls and prohibition. Patent reform is a potentially more promising but also more risky way of addressing high drug prices. If officials are unwilling to risk the benefits that pharmaceutical patents have enabled, they may also

[113] Maitland, "Priceless Goods."

[114] In this way, officials' deception may be similar to the kind of deception that Tamar Schapiro defends in circumstances of injustice, where refraining from deception would violate the spirit of moral requirements even though deception itself violates the letter of the moral law. Schapiro, "Kantian Rigorism and Mitigating Circumstances."

consider providing prizes for the development of lifesaving drugs that serve low-income populations. In any case, officials should proceed with great caution when enforcing or reforming intellectual property provisions for new drugs. In light of the moral risk associated with patent reform and the harms of existing regulations, officials may therefore reasonably prioritize policies that address high drug prices while also expanding patient's rights of self-medication.

7

Medical Autonomy
and Modern Healthcare

Imagine a world where people took rights of self-medication as seriously as they currently take informed consent requirements. It may not look very different for most people. Just as most patients continued to take their doctor's advice after the adoption of informed consent requirements, most patients might continue to consult medical experts before using unauthorized and untested drugs, even if they were legally permitted to decide differently. But as with informed consent, medicine would change at the margins. In those rare cases where patients refuse treatment, the doctrines of medical consent and informed consent now vest patients with that authority. Similarly, rights of self-medication would change medical practice only in those cases where a patient's judgment departs from a medical expert's.

Though rights of self-medication needn't change medical decision-making for most patients, rights of self-medication have the potential to transformation other aspects of healthcare as it is currently practiced. For example, if public officials respected patient's authority to make medical decisions without authorization from a regulator or a physician, then they should also respect patient's authority to choose to use unauthorized medical devices and medical providers. And regulators and physicians epistemic authority would be one of many sources of expertise that patients would have an interest in consulting. Just as rights of self-medication would expand the range of innovative treatments available to patients, they could also expand the range of innovative certifications and forms of medical information available to patients. And many of the same reasons in favor of rights of self-medication and against prohibitive regulations are also reasons to support patient's rights to access information about pharmaceuticals, including pharmaceutical advertisements.

One concern about rights of self-medication is that it could change the relationship between patients and physicians for the worse. For example, if patients were empowered to make their own medical choices, then health providers and patients might view their relationships in a more transactional light, just as they view other consumer products and services. Health workers may need to develop a new professional ethos that respects rights of self-medication while upholding widely held conceptions of professional virtue. Rethinking medical licensing and may go some way toward this end by enabling health workers to develop innovative standards of care that balance professional values and patient autonomy.

Rights of self-medication would also have revisionary implications for existing standards of medical liability. Existing approval and prescription requirements are ineffective and harmful, and they do not protect physicians or manufacturers from liability. Instead, tort law may serve the same functions as regulation while avoiding the dangers of regulatory capture, the harmful effects of drug lag and drug loss, and the violation of patient's rights that existing regulations entail. Tort law is not a perfect solution. Judges are also influenced by politics, and such an approach would not ensure the safety of all drugs. But the main advantage of tort law is that it can achieve many of the same goals of regulation without violating patient's rights to make their own medical choices.

It may seem that rights of self-medication, and a greater medical autonomy more generally, would imply that each person is on her own when it comes to medical decision-making. In response, I aim to show that rights of self-medication would give patients more resources, additional options, access to a wider range of information, and a greater diversity of providers than the existing system. Nor are rights of self-medication incompatible with a system of publically financed medical insurance. And like tort law, insurance providers could also further the aims of existing approval and prescription requirements by encouraging responsible self-medication in ways that do not violate patients' rights.

7.1 Markets and Medical Autonomy

In an earlier discussion of paternalism, I drew an analogy between the legal doctrine of coverture and policies that currently violate patients' rights of self-medication. Defenders of patriarchy argued that women were incapable of responsible financial decision-making just as defenders of medical paternalism argue that patients are incapable of making responsible decisions about their health. Today, men and women are free (for the most part) to invest their money in pension funds, to save it, or to spend it. But some people recognize that financial decisions are very complex, and when the stakes are high, they consult a financial advisor. Financial advisors adhere to either a suitability standard or a fiduciary standard. The suitability rule for financial brokers requires that brokers make recommendations that are in their clients' interests, but brokers are permitted to charge a fee for recommending particular funds or investments. In contrast, investment advisors, who adhere to the fiduciary standard, charge higher rates for their services, but they do not collect fees for particular recommendations. Financial decisions are complex, and different services are suitable for different investors. People may exercise their property rights to employ a broker, investment advisor, or they may elect to trade and invest without any advice despite the fact that it is usually a poor decision.[1]

Is there any reason to think that people are capable of managing hundreds of thousands of dollars of value in the form of mortgages, student loan debt, investments, credit cards, physical property, and contractual agreements; but that when it comes to choices about their bodies, they are generally incapable of deciding in their interests? In the absence of institutions that empower patients to make their own medical choices, we cannot know whether patients' relative lack of knowledge is insurmountable or whether patients could better exercise their rights of self-medication with greater knowledge and a system of regulation that empowered patients.

In contrast to policies that require public officials to approve choices before they are available to all citizens or patients, a certification system allows those who prefer their financial advisors and physicians to adhere to something like the fiduciary standard to continue to pay a fee to discuss their options without forcing that standard on everyone else. For those who value the current system, nothing about the relationship between these patients and their physicians would need to change—they could still adhere to regulatory guidelines and consult their physicians for advice, and their safety would be no more at risk than it currently is.

But while little is lost, much is gained because patients' rights of self-medication could also create new markets for patient choice, such as services that are analogous to the suitability standard. On this model, patients may visit lower cost pharmacists or physicians who are required to advise patients in light of their medical interests, but who may also collect a fee for prescribing certain drugs, which they disclose to the patient. Such a model could improve the current system, where all physicians and providers are provided with free meals and compensation, and patients are left to wonder whether their providers' prescribing decisions are influenced by factors other than their patients' interests.[2]

Alternatively, patients who are analogous to "expert investors" may choose to forgo the fees associated with seeking expert advice and make medical decisions

---

[1] I am grateful to Dana Howard for discussing this analogy with me.

[2] Marcia Angell, "Drug Companies & Doctors: A Story of Corruption," *New York Review of Books*, accessed April 6, 2016, http://www.nybooks.com/articles/2009/01/15/drug-companies-doctorsa-story-of-corruption/.

on their own. And patients who make pharmaceutical decisions to serve their recreational aims (who we may think of as analogous to recreational gamblers) may find that few advisors would recommend in favor of their choice, but no one would stop them either. In all cases, patients may either contract with advisors to waive their right to sue for adverse effects or pay more in exchange for the assurance that they can seek damages for malpractice.[3]

In addition to these new models of patient care, other knower organizations may develop in the absence of prohibitive safety and efficacy regulations. Daniel Klein develops the concept of a knower organization, which is a business that provides consumers with the assurance that the products they are using are safe and/or effective.[4] In addition to its prohibitive role, the FDA is also a knower organization. Rather than investing in and enforcing laws that violate patients' rights of self-medication, regulators could instead focus on post-market surveillance. Post-market information about typical use conditions and the effects of drugs in polypharmic patients is especially useful because clinical trials are typically unable to determine how drugs affect users outside the context of a clinical trial when the effects of drug depend on how it is used and whether it is used with other drugs.

Other markets related to expanded access could emerge as well. For example, just as people pay to access information about the quality of contractors and auto mechanics, they may also pay to access information about complex health decisions in lieu of seeing a physician. Brand names also provide assurance because large organizations have incentives to maintain patient trust.[5] Though it is common for proponents of drug safety to vilify the pharmaceutical industry, if there were policies that would permit people to import generic drugs from unlicensed manufacturers oversees, then large pharmaceutical companies would have incentives to compete by maintaining a reputation for producing safe drugs. In this way, pharmaceutical companies can maintain profitability, even if public officials allow more producers to manufacturer generic drugs or reform the patent system.

The point is that rights of self-medication give patients many ways to help patients learn about new drugs and become informed while a prohibitive approach allows just one. A certification system for drugs could also promote informed decision-making beyond safety considerations. For example, public and private agencies in the United States, Canada, and Europe currently certify food as humane or organic, and this information about values inform some

---

[3] Epstein, "Medical Malpractice."

[4] Daniel B. Klein, "The Demand for and Supply of Assurance," *Economic Affairs* 21, no. 1 (March 1, 2001): 4–11, doi:10.1111/1468-0270.00268.

[5] Daniel B. Klein, "How Trust Is Achieved in Free Markets," SSRN Scholarly Paper (Rochester, NY: Social Science Research Network, December 1, 2003), http://papers.ssrn.com/abstract=473442.

people's purchasing decisions, just as other people choose food based on health information or cost.

7.2 Pharmaceutical Marketing

If patients had rights of self-medication, then regulators' and physicians' judgments about the safety and efficacy of drugs would still inform many patient's decisions, but patients could consider other relevant information as well, including their values, tolerance for risk, and alternative sources of certification. Pharmaceutical advertising can also be a valuable source of information about new drugs. Yet officials in most countries limit manufacturers' freedom to advertise pharmaceuticals in ways that exceed the limits on advertising for other products. For example, though it is generally legal to advertise fast food, mountain bikes, alcohol, boxing gloves, rock-climbing equipment (and guns and cigarettes in some places), most countries strictly regulate pharmaceutical marketing and forbid manufacturers from direct-to-consumer (DTC) advertising or advertising drugs for off-label conditions.[6]

One rationale for advertising restrictions is that pharmaceutical marketing could make it difficult for patients to access high-quality information about new drugs in a climate of relentless advertising. On the other hand, online communities, public certification, and certificatory knower organizations could provide guidance in the context of advertising. More importantly, marketing restrictions censor information about potential opportunities for informed self-medication, which may be relevant to patients. Just as public officials are not entitled to paternalistically limit patient's access to pharmaceuticals, nor are they entitled to paternalistically limit access to information about pharmaceuticals. Like the argument for self-medication, the argument for pharmaceutical marketing is supported by rights-based considerations and empirical research that suggests that limiting patients' access to medical information can be harmful in ways that mirror the hazards of limiting rights of self-medication. Also like the argument for self-medication, the case for pharmaceutical marketing is gaining force within the United States, especially in light of recent judicial decisions.

Ethical justifications for freedom of speech often focus on the importance of self-expression for speakers and thinkers. As Seana Shiffrin argues, speech protections guard our interest in conveying our emotions, intellectual achievements, or moral relationships.[7] Commercial speech, it is generally assumed,

---

[6] New Zealand and the United States are the exceptions.

[7] Seana Valentine Shiffrin, "Thinker-Based Approach to Freedom Speech," *Constitutional Commentary* 27 (2010): 283.

doesn't reflect the mental contents of a person or thinker, so Shiffrin suggests that it merits fewer protections because it is less closely tied to a person's identity or deeply held commitments. However, though it is true that corporations do not have mental states that are communicated by corporate speech, commercial speech is also the speech of individuals who do wish to communicate their mental states. Though a team of copywriters is somewhat anonymous, individual salespeople and spokespersons directly express themselves to clients. In these cases commercial speech is tied to other aspects of the speaker's self-presentation and identity.

One seeming asymmetry between individuals' speech and commercial speech is that individuals identify with their own speech more than speech they are paid for. Yet even if most non-commercial speech doesn't reflect a person's deeply held commitments, the justification for permitting speech shouldn't rely on whether the speaker clearly identifies with speech and cares about it a lot. Also, other forms of paid expression, such as artistic performance and editorial writing, are considered forms of protected speech even though the speakers are paid for it. Moreover, some people's identities as marketing representatives, business owners, or product developers can be closely tied to their sense of themselves, and, in these cases, talking about a product can be a deeply important project.[8]

More importantly, freedom of speech should be protected for the sake of potential listeners. As Mill famously argues, people in the community have an interest in hearing different kinds of speech and benefit from the expression of many different ideas.[9] Even if commercial speakers are not entitled to honestly communicate information about new drugs, then patients, physicians, and others are entitled to access that information. Eugene Volokh highlights this point when he explores the justification for protecting speech for speakers who are dead.[10] Intuitively, it would be wrong to censor books written by Orwell or Marx, even though those authors are dead, because censorship also deprives potential listeners of the benefits of speech. Volokh extends this argument to commercial non-media speech when he argues that advertisements and other marketing also provide useful information to potential listeners.

Some may object that advertising is different because it is purely instrumental—rather than attempting to engage the listener's intellectual capacities, advertisers aim to limit the listener's perceptions of her options so she buys a particular product.[11] Yet some non-commercial speech surely plays

---

[8] John Tomasi, *Free Market Fairness* (Princeton University Press, 2012).

[9] Mill, *On Liberty and Other Essays*.

[10] Eugene Volokh, "Speech Restrictions That Don't Much Affect the Autonomy of Speakers," *Constitutional Commentary* 27 (2011): 347.

[11] C. Edwin Baker, "Autonomy and Free Speech," *Constitutional Commentary* 27 (2010): 251.

that role as well. Consider seduction, which seeks to sway a person's opinion via bypassing her intellectual capacities and engaging her emotions.[12] Furthermore, listeners may have an interest in commercial speech even if it isn't very intellectually engaging, just as people have an interest in reading superficial media or listening to uninteresting but entertaining music. Finally, in the case of pharmaceutical marketing, listeners' intellectual capacities are not bypassed by promotional claims. Pharmaceutical advertisements make scientific claims about the relative merits of a particular product. Though some pharmaceutical marketing does deploy celebrity endorsements and emotional appeals, even in these cases advertisers must convince consumers that their products are sufficiently safe and effective, even as they aim to use branding and endorsements to persuade consumers to use their drugs instead of alternatives. And marketing efforts for uncommon and life-threatening conditions do generally focus on evidence-based arguments in favor of a particular drug.

Another concern is that DTC pharmaceutical marketing would have very bad public health effects if combined with rights of self-medication. There is some evidence that DTC advertising could have good effects because it prompts people to make appointments with their physicians where they may receive a new diagnosis or discover a high-priority medical condition.[13] Other evidence suggests that pharmaceutical marketing could increase treatment compliance, perhaps by reminding people to take their medicine.[14] And DTC advertisements potentially destigmatize mental health conditions and encourage people to seek treatment for conditions they would not otherwise raise with a physician. If paired with rights of self-medication, DTC marketing could point people to the resources that enable them to make responsible drug choices. But, of course, any benefits of DTC pharmaceutical advertising may be mitigated or outweighed if a physician's visit were not required to access an advertised drug. On the other hand, the doctrine of informed consent requires that patients be informed about the risks and benefits all reasonable treatment options. So compared with other consumer goods, patients have especially strong rights to learn about pharmaceuticals because more general rights of informed consent are especially weighty. Furthermore, to the extent that public officials are entitled to censor manufacturers to promote public health, they should hold the pharmaceutical industry to the same standards as other industries. If paternalistic marketing restrictions of other industries would be impermissible, then even if DTC advertising paired

---

[12] Sarah Buss, "Valuing Autonomy and Respecting Persons: Manipulation, Seduction, and the Basis of Moral Constraints," *Ethics* 115, no. 2 (2005): 195–235.

[13] "Consumers' Reports on the Health Effects of Direct-to-Consumer Drug Advertising," *ProQuest. com* accessed November 1, 2016, http://search.proquest.com/openview/228b1121e635b4bfc30a-7b26a60b1ab9/1?pq-origsite=gscholar&cbl=36027.

[14] C. Lee Ventola, "Direct-to-Consumer Pharmaceutical Advertising: Therapeutic or Toxic?," *Pharmacy and Therapeutics* 36, no. 10 (2011): 669.

with rights of self-medication did have bad health effects, marketing restrictions would nevertheless be unwarranted.[15]

7.3 Off-Label Marketing

Pharmaceutical marketing restrictions that extend beyond fraud prohibitions are inconsistent with rights of self-medication and informed consent because they censor information that may be relevant to a patient's ability to make informed decisions about her body. The United States takes a notably permissive approach to pharmaceutical marketing because some forms of DTC marketing are permitted. But even in the United States, manufacturers are prohibited from marketing drugs for unapproved (off-label) uses and conditions. Limits on off-label marketing are generally accepted as permissible forms of public health regulation on the grounds that pharmaceutical marketing could compel consumers to make unhealthy decisions on the basis of false information. Yet marketing restrictions for pharmaceuticals are not limited to fraudulent or misleading advertisements; they also punish truthful speech that advocates for lawful conduct. For example, if a pharmaceutical representative in the United States discusses the off-label uses of a drug with a physician, he is subject to criminal penalties, even though off-label drug use is legal and even if the information about off-label uses is truthful. In this way, DTC and off-label marketing restrictions are not a form of anti-fraud regulation but a form of paternalistic censorship in behalf of patients.

Practices like off-label marketing remain illegal, but, in recent years, several pharmaceutical manufacturers and their representatives have challenged the FDA's enforcement of off-label marketing prohibitions on the grounds that these speech restrictions are inconsistent with longstanding constitutional protections for freedom of expression and commercial speech.[16] As these cases make their way through the courts, the legal status of off-label marketing is in flux. Consider the 2012 case of *United States v. Caronia* as an illustration of what is at stake in this debate. In 2005 pharmaceutical representative Alfred Caronia was charged with unlawfully promoting Xyrem for unapproved conditions. Though Xyrem is prescribed off-label for conditions such as fibromyalgia and chronic pain, it is only approved by the FDA for use in adult patients with narcolepsy.

---

[15] Elsewhere, I develop this point in more detail regarding tobacco advertisements. Flanigan, "Double Standards and Arguments for Tobacco Regulation."

[16] For example, in the most recent case, a US federal court recently ruled that truthful off-label promotion was legally permissible. Andrew Pollack, "Court Forbids F.D.A. from Blocking Truthful Promotion of Drug," *New York Times*, August 7, 2015, http://www.nytimes.com/2015/08/08/business/court-forbids-fda-from-blocking-truthful-promotion-of-drug.html.

Off-label prescribing is a pervasive and legal practice—even though the FDA has not approved off-label drugs as effective treatments for off-label conditions. However, off-label promotion is prohibited. And so when Caronia discussed the off-label uses of Xyrem in a meeting with a potential Xyrem customer, he was allegedly violating the federal Food, Drug, and Cosmetics Act (FDCA). Caronia's customer turned out to be an undercover federal investigator. In 2009 Caronia was found guilty of misdemeanor conspiracy to introduce misbranded drugs into interstate commerce. Caronia received probation and one hundred hours of community service.

At this point Caronia's story was not unusual. Off-label marketing prohibitions have been a significant constraint on the conduct of people in the pharmaceutical industry. Between 2004 and 2010 the government settled twenty-one off-label promotion cases and received over $7.9 billion in criminal fines and settlements.[17] For example, Eli Lilly paid $1.415 billion in a settlement related to off-label promotion of antipsychotic Zyprexa for treating dementia.[18] Pfizer paid $2.3 billion to resolve suits related to the off-label promotion of the arthritis drug Bextra, which was marketed to treat conditions such as postoperative pain.[19]

Yet Alfred Caronia's case was distinctive because he was prosecuted and charged as an individual. Manufacturers typically settle off-label promotion cases to avoid even more devastating penalties, but Caronia decided to take the case to trial. Though he was initially convicted of off-label marketing, when he appealed the ruling in 2012 the US Court of Appeals for the Second Circuit overturned Caronia's conviction.[20] The court's reasoning was that Caronia had not misrepresented the drug or promoted any unlawful uses of the drug, so the government did not have the authority to prosecute him for truthful off-label promotion. Though the case is limited to the Second Circuit, similar cases are making their way through the courts with differing results.

Since the court's reasons for siding with Caronia are valid, they would also justify legal off-label marketing and an end to the practice of penalizing manufacturers for other instances of off-label promotion. Some may reject my claim that the *Caronia* case was rightly decided on the grounds that commercial speech merits fewer protections than individual expression. The government's authority

---

[17] Antonia F. Giuliana, "Statistics for Off-Label Marketing Settlements Involving Prescription Drugs," *FCA Alert*, March 2, 2011, http://www.fcaalert.com/2011/03/articles/settlements-1/statistics-for-offlabel-marketing-settlements-involving-prescription-drugs/.

[18] US Department of Justice, "Eli Lilly and Company Agrees to Pay $1.415 Billion to Resolve Allegations of Off-Label Promotion of Zyprexa," Press Release 09-038, January 15, 2009.

[19] Gardiner Harris, "Pfizer Pays $2.3 Billion to Settle Marketing Case," *New York Times*, September 3, 2009, sec. Business, http://www.nytimes.com/2009/09/03/business/03health.html.

[20] United States v. Caronia, 576 F. Supp. 2d 385, 398-402 (EDNY 2008), rev'd, 703 F.3d 149 (2d Cir. 2012).

to bring off-label promotion suits and demand billions in settlements had gone practically unquestioned, seemingly for this reason.[21] The FDA is authorized to prohibit manufacturers from introducing new or misbranded drugs, but this authority doesn't clearly translate to the authority to punish pharmaceutical representative's speech or even promotional materials that tout off-label benefits.[22]

Despite aggressive restrictions on pharmaceutical marketing, recent legal developments have signaled a shift towards greater scrutiny of pharmaceutical marketing regulations.[23] And within the larger context of commercial speech, these developments fit with a trend towards greater recognition of advertising and marketing as a form of speech in the United States.[24] The United States is distinctive in that it permits a wider range of commercial speech than other countries. In the United States, speech restrictions must 1) support a substantial government interest, 2) directly advance that government interest, and 3) be narrowly tailored only to advance that interest.[25] While other jurisdictions are not so permissive of commercial speech (though I argue below that they ought to be), in the US, this test provides a good guide for evaluating whether off-label marketing restrictions are justified.

---

[21] These restrictions are enforced despite the fact that the FDA's mandate to regulate labeling does not explicitly authorize the agency to prohibit verbal communication or the creation and use of promotional materials that are currently classified as off-label marketing. The FDA is empowered by the FDCA to regulate the pharmaceutical industry. In this section, I address whether the FDCA also licenses marketing restrictions, and I conclude that it does not. The authors of the *FDA Law Blog* have provided a helpful analysis of the legal context of *Caronia*, which has informed this section. See especially "A Deep Dive into the Second Circuit's Caronia Decision, Potential Next Steps, and Potential Enforcement Fallout," *FDA Law Blog*, December 12, 2012, http://www.fdalawblog. net/fda_law_blog_hyman_phelps/2012/12/a-deep-dive-into-the-second-circuits-caronia-decision-potential-next-steps-and-potential-enforcement.html.

[22] 21 U.S.C. 352(f). A drug is classified as misbranded if it does not specify adequate directions for its use. Importantly, these directions must be limited to a product's intended use, defined in the as the condition and patient type that the drug was approved to treat. (21 C.F.R. §201.5).

[23] For example, in 2002 the Supreme Court ruled that compounding pharmacies were permitted to advertise compounded, unapproved new drugs because a prohibition on that advertising was too broad and a less restrictive policy was possible. There, the Court held that "fear that people would make bad decisions if given truthful information" cannot justify content-based limits on speech, and that speech should be protected, even if it does no more than propose a transaction. In 2011 the Court ruled that manufacturers could use records and information about prescribers for marketing purposes. There, the Court held that prescription drug marketing was sometimes beneficial to prescribers and patients and affirmed that, despite the potentially harmful effects of marketing, "speech in aid of pharmaceutical marketing however is a form of expression protected by the Free Speech Clause of the First Amendment" Thompson v. Western States Medical Center, 535 US 357 (Supreme Court 2002). Sorrell v. IMS Health Inc., 131 S. Ct. 2653 (Supreme Court 2011).

[24] Before 1980 commercial speech did not enjoy strong legal protections. Then, the US Supreme Court decided a landmark case, where they ruled that truthful commercial speech that advocates lawful conduct is generally protected. Central Hudson Gas & Elec. Corp. v. Public Serv. Comm'n of NY, 447 US 557 (Supreme Court 1980).

[25] Ibid.

By holding off-label marketing to an American commercial speech standard, it is clear that restrictions cannot be justified. First, consider the claim that there is a substantial government interest in prohibiting off-label promotion, such as the interest in promoting public health and patient safety. If the goal of marketing restrictions is to prevent patients from using potentially ineffective drugs off-label, then why not ban off-label *prescribing* directly? Yet the FDA acknowledges that it does not have a legitimate interest in discouraging off-label prescribing and that to do so would be to unjustifiably interfere with the practice of medicine and individual treatment decisions.[26] However, if the government's interest in patient safety and public health cannot justify restrictions on the prescription and use of off-label therapies, then it is unclear why the same interest justifies restrictions on off-label promotion, which also interfere with individual treatment decisions and the practice of medicine.

Second, off-label marketing restrictions are not necessary to protect consumers because there is not clear empirical evidence that advertising a product off-label is harmful while prescribing the product off-label is not harmful. Though the empirical effects of off-label marketing are controversial, there is some evidence that prohibitions of off-label advertising might *undermine* patients' health and safety because advertising makes it easier for patients and physicians to learn about new therapeutic uses for existing drugs.[27] For example, Dale Gerringer argues that at least four thousand deaths could have been prevented during seven months in 1981 had marketing approval for beta-blockers to be prescribed for the prevention of second heart attacks been allowed.[28] Even though beta-blockers were available off-label and cardiologists could legally

[26] In an e-mail correspondence with a public representative from the FDA's Center for Drug Evaluation and Research, the FDA official wrote: "The FDA is empowered by law to review drug products for safety and effectiveness. Once approved, a drug product may be prescribed by a licensed physician for any use that, based on the physician's professional opinion, is deemed to be appropriate [off-label]. This action is considered to be part of the practice of medicine. FDA does not regulate the practice of medicine and cannot comment on, or recommend, a course of treatment for any individual." E-mail correspondence with the author, October 25, 2012.

[27] There is some evidence in favor of this hypothesis, which pharmacologists William Wardell and Louis Lasagna illustrate via the example of beta-blockers. In the early 1960s, research suggested that beta-blockers, which diminish the effects of stress hormones like adrenaline, might be helpful for treating cardiovascular conditions, especially for preventing second heart attacks and lowering blood pressure. In 1965 beta-blockers were approved in the UK, but they were not approved in the United States until 1968, and even then, they were only approved for very limited conditions and not for the prevention of second heart attacks. Beta-blockers were only approved for the prevention of second heart attacks in 1981, seven months after a comprehensive study showed that 6,500–10,000 lives could be saved each year by beta-blockers used in this way. W. M Wardell and L. Lasagna, *Regulation and Drug Development* (Washington DC: American Enterprise Institute for Public Policy Research, 1975).

[28] Gerringer also claims that and at least 45,000 deaths could have been prevented had beta-blockers been initially approved for second heart attacks at the advice of cardiologists. Gieringer, "The Safety and Efficacy of New Drug Approval."

prescribe them for off-label use, off-label marketing restrictions affected the kinds of information accessible to practitioners and changed how physicians and patients made decisions. This example illustrates how prohibitions on information can cost lives.

On the other hand, critics of off-label promotion point to several public health hazards. Marketing influences physicians' prescribing choices, and some scholars worry that off-label marketing would encourage physicians to prescribe newer, more dangerous drugs with a less established safety record and more unknown side effects.[29] Another theoretical concern about off-label marketing is that it would contribute to increased healthcare costs because physicians would prescribe newer, more expensive drugs for a greater range of conditions.[30] One relevant feature of the controversy is that the potential harm done by off-label marketing restrictions is a result of the restrictions themselves—a lack of information for physicians, whereas the harm of permitting off-label marketing is associated with prescribing practices and patients' choices.

Moreover, insofar as regulators should avoid excessively punitive regulations when less coercive policies would do, marketing restrictions also are not the minimal necessary means of protecting consumers from unsafe prescriptions. Not only do pharmaceutical companies pay billions in fines for violating marketing regulations, but the regulations also can carry criminal penalties including jail time for pharmaceutical representatives. For example, criminal pleas were made in 72 percent of the off-label marketing cases settled between 2004 and 2010.[31] Marketing restrictions impose other burdens as well. Physicians who are asked to advise pharmaceutical manufacturers and colleagues about new drugs may not be permitted to give a complete assessment without running afoul of marketing regulations.[32] Yet public officials could alternatively inform physicians and patients when promotional claims are unapproved or limit off-label promotion to contexts where patients and physicians have an opportunity to learn more about the risks associated with a drug (such as in interactions with pharmaceutical representatives).[33]

---

[29] Aaron S. Kesselheim, "Off-Label Drug Use and Promotion: Balancing Public Health Goals and Commercial Speech," *American Journal of Law & Medicine* 37 (2011): 225.

[30] Ibid.

[31] Giuliana, "Statistics for Off-Label Marketing Settlements Involving Prescription Drugs."

[32] In some cases, this results in requirements that physicians who present information on behalf of drug manufacturers use the manufacturers' approved slides and materials. These regulations therefore have the effect of potentially undermining the public's trust in physicians while also preventing physicians from communicating their full and unfiltered judgments to drug developers, though communication between drug developers and physicians is clearly a worthy goal.

[33] In a complaint about off-label promotional restrictions filed by Allergan, the makers of Botox, the company proposed several alternatives to restrictions, including taxes on off-label uses or disclosure requirements for off-label promotional materials. Kesselheim, "Off-Label Drug Use and Promotion," 245.

For these reasons, the existing standards of commercial speech protection in the United States should also protect off-label marketing. But one may reply either that my interpretation of commercial speech law is overly permissive or that even if the off-label marketing should be legal under US law, that US law is overly permissive of commercial speech.[34] However, even if prohibitions of off-label marketing can be legally justified, prohibitions are not morally justified because off-label marketing enables consumers to better understand their pharmaceutical options. This is not to say that there is not a place for government in limiting what drug representatives can say—public officials can rightly prohibit fraudulent speech.[35] My claim is that government regulation of *truthful* off-label promotion is wrong, even if it is legal.

The moral reasons against off-label marketing prohibitions mirror the more general reasons against of pharmaceutical marketing restrictions. First, off-label marketing restrictions violate the speech rights of individual speakers who are paid to discuss new uses for drugs. At least some off-label marketing takes the form of oral communication by sales representatives, and, in these cases, there is an especially strong speaker-based interest in commercial speech protections. Off-label marketing restrictions also prohibit individual researchers and physicians from presenting off-label uses of drugs at industry-sponsored events, even if they clarify that off-label claims are not endorsed by sponsors and even if their own research and experience supports off-label claims. If researchers' and physicians' unpaid speech about off-label uses merit protection, so too should paid speech that says the same thing as long as it is truthful.

Second, for many patients, off-label treatment is a reasonable choice. In some cases, off-label therapies are the only choice because drugs are not approved for their patient-type and disease category. For example, very few drugs are approved for use in pregnant women, so most treatment for conditions during pregnancy are prescribed off-label. In these cases especially, respecting patients' rights to make treatment decisions may require information about legal off-label uses of drugs. Physicians would be obligated to disclose potential off-label uses if a reasonable patient would have an interest in knowing about it, but marketing restrictions would limit physicians' and patients' ability to know all relevant options so that the patient could make an informed choice.

---

[34] For example, the Caronia court ruled in favor of off-label marketing, but other circuits have upheld the prohibitions, so the legal questions about off-label marketing remain unsettled. See ibid.

[35] This appears to be the Ninth Circuit's recent strategy in upholding an off-label marketing conviction because a jury deemed the off-label statements false. See Harkonen v. US, 134 S. Ct. 824 (2013).

7.4 Professional Ethics

Patients' relationships with their physicians would change if physicians no longer controlled patient's access to pharmaceuticals and if information about treatment options were more widely available from multiple sources. But to the extent that physicians currently aspire to develop respectful, non-paternalistic relationships where their medical expertise is valued and rewarded, rights of self-medication are not in principle a threat to the fundamental values of the medical profession, which include respect for patient choice.

Some may worry that in practice, self-medication, an expansion in access to drugs for non-medical purposes, greater access to information about drugs, and advertising would effectively change the physician-patient relationship in ways that are morally worse. For example, several commentators express apprehension that consumer-oriented values are encroaching on the traditional physician-patient relationship. Arnold Relman suggests that market forces can undermine the physician-patient relationship by distorting physician's altruistic concern for patients.[36]. In a recent editorial, published in the *New England Journal of Medicine*, Pamela Hartzband, MD, and Jerome Groopman, MD, rejected what they call "The New Language of Medicine," which frames physicians as healthcare providers rather than as caretakers.[37] They worry that if medical professionals come to see patients as consumers, the caregiving relationship will suffer, medical care itself will suffer, and such a practice would demean both patients and doctors and "dangerously neglect the essence of medicine."[38] Paul Krugman worries, "The relationship between patient and doctor used to be considered something special, almost sacred. Now politicians and supposed reformers talk about the act of receiving care as if it were no different from a commercial transaction.... What has gone wrong with us?[39]

A related objection is that widespread access to pharmaceutical markets could potentially cause physicians to become callous and untrustworthy because they would see their patients as self-interested consumers or as potential sources of revenue, rather than as people in need. There is some evidence that markets do cause people to take a more instrumental approach toward others, so perhaps a more market-oriented approach to medicine would cause physicians to approach patients in an instrumental way.[40]

---

[36] A. S. Relman, "The Impact of Market Forces on the Physician-Patient Relationship," *Journal of the Royal Society of Medicine* 87, no. Suppl 22 (1994): 22–25.

[37] Pamela Hartzband and Jerome Groopman, "The New Language of Medicine," *New England Journal of Medicine* 365, no. 15 (October 13, 2011): 1372–73.

[38] Ibid.

[39] Paul Krugman, "Patients Are Not Consumers," *New York Times*, April 21, 2011, sec. Opinion, http://www.nytimes.com/2011/04/22/opinion/22krugman.html.

[40] Armin Falk and Nora Szech, "Morals and Markets," *Science* 340, no. 6133 (May 10, 2013): 707–11, doi:10.1126/science.1231566.

Three responses are available in behalf of self-medication in light of the concern that empowering patients to make medical decisions would corrupt the physician-patient relationship. First, these concerns rely on an empirical hypothesis about the likely effects of rights of self-medication on people's relationships. Yet there is some evidence that market norms promote honest, cooperative behavior and correct for patterns of discrimination.[41] And rights of self-medication could give physicians greater discretion to act in accordance with their fundamental professional values to the extent that it prompts people to seek out the counsel and care that physicians provide rather than consulting with physicians solely because of legal requirements.

Second, even if these concerns were warranted, they would not undermine the case for political rights of self-medication. People have rights to make their own pharmaceutical choices without legal interference, and even if exercising those rights did change their relationships, such changes would not be grounds for limiting the right of self-medication. Just as drug users are not liable to be interfered with on the grounds that drug use makes some of them callous friends and disagreeable family members, nor would they be liable to be interfered with on the grounds that their relationships with physicians changed because they were better able to exercise their rights of self-medication.

This is not to say that some forms of the physician-patient relationship are not better than others. Physicians who abide by professional norms that promote altruism, care, and empathy may be morally praiseworthy, compared with physicians who take an instrumental approach to patients and see them as a source of revenue. Recall the analogy to the suitability and fiduciary standards for financial advisors. The fiduciary standard may be a morally better professional norm for financial advisors while consumers may nevertheless be entitled to choose a financial advisor that operates only according to a suitability standard (perhaps because it is less costly). Some medical ethicists have argued that the physician-patient relationship is intrinsically a fiduciary one, but this conceptual claim is false.[42] There are many advantages to a fiduciary approach, and patients may choose physicians who are institutionally invested in their well-being and who hold themselves to a fiduciary standard. But patients may also choose to contract with physicians who only hold themselves to their

---

[41] Joseph Henrich et al., *Foundations of Human Sociality: Economic Experiments and Ethnographic Evidence from Fifteen Small-Scale Societies* (Oxford; New York: Oxford University Press, 2004); Dan Ariely et al., "The (True) Legacy of Two Really Existing Economic Systems," SSRN Scholarly Paper (Rochester, NY: Social Science Research Network, June 19, 2014), http://papers.ssrn.com/abstract=2457000.

[42] Allen Buchanan, "Principal/Agent Theory and Decisionmaking in Health Care," *Bioethics* 2, no. 4 (October 1, 1988): 317–33, doi:10.1111/j.1467-8519.1988.tb00057.x.

contractual obligations and legal standards that prohibit fraud and violations of informed consent.

Third, some of the arguments in favor of rights of self-medication and medical autonomy prompt a more general rethinking of ethical standards within the medical profession. So while rights of self-medication are not incompatible with the values that members of the medical profession currently uphold, they are incompatible with a legal requirement that patients must see only licensed physicians. Occupational licensing requirements for healthcare providers potentially have the same negative effects as licensing requirements for pharmaceuticals. Namely, licensing requirements may give patients a false sense of security about the quality of their physicians, while existing regulations do not ensure ethical standards or quality care in the health professions.[43] And like drug licensing, there are costs associated with medical licensing such as more expensive care, fewer available physicians, and the potential for less innovation in the provision of care. At the same time, a certification system for physicians, or multiple certification systems, could provide many of the benefits of a licensing system without imposing legal barriers that limit the supply of physicians. Most importantly though, like pharmaceutical regulations, medical licensing paternalistically limits the range of patients' treatment options and is therefore incompatible with the value of medical autonomy.[44]

In order to respect patients' rights of self-medication, physicians must rethink their professional role to the extent that existing practices empower physicians to paternalistically withhold access to drugs. Yet rights of self-medication would not necessarily change the valuable norms that physicians currently endorse, such as fiduciary, non-instrumental approaches to patient care. On the other hand, the reasons in favor of rights of self-medication are reasons to reject legal requirements that dictate the nature of patients' relationships with their physicians, as well as occupational licensing requirements. Many of the same arguments against approval requirements for drugs, for example, also call for public officials to rethink licensing requirements that paternalistically limit patients' choice of provider.

[43] Shirley Svorny et al., "Licensing Doctors: Do Economists Agree?," *Econ Journal Watch* 1, no. 2 (2004): 279–305.

[44] For more on the effects of occupational licensing in medicine see Marc T. Law and Sukkoo Kim, "Specialization and Regulation: The Rise of Professionals and the Emergence of Occupational Licensing Regulation," *The Journal of Economic History* 65, no. 3 (2005): 723–56; Marc T. Law and Mindy Marks, "The Effects of Occupational Licensing Laws on Minorities: Evidence from the Progressive Era," SSRN Scholarly Paper (Rochester, NY: Social Science Research Network, 2008), http://papers.ssrn.com/sol3/papers.cfm?abstract_id=943765; Adriana D. Kugler and Robert M. Sauer, "Doctors Without Borders? Relicensing Requirements and Negative Selection in the Market for Physicians," *Journal of Labor Economics* 23, no. 3 (2005): 437–65.

7.5 Torts and Product Liability

In the absence of preventive regulations that aim to protect patients from unsafe drugs and unqualified providers, tort law can protect patients' safety by deterring fraudulent, negligent, and coercive medical practices. Torts are violations of people's rights that result in civil liability. For example, if a physician negligently violates her patient's rights by failing to be sufficiently conscientious when providing care, then the patient would be entitled to seek compensation for damages or injury in court. Similarly, if a patient takes an uncertified drug that harms her, she can sue the manufacturer for damages if the harm was a result of negligence or fraudulent labeling and marketing.

Tort law must appeal to a conception of rights to establish whether an injured person is entitled to damages. I have argued that people have rights of self-medication, which include the right to assume risks as well as rights against fraud and deception. In light of these rights, manufacturers that take due care to accurately disclose and communicate the risks associated with their products ought to be protected by a legal presumption that consumers knowingly assumed the risks associated with a drug when they consented to use it. On this view, manufacturers' duties correspond to consumer's rights. People do not have rights against being injured by using dangerous drugs; they have rights against being injured by negligent or deceptively advertised drugs.

In other words, manufacturers conduct should be held to standards of fault liability, which subject them to a duty not to wrongfully injure people, rather than strict liability standards, which would subject them to a duty not to injure under any circumstances. Fault liability is also a more feasible standard for addressing injuries related to drug use because many drugs reliably injure some proportion of users, but users nevertheless have an interest in using them. If courts held manufacturers liable for all injuries that were caused by risky drugs, then there would be strong incentives not to create potentially beneficial drugs that were also very risky.

A benefit of using torts to address drug injuries is that the threat of a lawsuit encourages manufacturers to take steps to prevent harm. Standards of fault liability would encourage manufacturers to clearly disclose all known and theoretical risks and to take great care to avoid harmful negligence but would not discourage the sale of risky drugs. One may object that a mere fault liability standard is overly favorable to manufacturers, and that manufacturers ought to be held to standards of strict liability, which gives injured drug users a better baseline opportunity to seek damages. In response, officials might adopt standards of strict liability for injuries related to drug use while also allowing people to waive their entitlement to sue for damages in exchange for access to a dangerous drug.[45] More generally, whatever legal standards of product liability judges adopt, people ought to be permitted to forgo the benefits of tort action in exchange for expanded access. One may object that a contract that required people to waive their right to sue in the case of injury is unconscionable. Elsewhere, I argue against the unconscionability doctrine on the grounds that it is impermissibly paternalistic.[46] Just as patients can consent to the medical risks associated with using a drug, they should also be permitted to consent to legal risks associated with using drugs, such as the inability to sue in the event of injury.

Though the threat of legal penalties for wrongful injury could theoretically serve the same preemptive function as regulation in protecting patients, even if tort law did not effectively deter negligence or fraud, as Jason Solomon argues, the main advantage of using tort law to address drug injuries is that tort law empowers individuals to seek redress when they have been wronged.[47] Solomon argues that tort law gives injured people the chance to demand an explanation from wrongdoers and to publically hold them accountable. Drawing on Darwall's conception of respect, he suggests that judges not only affirm an injured person's dignity and self-respect by giving her the opportunity to seek damages, they also respect manufacturers by holding them to standards of mutual accountability.[48] In this sense tort law is a way of recognizing each person's equal membership in the moral and political community. In contrast, preemptive regulations, such as approval requirements and marketing restrictions, are paternalistic and thereby fail to hold all parties to equal standards of accountability and responsibility.

Tort law already functions to protect consumers in these ways, and while existing regulations set standards of safety, they do not protect manufacturers from liability.[49] In this way, public officials treat regulation as if it were necessary but insufficient to protect consumers from being wrongfully harmed by drugs.[50] Proponents of approval and prescription requirements have not established that preemptive regulations are necessary to protect consumers though, and torts and contracts may be jointly sufficient to protect people from wrongful harm while avoiding the detrimental effects of prohibitive regulations, which include drug lag, drug loss, and the violation of people's rights of self-medication.

---

[45] Richard Epstein discusses a similar proposal regarding medical malpractice. Epstein, "Medical Malpractice."

[46] Jessica Flanigan, "Rethinking Freedom of Contract," *Philosophical Studies*, May 17, 2016, 1–21, doi:10.1007/s11098-016-0691-6.

[47] Jason M. Solomon, "Equal Accountability Through Tort Law," *Northwestern University Law Review* 103 (2009): 1765.

[48] Ibid.; Stephen Darwall, *The Second-Person Standpoint: Morality, Respect, and Accountability* (Harvard University Press, 2009).

[49] Wyeth v. Levine, 129 S. Ct. 1187 (Supreme Court 2009).

[50] For a counterargument to my claim that tort law can replace regulation in these cases see Susan Rose-Ackerman, "Regulation and the Law of Torts," *The American Economic Review* 81, no. 2 (1991): 54–58.

This is not to suggest that tort law is always preferable to regulation. For example, environmental regulations may be necessary to prevent the diffuse but real harms caused by multiple polluters. And prescription requirements and other regulations for antibiotics may be justified on similar grounds. But for most drug sales, tort law is well suited to deter manufacturers from violating patients' rights against fraud and negligence. The advantage of tort law is that it can provide mechanisms for the victims of fraud and negligence to seek remedies without limiting access and innovation as much as regulation does.

7.6 Insurance and Social Costs

When a manufacture is not at fault for injuries associated with drug use, who should pay for the harms caused by risky drugs? A common justification for paternalism in medicine is that some people would become a burden to their fellow citizens if they were given the freedom to self-medicate and access any medical services because they would rely on other people to pay for at least some of their healthcare costs, either as members of an insurance pool or as taxpayers who collectively finance a national health insurance system. Put differently, even if we accept rights of self-medication and relatively unregulated markets in pharmaceuticals, I have not argued for an entirely free-market approach to health insurance and healthcare more generally. And as long as public officials tax citizens in order to provide healthcare to all or require citizens to purchase health insurance, people will be forced to pay the price for their fellow citizens' risky choices. This possibility is especially challenging if we assume, plausibly, that the same people who are likely to use uncertified drugs to save money are unlikely to be able to afford medical care or insurance, though this problem is not specific to unsafe pharmaceuticals.

Some proponents of prohibitive regulations cite the harmful effects of people's unhealthy choices as a justification for paternalistic policies, such as limits on self-medication. The argument goes like this. Taxpayers and members of insurance plans pay for each other's healthcare. When people make risky choices, they are likely to use more healthcare. More healthcare is expensive. The costs of healthcare are passed on to taxpayers and members of an insurance plan. Higher taxes and insurance premiums make people worse off. It is wrong to make people worse off in this way. Therefore, it is wrong to make risky choices, such as using unauthorized drugs. So public officials can limit people's rights of self-medication. Call this objection to self-medication the social costs objection—it states that public officials can limit people's rights of self-medication to prevent them from harming their fellow citizens by making risky choices.

Yet, even if policies that require taxpayers to finance a national health service and policies that require citizens to purchase insurance were justified, such policies could not justify limits on rights of self-medication or paternalistic regulations of the pharmaceutical industry. My response to the social cost argument has two steps. First, public officials might tax their citizens to provide healthcare or require that people purchase insurance on the grounds that citizens have enforceable rights to receive healthcare, and others are therefore liable to be coerced to provide them with it.[51] If so, then people may waive their right to healthcare. If the right to healthcare cannot be waived, those who use health insurance or public healthcare are nevertheless not liable to be interfered with on the grounds that they will subsequently exercise their rights to healthcare. Or if people do not have rights to healthcare, then public officials may either refuse to provide it or provide it out of beneficence. Either way, limits on rights of self-medication could not be justified on the grounds that people who misuse medication and subsequently injure themselves use publically funded health services.

Consider first the claim that all citizens have a right to healthcare and a duty to provide it to their compatriots, either by financing a national health service or by purchasing insurance.[52] According to this view, public officials may legitimately compel people to comply with their duty to provide each other with healthcare by becoming insured, paying taxes, and supporting public health efforts. It may then seem as if public officials could also compel people who make unhealthy choices to be healthier, for the sake of the public's interest in promoting everyone's health. For example, if a person used recreational drugs, became intoxicated, injured herself, and required hospitalization, her hospital stay would be subsidized by all taxpayers or members of an insurance pool and would divert resources from other efforts at providing people with healthcare.

However, even if people may be compelled to pay taxes to ensure access to healthcare for all, it wouldn't follow that other forms of coercion were permissible. For example, even if some people's decision to refuse to use statins caused a greater number of heart attacks, public officials could not compel people to

---

[51] I am skeptical that people have these rights, but many people who argue in favor of mandatory insurance or the public provision of healthcare say that people do. Norman Daniels, "Justice and Access to Health Care," in *The Stanford Encyclopedia of Philosophy*, ed. Edward N. Zalta, Spring 2013, http://plato.stanford.edu/archives/spr2013/entries/justice-healthcareaccess/.

[52] Though I am not committed to the claim that people have rights to healthcare in this way, many people hold this view. The consensus view that people have rights to healthcare is supported by several moral considerations. See for example, Allen E. Buchanan, "The Right to a Decent Minimum of Health Care," *Philosophy and Public Affairs* 13, no. 1 (1984): 55–78; Norman Daniels, "Health Care Needs and Distributive Justice," in *In Search of Equity* (Springer, 1983), 1–41, http://link.springer.com/chapter/10.1007/978-1-4684-4424-7_1. Norman Daniels, "Justice and Access to Health Care," in *The Stanford Encyclopedia of Philosophy*, ed. Edward N. Zalta, Spring 2011, 2011, http://plato.stanford.edu/archives/spr2011/entries/justice-healthcareaccess/.

self-medicate against their will. Similarly, even if taxation for the sake of public health and healthcare were permissible, limits on self-medication or recreational drug use are not. Many arguments in favor of universal health coverage appeal to a principle of egalitarianism. Taxes are a relatively egalitarian way of distributing the costs of providing for healthcare in a way that treats people in accordance with a principle of distributive justice. But paternalistic violations of people's rights against medical battery or rights of self-medication would not distribute the burdens of providing universal healthcare in an egalitarian way; they would excessively encumber the choices of those who are more likely to exercise their rights to use healthcare. But this principle would also justify imposing burdens on other groups that are likely to use healthcare, such as demographics that tend to make risky choices (e.g., young men) or conscientious demographics that tend to use health services (e.g., women). Yet, in all these cases, the fact that a person is more likely to exercise his or her right to healthcare does not make her liable to be preemptively penalized for her rights to be preemptively violated on the grounds that she is more likely to use healthcare.

Consider an analogy to other public services and important rights. Assume that freedom of expression is a basic right and that public officials use public funds to provide legal protections for journalists and artists and anyone else's speech too. Taxpayers and officials may notice that journalists who cover politically sensitive topics and controversial artists are more likely to use their right to a publically funded legal system that protects their freedom of expression. But people who produced controversial media or art would not be liable to be censored or disproportionately taxed to offset the fact that their actions were more costly to the public than others'. Similarly, people who make risky (but permissible) choices, such as walking through dangerous neighborhoods or having abrasive personalities, may require more police protection than their rural and conflict-averse compatriots. But taxpayers would not be entitled to restrict people's freedom of movement or expression on the grounds that certain people are more likely to use publically provided police protection. A person is not liable to bear greater limits of his rights in anticipation of their future use of police services.

A similar argument applies if citizens have rights to healthcare. To see why, imagine penalties were retroactive rather than preemptive. Public officials could penalize people who use the legal system, police services, or healthcare in cases where they determine that the use of public services was a result of a person's own choices. So journalists would be required to compensate the courts whenever they were sued for defamation; people in dangerous neighborhoods would be required to compensate fellow taxpayers for their decision to expose themselves to risks; and people who exercised their rights of self-mediation would pay their own hospital bills or a special fee for ambulance services and emergency care. But if people really have rights to public services like a legal system, police protection, and healthcare, then states cannot demand that people pay for exercising those rights. Consider what such a fee-for-service government would require to be effective. If such public services are rights, then even those who fail to pay the fee would nevertheless be entitled to access the service, so on what grounds could officials demand payment?

Yet, the same reasoning applies to preemptive penalties and regulations that limit people's other rights or force people to pay in advance for the increased costs they will impose on the public. Paternalistic regulations that limit people's rights of self-medication to avoid the costs of providing healthcare to unhealthy citizens amounts to a tax in advance on people who exercise their rights of self-medication for subsequently exercising their right to healthcare. But it is even worse than a tax because rights of self-medication are generally more weighty than rights against being taxed—if there are rights against being taxed at all. In sum, if healthcare is a right, then unhealthy citizens do not make themselves liable to preemptive or retroactive penalties or coercive restrictions simply because they tried or will try to exercise that right.[53]

The claim that all people have rights to healthcare whether their health needs are due to risky choices or factors beyond their control invokes the language of entitlement to explain people's claim to access public health services. But if healthcare is something that citizens are owed, then whoever owes it to citizens cannot place conditions on its use. If I owe twenty dollars to my friend Ernesto, then Ernesto is entitled to receive twenty dollars from me when my debt is due. I would not be entitled to restrict Ernesto's choices in ways that prevented him from requesting the money I owe him, and I shouldn't discourage him from collecting what I owe him. Similarly, if citizens were entitled to receive healthcare from their compatriots, then fellow taxpayers would not be entitled to discourage them from using healthcare.

One may reply to the foregoing argument by maintaining that rights to healthcare are not absolute, that people waive their rights to healthcare, or that people are not entitled to access healthcare under certain circumstances. For example, a jealous ex-husband may have the general right to freely associate with people, but he would waive his right to associate with his former spouse if he threatened her in ways that justified obtaining a restraining order. Though people are entitled to travel across borders, these rights can be limited to prevent fugitives from escaping punishment. Perhaps rights to healthcare are like this, and people who injure themselves by making risky medical choices waive their rights to use healthcare. For the sake of argument, suppose that people

---

[53] This arrangement is even harder to justify for rights of self-medication than for other rights because not all people who exercise their rights of self-medication will ultimately consume health services, though all would be subject to unilateral penalties if rights of self-medication were limited through paternalistic regulations.

who fail to use drugs that are recommended by a physician or pre-approved, waive their rights to healthcare because they potentially impose high costs on a public healthcare system. If so, then the social costs argument would not succeed because people could waive their rights to use public healthcare in exchange for the opportunity to smoke or eat fatty foods.

Or, one may deny that people have rights to use publically funded health services or insurance in the first place, or deny that people have rights to keep their insurance regardless of their conduct. Perhaps the principles of medical autonomy extend to health insurance, just as patients are entitled to make their own decisions about risks, finances, and the value of health with respect to drugs. If people do not have rights to use publically funded health services, then public officials may permissibly exclude people who make unhealthy decisions from the use of the public system. If people do not have rights to maintain insurance coverage under any circumstances, then insurance providers may permissibly exclude people who impose excessive burdens on the insurance pool, as long as they disclose that they will do so in advance and people are not legally required to have health insurance. On this view, taxpayers provide healthcare though people are not entitled to it, just as taxpayers provide public television or parks—benefits that all can enjoy but no one is owed. But if healthcare is a benefit of this sort, then they may permissibly exclude some people from using it, so they cannot claim that paternalistic limits on self-medication are necessary for the provision of healthcare. So again, such an argument could not justify limits on people's ability to purchase and use pharmaceuticals.

I do not mean to imply that people who do not voluntarily comply with the recommendations of regulatory agencies and their physicians should not receive publically subsidized healthcare on those grounds. Most likely, a policy that excluded people who exercised their rights of self-medication against experts' advice would excessively disadvantage people who cannot afford to see a physician or who are already socially marginalized. I raise these considerations only to show that people who do not comply with officials' and physicians' recommendations will use publically subsidized services does not justify limits on their right of self-medication.

One reason to provide people with publically financed healthcare is that people think it would be unacceptable to watch as people suffer and die because they failed to comply with their physician's recommendation or because they misused pharmaceuticals when their suffering and death could be easily prevented. But this argument for providing all people with healthcare appeals to a very narrow interest of people in a political community—their interest in avoiding the psychic costs of watching people suffer from preventable harms.[54] This interest is

[54] Grill, "Liberalism, Altruism and Group Consent," *Public Health Ethics* 2, no. 2 (2009): 146–57; Joel Feinberg, *Harm to Self* (New York, NY: Oxford University Press, 1986); Gerald Dworkin,

not a right though. If people were entitled to violate people's rights to avoid subsequent psychic costs, then such a view would seemingly justify an excessively prohibitive, perfectionistic legal system whereby prevailing attitudes set limits on everyone's conduct.

So, concerns about the cost of providing healthcare to people who injure themselves by using pharmaceuticals cannot justify prohibitive policies as a matter of principle. It also cannot justify limits on self-medication as a matter of practice. In some cases, rescinding prohibitive regulations and drug laws would save taxpayers money and reduce the burdens on the healthcare system, so the social cost argument also rests on a false empirical premise. For example, if citizens had rights of self-medication, taxpayers would not be required to subsidize policies related to approval, monitoring, enforcement, and drug-related incarceration. Furthermore, members of political communities may also save money by enforcing less prohibitive regulations, which would encourage pharmaceutical or meditech innovators to pursue development and approval in less prohibitive jurisdictions first, which could bring revenue to places that attract drug development.[55]

If the social cost argument were genuinely cited as a reason to limit people's rights of self-medication, such an argument also could not justify limits on deadly drugs or recreational drugs that are most likely to reduce life expectancy. In these cases, people's pharmaceutical choices would reduce their burdens on the healthcare system. But few proponents of paternalistic drug policies would make exceptions for deadly drugs and drugs that reduce life expectancy. This consideration shows that the social cost argument is often an indirect justification for paternalism and that calls for limits on self-medication are not motivated solely by concerns about fiscal solvency and the cost to one's fellow taxpayers. And even though drugs are expensive, pharmaceutical innovation and expanded access to pharmaceuticals also reduces the costs of providing healthcare on balance because it is generally less expensive to provide a person with access to a pill than access to a hospital bed.[56]

Nevertheless, public officials who remain concerned about pharmaceutical misuse may use the public provision of healthcare as a way to incentivize patients to use medically advisable drugs since public officials may permissibly require that patients consult with a physician and use only approved drugs

"Paternalism: Some Second Thoughts," in *The Theory and Practice of Autonomy*, Cambridge Studies in Philosophy (Cambridge University Press, 1988), http://dx.doi.org/10.1017/CBO9780511625206.009.

[55] Makower, Josh, Aabed Meer, and Lyn Denend. "FDA impact on US medical technology innovation: a survey of over 200 medical technology companies." *Advanced Medical Technology Association*, Washington, DC, available at: http://www.advamed.org/NR/rdonlyres/040E6C33-380B-4F6B-AB58-9AB1C0A7A3CF/0/makowerreportfinal.pdf (2010).

[56] J. D. Kleinke, "The Price Of Progress: Prescription Drugs In The Health Care Market," *Health Affairs* 20, no. 5 (September 1, 2001): 43–60, doi:10.1377/hlthaff.20.5.43.

to receive reimbursement or public coverage of their medical expenses. Such a system may limit patients' effective access to unapproved drugs, just as high drug prices limit patients' access. But unlike existing approval and prescription requirements, such an approach would promote prudent and informed self-medication in ways that did not violate patients' rights.

7.7 Conclusion

The value of medical autonomy is not limited to rights of self-medication and informed consent. In order to truly reject and limit medical paternalism, public officials also ought to rethink existing prohibitive approaches to certification, pharmaceutical marketing, and licensure in the health professions. Other industries may merit reconsideration on similar grounds too. For example, the same arguments against approval requirements for drugs extend to the approval requirements that limit patient's access to apps and medical devices. And the same considerations against paternalistic limitations on patient's access to information about drugs are also reasons to question paternalistic arguments for limiting access to genetic testing.[57] The broader message of this chapter is that rights of self-medication are not incompatible with non-coercive mechanisms for promoting informed and responsible pharmaceutical use. But coercive restrictions of the provision of drugs and limits on freedom of speech, which aim to mandate informed and responsible pharmaceutical use, are incompatible with rights of self-medication. Public officials should therefore devote resources to policies that encourage patients to use certified drugs and hold manufacturers accountable for fraud and negligence, while rethinking the paternalistic ethos that shaped health policy throughout the last century.

[57] See e.g., James P. Evans and Robert C. Green, "Direct to Consumer Genetic Testing: Avoiding a Culture War," *Genetics in Medicine: Official Journal of the American College of Medical Genetics* 11, no. 8 (August 2009): 568–69, doi:10.1097/GIM.0b013e3181afbaed.

8

Conclusion

I began this defense of rights of self-medication by arguing that the same considerations that justify rights of informed consent also support rights of self-medication. I then argued that paternalistic arguments in favor of restrictions of self-medication are unsuccessful in part because prohibitive pharmaceutical policies can do more harm than good. Next, I defended the claim that rights of self-medication support patients' rights to purchase and use almost all drugs, including deadly and recreational drugs and enhancements, without a prescription. But the most urgent rights are the rights of patients who suffer from life-threatening conditions to access potentially beneficial unapproved drugs. In these circumstances regulators are morally culpable for the harm and suffering they cause by enforcing prohibitive regulations.

Especially for patients who have the most urgent claims to use unapproved drugs, self-medication is a political cause and patient-driven drug development and protest are warranted responses to unjust drug regulations. I then discussed whether the pharmaceutical industry had special duties to facilitate access to drugs beyond self-medication and whether public officials could permissibly require them to provide affordable drugs. Though the pharmaceutical industry does not have special duties to provide affordable access to drugs and price controls are misguided, public officials may reform the patent system and remove regulatory barriers to drug development to address high drug prices. Some people object to self-medication on the grounds that the social costs of unrestricted access to drugs and relatively unregulated drug marketing would be unacceptable. In response, I argue that the cost of providing healthcare cannot justify limits on people's rights of self-medication and that a freer approach, including DTC drug marketing, could potentially empower patients and foster greater patient engagement and better communication.

At this point, the potentially revisionary implications of this thesis are clear, and the argument may be interpreted not as a defense of self-medication but as a reduction of informed consent. Yet, as I argued in the previous chapter, rights of self-medication only have revisionary implications to the extent that the current system coercively prevents pharmaceutical use in cases where people would otherwise choose to use an unauthorized drug. If officials, insurers, and citizens benefit from the current system, they can voluntarily maintain it through a public certification system and by subsidizing certified or prescribed drugs. It would be far more revisionary to abandon the doctrine of informed consent and embrace medical paternalism, which is not only likely to misfire but which also threatens the values of autonomy, equal treatment, and tolerance.

I imagine that rights of self-medication will still strike some readers as either trivial or dangerous. But to some patients who are dying of treatment-resistant diseases, those who wish to use unauthorized drugs to improve their well-being or prevent illness, and people who wish to die by using deadly drugs, the right of self-medication is not a trivial choice. And the penalties associated with unauthorized use and distribution are not trivial. Neither is the financial cost of existing regulations nor the number of drugs never developed a trivial amount. Though self-medication is sometimes dangerous, patients are able to consent to the dangers associated with pharmaceutical use and avoid the dangers if they choose. In contrast, no one can consent to the deadly system of existing regulations that violate patients' rights and cause death and suffering. For this reason, even those who do not wish to use unapproved pharmaceuticals should nevertheless support reforms that empower all patients by respecting people's rights of self-medication.

As recently as fifty years ago, people were skeptical of patients' ability to withstand hearing a terminal cancer diagnosis or to refuse life-sustaining treatment. Today we realize that informed consent is a fundamental ethical constraint that all physicians must respect, even when they disagree with a patient's choice. Outside the clinic, patients' rights are not similarly respected, so it's no wonder they so often seem ill equipped to decide when they are so often prohibited from meaningfully choosing how to manage their health. True patient empowerment requires more information, more trust, and more choice. Patients' rights profoundly expanded in the last century with the adoption of the doctrine of informed consent—rights of self-medication are the next step.

REFERENCES

Abigail Alliance v. Von Eschenbach, 445 F. 3d 470 (Court of Appeals, Dist. of Columbia Circuit 2006).

Adams, Christopher P., and Van V. Brantner. "Estimating the Cost of New Drug Development: Is It Really $802 Million?" *Health Affairs* 25, no. 2 (March 1, 2006): 420–28. doi:10.1377/hlthaff.25.2.420.

"A Deep Dive into the Second Circuit's Caronia Decision, Potential Next Steps, and Potential Enforcement Fallout." *FDA Law Blog*, December 12, 2012. http://www.fdalawblog.net/fda_law_blog_hyman_phelps/2012/12/a-deep-dive-into-the-second-circuits-caronia-decision-potential-next-steps-and-potential-enforcement.html.

Aids Healthcare Foundation. "FDA AIDS Protest Targets Approval of Gilead's Prevention Pill." AIDS Healthcare Foundation, January 23, 2012. http://www.aidshealth.org/#/archives/6488.

Alexander G., S. P. Kruszewski, and D. W. Webster. "Rethinking Opioid Prescribing to Protect Patient Safety and Public Health." *JAMA* 308, no. 18 (November 14, 2012): 1865–66. doi:10.1001/jama.2012.14282.

Alexander, Michelle, and Cornel West. *The New Jim Crow: Mass Incarceration in the Age of Colorblindness*. New York: New Press, 2012.

Allen, Arthur. "A Giant Pain in the Wallet." *Slate*, March 29, 2011. http://www.slate.com/articles/health_and_science/medical_examiner/2011/03/a_giant_pain_in_the_wallet.html.

Althaus, Scott. "Opinion Polls, Information Effects, and Political Equality: Exploring Ideological Biases in Collective Opinion." *Political Communication* 13, no. 1 (1996): 3–21.

Althaus, Scott L. *Collective Preferences in Democratic Politics: Opinion Surveys and the Will of the People*. Cambridge; New York: Cambridge University Press, 2003.

Anand, Geeta. "As Costs Rise, New Medicines Face Pushback." *Wall Street Journal*, September 18, 2007, sec. News. http://www.wsj.com/articles/SB119007210553130427.

Anderson, Elizabeth S. "What Is the Point of Equality?" *Ethics* 109, no. 2 (1999): 287–337.

Angell, Marcia. "Drug Companies & Doctors: A Story of Corruption." *New York Review of Books*, January 15, 2009. http://www.nybooks.com/articles/2009/01/15/drug-companies-doctorsa-story-of-corruption/.

———. *The Truth About the Drug Companies: How They Deceive Us and What to Do About It*. New York: Random House Trade Paperbacks, 2005.

annaedney, Anna Edney. "Shkreli's Strategy to Jack up Drug Prices May Be Curbed by FDA." *Bloomberg.com*. March 14, 2016. http://www.bloomberg.com/news/articles/2016-03-14/shkreli-s-strategy-to-jack-up-drug-prices-may-be-curbed-by-fda.

Anomaly, Jonny. "Combating Resistance: The Case for a Global Antibiotics Treaty." *Public Health Ethics* 3, no. 1 (April 1, 2010): 13–22. doi:10.1093/phe/phq001.

———. "Ethics, Antibiotics, and Public Policy." *Georgetown Journal of Law and Public Policy*, 2017.

Ariely, Dan, Ximena Garcia-Rada, Lars Hornuf, and Heather Mann. "The (True) Legacy of Two Really Existing Economic Systems." SSRN Scholarly Paper. Rochester, NY: Social Science Research Network, June 19, 2014. http://papers.ssrn.com/abstract=2457000.

Armstrong, Joanne. "Unintended Consequences—The Cost of Preventing Preterm Births after FDA Approval of a Branded Version of 17OHP." *New England Journal of Medicine* 364, no. 18 (May 5, 2011): 1689–91. doi:10.1056/NEJMp1102796.

Arundel, Anthony, and Isabelle Kabla. "What Percentage of Innovations Are Patented? Empirical Estimates for European Firms." *Research Policy* 27, no. 2 (1998): 127–41.

Aviv, Rachel. "Prescription for Disaster." *The New Yorker*, April 28, 2014. http://www.newyorker.com/magazine/2014/05/05/prescription-for-disaster.

Avorn, Jerry, and Aaron Kesselheim. "A Hemorrhage of Off-Label Use." *Annals of Internal Medicine* 154, no. 8 (April 19, 2011): 566. doi:10.7326/0003-4819-154-8-201104190-00010.

Baker, C. Edwin. "Autonomy and Free Speech." *Constitutional Commentary* 27 (2010): 251.

Bakke, Olav M. et al. "Drug Safety Discontinuations in the United Kingdom, the United States, and Spain from 1974 Through 1993: A Regulatory Perspective." *Clinical Pharmacology & Therapeutics* 58, no. 1 (July 1, 1995): 108–17.

Ballentine, Carol. "Taste of Raspberries, Taste of Death: The 1937 Elixir Sulfanilamide Incident." *FDA Consumer Magazine*, June 1981. http://www.fda.gov/aboutfda/whatwedo/history/productregulation/sulfanilamidedisaster/default.htm.

Barder, Owen, Michael Kremer, and Heidi Williams. "Advance Market Commitments: A Policy to Stimulate Investment in Vaccines for Neglected Diseases." *The Economists' Voice* 3, no. 3 (2006). http://www.degruyter.com/dg/viewarticle.fullcontentlink:pdfeventlink/$002fj$00 2fev.2006.3.3$002fev.2006.3.3.1144$002fev.2006.3.3.1144.pdf?t:ac=j$002fev.2006.3.3$0 02fev.2006.3.3.1144$002fev.2006.3.3.1144.xml.

Becker, Gary S., Michael Grossman, and Kevin M. Murphy. "An Empirical Analysis of Cigarette Addiction." Working Paper, National Bureau of Economic Research, April 1990. http://www.nber.org/papers/w3322.

Becker, Monica, Sally Edwards, and Rachel I. Massey. "Toxic Chemicals in Toys and Children's Products: Limitations of Current Responses and Recommendations for Government and Industry." *Environmental Science and Technology* 44, no. 21 (2010): 7986–91.

Beitz, Charles R. "The Moral Rights of Creators of Artistic and Literary Works." *Journal of Political Philosophy* 13, no. 3 (September 1, 2005): 330–58. doi:10.1111/j.1467-9760.2005.00226.x.

Belkin, Lisa. "Prematurity Drug Price Jumps Wildly." *New York Times*, April 1, 2011.

Belluck, Pam. "Birth Control Without Seeing a Doctor: Oregon Now, More States Later." *New York Times*, January 4, 2016. http://www.nytimes.com/interactive/2016/01/04/health/birth-control-oregon-contraception.html.

Berndt, Ernst R., Rachel Glennerster, Michael R. Kremer, Jean Lee, Ruth Levine, Georg Weizsacker, and Heidi Williams. "Advanced Purchase Commitments for a Malaria Vaccine: Estimating Costs and Effectiveness." National Bureau of Economic Research, 2005. http://www.nber.org/papers/w11288.

Bessen, James, and Michael James Meurer. *Patent Failure: How Judges, Bureaucrats, and Lawyers Put Innovators at Risk.* Princeton NJ: Princeton University Press, 2008.

"Best of the Biggest: How Profitable Are the World's Largest Companies?" *Forbes*, May 13, 2014. http://www.forbes.com/sites/liyanchen/2014/05/13/best-of-the-biggest-how-profitable-are-the-worlds-largest-companies/#1a3f0dd14c33.

Bhosle, M. J., and R. Balkrishnan. "Drug Reimportation Practices in the United States." *Therapeutics and Clinical Risk Management* 3, no. 1 (2007): 41.

"'Big Ideas,' by Gary S. Becker," *The Milken Institute Review*, June 2004, 93–94. UNZ.org. http://www.UNZ.org/Pub/MilkenInstituteRev-2004q2-00093.

Boldrin, Michele, and David K. Levine. *Against Intellectual Monopoly.* New York: Cambridge University Press, 2010.

Bostrom, Nick, and Toby Ord. "The Reversal Test: Eliminating Status Quo Bias in Applied Ethics." *Ethics* 116, no. 4 (2006): 656–79.

Bowie, Norman E. "Fair Markets." *Journal of Business Ethics* 7, no. 1/2 (1988): 89–98.

Bowie, Norman E., and Thomas W. Dunfee. "Confronting Morality in Markets." *Journal of Business Ethics* 38, no. 4 (July 2002): 381–93. doi:10.1023/A:1016080107462.

Brennan, Jason. *The Ethics of Voting*. New edition with a new afterword by the author. Princeton, NJ: Princeton University Press, 2012.

Brock, Dan W., and Allen E. Buchanan. "The Profit Motive in Medicine." *The Journal of Medicine and Philosophy* 12 (February 1987): 1–35. doi:10.1093/jmp/12.1.1.

Brock, Gillian. "Is Active Recruitment of Health Workers Really Not Guilty of Enabling Harm or Facilitating Wrongdoing?" *Journal of Medical Ethics* 39, no. 10 (2013): 612–14.

Buchanan, A. "Medical Paternalism." *Philosophy & Public Affairs* 7, no. 4 (1978): 370–90.

Buchanan, Allen. *Better than Human: The Promise and Perils of Enhancing Ourselves*. Oxford University Press, 2011.

———. "Principal/Agent Theory and Decisionmaking in Health Care." *Bioethics* 2, no. 4 (October 1, 1988): 317–33. doi:10.1111/j.1467-8519.1988.tb00057.x.

Buchanan, Allen, Tony Cole, and Robert O. Keohane. "Justice in the Diffusion of Innovation." *Journal of Political Philosophy* 19, no. 3 (September 1, 2011): 306–32. doi:10.1111/j.1467-9760.2009.00348.x.

Buchanan, Allen, and Matthew DeCamp. "Responsibility for Global Health." *Theoretical Medicine and Bioethics* 27, no. 1 (2006): 95–114. doi:10.1007/s11017-005-5755-0.

Buchanan, Allen E. "The Right to a Decent Minimum of Health Care." *Philosophy and Public Affairs* 13, no. 1 (1984): 55–78.

Buckley, Cara. "For Uninsured Young Adults, Do-It-Yourself Health Care." *New York Times*, February 18, 2009, sec. New York Region. http://www.nytimes.com/2009/02/18/nyregion/18insure.html.

Budish, Eric B., Benjamin N. Roin, and Heidi L. Williams. "Do Fixed Patent Terms Distort Innovation?: Evidence from Cancer Clinical Trials." SSRN Scholarly Paper. Rochester, NY: Social Science Research Network, September 5, 2013. http://papers.ssrn.com/abstract=2353471.

Bullough, Vern L. "Status and Medieval Medicine." *Journal of Health and Human Behavior* 2, no. 3 (October 1, 1961): 204–10.

Burger, Ludwig, and Torsten Severin. "Germany's Stance on Pricing Threatens Drug Firm Profits." *Reuters*, February 18, 2014. http://www.reuters.com/article/us-germany-drugs-analysis-idUSBREA1H09E20140218.

Burke, Lee, and Jeanne M. Logsdon. "How Corporate Social Responsibility Pays Off." *Long Range Planning* 29, no. 4 (August 1996): 495–502. doi:10.1016/0024-6301(96)00041-6.

Buss, Sarah. "Valuing Autonomy and Respecting Persons: Manipulation, Seduction, and the Basis of Moral Constraints." *Ethics* 115, no. 2 (2005): 195–235.

Cabrales, Antonio, and Sergi Jimenez-Martin. "The Determinants of Pricing in Pharmaceuticals: Are U.S. Prices Really Higher than Those of Canada?" SSRN Scholarly Paper. Rochester, NY: Social Science Research Network, April 1, 2007. http://papers.ssrn.com/abstract=1003132.

Calfee, J. E., and E. DuPre. "The Emerging Market Dynamics of Targeted Therapeutics." *Health Affairs* 25, no. 5 (2006): 1302–08.

Cantrell, Lee F. et al. "Death on the Doorstep of a Border Community—Intentional Self-poisoning with Veterinary Pentobarbital." *Clinical Toxicology* 48, no. 8 (September 2010): 849–50.

Caplan, Bryan. *The Myth of the Rational Voter: Why Democracies Choose Bad Policies*. New edition with a new preface by the author. Princeton, NJ: Princeton University Press, 2008.

Carpenter, Daniel. *Reputation and Power: Organizational Image and Pharmaceutical Regulation at the FDA*. Princeton University Press, 2014.

———. *Reputation and Power: Organizational Image and Pharmaceutical Regulation at the FDA (Princeton Studies in American Politics: Historical, International, and Comparative Perspectives*. Princeton University Press, 2010.

Carpenter, Daniel. "Free the F.D.A." *New York Times*, December 13, 2011, sec. Opinion. http://www.nytimes.com/2011/12/14/opinion/free-the-fda.html.

Carpenter, Daniel, and Gisela Sin. "Policy Tragedy and the Emergence of Regulation: The Food, Drug, and Cosmetic Act of 1938." *Studies in American Political Development* 21, no. 02 (September 2007): 149–80. doi:10.1017/S0898588X0700020X.

Carroll, John. "FDA Orders CytRx to Halt Patient Enrollment after Death of a Cancer Patient." *FierceBiotech*, November 18, 2014. http://www.fiercebiotech.com/story/fda-orders-cytrx-halt-patient-enrollment-after-death-cancer-patient/2014-11-18.

Cartwright, Will. "Killing and Letting Die: A Defensible Distinction." *British Medical Bulletin* 52, no. 2 (1996): 354–61.

Central Hudson Gas & Elec. Corp. v. Public Serv. Comm'n of NY, 447 US 557 (Supreme Court 1980).

Charlton, James. *Nothing About Us Without Us: Disability Oppression and Empowerment.* Berkeley: University of California Press, 2000.

Chartier, Gary. "Intellectual Property and Natural Law." *Australian Journal of Legal Philosophy* 36 (2011): 58.

Child, James W. "Can Libertarianism Sustain a Fraud Standard?" *Ethics* 104, no. 4 (1994): 722–38.

Christiano, Thomas. "The Authority of Democracy." *Journal of Political Philosophy* 12, no. 3 (2004): 266–90.

Cillers, L., and F. P. Retief. "Poisons, Poisoning, and the Drug Trade in Ancient Rome." *Akroterion* 45 (2000): 88–100.

Cleland, L. W. "Modern Bootlegging and the Prohibition on Fair Prices: Last Call for the Repeal of Pharmaceutical Price Gouging." *Bepress Legal Series*, 2004, 264.

Cohen, Joshua P, Cherie Paquette, and Catherine P Cairns. "Switching Prescription Drugs to over the Counter." *BMJ : British Medical Journal* 330, no. 7481 (January 1, 2005): 39–41.

Committee on Bioethics. "Informed Consent, Parental Permission, and Assent in Pediatric Practice." *Pediatrics* 95, no. 2 (February 1, 1995): 314–17.

Conly, Sarah. *Against Autonomy: Justifying Coercive Paternalism.* Cambridge: Cambridge University Press, 2012.

———. "The Case for Banning Cigarettes." *Journal of Medical Ethics*, March 30, 2016, medethics – 2016–103520. doi:10.1136/medethics-2016-103520.

Conrad, Peter, and Kristin K. Barker. "The Social Construction of Illness: Key Insights and Policy Implications." *Journal of Health and Social Behavior* 51, no. 1 suppl. (2010): S67–79.

"Consumers' Reports on the Health Effects of Direct-to-Consumer Drug Advertising." *ProQuest.com.* Accessed November 1, 2016. http://search.proquest.com/openview/228b1121e635b4bfc30a7b26a60b1ab9/1?pq-origsite=gscholar&cbl=36027.

Courtwright, David T. *Dark Paradise: A History of Opiate Addiction in America.* Harvard University Press, 2001.

Cowen, David L., and Donald F. Kent. "Medical and Pharmaceutical Practice in 1854." *Pharmacy in History* 39, no. 3 (January 1, 1997): 91–100.

Crisp, Roger. "Well-Being." In *The Stanford Encyclopedia of Philosophy*, Summer 2008. edited by Edward N. Zalta, http://seop.illc.uva.nl/archives/sum2008/entries/well-being/#4.1.

Cwik, Bryan. "Labor as the Basis for Intellectual Property Rights." *Ethical Theory and Moral Practice* 17, no. 4 (September 26, 2013): 681–95. doi:10.1007/s10677-013-9471-y.

Daemmrich, Arthur. "Invisible Monuments and the Costs of Pharmaceutical Regulation: Twenty-Five Years of Drug Lag Debate." *Pharmacy in History* 45, no. 1 (January 1, 2003): 3–17.

Dagger, Richard. "Membership, Fair Play, and Political Obligation." *Political Studies* 48, no. 1 (March 1, 2000): 104–17. doi:10.1111/1467-9248.00253.

Daniels, Norman. "Health-Care Needs and Distributive Justice." *Philosophy & Public Affairs* 10, no. 2 (1981): 146–79.

———. "Health Care Needs and Distributive Justice." In Ronald Bayer (ed) *In Search of Equity*, 1–41. Springer, 1983. http://link.springer.com/chapter/10.1007/978-1-4684-4424-7_1.

———. "Justice and Access to Health Care." In *The Stanford Encyclopedia of Philosophy*, edited by Edward N. Zalta, Spring 2011. http://plato.stanford.edu/archives/spr2011/entries/justice-healthcareaccess/.

———. "Justice and Access to Health Care." In *The Stanford Encyclopedia of Philosophy*, edited by Edward N. Zalta, Spring 2013. http://plato.stanford.edu/archives/spr2013/entries/justice-healthcareaccess/.

Dannon, Pinhas, Katherine Lowengrub, Ernest Musin, Yehudit Gonopolski, and Moshe Kotler. "Sustained-Release Bupropion Versus Naltrexone in the Treatment of Pathological

Gambling: A Preliminary Blind-Rater Study." *Journal of Clinical Psychopharmacology* 25, no. 6 (December 2005): 515–653.

Danzon, Patricia M., and Li-Wei Chao. "Cross-National Price Differences for Pharmaceuticals: How Large, and Why?" *Journal of Health Economics* 19, no. 2 (March 2000): 159–95. doi:10.1016/S0167-6296(99)00039-9.

Danzon, Patricia M., and Michael F. Furukawa. "Prices and Availability of Pharmaceuticals: Evidence from Nine Countries." *Health Affairs*, 2003, W3.

Danzon, Patricia M., and Eric Keuffel. "Regulation of the Pharmaceutical Industry." NBER Chapters. National Bureau of Economic Research, 2011. http://ideas.repec.org/h/nbr/nberch/12572.html.

Dare, Tim. "Parental Rights and Medical Decisions." *Pediatric Anesthesia* 19, no. 10 (October 1, 2009): 947–52. doi:10.1111/j.1460-9592.2009.03094.x.

Darrow, Jonathan J., Jerry Avorn, and Aaron S. Kesselheim. "New FDA Breakthrough-Drug Category—Implications for Patients." *New England Journal of Medicine* 370, no. 13 (March 27, 2014): 1252–58. doi:10.1056/NEJMhle1311493.

Darwall, by Stephen. "The Value of Autonomy and Autonomy of the Will." *Ethics* 116, no. 2 (January 1, 2006): 263–84. doi:10.1086/498461.

Darwall, Stephen. *The Second-Person Standpoint: Morality, Respect, and Accountability*. Harvard University Press, 2009.

Davis, Ryan. "The Moral Significance of Respect for Persons." Working Paper, Brigham Young University, 2015.

deBronkart, Dave. "How the E-Patient Community Helped Save My Life: An Essay by Dave deBronkart." *BMJ* 346 (April 2, 2013): f1990. doi:10.1136/bmj.f1990.

Dees, Richard H. "Better Brains, Better Selves? The Ethics of Neuroenhancements." *Kennedy Institute of Ethics Journal* 17, no. 4 (2007): 371–95. doi:10.1353/ken.2008.0001.

De George, Richard T. "Intellectual Property and Pharmaceutical Drugs: An Ethical Analysis." *Business Ethics Quarterly* 15, no. 04 (2005): 549–75.

DeJoy, David M. "The Optimism Bias and Traffic Accident Risk Perception." *Accident Analysis & Prevention* 21, no. 4 (1989): 333–40.

Dillon, Sir Andrew. "Carrying NICE over the Threshold." *NICE Blog*, February 19, 2015. https://www.nice.org.uk/news/blog/carrying-nice-over-the-threshold.

DiMasi, Joseph A., Ronald W. Hansen, and Henry G. Grabowski. "The Price of Innovation: New Estimates of Drug Development Costs." *Journal of Health Economics* 22, no. 2 (2003): 151–85.

Dockterman, Eliana. "People Want DEA Chief to Resign for Calling Medical Marijuana 'A Joke.'" *Time*, November 10, 2015. http://time.com/4107603/dea-medical-marijuana-joke-2/.

Domoslawski, Artur, Hanna Siemaszko, and Helsińska Fundacja Praw Czlowieka. "Drug Policy in Portugal: The Benefits of Decriminalizing Drug Use." Open Society Foundations, New York, 2011. https://www.tni.org/en/issues/decriminalization/item/2725-drug-policy-in-portugal.

Don and Iris Goodbye.wmv, 2011. http://www.youtube.com/watch?v=ChKa2b12Yhw&feature=youtube_gdata_player.

Douglass, Frederick. *Narrative of the Life of Frederick Douglass*. Unabridged edition. New York: Dover, 1995.

Douglas, Thomas. "Moral Enhancement." *Journal of Applied Philosophy* 25, no. 3 (2008): 228–45.

Dranove, David, Craig Garthwaite, and Manuel Hermosilla. "Pharmaceutical Profits and the Social Value of Innovation." Working Paper, National Bureau of Economic Research, 2014. http://www.nber.org/papers/w20212.

Duggan, Mark, Craig Garthwaite, and Aparajita Goyal. "The Market Impacts of Pharmaceutical Product Patents in Developing Countries: Evidence from India." Working Paper, National Bureau of Economic Research, 2014. http://www.nber.org/papers/w20548.

Dunning, David, Chip Heath, and Jerry M. Suls. "Flawed Self-Assessment Implications for Health, Education, and the Workplace." *Psychological Science in the Public Interest* 5, no. 3 (December 1, 2004): 69–106. doi:10.1111/j.1529-1006.2004.00018.x.

Dworkin, Gerald. "Paternalism." In *The Stanford Encyclopedia of Philosophy*, edited by Edward N. Zalta, Summer 2014. http://plato.stanford.edu/archives/sum2014/entries/paternalism/.

———. "Paternalism: Some Second Thoughts." In *The Theory and Practice of Autonomy*. Cambridge Studies in Philosophy, 121–130. Cambridge University Press, 1988.

Dworkin, Ronald. "Comment on Narveson: In Defense of Equality." *Social Philosophy and Policy* 1, no. 1 (September 1983): 24–40. doi:10.1017/S0265052500003307.

Earp, Brian D. "Love and Other Drugs." *Philosophy Now* 91 (2012): 14–17.

Edwards, Hayes. "Risky Business: How the FDA Overstepped Its Bounds by Limiting Patient Access to Experimental Drugs." *George Mason University Civil Rights Law Journal* 22 (2012): 389.

Eisenberg, Rebecca S. "Role of the FDA in Innovation Policy." *Michigan Telecommunications and Technology Law Review* 13 (2007): 345.

Epstein, Richard A. "Medical Malpractice: The Case for Contract." *American Bar Foundation Research Journal* 1, no. 1 (January 1, 1976): 87–149.

Epstein, Richard A. "Regulatory Paternalism in the Market for Drugs: Lessons from Vioxx and Celebrex." *Yale Journal of Health Policy, Law, and Ethics* 5 (2005): 741.

Epstein, Steven. *Impure Science: AIDS, Activism, and the Politics of Knowledge*. University of California Press, 1998.

Evans, James P., and Robert C. Green. "Direct to Consumer Genetic Testing: Avoiding a Culture War." *Genetics in Medicine : Official Journal of the American College of Medical Genetics* 11, no. 8 (August 2009): 568–69. doi:10.1097/GIM.0b013e3181afbaed.

"Experimental Vaccine Gives Father of the Bride Precious Time."*CNN.com*, September 9, 2010. http://www.cnn.com/2010/HEALTH/09/10/experimental.vaccine.delays.cancer/index.html.

Eyal, Nir. "Informed Consent." In *The Stanford Encyclopedia of Philosophy*, edited by Edward N. Zalta, Fall 2012. http://plato.stanford.edu/archives/fall2012/entries/informed-consent/.

Fabre, Cécile. *Whose Body Is It Anyway?: Justice and the Integrity of the Person*. eBook edition, 2008.

Falk, Armin, and Nora Szech. "Morals and Markets." *Science* 340, no. 6133 (May 10, 2013): 707–11. doi:10.1126/science.1231566.

"FAQs About Rx-to-OTC Switch." *CHPA.org*. Accessed April 6, 2016. http://www.chpa.org/SwitchFAQs.aspx#whatisswitch.

"FastStats." Accessed April 11, 2016. http://www.cdc.gov/nchs/fastats/accidental-injury.htm.

Faulmüller, Nadira, Hannah Maslen, and Filippo Santoni de Sio. "The Indirect Psychological Costs of Cognitive Enhancement." *The American Journal of Bioethics* 13, no. 7 (2013): 45–47.

Faupel, Charles E. "Heroin Use, Crime and Employment Status." *Journal of Drug Issues* 18, no. 3 (July 1, 1988): 467–79. doi:10.1177/002204268801800311.

Federal Trade Commission, "Health Claims" Media Resources https://www.ftc.gov/news-events/media-resources/truth-advertising/health-claims.

Feinberg, Joel. *Harm to Self*. New York, NY: Oxford University Press, 1986.

Feldman, Robin, and W. Nicholson Price. "Patent Trolling—Why Bio & Pharmaceuticals Are at Risk." *UC Hastings Research Paper*, no. 93 (2014). http://papers.ssrn.com/sol3/Papers.cfm?abstract_id=2395987.

Fields, Lisa. "FDA Says ADHD Drug Shortage to End in April." *Consumer Reports News*, April 5, 2012. http://www.consumerreports.org/cro/news/2012/04/fda-says-adhd-drug-shortage-to-end-in-april/index.htm.

Finkelstein, Amy. "Static and Dynamic Effects of Health Policy: Evidence from the Vaccine Industry." *The Quarterly Journal of Economics* 119, no. 2 (May 1, 2004): 527–64. doi:10.1162/0033553041382166.

Fisher III, William W., and Cyril P. Rigamonti. "The South Africa AIDS Controversy: A Case Study in Patent Law and Policy." *Documento de Trabajo, Facultad de Derecho de Harvard*, 2005. http://boris.unibe.ch/69881/1/South%20Africa.pdf.

Fischer, Severin et al. "Suicide Assisted by Two Swiss Right-to-Die Organisations." *Journal of Medical Ethics* 34, no. 11 (October 1, 2008): 810–14.

Flanagan, M. "Avastin's Progression." *Bio Century* 14, no. 11 (2006): A1–A5.

Flanigan, Jessica. "Adderall for All: A Defense of Pediatric Neuroenhancement." *HEC Forum* 25, no. 4 (August 20, 2013): 325–44. doi:10.1007/s10730-013-9222-4.

———. "A Defense of Compulsory Vaccination." *HEC Forum: An Interdisciplinary Journal on Hospitals' Ethical and Legal Issues* 26, no. 1 (March 2014): 5–25. doi:10.1007/s10730-013-9221-5.

———. "Double Standards and Arguments for Tobacco Regulation." *Journal of Medical Ethics*, April 5, 2016, medethics – 2016–103528. doi:10.1136/medethics-2016-103528.

———. "Public Bioethics." *Public Health Ethics* 6, no. 2 (July 1, 2013): 170–84. doi:10.1093/phe/pht022.

———. "Rethinking Freedom of Contract." *Philosophical Studies*, May 17, 2016, 1–21. doi:10.1007/s11098-016-0691-6.

———. "Review: Anne Phillips: *Our Bodies, Whose Property?*" *APA Newsletter on Feminism and Philosophy* 14, no. 1 (Fall 2014).

Flory, James H., and Philip Kitcher. "Global Health and the Scientific Research Agenda." *Philosophy & Public Affairs* 32, no. 1 (January 1, 2004): 36–65. doi:10.1111/j.1467-6486.2004.00004.x.

Flynn, Sean, Aidan Hollis, and Mike Palmedo. "An Economic Justification for Open Access to Essential Medicine Patents in Developing Countries." *The Journal of Law, Medicine & Ethics* 37, no. 2 (June 1, 2009): 184–208. doi:10.1111/j.1748-720X.2009.00365.x.

Foddy, Bennett, and Julian Savulescu. "Addiction and Autonomy: Can Addicted People Consent to the Prescription of Their Drug of Addiction?" *Bioethics* 20, no. 1 (2006): 1–15.

———. "A Liberal Account of Addiction." *Philosophy, Psychiatry, & Psychology* 17, no. 1 (March 1, 2010): 1–22. doi:10.1353/ppp.0.0282.

Frank, Cassie, David U. Himmelstein, Steffie Woolhandler, David H. Bor, Sidney M. Wolfe, Orlaith Heymann, Leah Zallman, and Karen E. Lasser. "Era of Faster FDA Drug Approval Has Also Seen Increased Black-Box Warnings and Market Withdrawals." *Health Affairs* 33, no. 8 (August 1, 2014): 1453–59. doi:10.1377/hlthaff.2014.0122.

Franke, Norman H. "Pharmaceutical Conditions and Drug Supply in the Confederacy." *The Georgia Historical Quarterly* 37, no. 4 (December 1, 1953): 287–98.

Freeman, R. Edward. *Strategic Management: A Stakeholder Approach.* Cambridge University Press, 2010.

Freeman, Samuel. "Liberalism, Inalienability, and Rights of Drug Use." In *Drugs and the Limits of Liberalism: Moral and Legal Issues*, edited by Pablo De Greiff, 110–132. Cornell University Press, 1999.

Freiman, Christopher, and Adam Lerner. "Self-Ownership and Disgust: Why Compulsory Body Part Redistribution Gets under Our Skin." *Philosophical Studies* 172, no. 12 (March 11, 2015): 3167–90. doi:10.1007/s11098-015-0463-8.

Fricker, Miranda. *Epistemic Injustice: Power and the Ethics of Knowing.* Oxford; New York: Oxford University Press, 2009.

Friedersdorf, Conor. "Ted Cruz's Best Idea for Overhauling the FDA." *The Atlantic*, December 18, 2015. http://www.theatlantic.com/politics/archive/2015/12/ted-cruzs-best-idea-for-overhauling-the-fda/421158/.

Friedman, Andrew L., and Samantha Miles. "Developing Stakeholder Theory." *Journal of Management Studies* 39, no. 1 (January 1, 2002): 1–21. doi:10.1111/1467-6486.00280.

Gaffney, RAC, Alexander. "From 100 Hours to 1: FDA Dramatically Simplifies Its Compassionate Use Process." Regulatory Affairs Professionals Society, February 4, 2015. http://www.raps.org/Regulatory-Focus/News/2015/02/04/21243/From-100-Hours-to-1-FDA-Dramatically-Simplifies-its-Compassionate-Use-Process/.

Galasso, Alberto, and Mark Schankerman. "Patents and Cumulative Innovation: Causal Evidence from the Courts." Working Paper, National Bureau of Economic Research, July 2014. http://www.nber.org/papers/w20269.

Galloway, Jim. "The Next Stage of Medical Marijuana Debate: Civil Disobedience." Political Insider Blog, 2016. http://politics.blog.ajc.com/2016/01/20/the-next-stage-of-medical-marijuana-debate-civil-disobedience/.

Gallup. "CDC Tops Agency Ratings; Federal Reserve Board Lowest." *Gallup.com*, July 10, 2009. http://www.gallup.com/poll/121886/CDC-Tops-Agency-Ratings-Federal-Reserve-Board-Lowest.aspx.

"Generic Drug Regulation and Pharmaceutical Price-Jacking." *Marginal REVOLUTION*, September 24, 2015. http://marginalrevolution.com/marginalrevolution/2015/09/generic-drug-regulation.html.

Ghinea, N., W. Lipworth, I. Kerridge, and R. Day. "No Evidence or No Alternative? Taking Responsibility for off-Label Prescribing." *Internal Medicine Journal* 42, no. 3 (March 1, 2012): 247–51. doi:10.1111/j.1445-5994.2012.02713.x.

Gibson, Kevin. "The Moral Basis of Stakeholder Theory." *Journal of Business Ethics* 26, no. 3 (August 2000): 245–57. doi:10.1023/A:1006110106408.

Gieringer, D. H. "The Safety and Efficacy of New Drug Approval." *Cato Journal* 5, no. 1 (1985): 177–201.

Giuliana, Antonia F. "Statistics for Off-Label Marketing Settlements Involving Prescription Drugs." *FCA Alert*, March 2, 2011. http://www.lexology.com/library/detail.aspx?g=df7747e8-dd57-454d-a29d-3f59baed69c4.

Glennerster, Rachel, Michael Kremer, and Heidi Williams. "Creating Markets for Vaccines." *Innovations* 1, no. 1 (2006): 67–79.

Golden, M., and T. Zoanni. "Killing Us Softly: The Dangers of Legalizing Assisted Suicide." *Disability and Health Journal* 3, no. 1 (2010): 16–30.

González, Ángel. "Protesters Demand New Cancer Drugs." *Seattle Times*, September 19, 2007. http://www.seattletimes.com/business/protesters-demand-new-cancer-drugs/.

Good, Chris. "White House Protesters Blast Prescription Drug Policy." *ABC News*, September 28, 2014. http://abcnews.go.com/blogs/politics/2014/09/at-white-house-prescription-drug-protesters-call-for-new-fda-chief/.

Goodin, Robert E. "The Ethics of Smoking." *Ethics* 99, no. 3 (1989): 574–624.

——. *Utilitarianism as a Public Philosophy.* Cambridge University Press, 1995.

Gordon, Wendy J. "A Property Right in Self-Expression: Equality and Individualism in the Natural Law of Intellectual Property." *Yale Law Journal* 102, no. 7 (1993): 1533–1609.

Grabowski, Henry. "Patents, Innovation and Access to New Pharmaceuticals." *Journal of International Economic Law* 5, no. 4 (2002): 849–60.

Grabowski, Henry G., and John Mitcham Vernon. *The Regulation of Pharmaceuticals: Balancing the Benefits and Risks.* Washington DC: American Enterprise Institute for Public Policy Research, 1983.

Grabowski, Henry G., John M. Vernon, and Lacy Glenn Thomas. "Estimating the Effects of Regulation on Innovation: An International Comparative Analysis of the Pharmaceutical Industry." *Journal of Law and Economics* 21, no. 1 (April 1, 1978): 133–63.

Grabowski, Henry, and Y. Richard Wang. "Do Faster Food and Drug Administration Drug Reviews Adversely Affect Patient Safety? An Analysis of the 1992 Prescription Drug User Fee Act." *Journal of Law and Economics* 51, no. 2 (May 1, 2008): 377–406.

Grabowski, H. G. "Increasing R&D Incentives for Neglected Diseases: Lessons from the Orphan Drug Act." In *Increasing R&D Incentives for Neglected Diseases: Lessons from the Orphan Drug Act,* edited by Keith Maskus and Jerome Reichman. Cambridge University Press, 2005. http://dukespace.lib.duke.edu/dspace/handle/10161/7359.

Greenberg, Jeff, Tom Pyszczynski, Sheldon Solomon, Abram Rosenblatt, Mitchell Veeder, Shari Kirkland, and Deborah Lyon. "Evidence for Terror Management Theory II: The Effects of Mortality Salience on Reactions to Those Who Threaten or Bolster the Cultural Worldview." *Journal of Personality and Social Psychology* 58, no. 2 (1990): 308.

Greenwald, Glenn. "Drug Decriminalization in Portugal: Lessons for Creating Fair and Successful Drug Policies." Cato Institute Whitepaper Series, April 2, 2009. http://papers.ssrn.com/sol3/papers.cfm?abstract_id=1464837.

Grill, Kalle. "Liberalism, Altruism and Group Consent." *Public Health Ethics* 2, no. 2 (2009): 146–57.

Grill, Kalle, and Kristin Voigt. "The Case for Banning Cigarettes." *Journal of Medical Ethics*, November 17, 2015, medethics – 2015-102682. doi:10.1136/medethics-2015-102682.

Grootendorst, P. V., and A. Edwards. "Patents and Other Incentives for Pharmaceutical Innovation." *Encyclopedia of Health Economics* 2 (2014): 434–42.

Guerrero, Alexander A. "Don't Know, Don't Kill: Moral Ignorance, Culpability, and Caution." *Philosophical Studies* 136, no. 1 (2007): 59–97.

Haidt, Jonathan, Clark McCauley, and Paul Rozin. "Individual Differences in Sensitivity to Disgust: A Scale Sampling Seven Domains of Disgust Elicitors." *Personality and Individual Differences* 16, no. 5 (May 1, 1994): 701–13. doi:10.1016/0191-8869(94)90212-7.

Hall, Alicia. "Financial Side Effects: Why Patients Should Be Informed of Costs." *Hastings Center Report* 44, no. 3 (2014): 41–47.

Hamilton, Bernice. "The Medical Professions in the Eighteenth Century." *The Economic History Review* 4, no. 2 (1951): 141–69.

Hamilton, Walton H. "The Ancient Maxim Caveat Emptor." *Yale Law Journal* 40 (1931): 1133.

Hardimon, Michael O. "Role Obligations." *Journal of Philosophy* 91, no. 7 (1994): 333–63.

Harkonen v. US, 134 S. Ct. 824 (Supreme Court 2013).

Harman, Elizabeth. "Does Moral Ignorance Exculpate?," *Ratio* 24, no. 4 (November 9, 2011): 443–68.

Harris, Gardiner. "F.D.A. Finds Short Supply of Attention Deficit Drugs." *New York Times*, December 31, 2011, sec. Health/Money & Policy. http://www.nytimes.com/2012/01/01/health/policy/fda-is-finding-attention-drugs-in-short-supply.html.

———. "Pfizer Pays $2.3 Billion to Settle Marketing Case." *New York Times*, September 3, 2009, sec. Business. http://www.nytimes.com/2009/09/03/business/03health.html.

Hartzband, Pamela, and Jerome Groopman. "The New Language of Medicine." *New England Journal of Medicine* 365, no. 15 (October 13, 2011): 1372–73.

Hassoun, Nicole. "Global Health Impact: A Basis for Labeling and Licensing Campaigns?" *Developing World Bioethics* 12, no. 3 (December 1, 2012): 121–34. doi:10.1111/j.1471-8847.2011.00314.x.

Hawk, William. "Review of Douglas Husak, Peter de Marneffe, *The Legalization of Drugs: For & Against.*" *Notre Dame Philosophical Reviews* 2006, no. 8 (2006).

Hawley, Chris, and News Services. "'An Epidemic': Pharmacy Robberies Sweeping US." *NBC News*, June 25, 2011. http://www.nbcnews.com/id/43536286/ns/us_news-crime_and_courts/t/epidemic-pharmacy-robberies-sweeping-us/.

Healy, Patrick, and Margot Sanger-katz. "Hillary Clinton Proposes Cap on Patients' Drug Costs as Bernie Sanders Pushes His Plan." *New York Times*, September 22, 2015. http://www.nytimes.com/2015/09/23/us/politics/hillary-rodham-clinton-proposes-cap-on-patients-drug-costs-as-sanders-pushes-his-plan.html.

Heller, Michael A., and Rebecca S. Eisenberg. "Can Patents Deter Innovation? The Anticommons in Biomedical Research." *Science* 280, no. 5364 (May 1, 1998): 698–701. doi:10.1126/science.280.5364.698.

Hemphill, Thomas A. "Extraordinary Pricing of Orphan Drugs: Is It a Socially Responsible Strategy for the U.S. Pharmaceutical Industry?" *Journal of Business Ethics* 94, no. 2 (November 18, 2009): 225–42. doi:10.1007/s10551-009-0259-x.

Henrich, Joseph, Robert Boyd, Samuel Bowles, Colin Camerer, Ernst Fehr, and Herbert Gintis. *Foundations of Human Sociality: Economic Experiments and Ethnographic Evidence from Fifteen Small-Scale Societies.* Oxford; New York: Oxford University Press, 2004.

Hidalgo, Javier. "Resistance to Unjust Immigration Restrictions." *Journal of Political Philosophy* 23, no. 4 (December 1, 2015): 450–70. doi:10.1111/jopp.12051.

———. "The Case for the International Governance of Immigration." *International Theory* 8, no. 1 (March 2016): 140–70. doi:10.1017/S1752971915000226.

———. "The Duty to Disobey Immigration Law." *Moral Philosophy and Politics* 3, no. 2 (2016): 165–86.

Hill Jr, Thomas E. "Moral Responsibilities of Bystanders." *Journal of Social Philosophy* 41, no. 1 (2010): 28–39.

Holland, Julie. *Moody Bitches: The Truth About the Drugs You're Taking, the Sleep You're Missing, the Sex You're Not Having, and What's Really Making You Crazy.* Reprint. Penguin Books, 2016.

Hollis, Aidan. "An Efficient Reward System for Pharmaceutical Innovation." Draft, University of Calgary, June 10, 2004. http://cdrwww.who.int/entity/intellectualproperty/news/Submission-Hollis6-Oct.pdf.

Hollis, Aidan, and Thomas Pogge. "The Health Impact Fund: Making New Medicines Accessible for All." 2008. http://www.popline.org/node/210204.

Holton, Richard. "Rational Resolve." *Philosophical Review* 113, no. 4 (2004): 507–35.

———. *Willing, Wanting, Waiting.* Oxford: Oxford University Press, 2009.

Horton, John. "In Defence of Associative Political Obligations: Part One." *Political Studies* 54, no. 3 (October 2006): 427–43.

————. "In Defence of Associative Political Obligations: Part Two." *Political Studies* 55, no. 1 (2007): 1–19.

Howard-Snyder, Frances. "Doing vs. Allowing Harm." In *The Stanford Encyclopedia of Philosophy*, edited by Edward N. Zalta, Winter 2011. http://plato.stanford.edu/archives/win2011/entries/doing-allowing/.

Hsiao, William C. "When Incentives and Professionalism Collide." *Health Affairs* 27, no. 4 (2008): 949–51.

Huebner, James M. "Moral Psychology and the Intuition That Pharmaceutical Companies Have a 'Special' Obligation to Society." *Journal of Business Ethics* 122, no. 3 (June 15, 2013): 501–10. doi:10.1007/s10551-013-1773-4.

Huemer, Michael. "Is There a Right to Own a Gun?." *Social Theory and Practice* 29 (2003): 297–324.

————. *The Problem of Political Authority: An Examination of the Right to Coerce and the Duty to Obey*. Houndmills, Basingstoke, Hampshire; New York: Palgrave Macmillan, 2012.

Hughes, Caitlin Elizabeth, and Alex Stevens. "A Resounding Success or a Disastrous Failure: Re-Examining the Interpretation of Evidence on the Portuguese Decriminalisation of Illicit Drugs." *Drug and Alcohol Review* 31, no. 1 (January 1, 2012): 101–13. doi:10.1111/j.1465-3362.2011.00383.x.

Hurst, S. A., and A. Mauron. "The Ethics of Palliative Care and Euthanasia: Exploring Common Values." *Palliative Medicine* 20, no. 2 (2006): 107–112.

Husak, Douglas. *Overcriminalization: The Limits of the Criminal Law*. New York; Oxford University Press, 2008.

Husak, Douglas N. "Guns and Drugs: Case Studies on the Principled Limits of the Criminal Sanction." *Law and Philosophy* 23, no. 5 (2004): 437–93.

————. "Recreational Drugs and Paternalism." *Law and Philosophy* 8, no. 3 (December 1, 1989): 353–81. doi:10.2307/3504593.

Husak, Douglas, and Peter de Marneffe. *The Legalization of Drugs*. (Cambridge, UK: Cambridge University Press, 2005).

Hvide, Hans K., and Benjamin F. Jones. "University Innovation and the Professor's Privilege." Working Paper, National Bureau of Economic Research, March 2016. http://www.nber.org/papers/w22057.

"If A Drug Is Good Enough For Europeans, It's Good Enough For Us." *Health Affairs*. Accessed April 7, 2016. http://healthaffairs.org/blog/2014/02/14/if-a-drug-is-good-enough-for-europeans-its-good-enough-for-us/.

"Illicit Drugs: The WHO Calls for Decriminalisation." *The Economist, Newsbook blog*, Accessed April 11, 2016. http://www.economist.com/blogs/newsbook/2014/07/illicit-drugs.

In re Schloendorffv. Society of New York Hospital. (NYS 1914).

International, United Press. "Police Arrest AIDS Protesters Blocking Access to FDA Offices." *Los Angeles Times*, October 11, 1988. http://articles.latimes.com/1988-10-11/news/mn-3909_1_police-arrest-aids-protesters.

Jefferson, Erica. "FDA Approves Plan B One-Step Emergency Contraceptive for Use Without a Prescription for All Women of Child-Bearing Potential." Press Announcements. June 20, 2013. http://www.fda.gov/NewsEvents/Newsroom/PressAnnouncements/ucm358082.htm.

Jefferson, Thomas. *Notes on the State of Virginia*, edited by Frank Shuffelton. New York, NY: Penguin Classics, 1998.

Jensen, Elizabeth J. "Research Expenditures and the Discovery of New Drugs." *The Journal of Industrial Economics* 36, no. 1 (1987): 83–95. doi:10.2307/2098598.

Jr, Howard McGary, and Bill E. Lawson. *Between Slavery and Freedom: Philosophy and American Slavery*. Indiana University Press, 1993.

"Judge Who Shelved Apple Trial Says Patent System out of Sync." *Reuters*, July 5, 2012. http://www.reuters.com/article/us-apple-google-judge-idUSBRE8640IQ20120705.

Kaitin, Kenneth I., and Jeffrey S. Brown. "A Drug Lag Update." *Drug Information Journal* 29, no. 2 (April 1, 1995): 361–73. doi:10.1177/009286159502900203.

Kaufman, D. B. "Poisons and Poisoning Among the Romans." *Classical Philology* 27, no. 2 (1932): 156–67.

Kaufman, Marc. "9 Arrested Protesting Morning-After Pill Plan." *Washington Post*, January 8, 2005, sec. Nation. http://www.washingtonpost.com/wp-dyn/articles/A57879-2005Jan7.html.

Kelsey, Frances O. "Thalidomide Update: Regulatory Aspects." *Teratology* 38, no. 3 (June 6, 2005): 221–26.

Kendrick, Dawn. "Emergency Insulin Could Have Saved Man's Life." *WKYC*, February 12, 2015. http://www.wkyc.com/story/news/health/2015/02/11/emergency-insulin/23276399/.

Kerr, James J. "Notes on Pharmacy in Old Dublin." *Dublin Historical Record* 4, no. 4 (1942): 149–59.

Kesselheim, Aaron S. "Off-Label Drug Use and Promotion: Balancing Public Health Goals and Commercial Speech." *American Journal of Law & Medicine* 37 (2011): 225.

Kessler, David. "Statement to the US House Committee on Oversight and Government Reform," 110 Congress, Second Session, May 14, 2008 Serial No. 110–201.

Khazan, Olga. "Why Medicine Is Cheaper in Germany." *The Atlantic*, May 22, 2014. http://www.theatlantic.com/health/archive/2014/05/why-medicine-is-cheaper-in-germany/371418/.

Kinsella, Stephan. "The Case Against Intellectual Property." In Lütge, Christoph, (ed) *Handbook of the Philosophical Foundations of Business Ethics*, 1325–57. Springer, 2013. http://link.springer.com/10.1007/978-94-007-1494-6_99.

Kjærsgaard, Torben. "Enhancing Motivation by Use of Prescription Stimulants: The Ethics of Motivation Enhancement." *AJOB Neuroscience* 6, no. 1 (January 2, 2015): 4–10. doi:10.1080/21507740.2014.990543.

Klein, Daniel B. "Colleagues, Where Is the Market Failure? Economists on the FDA." *Econ Journal Watch* 5, no. 3 (2008): 316–48.

———. "How Trust Is Achieved in Free Markets." SSRN Scholarly Paper. Rochester, NY: Social Science Research Network, December 1, 2003. http://papers.ssrn.com/abstract=473442.

———. "The Demand for and Supply of Assurance." *Economic Affairs* 21, no. 1 (March 1, 2001): 4–11. doi:10.1111/1468-0270.00268.

Klein, Daniel B., and Alexander Tabarrok. "Do Off-Label Drug Practices Argue Against FDA Efficacy Requirements? A Critical Analysis of Physicians' Argumentation for Initial Efficacy Requirements." *American Journal of Economics and Sociology* 67, no. 5 (2008): 743–75.

———. "FDA Review." The Independent Institute, 2016. http://www.fdareview.org/09_reform.php#3.

Kleinfield, N. R. "Anxious Days for Long Island Pharmacies." *New York Times*, January 8, 2012, sec. N.Y./Region. http://www.nytimes.com/2012/01/09/nyregion/anxious-days-for-long-island-pharmacies.html.

Kleinke, J. D. "The Price of Progress: Prescription Drugs in the Health Care Market." *Health Affairs* 20, no. 5 (September 1, 2001): 43–60. doi:10.1377/hlthaff.20.5.43.

Klosko, George. "Presumptive Benefit, Fairness, and Political Obligation." *Philosophy & Public Affairs* 16, no. 3 (1987): 241–59.

Knobe, Joshua. "Folk Psychology, Folk Morality." PhD diss., Princeton University, 2006. http://148.216.10.92/archivos%20PDF%20de%20trabajo%20UMSNH/Aphilosofia/folkpsychology.pdf.

Koehler, Jonathan J., and Andrew D. Gershoff. "Betrayal Aversion: When Agents of Protection Become Agents of Harm." *Organizational Behavior and Human Decision Processes* 90, no. 2 (2003): 244–61.

Kopel, David B. "Trust the People: The Case Against Gun Control." *Journal on Firearms & Public Policy* 3 (1990): 77.

Korsgaard, Christine M. *Creating the Kingdom of Ends*. Cambridge University Press, 1996.

———. "Personal Identity and the Unity of Agency: A Kantian Response to Parfit." *Philosophy & Public Affairs* 18, no. 2. (1989): 101–32.

———. "The Right to Lie: Kant on Dealing with Evil." *Philosophy & Public Affairs* 15, no. 4 (October 1, 1986): 325–49.

Kremer, Michael. "Patent Buyouts: A Mechanism for Encouraging Innovation." *The Quarterly Journal of Economics* 113, no. 4 (November 1, 1998): 1137–67. doi:10.1162/003355398555865.

Kruger, Justin, and David Dunning. "Unskilled and Unaware of It: How Difficulties in Recognizing One's Own Incompetence Lead to Inflated Self-Assessments." *Journal of Personality and Social Psychology* 77, no. 6 (1999): 1121–34. doi:10.1037/0022-3514.77.6.1121.

Krugman, Paul. "Patients Are Not Consumers." *New York Times*, April 21, 2011, sec. Opinion. http://www.nytimes.com/2011/04/22/opinion/22krugman.html.

Kugler, Adriana D., and Robert M. Sauer. "Doctors Without Borders? Relicensing Requirements and Negative Selection in the Market for Physicians." *Journal of Labor Economics* 23, no. 3 (2005): 437–65.

Lacey, Marc. "In Tijuana, a Market for Death in a Bottle." *New York Times*, June 21, 2008, sec. International/Americas. http://www.nytimes.com/2008/07/21/world/americas/21tijuana.html.

LaFollette, Hugh. "Gun Control." *Ethics* 110, no. 2 (2000): 263–81.

Lanjouw, Jean O. "Intellectual Property and the Availability of Pharmaceuticals in Poor Countries." NBER Chapters. National Bureau of Economic Research, Inc, 2003. https://ideas.repec.org/h/nbr/nberch/10794.html.

———. "The Introduction of Pharmaceutical Product Patents in India:" Working Paper, National Bureau of Economic Research, January 1998. http://www.nber.org/papers/w6366.

Lanjouw, Jean O., and Mark Schankerman. "Characteristics of Patent Litigation: A Window on Competition." *The RAND Journal of Economics* 32, no. 1 (2001): 129–51. doi:10.2307/2696401.

Lasagna, L., and W. M. Wardell. "The FDA, Politics, and the Public." *JAMA* 232, no. 2 (April 14, 1975): 141–42. doi:10.1001/jama.1975.03250020015015.

Law, Marc T., and Sukkoo Kim. "Specialization and Regulation: The Rise of Professionals and the Emergence of Occupational Licensing Regulation." *The Journal of Economic History* 65, no. 03 (2005): 723–56.

Law, Marc T., and Mindy Marks. "The Effects of Occupational Licensing Laws on Minorities: Evidence from the Progressive Era." SSRN Scholarly Paper. Rochester, NY: Social Science Research Network, November 1, 2008. http://papers.ssrn.com/sol3/papers.cfm?abstract_id=943765.

Laxminarayan, Ramanan, Zulfiqar Bhutta, Adrian Duse, Philip Jenkins, Thomas O'Brien, Iruka N. Okeke, Ariel Pablo-Mendez, and Keith P. Klugman. "Drug Resistance." In *Disease Control Priorities in Developing Countries*, edited by Dean T. Jamison, Joel G. Breman, Anthony R. Measham, George Alleyne, Mariam Claeson, David B. Evans, Prabhat Jha, Anne Mills, and Philip Musgrove, 2nd ed. Washington, DC: World Bank, 2006. http://www.ncbi.nlm.nih.gov/books/NBK11774/.

Lemmens, Trudo, and Carl Elliott. "Justice for the Professional Guinea Pig." *American Journal of Bioethics* 1, no. 2 (2001): 51–53.

Lev, Ori. "Should Children Have Equal Access to Neuroenhancements?" *AJOB Neuroscience* 1, no. 1 (February 10, 2010): 21–23. doi:10.1080/21507740903504442.

Levenstein, Margaret. "Mass Production Conquers the Pool: Firm Organization and the Nature of Competition in the Nineteenth Century." *The Journal of Economic History* 55, no. 3 (1995): 575–611.

Lewis, Neil A. with Robert Pear. "U.S. Drug Industry Fights Reputation for Price Gouging." *New York Times*, March 7, 1994, sec. U.S. http://www.nytimes.com/1994/03/07/us/us-drug-industry-fights-reputation-for-price-gouging.html.

Liao, S. Matthew. "Intentions and Moral Permissibility: The Case of Acting Permissibly with Bad Intentions." *Law and Philosophy* 31, no. 6 (2012): 703–24.

Lichtenberg, Frank R. "Importation and Innovation." Working Paper, National Bureau of Economic Research, September 2006. http://www.nber.org/papers/w12539.

———. "Pharmaceutical Innovation and Longevity Growth in 30 Developing and High-Income Countries, 2000–2009." *Health Policy and Technology* 3, no. 1 (2014): 36–58.

———. "Pharmaceutical Innovation, Mortality Reduction, and Economic Growth." Working Paper, National Bureau of Economic Research, May 1998. http://www.nber.org/papers/w6569.

Lidegaard, Øjvind, Ellen Løkkegaard, Aksel Jensen, Charlotte Wessel Skovlund, and Niels Keiding. "Thrombotic Stroke and Myocardial Infarction with Hormonal Contraception." *New England Journal of Medicine* 366, no. 24 (June 14, 2012): 2257–66. doi:10.1056/NEJMoa1111840.

Loftus, Peter. "Lipitor: Pfizer Aims to Sell Over-the-Counter Version." *Wall Street Journal*, March 2, 2014, sec. Business. http://www.wsj.com/articles/SB10001424052702304071004579410930136742414.

Lombardo, Paul A. "Phantom Tumors and Hysterical Women: Revising Our View of the Schloendorff Case." *The Journal of Law, Medicine & Ethics: A Journal of the American Society of Law, Medicine & Ethics* 33, no. 4 (2005): 791–801.

Mackey, Tim K., and Virginia J. Schoenfeld. "Going 'social' to Access Experimental and Potentially Life-Saving Treatment: An Assessment of the Policy and Online Patient Advocacy Environment for Expanded Access." *BMC Medicine* 14 (February 2, 2016). doi:10.1186/s12916-016-0568-8.

Magyar, Heidi. "Bupropion: Off-Label Treatment for Cocaine and Methamphetamine Addiction." *Current Psychiatry* 9, no. 7 (July 2010). http://www.currentpsychiatry.com/index.php?id=22661&tx_ttnews%5Btt_news%5D=175212.

Maitland, Ian. "Priceless Goods: How Should Life-Saving Drugs Be Priced?" *Business Ethics Quarterly* 12, no. 4 (October 2002): 451–80. doi:10.2307/3857995.

Makower, Josh, Aabed Meer, and Lyn Denend. "FDA impact on US medical technology innovation: a survey of over 200 medical technology companies." *Advanced Medical Technology Association*, Washington, DC, available at: http://www.advamed.org/NR/rdonlyres/040E6C33-380B-4F6B-AB58-9AB1C0A7A3CF/0/makowerreportfinal. pdf (2010).

Mandel, Michael. "How the FDA Impedes Innovation: A Case Study in Overregulation." Policy Brief, Progressive Policy Institute, June 2011.

Manson, Neil C., and Onora O'Neill. *Rethinking Informed Consent in Bioethics*. Cambridge; New York: Cambridge University Press, 2007.

Marcus, Amy Dockser. "Deaf or Death? In Drug Trial, Parents Weigh Life vs. Hearing Loss." *Wall Street Journal*, March 2, 2015, sec. Business. http://www.wsj.com/articles/deaf-or-death-in-drug-trial-parents-weigh-life-vs-hearing-loss-1425267002.

———. "Niemann-Pick Type C: A Fight to Save Children with a Drug." *Wall Street Journal*. Accessed March 10, 2015. http://on.wsj.com/1due624.

———. "The Loneliness of Fighting a Rare Cancer." *Health Affairs* 29, no. 1 (January 1, 2010): 203–6. doi:10.1377/hlthaff.2009.0470.

Mariani, Mike. "Why So Many White American Men Are Dying." *Newsweek*, December 23, 2015. http://www.newsweek.com/2016/01/08/big-pharma-heroin-white-american-mortality-rates-408354.html.

Marks, H. M. "Revisiting 'the Origins of Compulsory Drug Prescriptions.'" *American Journal of Public Health* 85, no. 1 (January 1995): 109–115.

Marneffe, Peter de. *Liberalism and Prostitution*. Reprint. New York; Oxford: Oxford University Press, 2012.

———. "Self-Sovereignty and Paternalism." In *Paternalism: Theory and Practice*, edited by Christian Coons and Michael Weber, 56–73. Cambridge University Press, 2013.

Masters, Alexander. "A Plutocratic Proposal." *Mosaic*, April 7, 2015. http://mosaicscience.com/story/plutocratic-proposal.

McCabe, Christopher, Richard Edlin, and Jeff Round. "Economic Considerations in the Provision of Treatments for Rare Diseases." In *Rare Diseases Epidemiology*, 211–22. Springer, 2010. http://link.springer.com/chapter/10.1007/978-90-481-9485-8_13.

McGraw, A. Peter, Janet A. Schwartz, and Philip E. Tetlock. "From the Commercial to the Communal: Reframing Taboo Trade-Offs in Religious and Pharmaceutical Marketing." *Journal of Consumer Research* 39, no. 1 (June 1, 2012): 157–73. doi:10.1086/662070.

McMahan, Jeff. "Killing, Letting Die, and Withdrawing Aid." *Ethics* 103, no. 2 (1993): 250–79.

McNeill, Paul. "Paying People to Participate in Research: Why Not?" *Bioethics* 11, no. 5 (1997): 390–96.

Meis, P. J. et al. "Prevention of Recurrent Preterm Delivery by 17 Alpha-hydroxyprogesterone Caproate." *New England Journal of Medicine* 348, no. 24 (2003): 2379–85.

Merrill, R. A. "Regulation of Drugs and Devices: An Evolution." *Health Affairs* 13, no. 3 (May 1, 1994): 47–69. doi:10.1377/hlthaff.13.3.47.

Miller, Henry. *To America's Health: A Proposal to Reform the Food and Drug Administration*. Hoover Institution Press, 2000.

Mill, John Stuart. *On Liberty and Other Essays*. Edited by John Gray. Oxford; New York: Oxford University Press, 2008.

Miller, T. Christian, and Jeff Gerth. "Dose of Confusion." *ProPublica*, September 20, 2013. http://www.propublica.org/article/tylenol-mcneil-fda-kids-dose-of-confusion.

Mitchell, Martha Carolyn. "Health and the Medical Profession in the Lower South, 1845–1860." *The Journal of Southern History* 10, no. 4 (1944): 424–46.

Moller, D. "Abortion and Moral Risk." *Philosophy* 86, no. 3 (July 2011): 425–43. doi:10.1017/S0031819111000222.

Moody, L. E., J. Lunney, and P. A. Grady. "Nursing Perspective on End-of-Life Care: Research and Policy Issues, A." *Journal of Health Care Law & Policy* 2 (1998): 243.

Moore, Adam D. "Lockean Theory of Intellectual Property, A." *Hamline Law Review* 21 (1997): 65.

Moore, Adam, and Ken Himma. "Intellectual Property." In *The Stanford Encyclopedia of Philosophy*, edited by Edward N. Zalta, Winter 2014. http://plato.stanford.edu/archives/win2014/entries/intellectual-property/.

Moriarty, Jeffrey. "How Much Compensation Can CEOs Permissibly Accept?" *Business Ethics Quarterly* 19, no. 2 (2009): 235–50.

Morrow, K. John. "Drug Development in the Age of Social Media." *Life Science Leader*, April 25, 2015.

Moynihan, Ray, Iona Heath, and David Henry. "Selling Sickness: The Pharmaceutical Industry and Disease Mongering." *British Medical Journal* 324, no. 7342 (April 13, 2002): 886–91.

Murray, Fiona, Philippe Aghion, Mathias Dewatripont, Julian Kolev, and Scott Stern. "Of Mice and Academics: Examining the Effect of Openness on Innovation." Working Paper, National Bureau of Economic Research, March 2009. http://www.nber.org/papers/w14819.

Murray, Fiona, and Scott Stern. "Do Formal Intellectual Property Rights Hinder the Free Flow of Scientific Knowledge?: An Empirical Test of the Anti-Commons Hypothesis." *Journal of Economic Behavior & Organization* 63, no. 4 (2007): 648–87.

Musick, Nathan, and Phillip Webre. "Federal Policies and Innovation." Congressional Budget Office, November 17, 2014. https://www.cbo.gov/publication/49487.

New, Bill. "Paternalism and Public Policy." *Economics and Philosophy* 15, no. 1 (April 1999): 63–83. doi:10.1017/S026626710000359X.

Novak, William. *The People's Welfare: Law and Regulation in Nineteenth-Century America*. Chapel Hill: University of North Carolina Press, 1996.

Nozick, Robert. *Anarchy, State, and Utopia*. 2nd ed. New York: Basic Books, 2013.

Nussbaum, Martha C. "Danger to Human Dignity: The Revival of Disgust and Shame in the Law." *Chronicle of Higher Education*, August 6, 2004.

Nutt, Amy Ellis, and Dennis. "ALS Patients Press FDA for Quick Access to Controversial Biotech Drug." *Washington Post*, April 3, 2015, sec. Health and Science. https://www.washingtonpost.com/national/health-science/als-patients-press-fda-for-quick-access-to-controversial-biotech-drug/2015/04/03/fb954618-d220-11e4-a62f-ee745911a4ff_story.html.

Nutton, Vivian. *Ancient Medicine*. London; New York: Routledge, 2012.

Okie, Susan. "Access Before Approval—A Right to Take Experimental Drugs?" *New England Journal of Medicine* 355, no. 5 (2006): 437–40.

Oliphant, James. "Activist Takes on FDA for Experimental Drugs." *Chicago Tribune*, August 21, 2007. http://www.montereyherald.com/article/ZZ/20070821/NEWS/708219923.

Olsaretti, Serena. "Freedom, Force and Choice: Against the Rights-Based Definition of Voluntariness." *Journal of Political Philosophy* 6, no. 1 (March 1, 1998): 53–78. doi:10.1111/1467-9760.00046.

Olsen, Darcy. *The Right to Try: How the Federal Government Prevents Americans from Getting the Lifesaving Treatments They Need*. 1st ed. New York, NY: Harper, 2015.

Pagel, Walter. "Prognosis and Diagnosis: A Comparison of Ancient and Modern Medicine." *Journal of the Warburg Institute* 2, no. 4 (April 1, 1939): 382–98.

Palmer, Brian. "The $8,000 Pill." *Slate*, August 16, 2010. http://www.slate.com/articles/news_and_politics/explainer/2010/08/the_8000_pill.html.

Parfit, Derek. *Reasons and Persons*. Oxford: Oxford University Press, 1986.

Pear, Robert. "Medicaid Pays Less Than Medicare for Many Prescription Drugs, U.S. Report Finds." *New York Times*, August 15, 2011. http://www.nytimes.com/2011/08/16/us/16drug.html.

Peltzman, Sam. "An Evaluation of Consumer Protection Legislation: The 1962 Drug Amendments." *Journal of Political Economy* 81, no. 5 (1973): 1049–91.

———. "The Health Effects of Mandatory Prescriptions." *Journal of Law and Economics* 30, no. 2 (October 1, 1987): 207–38.

Perfetto, Eleanor M., Laurie Burke, Elisabeth M. Oehrlein, and Robert S. Epstein. "Patient-Focused Drug Development: A New Direction for Collaboration." *Medical Care* 53, no. 1 (January 2015): 9–17. doi:10.1097/MLR.0000000000000273.

Persson, Ingmar, and Julian Savulescu. "The Perils of Cognitive Enhancement and the Urgent Imperative to Enhance the Moral Character of Humanity." *Journal of Applied Philosophy* 25, no. 3 (2008): 162–77.

"Pharmaceutical HTA and Reimbursement Processes—Switzerland." April 2011. https://www.ispor.org/HTARoadMaps/SwitzerlandPH.asp.

Philipson, Tomas J., Ernst R. Berndt, Adrian H. B. Gottschalk, and Matthew W. Strobeck. "Assessing the Safety and Efficacy of the FDA: The Case of the Prescription Drug User Fee Acts." Working Paper, National Bureau of Economic Research, 2005. http://www.nber.org/papers/w11724.

Phillips, Anne. *Our Bodies, Whose Property?* Princeton, NJ: Princeton University Press, 2013.

Pogge, Thomas. "The Health Impact Fund: Enhancing Justice and Efficiency in Global Health." *Journal of Human Development and Capabilities* 13, no. 4 (2012): 537–59.

Pollack, Andrew. "Court Forbids F.D.A. from Blocking Truthful Promotion of Drug." *New York Times*, August 7, 2015. http://www.nytimes.com/2015/08/08/business/court-forbids-fda-from-blocking-truthful-promotion-of-drug.html.

———. "Deal by Cystic Fibrosis Foundation Raises Cash and Some Concern." *New York Times*, November 19, 2014. http://www.nytimes.com/2014/11/19/business/for-cystic-fibrosis-foundation-venture-yields-windfall-in-hope-and-cash.html.

———. "Drug Goes From $13.50 a Tablet to $750, Overnight." *New York Times*, September 20, 2015. http://www.nytimes.com/2015/09/21/business/a-huge-overnight-increase-in-a-drugs-price-raises-protests.html.

Powell, David, Rosalie Liccardo Pacula, and Mireille Jacobson. "Do Medical Marijuana Laws Reduce Addictions and Deaths Related to Pain Killers?" Working Paper, National Bureau of Economic Research, July 2015. http://www.nber.org/papers/w21345.

"FDA Commissioner Removes Breast Cancer Indication from Avastin Label." Press Announcements. Accessed May 30, 2016. http://www.fda.gov/NewsEvents/Newsroom/PressAnnouncements/ucm279485.htm.

PTI. "39 More Drugs to Become Affordable; Diabetes, Digestive Disorder Medicines in Price Control List." *Times of India*. July 16, 2015. http://timesofindia.indiatimes.com/india/39-more-drugs-to-become-affordable-diabetes-digestive-disorder-medicines-in-price-control-list/articleshow/48097256.cms.

Qian, Yi. "Do National Patent Laws Stimulate Domestic Innovation in a Global Patenting Environment? A Cross-Country Analysis of Pharmaceutical Patent Protection, 1978–2002." *The Review of Economics and Statistics* 89, no. 3 (2007): 436–53.

Quinn, Warren S. "Actions, Intentions, and Consequences: The Doctrine of Double Effect." *Philosophy & Public Affairs* 18, no. 4 (October 1, 1989): 334–51.

Quong, Jonathan. *Liberalism Without Perfection*. Oxford; New York: Oxford University Press, 2011.

Ramsey, Matthew. "Medical Power and Popular Medicine: Illegal Healers in Nineteenth-Century France." *Journal of Social History* 10, no. 4 (1977): 560–87.

Rasmussen Reports. "74% Want to Audit the Federal Reserve," November 8, 2013. http://www.rasmussenreports.com/public_content/business/general_business/november_2013/74_want_to_audit_the_federal_reserve.

Rawls, John. *A Theory of Justice*. Harvard University Press, 1971.

Reichbach, Gustin L. "A Judge's Plea for Medical Marijuana." *The New York Times*, May 16, 2012. http://www.nytimes.com/2012/05/17/opinion/a-judges-plea-for-medical-marijuana.html.

Relman, A S. "The Impact of Market Forces on the Physician-Patient Relationship." *Journal of the Royal Society of Medicine* 87, no. Suppl 22 (1994): 22–25.

Relman, Arnold S. "Eliminate the Profit Motive in Health Care," Physicians for a National Health Program. September 28, 2011. http://www.pnhp.org/news/2011/september/eliminate-the-profit-motive-in-health-care.

"Remarks by the President at a Campaign Event in Roanoke, Virginia." *Whitehouse.gov*, July 13, 2012. https://www.whitehouse.gov/the-press-office/2012/07/13/remarks-president-campaign-event-roanoke-virginia.

Resnik, David B. *The Price of Truth: How Money Affects the Norms of Science*. Oxford University Press, 2006.

Riddle, John M. "Theory and Practice in Medieval Medicine." *Viator* 5, no. 1 (January 1, 1974): 157–84.

Roan, Shari. "Swine Flu 'Debacle' of 1976 Is Recalled." *Los Angeles Times*, April 27, 2009. http://articles.latimes.com/2009/apr/27/science/sci-swine-history27.

Rose-Ackerman, Susan. "Regulation and the Law of Torts." *The American Economic Review* 81, no. 2 (1991): 54–58.

Rosen, Gideon. "Culpability and Ignorance." *Proceedings of the Aristotelian Society* 103, New Series (January 1, 2003): 61–84.

Rosenthal, Elisabeth. "Officials Question the Rising Costs of Generic Drugs." *New York Times*, October 7, 2014. http://www.nytimes.com/2014/10/08/business/officials-question-the-rising-costs-of-generic-drugs.html.

———. "The Soaring Cost of a Simple Breath." *New York Times*, October 12, 2013, sec. U.S. http://www.nytimes.com/2013/10/13/us/the-soaring-cost-of-a-simple-breath.html.

Rosner, F. "Moses Maimonides' Treatise on Asthma." *Thorax* 36, no. 4 (April 1981): 245–51.

Roxborough, Craig, and Jill Cumby. "Folk Psychological Concepts: Causation." *Philosophical Psychology* 22, no. 2 (April 1, 2009): 205–13. doi:10.1080/09515080902802769.

Royal Society of Chemistry. "Medicine Gets Personalised." July 2015. http://www.rsc.org/chemistryworld/Issues/2005/July/Medicine_personalised.asp.

Russell, Bertrand. *The Conquest of Happiness*. Lulu Press, 2015.

Sage Bionetworks. "Current Bridge Studies." 2016. http://sagebase.org/bridge/.

———. "Press Release: Sage Bionetworks Announces Program to Develop BRIDGE: An IT Platform That Leverages Patient Wisdom and Data for 21st Century Biomedical Research." *MarketWatch*. September 27, 2013. http://www.marketwatch.com/story/sage-bionetworks-announces-program-to-develop-bridge-an-it-platform-that-leverages-patient-wisdom-and-data-for-21st-century-biomedical-research-2013-09-27.

Samuels, Alec. "Complicity in Suicide." *Journal of Criminal Law* 69, no. 6 (2005): 535–9.

Sandel, Michael. "The Case Against Perfection." *Atlantic Monthly* 293, no. 3 (2004): 51–62.

Sandora, Thomas J., and Donald A. Goldmann. "Preventing Lethal Hospital Outbreaks of Antibiotic-Resistant Bacteria." *New England Journal of Medicine* 367, no. 23 (December 6, 2012): 2168–70. doi:10.1056/NEJMp1212370.

Scanlon, T. M., and Jonathan Dancy. "Intention and Permissibility." *Proceedings of the Aristotelian Society, Supplementary Volumes* 74 (January 1, 2000): 301–38.

Scanlon, T. M., and Thomas Scanlon. *Moral Dimensions*. Harvard University Press, 2009.

Schapiro, Tamar. "Kantian Rigorism and Mitigating Circumstances." *Ethics* 117, no. 1 (2006): 32–57. doi:10.1086/508036.

———. "What Is a Child?" *Ethics* 109, no. 4 (July 1, 1999): 715–38. doi:10.1086/233943.

Scheffler, Samuel. "Doing and Allowing." *Ethics* 114, no. 2 (January 1, 2004): 215–39. doi:10.1086/379355.

Scheffler, Samuel. "Relationships and Responsibilities." *Philosophy & Public Affairs* 26, no. 3 (July 1, 1997): 189–209. doi:10.1111/j.1088-4963.1997.tb00053.x.

Schifrin, L. G., and J. R. Tayan. "The Drug Lag: An Interpretive Review of the Literature." *International Journal of Health Services: Planning, Administration, Evaluation* 7, no. 3 (1977): 359–81.

Schnall, Simone, Jonathan Haidt, Gerald L. Clore, and Alexander H. Jordan. "Disgust as Embodied Moral Judgment." *Personality and Social Psychology Bulletin*, May 27, 2008. doi:10.1177/0146167208317771.

Schuklenk, Udo. *Access to Experimental Drugs in Terminal Illness: Ethical Issues* (Binghamton, NY: Pharmaceutical Products Press/Haworth Press, 1998).

Scoccia, Danny. "In Defense of Hard Paternalism." *Law and Philosophy* 27, no. 4 (July 1, 2008): 351–81. doi:10.1007/s10982-007-9020-8.

———. "The Right to Autonomy and the Justification of Hard Paternalism." In *Paternalism: Theory and Practice*, edited by Christian Coons and Michael Weber, 74–92. Cambridge University Press, 2013.

Seal, Karen H., Robert Thawley, Lauren Gee, Joshua Bamberger, Alex H. Kral, Dan Ciccarone, Moher Downing, and Brian R. Edlin. "Naloxone Distribution and Cardiopulmonary Resuscitation Training for Injection Drug Users to Prevent Heroin Overdose Death: A Pilot Intervention Study." *Journal of Urban Health : Bulletin of the New York Academy of Medicine* 82, no. 2 (June 2005): 303–11. doi:10.1093/jurban/jti053.

Seale C., and J. Addington-Hall. "Euthanasia: The Role of Good Care." *Social Science & Medicine* 40, no. 5 (1995): 581–7.

Sharot, Tali. "The Optimism Bias." *Current Biology* 21, no. 23 (2011): R941–45.

Shepherd, Greene, and Brian C. Ferslew. "Homicidal Poisoning Deaths in the United States 1999–2005," *Clinical Toxicology (Philadelphia, Pa.)* 47, no. 4 (April 2009): 342–47. doi:10.1080/15563650902893089.

Shiffrin, Seana. "Intellectual Property." SSRN Scholarly Paper. Rochester, NY: Social Science Research Network, 2007. http://papers.ssrn.com/abstract=2679176.

Shiffrin, Seana Valentine. "Paternalism, Unconscionability Doctrine, and Accommodation." *Philosophy & Public Affairs* 29, no. 3 (2000): 205–50. doi:10.1111/j.1088-4963.2000.00205.x.

———. "Thinker-Based Approach to Freedom Speech." *Constitutional Commentary* 27 (2010): 283.

———. "Wrongful Life, Procreative Responsibility, and the Significance of Harm." *Legal Theory* 5, no. 02 (1999): 117–48.

Simmons, A. John. "Justification and Legitimacy." *Ethics* 109, no. 4 (1999): 739–71. doi:10.1086/233944.

Singer, Peter. "Voluntary Euthanasia: A Utilitarian Perspective." *Bioethics* 17, nos. 5–6 (2003): 526–41.

Smith, Michael. "Two Kinds of Consequentialism." *Philosophical Issues* 19, no. 1 (October 1, 2009): 257–72. doi:10.1111/j.1533-6077.2009.00169.x.

Snyder, Jeremy. "Disregard and Dependency." *Business Ethics Journal Review* 1, no. 13 (May 20, 2013): 82–85.

———. "Needs Exploitation." *Ethical Theory and Moral Practice* 11, no. 4 (2008): 389–405.

Sofer, Gideon J. "The FDA Is Killing Crohn's Patients." *Wall Street Journal*, December 30, 2008, sec. Opinion. http://www.wsj.com/articles/SB123059825583441193.

Solomon, Jason M. "Equal Accountability Through Tort Law." *Northwestern University Law Review* 103 (2009): 1765.

Solomon, Kenneth. "Social Antecedents of Learned Helplessness in the Health Care Setting." *The Gerontologist* 22, no. 3 (June 1, 1982): 282–87. doi:10.1093/geront/22.3.282.

Sorrell v. IMS Health Inc., 131 S. Ct. 2653 (Supreme Court 2011).

Spinello, Richard A. "Ethics, Pricing and the Pharmaceutical Industry." *Journal of Business Ethics* 11, no. 8 (August 1992): 617–26. doi:10.1007/BF00872273.

Stafford, R. S. "Regulating off-Label Drug Use—Rethinking the Role of the FDA." *New England Journal of Medicine* 358, no. 14 (2008): 1427–29.

Standen, Amy. "Should Severe Premenstrual Symptoms Be a Mental Disorder?" *NPR. org*, October 21, 2013. http://www.npr.org/blogs/health/2013/10/22/223805027/should-disabling-premenstrual-symptoms-be-a-mental-disorder.

Stein, Rob. "Critics Slam Cost of FDA-approved Drug to Prevent Preterm Births." *Washington Post*, April 1, 2011.

Stemplowska, Zofia, and Department of Philosophy, Florida State University. "What's Ideal About Ideal Theory?" Edited by Margaret Dancy, Victoria Costa, and Joshua Gert. *Social Theory and Practice* 34, no. 3 (2008): 319–40. doi:10.5840/soctheorpract200834320.

Stilz, Anna. *Liberal Loyalty: Freedom, Obligation, and the State*. Reprint. Princeton, NJ: Princeton University Press, 2011.

Sulmasy, D. P. "Managed Care and Managed Death." *Archives of Internal Medicine* 155, no. 2 (1995): 133.

Sunstein, Cass R. "Legal Interference with Private Preferences." *University of Chicago Law Review* 53, no. 4 (1986): 1129–74.

Svorny, Shirley, et al. "Licensing Doctors: Do Economists Agree?" *Econ Journal Watch* 1, no. 2 (2004): 279–305.

Swift, Adam. *How not to Be a Hypocrite: School Choice for the Morally Perplexed Parent.* Psychology Press, 2003.

Tabarrok, Alex. *Launching the Innovation Renaissance: A New Path to Bring Smart Ideas to Market Fast.* TED Books, 2011.

Tabarrok, A. T. "Assessing the FDA via the Anomaly of Off-Label Drug Prescribing." *Independent Review* 5, no. 1 (2000): 25–53.

Takayama, Akane, and Mamoru Narukawa. "Pharmaceutical Pricing and Reimbursement in Japan for Faster, More Complete Access to New Drugs." *Therapeutic Innovation & Regulatory Science*, December 23, 2015. doi:10.1177/2168479015619202.

Tanda, Gianluigi, and Gaetano Di Chiara. "A Dopamine-μ1 Opioid Link in the Rat Ventral Tegmentum Shared by Palatable Food (Fonzies) and Non-Psychostimulant Drugs of Abuse." *European Journal of Neuroscience* 10, no. 3 (1998): 1179–87.

Taylor A. L., L. O. Gostin, and K. A. Pagonis. "Ensuring Effective Pain Treatment: A National and Global Perspective." *JAMA* 299, no. 1 (January 2, 2008): 89–91. doi:10.1001/jama.2007.25.

Temin, Peter. "Costs and Benefits in Switching Drugs from Rx to OTC." *Journal of Health Economics* 2, no. 3 (1983): 187–205.

———. "Realized Benefits from Switching Drugs." *Journal of Law and Economics* 35, no. 2 (1992): 351–69.

The Editorial Board. "No Justification for High Drug Prices." *New York Times*, December 19, 2015. http://www.nytimes.com/2015/12/20/opinion/sunday/no-justification-for-high-drug-prices.html.

"The Shame of Filling a Prescription." *Well.* Accessed December 30, 2014. http://well.blogs.nytimes.com/2012/01/05/the-shame-of-filling-a-prescription/.

Thompson v. Western States Medical Center, 535 US 357 (Supreme Court 2002).

Thomson, Judith Jarvis. "A Defense of Abortion." *Philosophy & Public Affairs* 1, no. 1 (1971): 47–66.

———. "Self-Defense." *Philosophy & Public Affairs* 20, no. 4 (1991): 283–310.

Thoreau, Henry David. *Civil Disobedience and Other Essays.* Courier, 2012.

Tierney, John. "The Rational Choices of Crack Addicts." *New York Times*, September 16, 2013, sec. Science. http://www.nytimes.com/2013/09/17/science/the-rational-choices-of-crack-addicts.html.

"Timeline: The Battle for Plan B." *Time.com*, June 11, 2013. http://healthland.time.com/2013/06/11/timeline-the-battle-for-plan-b/.

Tomasi, John. *Free Market Fairness.* Princeton University Press, 2012.

Topol, Eric J. "Intensive Statin Therapy—A Sea Change in Cardiovascular Prevention." *New England Journal of Medicine* 350, no. 15 (2004): 1562–64.

———. *The Patient Will See You Now: The Future of Medicine Is in Your Hands.* New York: Basic Books, 2015.

Trussell, J., F. Stewart, M. Potts, F. Guest, and C. Ellertson. "Should Oral Contraceptives Be Available Without Prescription?" *American Journal of Public Health* 83, no. 8 (August 1993): 1094–99.

Tversky, Amos, and Daniel Kahneman. "Availability: A Heuristic for Judging Frequency and Probability." *Cognitive Psychology* 5, no. 2 (September 1973): 207–32. doi:10.1016/0010-0285(73)90033-9.

United Nations Office on Drugs and Crime. "Discussion Paper: From Coercion to Cohesion: Treating Drug Dependence Through Health Care, Not Punishment." Vienna: United Nations, 2009. https://www.unodc.org/docs/treatment/Coercion_Ebook.pdf.

———. "The International Drug Control Conventions." Final Acts and Resolutions. New York, NY: United Nations, 1988 1961). https://www.unodc.org/documents/commissions/CND/Int_Drug_Control_Conventions/Ebook/The_International_Drug_Control_Conventions_E.pdf.

————. "World Drug Report." Vienna: United Nations, 2014. https://www.unodc.org/documents/data-and-analysis/WDR2014/World_Drug_Report_2014_web.pdf.

United Press International. "Police Arrest AIDS Protesters Blocking Access to FDA Offices." *Los Angeles Times*, October 11, 1988. http://articles.latimes.com/1988-10-11/news/mn-3909_1_police-arrest-aids-protesters.

United States v. Oakland Cannabis Buyers' Cooperative, 532 US 483 (Supreme Court 2001).

University of Michigan Health System. "U-M Team Seeks to Outsmart C Difficile with New $92 Million Effort." *ICT.com*, March 9, 2016. http://www.infectioncontroltoday.com/news/2016/03/um-team-seeks-to-outsmart-c-difficile-with-new-92-million-effort.aspx.

US Department of Justice. "Eli Lilly and Company Agrees to Pay $1.415 Billion to Resolve Allegations of Off-Label Promotion of Zyprexa." January 15, 2009.

US Food and Drug Administration. "Using Innovative Technologies and Other Conditions of Safe Use to Expand Drug Products Considered Nonprescription." February 28, 2012. http://www.regulations.gov/#!documentDetail;D=FDA-2012-N-0171-0001.

Valentini, Laura. "Ideal vs. Non-Ideal Theory: A Conceptual Map." *Philosophy Compass* 7, no. 9 (September 1, 2012): 654–64. doi:10.1111/j.1747-9991.2012.00500.x.

————. "On the Apparent Paradox of Ideal Theory." *Journal of Political Philosophy* 17, no. 3 (September 1, 2009): 332–55. doi:10.1111/j.1467-9760.2008.00317.x.

VanDeVeer, Donald. "Autonomy Respecting Paternalism." *Social Theory and Practice* 6, no. 2 (July 1, 1980): 187–207.

Veatch, Robert M. "Abandoning Informed Consent." *Hastings Center Report* 25, no. 2 (1995): 5–12. doi:10.2307/3562859.

Velleman, J. David. "A Right of Self-Termination?" *Ethics* 109, no. 3 (April 1, 1999): 606–28. doi:10.1086/et.1999.109.issue-3.

Velleman, J. David. "Against the Right to Die." *Journal of Medicine and Philosophy* 17, no. 6 (1992): 665–81.

————. "A Right of Self-Termination?" *Ethics* 109, no. 3 (April 1, 1999): 606–28. doi:10.1086/233924.

Ventola, C. Lee. "Direct-to-Consumer Pharmaceutical Advertising: Therapeutic or Toxic?" *Pharmacy and Therapeutics* 36, no. 10 (2011): 669.

Volokh, Eugene. "Medical Self-Defense, Prohibited Experimental Therapies, and Payment for Organs." *Harvard Law Review* 120, no.7 (2007): 1813–46.

————. "Speech Restrictions That Don't Much Affect the Autonomy of Speakers." *Constitutional Commentary* 27 (2011): 347.

Voorhoeve, Alex. "In Search of the Deep Structure of Morality: An Interview with Frances Kamm." *Imprints* 9, no. 2 (2006): 93–117.

Vossen, Bas van der. "Associative Political Obligations." *Philosophy Compass* 6, no. 7 (2011): 477–87.

Wall, Steven. "Self-Ownership and Paternalism." *Journal of Political Philosophy* 17, no. 4 (2009): 399–417.

Wardell, W. M. "The Drug Lag Revisited: Comparison by Therapeutic Area of Patterns of Drugs Marketed in the United States and Great Britain from 1972 Through 1976." *Clinical Pharmacology and Therapeutics* 24, no. 5 (1978): 499.

Wardell, W. M., and L. Lasagna. *Regulation and Drug Development*. Washington DC: American Enterprise Institute for Public Policy Research, 1975.

Waring Joseph I. "Colonial Medicine in Georgia and South Carolina." *The Georgia Historical Quarterly* 59 (January 1, 1975): 141–53.

Watts, T. D. "The For-profit Social Welfare Policy Sector and End-of-life Issues: A Troublesome Ethical Mixture." *Catholic Social Science Review* 12 (2007): 351–69.

Wellman, Christopher H. "Liberalism, Samaritanism, and Political Legitimacy." *Philosophy & Public Affairs* 25, no. 3 (1996): 211–37.

Wertheimer, Alan. "Liberty, Coercion, and the Limits of the State." *The Blackwell Guide to Social and Political Philosophy*. Oxford, UK: Blackwell, 2002.

Wertheimer, Alan, and Matt Zwolinski. "Exploitation." In *The Stanford Encyclopedia of Philosophy*, edited by Edward N. Zalta, Spring 2013. http://plato.stanford.edu/archives/spr2013/entries/exploitation/.

Wiggins, Steven N. "Product Quality Regulation and New Drug Introductions: Some New Evidence from the 1970s." *The Review of Economics and Statistics* 63, no. 4 (November 1, 1981): 615–19. doi:10.2307/1935858.

Wilkinson, Martin, and Andrew Moore. "Inducement in Research." *Bioethics* 11, no. 5 (1997): 373–89. doi:10.1111/1467-8519.00078.

Williams, Bernard. "Consequentialism and Integrity." In *Consequentialism and Its Critics*, edited by Samuel Scheffler, 20–50. Oxford University Press, 1988. http://philpapers.org/rec/WILCAI.

Wilson, James. "Paying for Patented Drugs Is Hard to Justify: An Argument About Time Discounting and Medical Need." *Journal of Applied Philosophy*, 2012. http://onlinelibrary. wiley.com/doi/10.1111/j.1468-5930.2012.00567.x/full.

———. "Why It's Time to Stop Worrying About Paternalism in Health Policy." *Public Health Ethics* 4, no. 3 (November 1, 2011): 269–79. doi:10.1093/phe/phr028.

Wilson, Renate, and Woodrow J. Savacool. "The Theory and Practice of Pharmacy in Pennsylvania: Observations on Two Colonial Country Doctors." *Pennsylvania History: A Journal of Mid-Atlantic Studies* 68, no. 1 (2001): 31–65.

W., Justin. "Philosophers on Drug Prices." *Daily Nous*, September 28, 2015. http://dailynous. com/2015/09/28/philosophers-on-drug-prices/.

Wyeth v. Levine, 129 S. Ct. 1187 (Supreme Court 2009).

Yen, Alfred C. "Restoring the Natural Law: Copyright as Labor and Possession." *Ohio State Law Journal* 51 (1990): 517–59.

Young, James Harvey. *American Self-Dosage Medicines: An Historical Perspective*. Coronado Press, 1974.

Young, Robert. "Informed Consent and Patient Autonomy." In *A Companion to Bioethics*, edited by Helga Kuhse and Peter Singer, 530–40. Chichester: Wiley-Blackwell, 2009. http://onlinelibrary.wiley.com/doi/10.1002/9781444307818.ch44/summary.

Zwolinski, Matt. "Are Usurious? Another New Argument for the Prohibition of High Interest Loans?" *Business Ethics Journal Review* 1, no. 4 (2013): 22–27.

———. "Price Gouging, Non-Worseness, and Distributive Justice." SSRN Scholarly Paper. Rochester, NY: Social Science Research Network, February 4, 2009. http://papers.ssrn.com/abstract=1337654.

———. "The Ethics of Price Gouging." SSRN Scholarly Paper. Rochester, NY: Social Science Research Network, March 3, 2008. http://papers.ssrn.com/abstract=1099567.

Zylicz, Z., and I. G. Finlay. "Euthanasia and Palliative Care: Reflections from The Netherlands and the UK." *Journal of the Royal Society of Medicine* 92, no. 7 (1999): 370.

INDEX